College Hookup Culture
and Christian Ethics

College Hookup Culture and Christian Ethics

The Lives and Longings of Emerging Adults

JENNIFER BESTE

OXFORD
UNIVERSITY PRESS

OXFORD
UNIVERSITY PRESS

Oxford University Press is a department of the University of Oxford. It furthers
the University's objective of excellence in research, scholarship, and education
by publishing worldwide. Oxford is a registered trade mark of Oxford University
Press in the UK and certain other countries.

Published in the United States of America by Oxford University Press
198 Madison Avenue, New York, NY 10016, United States of America.

© Oxford University Press 2018

Sections of chapter 7 were first published as "Poverty of Spirit within Party and
Hookup Culture: Undergraduates' Engagement with Johann Metz," Horizons, v. 44.1
(June 2017): 108–136. Reprinted with permission from Horizons: The Journal
of the College Theology Society.

Ideas and sections of the manuscript were first published in "Longing for More:
College Hookup Culture," International Journal for Theology, Concilium: Young
Catholics Reshaping the Church, eds. Solange Lefebvre, Maria Clara Bingemer,
and Silvias Scatena (2015/2), London: SCM Press, 94–106.

Library of Congress Cataloging-in-Publication Data
Names: Beste, Jennifer Erin, author.
Title: Christian ethics and college hookup culture / Jennifer Beste.
Description: New York : Oxford University Press, 2017. |
Includes bibliographical references. Identifiers: LCCN 2017000263 (print) |
LCCN 2017039706 (ebook) | ISBN 9780190268510 | ISBN 9780190268527 |
ISBN 9780190268534 | ISBN 9780190268503
Subjects: LCSH: Christian college students–Religious life. |
Christian college students–Sexual behavior. | Christian college students–Social life
and customs. | Christian ethics. Classification: LCC BV4531.3 (ebook) |
LCC BV4531.3 .B47 2017 (print) | DDC 248.8/34–dc23
LC record available at https://lccn.loc.gov/2017000263

1 3 5 7 9 8 6 4 2

This book is dedicated to all my former students. Since fall semester 2003, the beginning of my teaching career, I have remained in awe of your courage to share personal stories and reflect deeply and honestly about your lived experiences. Because you risked the vulnerability that this book celebrates, others can be empowered to make decisions that improve their lives and advance the cause of justice on their campuses.

Contents

PART III: *Sexual Justice: A Call to Action*

Acknowledgments

IT IS EXCITING and humbling to reach the point in a project of this magnitude where I can ponder and appreciate the myriad stars that aligned to make it all possible. Many heartfelt thanks are in order, first and foremost to the students I have taught since 2003 who were willing to share their stories and experiences, reflections and analyses, and ongoing feedback as my visions for this book progressed. If my 126 student ethnographers featured in part I and my 150 students mentioned in part II steal the show— because it is their voices that readers will encounter most directly in this book—I must emphasize that there's only a show to steal because of the students who preceded and followed them. At the beginning of my teaching career, for example, I received messages from several graduates about what was "really going on" on our campus. Inspired by students who continued to share, confidentially, their experiences of real-life dynamics of party and hookup culture, a graduate student and I interviewed student volunteers willing to participate in a video about hookup culture, sexual violence, and sexual justice that was shown to all first-year college students from 2009 to 2011. In turn, those student volunteers and over 1,000 first-year students who participated in this program validated and gave direction to my plans for *College Hookup Culture and Christian Ethics*. Much later, after chapter drafts had taken shape, I benefited again from students as they read my work and provided valuable feedback. Sincere thanks both to students in the classroom and student workers throughout the years who lent their many talents to this project: Esther Cleary, Katie Keller, Brian VanderHeiden, Laura Hey, Devin Roll, Natalie Hager, Emily Doyle, Emily Thornton, and Mary Lindell.

I also wish to express my gratitude to the Louisville Institute for granting me a sabbatical spring semester of 2012, and to the Collegeville Institute at St. John's University in Collegeville, Minnesota, for accepting me as a scholar in residence during the fall of 2012. A special thank-you to Don Ottenhoff, Executive Director of the Collegeville Institute, and to my Collegium colleagues that semester. Regular feedback and wonderful camaraderie with such diverse and talented scholars was just what this project and I needed.

Next, I cannot imagine what I would have done without the support, encouragement, and brilliance of the professional colleagues I am blessed to count as friends. Thank you Margaret Farley, Dan Finn, Todd Whitmore, Jean Keller, Kathy Coffey-Guenter, Charlie Camosy, Gillian Ahlgren, and Heidi Park for your generosity. I am likewise tremendously grateful to Judy Shank for assistance with editing and preparations of the manuscript, and to Cynthia Read, Executive Editor at Oxford University Press, for the patience and expertise that have defined her commitment to me and my scholarship not just once, but twice now.

Finally, I thank the people closest to me who have loved and supported me through the joys and trials of writing this book: my son Jamison for his sense of humor and playfulness, my daughter Anna for believing in me and taking on extra household chores, and my husband Steve for his unfailing enthusiasm for my research and willingness to edit chapter drafts.

*College Hookup Culture
and Christian Ethics*

Introduction

How can academic researchers really understand our experiences of hooking up and the dynamics of hookup culture? They aren't college students. They didn't grow up with the same media. They don't live in the res. halls and go to parties. They just don't live our reality day in and day out. I doubt their analyses are accurate.

ZACH, undergraduate,[1]
Christian sexual ethics seminar

MY INITIAL REACTION to the skepticism of Zach and many of his peers was dismay. Anticipating student buy-in and enthusiasm about analyzing college sexual culture in a theological ethics course, I had looked forward to seeing how students would process the best available research on hookup culture.[2] Studies indicate that hookups, defined as sexual activity devoid of commitment and emotional investment, are becoming normative on U.S. college campuses.[3] While students acknowledged the value of quantitative and qualitative research on this topic, they did not find it sufficient to explain the complex dynamics of their lived experience. In their view, a truly accurate understanding would need a full, respectful consideration of their own perspectives. Without this, a theological and ethical analysis of hookup and party culture would be incomplete.

Regularly feeling unsettled after class during the next few weeks, I sensed that my students were on to something too important to ignore. They were, after all, correct: despite years of leading seminar-style discussions and assigning anonymous papers and surveys about sexuality and relationships, neither I nor the other scholars who were publishing on hookup culture had lived and breathed contemporary college students' reality "day in and day out." My ability to engage students in theological and ethical analyses of contemporary social and sexual norms was admittedly compromised. Students seemed to require a new paradigm for teaching and learning about these issues, but what would that look like?

I found myself seriously contemplating the implications of changes that had occurred in only a single generation. During my own college years, the Internet and social media did not exist. Compared to an earlier era (when I grew up), changes in popular culture and media after the mid-nineties (when my students grew up) undoubtedly led to very different experiences of gender and sexual socialization through childhood, adolescence, and young adulthood. Undergraduates' accounts of college culture were particularly striking in terms of the social and sexual norms of our two college social realities. In the early nineties, on my college campus, informal dating and romantic relationships were the sexual and relational norm; casual sex occurred, but it was neither expected nor a normative part of the "typical college experience." This has changed dramatically.

Complicating my challenge to improve my Christian sexual ethics seminar was millennial students' skepticism about religious authorities and educators, particularly when these adults addressed sexuality and relationships.[4] Years of teaching Christian sexual ethics had made it clear that many college students who grew up Christian (particularly Catholic) expressed weariness if not resentment about being told what to think and how to behave sexually. Having been lectured too often and solicited too little for their questions, experiences, and concerns, the majority of my students regarded their Christian denominations' teachings on sexuality and gender as sex-negative, judgmental, or simply irrelevant to their lives. Facing these obstacles, how could I teach my course in such a way that Christian and non-Christian students alike might experience Christian ethics as a rich context for thought-provoking questions and life-giving insights about who they are, how they should relate to others, and what really matters in life?

The next semester, I took these challenges to heart and radically altered how we studied hookup culture and Christian ethics. For starters, we partnered in a more dynamic process of teaching and learning by each playing to our particular strengths. While mine included expertise in Christian theology and ethics, as well as a honed ability to ask questions and read texts critically, my students' unique strengths consisted of "insider" knowledge of college culture and their native fluency with the narratives of sex, gender, relationships, and fulfillment circulating in popular culture and social media. Instead of beginning the course with social scientific research and theories on sexuality, gender, and hookup culture, I tried a new assignment on the first day of class. My students' task over the next two weeks was to become ethnographers who would attend, observe, and analyze eight to ten hours of college parties.

More specifically, I decided each student's field research would culminate in a twelve-page paper.[5] In addition to describing how their peers acted at college parties, students would hypothesize about why their peers act the way they do and analyze power dynamics among different social groups based on race and ethnicity, sexual orientation, and gender. Lastly, they would reflect on whether they thought their peers were happy at parties. My pedagogical objective was to allow the class to compare their own ethnographic findings with sociological readings on gender, sexuality, and hookup culture. At that point, we would be ready to move beyond mainly phenomenological issues to pursue our emerging theological and ethical questions and concerns.

I was surprised when reading the first set of seventy-five papers. Students' observations and analyses were fascinating and thought-provoking, but even more striking was the degree to which students embraced their roles as sober ethnographers (they weren't allowed to consume alcohol) and used highly creative methods to obtain their data. In addition to direct observation, many chose to interview friends before, during, and/or after parties. Some posed the assignment's questions to acquaintances or even strangers at parties, and others maintained communication with partiers via text messages, treating their text threads as extended, eighteen-hour interviews connecting pregame festivities with the morning after. While some students asked their friends for help with observation and analysis, others went completely "under cover" and made up excuses about why they weren't drinking that evening.

As I read their papers and listened to the students in class, I was deeply impressed by how much they learned in their role as ethnographers, and how students began questioning things they previously had taken for granted or had never noticed. Those who identified themselves as regular partiers expressed the greatest surprise about what they actually noticed and realized when they adopted the ethnographer role compared to their usual experiences as drunken participants.

It is important to acknowledge, of course, that my student ethnographers' analyses of college parties did not represent all students' social reality. Not all college students hook up or even attend college parties.[6] For instance, in an April 2010 anonymous survey I conducted at my university, only 40% of first-year women and 42% of men reported that they had hooked up once or more by the end of their freshman year.[7] Some students in my classes had never attended college parties before receiving my assignment, and they expressed distaste about the whole idea of hooking up. One young man found the prospect of observing eight to ten hours of college parties so distasteful that he dropped the course.

Beginning my sexual ethics course with this assignment during the next two years, I began to recognize that consistent themes about party culture were emerging semester after semester. Taking into consideration everything my students and I learned from their ethnographies, and our subsequent discussions about theology and ethics, I seized opportunities to lecture at various universities about my students' research. As it turned out, everywhere I spoke students were curious about what their peers privately thought about college parties and hookups, and were open to exploring the intersection between sexuality and Christian theology. Many undergraduates expressed a deep longing for more than their social and sexual norms were providing them. They also responded positively to the way in which I wove college students' insights into my theological and ethical reflections about human fulfillment and justice within the college party context. My qualitative analysis[8] of students' ethnographies and perspectives was resonating, and I found that many students were intrigued and motivated by the idea of transformation—not just in their own lives but also in the entire college culture.

As I engaged in conversations with undergraduates about college sexual culture, theology, and ethics, I decided to write a new kind of Christian ethics text—one that regarded college students' reflections on their experiences and social realities as a legitimate source of knowledge. I also hoped that, by weaving "insider" voices with the perspectives of Christian theologians, the resulting text would be more relevant and valuable to undergraduates (and other readers) than an approach that simply, and more traditionally, applied Christian teachings on sexuality and relationships to hookup culture.

Methodology

At a Midwestern Catholic university (referred to as "University A"), I asked my students for their consent to analyze their written work for research and educational purposes. University A has 4,000 to 5,000 undergraduates, participates in Division 1 athletics, and does not have fraternities or sororities. I received Institutional Review Board (IRB) approval to analyze their writings.[9] Part I of this book offers an account and analysis of contemporary party and hookup culture based on my qualitative analysis of the 126 ethnographies that I collected.[10] Together, chapters 1 to 4 aim to create a space for lively dialogue about sex, gender, power, relationships, and happiness.

Prior to entering these conversations, I wish to address four potential concerns regarding methodology. First, under ideal conditions, this project would have involved recruiting undergraduates from a variety of public and private universities in all major U.S. geographic locations. Lacking sufficient resources, I instead utilized a convenience sample. Thus, even though collectively my ethnographers were more adventurous than I anticipated, and they observed college parties at a variety of private and public universities in seven states (Tennessee, Missouri, South Carolina, Ohio, Indiana, Illinois, and Kentucky), my sample is limited to undergraduates attending a single university. Intended as qualitative and exploratory, this ethnographic study examined in part I investigates the general patterns, themes, and constructs that emerge from studying in depth one particular group of undergraduates. I leave it to my readers to render their own judgments about whether they recognize the experiences and struggles of their own, their friends, acquaintances, or family members within this account of contemporary college party culture and the broader cultural trends that influence us all.

Second, since students were assigned a grade for the paper, one might question whether the power differential between the students and their professor compromised the trustworthiness of their observations and analyses. Were ethnographers free and comfortable enough to be honest in their party descriptions and analyses, or did they simply write what they thought their professor wanted to hear in an attempt to receive a higher grade? When explaining this assignment to my students each semester, I addressed this issue directly. Obviously the value of this project depended on their freedom to generate competent analysis based on honest observations. As the condition for gaining deeper understanding, students' honesty was essential to determine, eventually, the extent to which undergraduate ethnographers' findings were either aligned with or distinct from the existing literature of "adult" researchers on hookup culture. Ultimately, given the descriptive and exploratory nature of their task, it was not clear to my students or even to me what I as a professor would "want to hear." Echoing the assurance of academic freedom for this assignment that I provided in writing, I also guaranteed students in class that their personal analysis or the content of their observations would have no bearing on grades. Furthermore, this assignment was situated within the broader context of my ordinary pedagogical commitments, among which is my uncompromising pledge to honor academic freedom and to create a respectful space where students can express their views honestly and without fear of reprisal. By posing the following question every semester, I encouraged my students to assess for themselves the trustworthiness of their data: "Given that the assignment was graded and part of an ethics course, was your ability to be frank in your descriptions and analysis of college parties compromised? Reflecting on your experiences at the parties, are there any events that you omitted or overlooked in your ethnography paper?" Throughout the semesters, students discussing this in small groups consistently reported comfort with being honest in their writing, and at the end of the course, the ethnography paper was regularly ranked in an anonymous evaluation as the most pedagogically effective, thought-provoking assignment of the course.[11]

Third, some might question whether the data is trustworthy, since the ethnographies were written by students enrolled in a Christian sexual ethics course. Were students who took this particular course representative of the wider student body at their university, or did this course attract a unique social group of undergraduates? Were students drawn to the class either because they were more interested in religion and theology, or in gender and sexuality, than most of their peers? Were they more or less religiously conservative than the student body as a whole? According to self-reports on the first day of class each semester, most students' primary motivation for selecting my course over other third-level theology courses was to satisfy two course requirements simultaneously: one upper-level theology and one gender studies requirement. From a research perspective, this was good news, as the course attracted a diverse set of majors from arts and sciences, social sciences, and business. Furthermore, students possessed a diverse range of beliefs and attitudes regarding sex, gender, relationships, religion, and ethics. As for gender and ethnic diversity among the research sample, 56% were female and 44% were male, and 92% were Caucasian, 6% African American, and 2% Asian American. The lack of ethnic diversity in my sample, a limitation of this study, reflected the broader population of this university.

Fourth, millennial readers especially may question my competence as an adult researcher to code and interpret the data in a way that accurately reflects the views and perspectives of 126 undergraduate ethnographers.

Though it is impossible for a qualitative researcher to interpret data with pure objectivity, it is possible to be self-reflexive, aware of how subjectivity and biases can influence the process of interpretation. Throughout the coding process, I intentionally utilized multiple procedures to check that my interpretations of repeated themes and theoretical constructs were grounded in the data itself, and not simply an imposition of my own biases and perspectives. To ensure that my qualitative analysis represented as accurately as possible the ethnographers' collective account of their social reality, I asked for feedback from students in my sexual ethics courses from 2010 to 2012. During every semester that I read ethnography assignments, I took notes on reoccurring ideas, themes, and particular quotations, later checking with students on which ideas were representative of their college party culture and which appeared as exaggerations. When classes came to a consensus that a particular description of a party behavior or sexual act was extreme and not representative of typical college parties, I deleted it.[12] Lastly, besides my own qualitative coding, I hired two students—one Caucasian female undergraduate and one white male undergraduate from a different university (neither of whom took my sexual ethics course)— to code portions of the relevant text and identify repeating ideas and themes. In addition to discussing our coding outlines of repeating ideas and themes, the male undergraduate[13] later read and evaluated drafts of my four chapters in part I. His primary task was to identify any ideas or themes not adequately grounded in the data that could represent an imposition of my own biases and concerns.

Given the lack of ethnic diversity among my students and the larger student body at University A, it is crucial to acknowledge that Caucasian students provide most of this book's accounts of party culture and also helped determine which party descriptions count as representative. The majority of these students, furthermore, revealed their interest in the opposite sex.[14] Thus, the understanding of college party culture emerging from the ethnographies could have been much different if the student body had been more diverse in regard to race and ethnicity or sexual orientation.

Organization

Part I of this book takes seriously students' observations and analyses of their own social realities and encourages conversations in the remainder of the book that I believe we ignore at our own peril. Far from wishing to sensationalize "the secret lives of college students after dark," I allow chapters 1 through 4 to set the stage for exploring solutions to the dangers and injustices of party and hookup culture that students bring to light. As most student ethnographers show with remarkable consistency, many of their peers who throw themselves into being "so college" by partying hard and hooking up regularly are surprised when the social dynamics of college that they anticipated so eagerly leave them disillusioned, unfulfilled, and positively longing for more.

Part II brings students (likewise, readers) into conversation with Christianity's countercultural narrative of what it means to become fully human and experience genuine joy and fulfillment. By many accounts—and as my college students testify—the dominant U.S. cultural narrative that most people encounter daily is relentless and persuasive: independence, competitive success, wealth, and social status equal happiness and fulfillment. Meanwhile, for Christians, the life of Jesus Christ is the source of truth about how to discern life's purpose and experience joy and fulfillment. The spokesperson for this vision in chapters 5 through 7 is theologian Johann Metz, whose portrait of Jesus enduring his desert temptations and becoming "fully human"[15] begins to address questions about students' dissatisfaction and helps them recognize the obstacles to their joy and fulfillment. Unfortunately, such obstacles are woven into the fabric of popular culture's dominant narrative, which many have internalized not only deeply but also unconsciously and uncritically. For a great many of my students who have compared Jesus's way of being in the world with their own way of being, the authenticity, relevance, and hope they discover in Metz's *Poverty of Spirit* is attractive and compelling.

Preparing students for this part of our semester, I explain that, central to Metz's theological framework[16] is the belief that God has created us out of love; and throughout our lives we are all confronted with a fundamental decision to accept or reject God's ongoing gift of self and invitation for a relationship. We reach our potential and become fully human through freely living out a "yes" to God's offer, but what does this look like in real life? Seeking answers in the context of college culture, my students and I have been drawn to three interrelated aspects of Jesus's poverty in Metz's *Poverty of Spirit* that are crucial to the meaning of "fully human": (1) interdependence on God and others (resisting hyper-individualism); (2) self-love (accepting human finitude and honoring one's unique calling); and (3) love of neighbor as self (letting go of egoism in favor of encounter, respect, and care for others as distinct others).

In *College Hookup Culture and Christian Ethics*, I focus on Metz's theological meditations on Jesus Christ[17] and his broader theology for four main reasons. First, regardless of whether they identify as Christian, religious, or nonreligious, the majority of college students in my ethics courses for the last six years have found *Poverty of Spirit* deeply relevant to the dynamics and struggles in both their "day" lives and their "party" lives. In fact, many rank it as the most influential text they read with me, and nearly all recommend keeping it for future sections. More specifically, students have been attracted to and challenged by Metz's account of Christ's way of becoming fully human, his capacity for authenticity, and his willingness to love self and others whole-heartedly.

Second, in addition to its relevant content, *Poverty of Spirit* is beautifully written: Metz's imaginative, poetic, and evocative language engages readers intellectually, spiritually, and ethically, and successfully draws them into meaningful discussions about the purpose of life and who they truly want to be. Third, students are drawn to the "realness" of Metz's theology and his grasp on our struggles to act justly in relationship with others, ourselves, and God. Across the spectrum of his writings, Metz captures our human capacity for both boundless love and unspeakable evil, and he wrestles openly and honestly with God about the depth of human suffering in our world throughout history and in the present. Fourth, Metz's vision of becoming fully human does not depend on a framework of strict gender binaries or an essentialist "complementarity" framework, which can promote exclusionary or unjust relational dynamics. Such gender essentialism also alienates many students, fostering skepticism that Christian theology can be a resource for truth and wisdom concerning sexuality, relationships, and fulfillment.

At a different Catholic university (referred to as "University B"), I asked my students to imagine the following scenario after they had read *Poverty of Spirit* and interpreted Metz's distinctive theological vocabulary: Metz's Jesus returns to our world as a twenty-year-old African American male transfer student at their university,[18] where they meet and recognize him at a college party and have a conversation about becoming fully human and embracing poverty of spirit in the context of college party culture. How would that conversation unfold? My intention was, in Ignatian spiritual terms, to invite them into a "composition of place," an encounter with Jesus in the context of a college party. I received approval to collect students' papers in class for research and subsequently engaged in qualitative analysis of 150 student reflections.[19]

University B is similar to University A in terms of the following demographics: it is Catholic, has approximately 3,500 to 4,000 undergraduates (the majority from midwestern states), and does not have fraternities or sororities. A main difference is that University B offers Division 3 athletics.[20] Among my research sample, 66% were female and 34% were male. As for ethnic diversity among the research sample, 92% were Caucasian, 2.7% African American, and 3.3% Asian American, .7% Hispanic, and 1.3% were international students. As at University A, my students at University B reflected the broader student population of their university. Furthermore, students at University B were motivated to take Christian Sexual Ethics in order to satisfy two course requirements: one upper-level theology and one gender studies requirement. Consequently, students in my classes at University B also pursued a wide range of majors and had diverse beliefs and attitudes regarding sex, gender, relationships, religion, and ethics. The qualitative data and findings from my study may have differed, of course, if my student sample had been more ethnically, religiously, and geographically diverse. During the years of my study, 52% of the student body identified as Catholic, 30% as Protestant, and 2% as members of other world religions; 16% declared no religious affiliation.[21]

While these students at University B were asked very different questions from the student ethnographers at University A, readers will recognize similar analyses about party and hookup culture dynamics and the ways in which broader cultural attitudes and norms undergird and fuel party and hookup culture. Comparing and contrasting Jesus's way of being in the world with the typical college students' ways of being, students quoted in part II highlight how it is especially challenging for them to be countercultural and follow the path of Christ.

Part III culminates in a call to action on college campuses involving collaboration between undergraduates, administrators, faculty, and staff. This section acquires urgency from our understanding of normative party and hookup behavior gained in part I, and from analysis of the three aspects of poverty of spirit explored in part II, particularly an understanding of neighbor-love that demands the pursuit of justice for—and in solidarity with—our neighbor. More specifically, chapters 8 through 11 draw on diverse sources to examine what it means to treat others and oneself justly in the context of sexuality and relationships (Margaret Farley's *Just Love*, social scientific studies, and more student reflections); then explores obstacles to sexual justice on college campuses, focusing especially on the high prevalence of sexual violence and its traumatic impact on sexual assault survivors; and finally identifies three commitments necessary to create a sexually just culture on college campuses.

Distinctive Contributions

Throughout this work, voices from the academic fields of theology, ethics, sociology, and psychology blend with the voices of today's college students, whose ethnographies and personal reflections give rise to a distinct set of questions and issues. The dialogue born from these exchanges is not just fascinating intellectually but also truly helpful for students hoping to integrate faith or spirituality with their sexual and social lives. The value of this aspect of *College Hookup Culture and Christian Ethics* is perhaps best seen in light of the findings of Donna Freitas in her book *Sex and the Soul*,[22] which explores the relationship between students' religious and spiritual beliefs and their sexual attitudes and behavior. With the exception of students at evangelical colleges, college students reported that their religious beliefs had little to no influence on their sexual and social lives. Catholics in particular viewed their tradition's teachings against premarital sex and birth control as unrealistic, irrelevant, and outdated. Freitas argues that, given most Christian denominations' failure to communicate their teachings about sexuality in compelling terms, both Catholics and mainline Protestants remain confused about how to relate sex and the soul. Consequently, they compartmentalize religion and spirituality from their sexual and social lives. A unique aspect of *College Hookup Culture and Christian Ethics* is its exploration of how college students (and other readers) can integrate these important aspects of human experience in order to live fully and flourish.

Another unique aspect of this book is the contribution it makes to the field of Christian ethics by advancing the growing subdiscipline of Christian ethics and ethnography. Christian Scharen and Aana Marie Vigen's *Ethnography as Christian Theology and Ethics* begins to chart a path for how ethnographic research can be a distinctive form of Christian ethics.[23] Christian theologians and ethicists interested in integrating ethnographic methods with their scholarship share two main commitments: (1) a methodological commitment to broaden sources of knowledge beyond theological texts to include the experiences and perspectives of non-academicians (especially groups who have been marginalized or neglected by the theological academy); and (2) a desire to make theology relevant to contemporary Christians by attending to the diversity and complexity of lived experiences. No other Christian ethicist, to my knowledge, has systematically utilized college students' critical reflections on their experiences (part I), theological analyses of party and hookup culture (part II), and ethical analyses of sexual and relational norms (part III) as legitimate sources of knowledge alongside reason, Scripture, and tradition. Yet my ethical methodology—far from rogue—remains grounded in the Catholic tradition's affirmation that critical reflection[24] of our own and others' experiences offers insights about human fulfillment, justice, and God's desires for us.

This volume also makes several distinct and valuable contributions to the growing body of research on party and hookup culture. The book directly poses open-ended questions to undergraduates that few, if any, social scientific researchers have asked. In contrast to generalized answers solicited by most quantitative research on hookup culture, my assignments provided students time and opportunity to write as extensively as they wished. As expected, the qualitative components of this research yielded distinct and valuable insights about the dynamics of party and hookup culture and college students' private assessments of their social, gender, and sexual norms. Furthermore, this book is the first to involve undergraduates as co-researchers who observe and analyze peers at college parties. How do college students perceive the dynamics of their own social reality when they enter the research field of parties as sober ethnographers? Since undergraduate ethnographers collectively have been exposed to U.S. popular culture, and other cultural influences on sexual and gender socialization similar to the peers they observe, they have the potential to offer a unique "insider" account of the social imaginary underlying the attitudinal and behavioral norms of college party culture. Charles Taylor defines social imaginary as "the ways people imagine their social existence, how they fit together with others, how things go on between them and their fellows, the expectations that are normally met, and the deeper normative notions and images that underlie these expectations."[25]

As I analyzed this project's rich data and engaged in conversation with undergraduates, faculty, and people of all ages, I realized that, insofar as authenticity, justice, and fulfillment matter to most people, this book's purview and audience are much broader than simply the population it directly studies. The cultural influences on undergraduates impact today's younger teenagers, as well as adults of all ages, as we seek authenticity, meaning, and fulfillment in our sexual and relational lives.

To my readers about to embark on this journey, I present the same challenge that I give to my students each semester: as you read, suspend or let go of previously held moral assumptions and judgments about men and women who drink to get wasted and/or hook up. While this may be difficult, I have found this step crucial because snap moral judgments blind us to the more complex and heartbreaking social dynamics that exist not only in party and hookup culture but also in broader U.S. culture. Remaining locked into the thoughts and emotions we experience when judging others (labeling women sluts or whores, for example) distracts us from the more significant questions and insights that arise when we are instead curious and compassionate. Without question, my own empathy for college students has grown exponentially as I have listened to their stories and perspectives for the past thirteen years. The fact that so many have suffered profoundly from hookup norms, and the forms of sexual violence that frequently occur at parties, signals an urgency to establish safe and just campuses and to persuade universities to view their educational mission more holistically. Colleges and universities, I believe, must be in the business of fostering students' intellectual, psychological, social, spiritual, and sexual maturity and development simultaneously. To better understand the world of many college undergraduates and learn why theological and ethical consideration of their social reality is so important, let us begin with the student voices awaiting us in chapter 1.

PART I

Through Their Own Eyes

Undergraduate Ethnographies and Analyses
of Party and Hookup Culture

I
———————

College Students' Ethnographic Observations of Parties and Hookups

ACCORDING TO STUDENT ETHNOGRAPHERS, being a college student today often involves negotiating between two identities. In the daytime, you're the responsible young adult who successfully manages the myriad demands of classes, jobs, extracurricular activities, and social life. In academic settings, peers and professors alike recognize you as attentive, respectful, appreciative of differences, and smart. You are also the daughter or son who texts or calls home during the fifteen-minute break between classes. Mom and Dad are proud of you, no doubt, especially because daylight makes no mistake: their talented child is likely some hybrid of a talented athlete, budding scholar, moral exemplar, religious role model, creative entrepreneur, dedicated volunteer, lover and protector of the environment, and so on.

After the sun sets, on a party night, however, you may find yourself adopting an alternate persona. Thanks in large part to the alcohol, your behavior and attire are suddenly following a completely different value set and social script: seeking freedom from school pressures, life stresses, and normal inhibitions, you make one choice after another that fails the grandmother test: Would I say or wear or do this in front of grandma? This second social script finds fun, humor, and stress relief in carefree or reckless behavior that often involves excessive drinking and hooking up. Many student ethnographers repeatedly described how peers who were introverted during the day would drink copious amounts of alcohol in order to fit in with their more outgoing partying peers at night. Dominic notes, for instance, "Having had a class with Tanya, examining the stark difference in behavior between the reserved, shy girl in class and the wild and crazy partier was quite astounding. Throughout the rest of the evening she continued acting with unrestricted inhibitions, displaying an entirely different persona than the one she had shown in class."

My student ethnographers also emphasized how normal it has become for many peers to jettison their "morals" and religious values when they embrace their "night identities" as college partiers:

> People lose themselves in the party scene; they disregard whatever values and standards they hold themselves and others to when they are sober and out in the real world, and enter the party world acting with a degree of carelessness that would be unlike them in the normal day-to-day. While this most certainly applies to relationships, it also applies to sexuality. (Katherine)

> Most moral beliefs or attitudes towards sex are thrown out the window. (Austin)

> Students who seem so moral in the light of day do crazy things in the middle of a dark house on a Friday night. Students were grinding on one another and many were hooking up. No one seemed to care about privacy. (Adele)

> It's a Catholic University, so many students here possess a strict moral compass. However, during the time period I observed, this moral compass was forgotten. For instance, the male I observed dancing on the empty keg shell and taking off his shirt and his partner's shirt had a girlfriend who was not the girl he was undressing on top of the keg shells. I know this guy very well and I know how he sticks to his morals and values every day. However, at the time I was observing him, I cannot say the same. I noticed that some of my good friends were just looking for a guy or girl to hook up with for the night, having zero respect for their morals, while others were completely ignoring the fact that their "significant other" existed. One friend came up to me and said, "Find me a boy for the night." Without doubt, I know I have said the same thing before, but hearing it from her was shocking. This girl was the most innocent girl I have ever met. She has a very close relationship with God and would never have acted like this if she had not consumed heavy amounts of alcohol. For the night, her attitudes and beliefs about sexuality completely changed. (Annie)

No one, I believe, has the potential to speak more credibly and authentically to the related phenomena of split identities, peer influence, and social pressures than college students themselves. To gain insight into college party and hookup culture, I invite readers to place themselves imaginatively into the scenes of contemporary college parties described here by my undergraduate ethnographers.[1]

Before the Party

As today's average college student knows well, partying does not begin at the actual party but with so-called pregaming, as Macy notes: "It all starts in the dorms or the apartments that people live in—the idea being that no one wants to show up at a party sober." All student ethnographers identified striking differences in how men and women prepare and dress for parties. College men typically spend ten minutes at most getting ready, and then relax and pregame with friends. Consider the following typical description of male pregaming and the frequent competition to see who can become the most impaired in the least amount of time:

> Rob was drinking Bacardi 151 and was taking shots of it. He claimed that he was trying to get "f**d up tonight." John, Ed, and Pete were drinking beer and taking them down very fast. Chris was drinking regular vodka and he took a shot every ten minutes or so. This continued as time went on. They made jokes about hooking up with chicks (some were not so much jokes), while others talked about how belligerent they were going to be at the party. When they were all about 7-10 drinks deep, they decided they were drunk enough to head out to an actual party. (Theo)

Besides hanging out with their "bros," male ethnographers also observed their friends inviting girlfriends or women they are interested in to pregame before leaving for parties. For instance, Derek describes how his friend Kevin was scoping out women during dinner in the cafeteria in the hopes that he could invite some over to pregame. He was excited when he spotted Holly, a particularly attractive acquaintance:

> Kevin invited Holly and her friends over for the pregame, and the girls accepted the invitation. As Kevin left the cafeteria he was excited and felt accomplished. Kevin leaned over to one of his friends and said, "Did you see that? She wants me. Tonight is going to be a good night." While hanging out with his friends later and waiting for Holly to show, Kevin receives a text from Holly: "I do not

think we are going to make it to your place tonight, but maybe we will see you a little later at the party." Kevin is not happy with this obviously, but shrugs it off and tries to downplay it to the room. He makes the comment, "Bitch."

In contrast to guys' preparation for the party, student ethnographers describe college women's "pregame" as a two- to three-hour affair. Much time is needed to fix their hair, apply makeup, try on multiple outfits, and seek their friends' advice about which outfit looks hottest, sexiest, or "sluttiest":

> My roommate Kara comes in and she is wearing a tiny black shirt and a push-up bra, making half of her chest hang out. "Does this look okay?" she asks me. "I feel like I don't look slutty enough." I assure her she looks great, in particular complimenting how great her boobs look and add that she would most definitely get hit on. My roommate Kelly comes downstairs. She is wearing a black mini dress, the material of which is spread so threadbare across her skin that I can see her thong even in the dim lighting of our front porch. She goes straight to the freezer and grabs the bottle of 99 Berries she had bought earlier that afternoon. "I've gotta catch up fast," she says as she throws back two shots, one right after the other. (Nora)

Men who observed women friends prepare for parties reported similar rituals and expressed surprise at how long it took to get ready and the lengths that women will go to in their attempts to appear sexy or slutty:

> I had lounged on Jane's couch for an hour as she agonized over what to wear. Dress and leggings, blouse and leggings, blouse and skinny jeans, and all other permutations imaginable were considered. Then there was the less difficult question: "Cute or slutty?" Over the next hour, I found that the terms sexy and slutty were used more or less interchangeably. Jane would ask Sally how slutty her outfit was in a text and then turn to ask me "Is this sexy enough?" She added jeans so tight that she later complained of not being able to sit down properly. Jane and Sally both have boyfriends and were going out without their boyfriends for the first time of the New Year. Sally was agonizing over whether her top was "too slutty" to

wear without her boyfriend nearby to mark his territory. She finally decided on a delicate pink top and went with jeans tighter than Jane, if that was at all possible. (Max)

Max expressed surprise that Jane and Sally would obsess so much about looking "sexually enticing" when they were not even going to see their boyfriends that evening. After finally being ready to go out, Jane and Sally needed to drink before arriving at the party, so they went downstairs where a crowd of friends and acquaintances had gathered to pregame. They talked Max into playing "Never Have I Ever":

> It is a simple game; I say something I have never done and if they have, they take a drink. I began listing off a series of unperformed acts as the two began sucking down their beers as fast as they could. The guys began to cheer and laugh as they quickly learned things about Sally and Jane that they had not known before. "Never have I ever given oral sex. Never have I ever had sexual intercourse. Never have I ever worn a bra. Never have I ever smoked marijuana. Never have I ever kissed a member of my own sex." The list went on and on and the girls kept drinking. It occurred to me how ridiculous it was that, by drinking, they admitted all these things in front of guys they did not even know. It kept going with occasional interjections from the crowd— "Never have I ever sucked a dick! Yeah! You drink that beer!"—until the two were done and trying to hold in burps.

Such description among ethnographers of drinking games where all share the most intimate details of their sexual histories were commonplace during pregaming. As for why college students (mostly women) are so willing to divulge what they have done to others who barely know them—if at all, Nora sums it up without mincing words: "It is often the women who reveal the most about their sexual history, in hopes that the men will notice and perhaps pursue them or at least view them as sexually experienced."

Observing College Parties Sober

By the time they arrive at parties, many students are highly intoxicated and typically make their way to the keg or bar area. Student ethnographers noticed that their peers often stuck with their own friend groups, with the genders mostly segregated until they all had more alcohol in their systems.

All student ethnographers emphasized the expectations for heterosexual men in comparison to heterosexual women when it comes to dress, body language, and behavior. Similar to pregaming observations, they emphasized the extremes to which women go in their quest to appear "hot" and sexy at parties in order to gain attention and approval from college men:

> Girls are always trying to present themselves in a way that is sexually arousing to men. Appearance is everything. If a girl does not look hot at a party, the chances of a guy being interested in talking to her are slim. (Derek)

> The girls dress in very revealing clothing. Most put on heavy makeup and try to look as close to a guy's view of "perfection" as possible. Women are expected to display their features, and anything less just seems to be out of place. (Harry)

> I thought half the girls were going to rip their dresses they were so tight and short. All of the girls were wearing some top that accentuated their cleavage and some skirt that almost showed their butt, but not quite. It looked impossibly uncomfortable. (Mindy)

Many student ethnographers noticed how women all seemed to be after the same sexy and voluptuous look, wearing the least amount of clothing possible to accentuate their cleavage and butt. Uniformity of dress was most extreme for women in sororities, as seen in the following observations from a Greek party:

> Tight white pants, low-cut tank tops, short-shorts, and either strappy sandals or wedges were all the rage. Many women also wore sundresses or skirts. I was shocked by the similarities in overall look of the women; it was as if they had a prototype to follow. Outfits aside, these women still looked the same. They were incredibly thin and in shape, tan, mostly bleached blonde, had perfectly plucked eyebrows, poker straight hair, and at least three pounds of make-up. In the eyes of society, these women were absolutely flawless. (Kelly)

Many male ethnographers marveled at or were simply critical of the discomfort women will endure in their quest to appear sexy:

> I have never talked to any girl who said dressing up the way they do is comfortable. The first thing any girl wants to do after a party is

ditch the heels. Often as soon as they return home, the nice clothes come off and the sweats go back on. I have learned that it is also not that rare for a girl to tape her breasts together before going out. As a male, this is such a foreign concept. It is difficult enough to grasp the makeup concept, but living our whole lives surrounded by it, it is just accepted. The clothes, the heels, and the tape, are a different story. Women go to such extremes to make themselves look good, and what do men do? Men take a shower, throw on a t-shirt, make sure their hair is not a complete mess, and go have a good time. (Harry)

If at least three hours' notice is not given to a woman, then I am being unreasonable. I cannot imagine such a life. This process is extended to other areas of female life in the countless hours spent at shopping malls and clothing boutiques. The pains that go into the female dress are almost nauseating to me. The different ways women attempt to do their hair, the fashion show of outfits they have to parade, are all endured in an effort to look like some alabaster goddess. The sad thing is when women do this and they still end up not looking all that great. Men can look just so impossibly mediocre and still be able to go home with a girl that is far better looking than them. (Kyle)

While most male ethnographers commented that they felt no need to conform to a particular appearance expectation, some perceived that college men were subject to an opposite norm of appearing as though they couldn't care less about their appearance or the desire to impress anyone. Dominic, for instance, notes: "More casual attire for men is not only accepted but also promoted, as it properly displays the lack of care they have invested into the current social scene." When men act outside this social script and put more effort into their appearance, they are at times "disciplined" by having their heterosexuality called into question.

Ethnographers noticed how both genders often stuck together to scope out and evaluate the opposite sex. Further, men wanted to gain their "bro's opinion" of women's level of "hotness" before pursuing anyone:

The men banded together, basically claiming the women they would pursue that night. Without saying her name, guys would encourage other guys to pursue a particular girl based solely on appearance. "Did you see her ass? The blonde," one guy said. His friend responded: "Yeah, go talk to her." Many of the guys reduced a woman to her attractive body parts, transparently showing their interests and motivations. Though not as blunt, women also engaged in similar behavior, pointing out or "claiming" a guy based on his physical appearance. From previous experiences, the following morning after a night out, girls and guys still refer to that person as the "short brunette" or "big Titties" or "blue V-neck," disregarding their names all together. (Teagan)

Male and female ethnographers also frequently commented on how much "work" women did at the very beginning of parties to be engaging while men initially tended to act casual, indifferent, or aloof:

The courting seemed to begin with a bunch of flirtation on the girl's part and a casual indifference on the guy's part. Eventually, the guy's casual indifference turned into a profound bravado. His bravado stemmed from a variety of things: his prowess at drinking games such as the winning shot of beer pong, the sheer volume of alcohol he consumed, how many people he knew, anything that seemed worthy of conversations. Girls seemed more intent on listening to the guys and having a very engaging posture. They were looking at the guy's face, had their body leaned in towards him, often touched him and laughed or giggled at silly things he said. Girls expect guys to be hypersexual, so they believe physically touching, hanging on or falling into a guy will help increase their chances that they will start something with the guy. (Alec)

At many parties, student ethnographers also observed women seeking male attention and approval by engaging in "girl on girl" action:

Some women did a dance with each other, and if they were really drunk, gave in to peer pressure and even kissed. (Anthony)

Sally was resting her sore feet and Jane was giving her a lap dance. A crowd of guys had stopped rolling their hips to the music to see the girls grind their pelvises against each other and cheer for the homosexual antics. The guys were cheering out, "Fuck her." "Yeah get it." "Rub it all over her!" (Max)

When enough fierce beer pong games had been played and enough alcohol consumed, student ethnographers began to observe many peers dancing, which largely consists of bumping and grinding:

The music is turned up as loud as it can go and then the dancing begins. Girls are so ridiculous—butts are shaking, arms are flailing, and lips are pouting. If this is a legitimate attempt at sexy, I think they need to seriously look in a mirror. It is then that I noticed that a lot of guys are not dancing. The men are just watching the women. This is creepy. A few girls start to reach obliteration and lose control of what they are doing. They begin with dance wildly and grind on anyone in sight, man or woman. At this point, people begin making out all over the place and heading to bedrooms. (Erin)

The girls were dancing on guys, other girls, and walls. They were dancing in a very sexual and "slutty" way. One girl was wearing a tight shirt that showed her midriff, a tight, very short skirt, and high heels. She looked as if she was having sex with whatever or whomever she was dancing on. She would go up to guys, grab them, and then start dancing on them as if she was an object. (Elena)

Dancing consisted of girls grinding up on guys and just rubbing their butts all over the guys' lower regions. It was pretty raunchy and incredibly sexual. (Theo)

According to students, college men and women tend to interpret the motivations of grinding differently. While most guys interpreted dancing as a girl's desire to hook up and have sex, women often claimed that their motivation was to attract male attention, dance provocatively in order to fit in, or to have fun:

I would describe dancing at a party as having sex with clothes on. The amount of humping and touching certain body parts is unbelievable. However, I don't think dancing like a "slut" means a girl is one. Some girls enjoy dancing and feeling a connection through dance. I think most guys would not agree with me in regards to this. When a guy dances with a girl, especially a random girl, he thinks she wants him sexually. This is a common misconception. Numerous times I noticed the girl would walk away and the guy would chase after her. (Preston)

When I go out to parties I do not really enjoy grinding on my boyfriend because I feel like touching in that way should not be shared with the entire world. It is not anyone's business what my boyfriend and my physical relationship consists of. This is something for private, not the public eye. Yet, when we go to parties I always end up grinding on him because I want to fit in with everyone else. (Tammy)

Observations About Race and Ethnicity at College Parties

While all ethnographers wrote about male–female interactions and the different ways in which men's and women's bodies were depicted at parties, they did not consistently include thoughts and observations pertaining to the relevance of race and ethnicity in students' interactions and behavior. Among all 126 ethnographers, 30% did not answer or address the question about race and ethnicity. One percent noted that they could not answer owing to lack of diversity at their parties, 17% perceived no difference in the behavior and interactions between students of different ethnicities, and 52% perceived differences that they described. If we separate ethnographers according to ethnicity, 92% were Caucasian, 6% were African American, and 2% were Asian American. Among those who were Caucasian, 33% did not answer or address the question about race and ethnicity, 1% noted that they could not answer due to lack of diversity at their parties, 18% perceived no difference in the behavior and interactions between students of different ethnicities, and 49% perceived differences. Of the 8% of ethnographers who identified as either African American or Asian American, all answered the question about race and ethnicity. One student perceived no difference in the behavior and interactions between students of different ethnicities, and nine students perceived differences. Certain observations and analyses will be offensive and ethically problematic for many readers; it is important to remember that the vast majority of ethnographers were Caucasian, and their perceptions were influenced by white privilege and deeply entrenched racist stereotypes about African Americans' bodies and sexuality.

The most prominent theme among ethnographers (regardless of their own ethnicity) was segregation. Most often, they reflected upon the lack of ethnic diversity at parties:

At both parties, I was quick to realize there were few minorities at the parties. All of the parties consisted of whites and maybe a few Asians or Hispanics. I think I only saw about two or three blacks.

On top of that, two of them were the same people on both nights. My friend informed me that most black students had their own parties. He said the two types of parties were pretty segregated. (Alec)

Race never seems to be a huge issue at the parties I have attended, but maybe that is because the parties are usually separate. At the parties I attend, the occasional black, Hispanic, or other ethnic person may be there. But for the most part, white people go to one group of parties and blacks go to another group. I have noticed that white males, as a whole, talk to mostly white females. (Simone)

There were hardly any individuals of minority race or ethnicity at either of the parties. I found that very telling itself. I think, oftentimes in [University A's] social culture, ethnic groups tend to separate themselves. We intermix easily in clubs and other events, but when we are given a choice of parties to attend, we seem to drift into a more segregated atmosphere. (Bailey)

When these ethnographers did observe ethnic diversity at college parties, most focused solely on observing the behavior and interactions of Caucasian and African Americans, and were silent about students of other ethnicities.[2] Many ethnographers again observed that students tended to self-segregate according to ethnicity.

African Americans only socialized in groups with other African Americans. There seemed to be no interracial bonding at all during this party. No whites wanted to branch out and talk to blacks, and no blacks wanted to branch out and talk to whites. (Eric)

One of my white roommates is very interested in African American men, so occasionally there will be a few at our parties. They are always differently dressed than the white boys, usually wearing baggy jeans with a colored t-shirt, and a hat and gym shoes of the same color. Honestly, they tend to stick together. They usually come over, sit on the couch with Katie, talk and have a few drinks. They don't usually participate in the drinking games or really associate with anyone else. The atmosphere was clearly dominated by white males and females, making anyone who did not fit that mold feel semi-awkward. Instead of drawing attention to themselves, students seemed to stay in their various niches, associating with the people with whom they felt relaxed. (Nora)

I saw that many of the different ethnic groups did not interact with each other but rather stayed within their own group of friends. I saw that many of the white males only interacted with white women and it was similar with African American males: they only interacted with girls of their same ethnic background. (Marek)

Out of all of the ethnic groups, black women and white men interacted the least and tended to self-segregate. Black women were frequently observed as "sticking together" or as only being interested in African American men. With only a few exceptions, ethnographers observed white men flirting and socializing solely with white women:

The three single female friends that came with my girlfriend were all black, and only black men attempted to dance with them. (Isaac)

The white men were not very forward, and stuck to talking to white girls in the non-confrontational setting. The Caucasian men also seemed to only be interested in girls of the same race. (Emmie)

Black men often target or talk to the best looking white women. This is the opposite for the white men. It seems like the white men are more intimidated by the black women and don't seem to talk to them. However, it could also just mean that they are not interested in them. (Derek)

Ethnographers' observations about African American men were more mixed. While some ethnographers observed them self-segregating, others noticed them flirting with women of all ethnicities. A small minority of ethnographers observed white women flirting back and eagerly dancing with African American men (especially if they were high-profile athletes), but the majority perceived white women as avoiding or rejecting black men's advances:

Caucasian women treated African American men differently than Caucasian men. Most women were not open to talking to African American men and were especially standoffish towards them. They were more likely to talk to and dance with Caucasian men than African American men. I have thought about a few reasons why this might be. One is because there were not as many African American men there as there were Caucasian. It is hard to accurately measure how women in general treat African American men as opposed to Caucasian. The second is because of the stereotypes of African American men, especially in this neighborhood. Most women look at African American men as predators. A lot of this neighborhood's residents are African American men who are a little rough on the outside. I honestly believe some women are afraid of what may happen if they open up to an African American man. (Sophie)

At this party, the white girls in general stayed close to the white men. The African American male students were very forward with all of the women at the party. Instead of being concerned mainly with the drinking games, they focused their efforts on flirting with as many women as possible. Unfortunately, their efforts were rarely rewarded since most of the girls blew them off. Nonetheless, despite all the rejections, some subtle while others glaringly obvious, the African American males continued to 'cat call' to the women walking by. (Emmie)

Another theme that arose in some students' reports is that African American men exuded more confidence than white men at college parties:

Black people tend to have a much cockier attitude when at parties and unlike the white people, they do not try and act within the social norm; they have their own distinct way of enjoying parties. They tend to hang out with one another and do not really acknowledge or care what everyone else is doing around them. White people, on the other hand, are constantly trying to conform themselves to what is popular at the time. (Scott)

Black males seem to be more comfortable with their body language and know how to utilize it well to keep the attention of the women they are interacting with. They also seem to have more confidence in their delivery when speaking to white women. White males seem less confident. (Miley)

Out on the dance floor I noticed right away that the African American men were the first out there. They would approach women from behind with confidence. They did not seem to discriminate racially and just enjoyed the company. (Emmie)

Ethnographers were mixed in their views about whether white and black men interacted the same or differently in their flirtations with women. Some noted that white men were more aggressive while others perceived that black men were more forward in their interactions with women:

> The black guys were the most aggressive. . . . I found out later from my sister that black guys wear sweatpants so that when the girls grind on them they could feel their genital area. Their main aim is just to get a girl to dance on them. They would huddle in a circle and watch as different guys got twerked on by girls. They would also chant very loudly when it was over, and the guys would high-five each other. The black men had a cocky attitude and they were not afraid to approach any of the girls. (Merida)

> In my observation, it appeared that white men treated girls possibly worse than black men, with their constant efforts to get girls drunk and hook up with them. Black men seemed more passive and had the attitude that girls would come to them. (Scott)

Very few ethnographers compared African American women's and white women's interactions with men. For those who did, some perceived that black women demanded more respect from men than white women do:

> The aggressiveness did not sit overly well with other black women I observed at the party. The black girls did not like when the white guys were touching all over them while dancing. It was obvious that white guys were not used to rejection whatsoever. I noticed black girls typically give more attitude than necessary to men approaching them. (Adaline)

> White women seem more willing to make themselves subservient to men than black women. They seem much more eager to please their partner than black women do. (Rob)

As I coded students' observations and analyses of racial and ethnic interactions at college parties, I was struck by the stark contrast between (1) Caucasian students' private, written observations and analyses on the intersection between racism and sexuality; and (2) their public comments in class discussions. Several weeks after submitting their ethnography papers, students read Kelly Brown Douglas's *Sexuality and the Black Church*, which argues that one of the most effective ways to disempower and denigrate a social group's collective identity is to attack or denigrate their sexuality and bodies. Using powerful historical examples, Douglas demonstrates how U.S. whites created a dominant narrative about the differences between white and black sexuality and bodies in order to legitimize slavery, lynching, castration, and subsequent social and economic oppression of African Americans.[3] White students consistently expressed horror at past unjust practices of demeaning African American sexuality but had trouble identifying how white culture today denigrates minority groups' bodies and sexuality. When asked to reflect on manifestations of racism within their own social culture, white students typically expressed that their generation is distinct from prior generations in their lack of racism and affirmation of ethnic diversity. White students did not perceive themselves as denigrating African Americans in any way, and some were offended by Douglas's descriptions of white culture. Yet their analyses of the two forms of segregation at parties (separate parties and the self-segregation at common parties) sharply challenged their own optimistic sentiments of their generation's "lack of racism." Their lack of analysis of the segregation they were observing is also worth noting. Only a minority of students who mentioned segregation sought an explanation, and most avoided any references to racism:

I didn't see much interracial mingling, but I didn't get the impression that this was due to discrimination or judgments. It just seemed that people were socializing in their friend groups. (Tessa)

I asked some of the guys at the party: "Why is it so that people who have the same color or nationality stay and interact with each other at parties and not with other groups?" The main responses were: "Because we feel comfortable with the people of our same group and the language of our group" and "We feel like we are all in a bubble and that if we try to approach and interact with another group's bubble, this is viewed as a threat to them and less comfortable." (Tucker)

As for the people who stick with other members of their same race, I think that they did that for one simple reason: comfort. Everyone likes to have something undeniably familiar to fall back on. (Rosie)

From my understanding, people feel safer when they are surrounded with people who look like them, so that had to be the explanation for this lack of bonding. (Eric)

Such an explanation about safety and comfort by Caucasian students raises the question: What social beliefs, attitudes, histories, current practices, and developmental processes influence Caucasian students to feel more comfortable and safer around people who "look like them?"[4] How does this explanation square with Caucasian college students' belief that they are more comfortable and affirming of diversity than prior generations? Only four Caucasian ethnographers[5] hinted at racist dynamics when describing interactions at college parties:

> The dynamic between black and white still seems to be rough and it is hard to cross the racial barrier in a sexual manner still in today's society. (Derek)

> The black and white males kept to their separate groups, but the white girls seemed to mingle with the black males who were also football players. There was a lot of diversity on the dance floor, black males dancing with white females, white females with white males and even white females with other white females. This dynamic seems to be pretty typical in college especially at a white racially dominated party. One part of me felt uneasy about the racial dynamic, but then the other side of me was not surprised one bit by the dynamic. It made me feel uneasy because it showed that the racial stereotypes we deal with in society are embedded in us because they are very much alive in our social scene. (Jill)

> Something interesting occurred when minorities interacted with whites. They often seemed to display a stronger personality than their white counterparts and were more proactive in their pursuit of the other gender at the parties. Perhaps one reason is that many minorities feel they must overcome a disadvantage in order to get noticed by their white peers. Black men may feel like they have trouble competing with white men for white women, so they try extra hard to woo a girl in a predominantly white community. One final explanation is that the minorities at the parties had felt that they must overcome any stereotypes subjugated to them by the majority, thus trying to embody the ideal party goer. The boys tried to be ultra-masculine in terms of white culture while girls tried to be ultra-feminine in terms of white girl culture. This could all be an attempt to fit in with everyone else and win someone over of the opposite sex. (Alec)

Even today, women who hook up with black men are slightly looked down upon even though most will not admit to this prejudice; my party observations might prove this theory. In general, it seemed to me that white women seemed to steer away from black men at the party and most only were interested in white men. The black men and women stayed together and the white men and women stayed together besides a few exceptions. (Tammy)

Despite my study's small sample of student ethnographers who were ethnic minorities—eight African Americans and two Asian Americans—I was curious about similarities and differences in themes that might emerge when I compared their analysis of parties with voices from the Caucasian majority. Mindful that the perspectives of only ten students obviously cannot be taken to represent entire minority groups, I also understood that failure to analyze their group perspectives would be to silence these students in some respects. Examining this group's analysis of the impact of race and ethnicity on social interactions, I was struck first by significant similarities. Ethnic minority students also noted segregation at parties:

I rarely witnessed a moment when the white males would talk to the black females. It was clear that they noticed them dancing in the crowd or retrieving a drink, but I hardly saw any white male approach a black female to talk. (Maria)

I noticed that we [black men] were being glanced at while partying. I think this happened because we were the only black males at the party. I felt a sense of responsibility because I was black. I felt like I couldn't actually party and have as much of a good time as others because of this. I noticed that the white students were initially turned off by the thought of meeting someone of different skin color. I don't want to say that this governed the experience completely but I did notice the looks and glances. The white women seemed more willing to meet a new person whereas the white men stayed confined in their group and watched from a distance.... There is definitely a difference in interaction between races and between genders. I often find myself frustrated because I don't think at this point in time there should be an emphasis on approachability based on skin color differences. (Mitchell)

Some African American ethnographers chose to spend one evening at a predominantly black party and their other evening at a predominantly white party. They observed that women at both parties dressed sexily to receive attention and attract men, witnessed black males flirting with white females, and regularly noticed students behaving sexually and hooking up:

> Women at both white and black parties dressed with one intention in mind which is to get the guy. (Adaline)

> The black girls definitely dress more provocatively. They stayed with their friends a lot. The black girls are generally the ones who would twerk and grind on the guys. They would literally put their hands on their knees, bend over, and start dancing on guys. The black girls also gravitated towards their friends more. They stayed in packs and definitely seemed more afraid to branch out and talk to other people. (Merida)

> When I was observing the African American males, I'd notice that they just wanted to hook up with any white girl who was there. They would dance with them and talk to them trying to get their number. The white women were trying to hook up with some of the African American men. They especially tried to hook up with the athletes that were there that night. (Saige)

Most ethnic minority students noted a difference in the drinking culture: students drank more excessively at white parties. Black students perceived that black men focused on flirting with women and hooking up, whereas white men were interested in both drinking beer with male peers and hooking up:

> At the white party, the aim seemed to be drink as much as you can handle, then keep drinking. I saw multiple people throwing up in the backyard of the party. Alcohol is everywhere and plays a key factor in the happenings at parties. Intentions at the black party were leaning more toward sex instead of drinking. There was still a large amount of liquor at the party but nobody was beyond drunk. The liquor seemed to break the ice at the party. All the males at the party seemed to come in with one thing on their mind and that was which girl they are leaving with tonight. Girls and guys grinding all over each other was a quick indication. It was like they were having

sex on the dance floor with clothes on. The black party didn't really seem to be based on relationships. It was more of a one-night stand situation going on. (Adaline)

When considering student ethnographers' observations and analyses at University A about race and ethnicity, it is, of course, possible that the culture they describe is not nationally representative of most college party cultures; however, recall that ethnographers observed these dynamics at public and private universities in seven states. Furthermore, research on racially themed parties and racist incidents at universities suggests that ethnographers' observations of racial and ethnic segregation and racist dynamics likely pervade many college parties nationwide.[6]

Observations and Analysis of Interactions According to Sexual Orientation

When I asked student ethnographers to observe interactions between and among heterosexual men and women and LGBTQ individuals, 61% of ethnographers found something substantive to share. Out of the 39% of students who did not address questions pertaining to sexual orientation, it is difficult to know whether this was due to lack of interest, discomfort with the topic, or their perception that they were observing only heterosexual students. A total of 15% reported that they could not answer the question due to lack of LGBTQ students at their parties, 9% observed no differences, and 37% observed and analyzed differences in interactions and behavior. Although my students were not asked to reveal their sexual orientation for this assignment, it is most likely that the majority of ethnographers identified as heterosexual; only 2% voluntarily identified as LGBTQ and the majority gave the impression of identifying as heterosexual by alluding in their papers to prior hookups or relationships with the opposite sex. Recall, as with earlier material in this chapter on sexism and racism, that students' cultural biases influence their observations and analyses. When it comes to ethnographers' writing about sexual orientation, readers may find certain comments offensive.

As for those students who perceived no differences among students according to sexual orientation, the dominant theme was that alcohol has the same loosening-up effect on LGBTQ students as on heterosexuals:

The dynamics of straight couples and gay couples is not that different because alcohol makes both straight and gay people more outgoing and more willing to toss morals aside in the hopes that their outgoing behavior will lead them to looking more attractive and therefore hooking up with new people. (Dave)

I found that the homosexual boys were very touchy-feely. Almost every private interaction between the two of them involved some sort of bodily touching, the most common being holding hands. Being the detective that I was, I asked an individual who knew the couple if they normally behaved like that. She informed me that it was very uncommon for them to show affection outside of private rooms when they were sober; however, as soon as they became intoxicated, all their inhibitions flew out the window. The woman told me that the two homosexual boys feel awkward when they receive dirty looks from their peers while publicly displaying their affection and that alcohol throws these worries away. (Frank)

While several students expressed that LGBTQ persons could freely express themselves because their generation affirms diversity, tolerance, and acceptance, most ethnographers who detected differences in interactions perceived that many LGBTQ students were not as comfortable as heterosexuals. They perceived that it is risky for them to reveal their sexual orientation publicly at the college party scene because there is the potential of harassment and hostile repercussions:

There did not appear to be a significant difference in how heterosexual bodies were depicted in relation to homosexual bodies. This makes finding same-sex couples difficult to pick out, as their out-of-the-norm behavior is often suppressed due to their surroundings. This likely conveys the need for homosexuals to repress their true selves in an attempt to fit in and coexist with those around them, so as not to stand out—the ultimate punishment in the identity-obsessed world of the party scene. (Dominic)

I observed one homosexual couple. They are not openly gay. This couple certainly acted differently than a heterosexual couple. In particular, this couple kept their distance from each other—they were not very touchy-feely like some heterosexual couples can be in public. This could be because they are not sure how everyone would react to an openly gay couple at a house party. They could be more reserved in their actions because they don't want negative reactions. (Percy)

Homophobia, although less at [University A], greatly determines the behavior of many homosexuals. Many fear to be open about their sexuality for fear of being harassed. I spoke with a gay friend of mine throughout the evening, and I asked him what it is like to be gay at these parties. He flatly told me that it was awful. He said that few people were openly gay at college parties and even if they were, there was very little open flirting and definitely not anything more. He told me that some gay guys were sexually active, but they went to gay bars or clubs where it was much easier to find someone without fear of being harassed. (Alec)

There were no openly LGBTQ couples at this party. A few gay friends were in attendance but did not interact in any type of sexual manner with their same sex. Most of my gay friends pretend to be straight. [University A] claims to accept the LGBTQ community but not many kids do; everyone is very judgmental. (Nikki)

Although college is often thought of as a time of growth and exploration, coming out as a homosexual is still a risky move. Prejudice and discrimination towards gay people, while getting better, is still a prevalent part of our society. Some homosexuals may not feel comfortable enough to let their sexual orientation be known. (Michelle)

Some ethnographers also noted that gay men acted more uncomfortably around heterosexual men than around women:

This gay man spent most of the time talking and being a part of the group of heterosexual females. He laughed, talked, and moved just liked the females did. When he did talk to a heterosexual male his total mood changed. He became more reserved and not flamboyant at all. The heterosexual males who were talking to him didn't seem to change their line of communication at all. (Ian)

The one gay student danced and mingled with a group of girls all night. He may mingle with the girls because he is unsure of how guys would react to being approached by a guy who is openly gay. Dancing is also a way he can express himself, and he seemed to be having a great time dancing and talking with his girlfriends. (Spencer)

Interestingly, in class discussions on sexual orientations, heterosexual students again express that their generation is more progressive on LGBTQ rights. And yet, according to student ethnographers, their college campus and party scene is not perceived as a safe environment for many LGBTQ students to "come out" and be themselves.

College Party Hookups: Expected and Normative?

There was a consensus among student ethnographers that their peers began hooking up as the partying and drinking continued. A dominant emphasis in ethnographers' accounts included the idea that alcohol gave students the "liquid courage" to act in ways they normally would not feel comfortable acting while sober. Consider Erin's story of her friends Mary and Nathan:

> Mary has the reputation for being a "party girl" so I knew I could count on her to go out on a Tuesday night. Mary, the seasoned drinker, typically downs about four to five shots before we go out. Mary becomes a different person when she drinks and so does my other friend—we will call him Nathan. They are both very sweet and shy individuals when they are sober, but when they have had a few drinks they are loud and for lack of a better term, "horny." Sober, Nathan was completely friendly and nonsexual towards Mary. Nathan was sympathetic toward her ex-boyfriend situations. Mary made it clear that she was not ready to be with anyone else physically or emotionally. As soon as they started drinking heavily, the way that Nathan and Mary usually acted changed. Since Nathan knew how sad and upset Mary was about her breakup, he also knew how vulnerable she was. It was clear that Nathan was hardcore flirting with Mary and it was also clear that Mary was interested. Mary laid down on one of the couches and closed her eyes. Nathan sat there for a while; he looked like he was in an internal struggle. He got up and went to the bathroom. When Nathan returned, he went straight to the couch that Mary was on and laid on top of her. It was obvious that both Mary and Nathan were extremely drunk. They started making out. Naturally, I began to feel really uncomfortable and awkward. I didn't know what to do—I had to see if Mary was okay. I went to the bathroom and slammed the door. They flew apart

so fast Nathan fell to the ground. Both were laughing hysterically. I apologized and told Mary I was leaving. She winked at me and waved. Mary and Nathan, under the influence of alcohol, were very forward and were not concerned with feelings or emotions that could catch up with them later.

Ethnographers also described how college men typically were the ones who initiated hookups and how they became more flirtatious, attentive, and very touchy with the woman they wanted to bring home: "They bring her drinks, dance on her, cheer her up with what they think she wants to hear. By doing these things the guys think girls will just fall for them and have sex with them" (Elena). Many ethnographers repeatedly mentioned men acting aggressively in the pursuit of a hookup; such behavior appeared to be the norm of college parties:

> Male attitudes were also very aggressive; it appeared as though the main goal for males was to get as drunk as possible and to pick up girls for their own enjoyment, so that they could brag about it to their friends and build up their own reputations. Males are predatory toward females. One guy brought along a funnel, which is used to drink beer extremely efficiently in an attempt to get drunk faster. He challenged one girl to see who could do it faster, and the male student clearly won. After this challenge, he began to talk to the girl in what appeared to be an attempt to convince her to hook up with him. This sort of thing happened everywhere—females whose alcoholic tolerance is not nearly to the level of males are always given drinks and will have their cup filled up long before a male's cup. One of the more attractive girls voiced how she had just finished her last beer and within a matter of seconds a male had brought her one from his case. After this happened the girl began to dance or "grind" with the male as some sort of repayment. (Scott)

> Overall, the men behaved very aggressively and came on very strongly toward the women, as they felt they had the right to touch women whenever they pleased. The men also had this sense of pride about them, like they were entitled to something (I'm not sure what) and like they were superior to women. (Kelly)

In the minority of instances in which women were the sexual initiators, peers were quick to comment on how slutty or drunk they were. As Derek wrote, "Women will be looked down upon or looked at differently if they are the ones who go after the men."

Student ethnographers regularly described peers going upstairs to bedrooms or bathrooms for quick hookups, engaging in sexual behavior publicly on sofas and floors or in house corners, leaving to hook up outside, or heading to the guy's place. They also emphasized that conversations about hooking up and actual acts of hooking up are intentionally part of the public domain of college parties:

> I was talking to an individual who suddenly grabbed me and began telling me which women would do what sexual acts (most of which consisted of oral sex) if you did certain things for them. He was not concerned about talking about these women once they left the room, and everyone around us viewed this as an ordinary event. The casual talking about sex and who will do what promotes this kind of culture. By observing the ways people danced and "made out" wherever they could find a spot, there was no concern about others watching or judging their actions. In fact, this short-term sexual pleasure was celebrated. (Colter)

> There was no place that seemed inappropriate to touch another person even in a public setting, and there seemed to be no shame in making out or going even further with someone they did not know. Some people were on the couches and seemed to be close to having sex right on the couch in front of everyone. Those who were on the couches seemed to have no care in the world that others were learning about their sex life as they walked by. They just went along with their business as if they were in their own bedroom. (Tammy)

> Sex is an act that is very public. . . . Sex at this party seemed to be just something you do. Everyone was talking about who had screwed around with whom. To have sex with someone, you don't even really have to know their name. (Mindy)

> Students think that in college random hookups are okay, because in today's society sex is more physical than it is intimate. (Duke)

Concerning the frequency of observed hookups, students repeatedly revealed a nonchalant attitude, suggesting they believed nothing extraordinary or shocking was occurring:

Sex is a normal thing, or at least, hookups are. (Nora)

The college hookup scene dictates that even sex can be casual, over and done with, and never thought of again. (Helen)

From friends' stories it is apparent that one night stands or hooking up is as common and harmless as eating peanut butter and jelly sandwiches. (Sam)

It is a part of human nature to hook up, and knocking back a few brews can make hooking up even more fun. (Nolan)

Some male undergraduate ethnographers who focused on following their friends and interviewing them during consecutive evenings and weekends of college parties noted that some men hooked up with a different woman each night. For instance, Collin observed his friend Rob "seal the deal" and have sex on Friday with Kate—a girl he had talked about for weeks. On Saturday night, Collin continued to watch Rob interact flirtatiously with Kate and a few other women at the party. Collin writes:

By now it's about 11:00 p.m. and Rob had disconnected from Kate, talked to a few other girls, but made his way back to her. It seemed Rob had searched the party for something different but couldn't find anything, so he came back. This time Rob and Kate stood in the corner talking a little more closely. After a while, Jessica hurried over to see him. I thought to myself, "It's almost like he has these girls on tap." . . . The situation seemed to unfold just like Friday night with Kate. Jessica and Rob hung around with the rest of us in the family room, but eventually went upstairs and disappeared. The next morning, Rob walked out of his room with a casual smile and I asked him straight out, "Are you going to tell me what happened?" And Rob responded, "I had sex with her." He had just pulled two girls on back-to-back nights and acted so casually about it.

Student ethnographers frequently observe that, within this culture, choosing not to have sex when the opportunity arises is viewed as strange or odd, and usually results in subtle or blatant negative social consequences. As Percy notes: "It is far too commonly assumed that people should be having sex, and something isn't 'normal' if an individual is not having sex, or does not have a sexual history."

For instance, Cameron recounts how a very drunk woman approached his friend Jim at a party. They were in a class together and she asked if he could walk her home because she did not want to walk home by herself. Jim appeared reluctant to leave the party, but walked her home. When he returned to his friends at the party, they eagerly asked him if he "got some":

> Jim told us that when they got back to her house, he got her some water, and they talked for a few minutes. Then he made sure she got into bed all right. As he was leaving, she said to him that he could stay if he wanted to. I asked what he said, and he told her that he needed to get back to the party with his friends. At this moment another one of our friends gave Jim a hard time for not hooking up with her when she obviously wanted it, even went as far as calling him a "pussy."

Female ethnographers also acknowledge how a choice not to "put out" labels you a "prude" or a "freezer," and this reputation typically results in social suicide among male peers. As Erin comments, "Prudes get no attention from guys because the guys know it is not going anywhere. It is horrible to say but in college it is reality." A consistent theme is that women who don't hook up are at risk of being on "the outside" of the party scene and appearing less attractive to men.

Furthermore, within this social context that celebrates college as *the* time to experiment sexually and be wild, desiring to have sex within a committed relationship rather than simply wanting hookups can earn a college student the reputation of being too clingy or having "way too high" expectations. Student ethnographers frequently observe that many couples in a relationship display ambivalence about their relationship status by flirting with others or cheating on their significant other:

> Being in college, you are told to experiment and test the waters. Being in a relationship in college seems to be looked down upon because people view college as a way to have fun. When I see people act unfaithful at parties I immediately think they are feeding into the college way of life, and they don't want to come across as wanting to settle down. (Merida)

> Ryan was talking with a simply dressed girl wearing jeans, a nice shirt, and flip-flops. He slowly brushed her face and I could tell he

said, "Wow! You are beautiful." However, this girl was not letting it get to her. She continued speaking with him, but she was smart enough to shrug off his sweet talk. I could tell this made him angry. When I went over to talk to him about it, he just kept texting and saying, "She ain't shit" and "She was ugly anyway." I asked him who he was texting, his face lit up and said, "My girlfriend. She is about to come here from another party." At this point I started to get mad. I could not even imagine how angry I would be if my boyfriend was acting like that with another girl. I was livid that people in relationships were doing this to each other. (Ellen)

Descriptions of Predatory Behavior at College Parties: A Pervasive Underlying Theme

While college parties are viewed and celebrated by most as a place to be freed from daily stressors and have fun, many ethnographers, both male and female, noted an underside to this carefree party scene: it fosters aggressive male behavior that often results in unwanted sexual experiences that meet legal definitions of sexual assault—a topic I address in chapter 9. Among student ethnographers, there was not a clearly identified line between normal aggressive behavior and behavior that was unacceptably wrong, including rape. Consider how a common theme among ethnographers was not merely the aggressiveness of men but also the use of images of women as prey and men as predators, hunters, or lions who stalk their prey:

> The women were all dressed scandalously, thus making the girls the "bait or prey" for the guys. The girls seemed to be parading around in order "to get caught" by the nearest guy. These girls acted weak and were able to be manipulated by the guys. At the party, some girls enjoyed the advances and flirting by guys. (Tracy)

> Men are like wild animals looking for food. They will do everything and anything they want until something negative comes from it. Men were clearly more dominant and aggressive compared to the women. I noticed that women were often subject to the behavior of the men. At times I felt like I was watching the predator stalk and then eat its prey. (Preston)

Men were seen as the pursuers. They were the hunters in this situation, going out to find a girl that they want. The girls of course were the hunted. This idea would seem to give the power to the guys. The hunters are seen as the people who control the situation and ultimately the outcome. (Mike)

My friend Austin could be considered one of the hunters in respect to females. Through behaviors such as obnoxious celebrations, he was trying to attract someone of the opposite sex from the minute that he entered the party, and succeeded. Derek's girlfriend is also surrounded by a group of other college males, all encouraging her alcohol consumption and studying her like a group of hungry lions before they pounce on their prey. (Riley)

Although drinking and casual sex are viewed as normal at college parties, many students noted that it is dangerous for women to get really drunk because they become a "target" for many guys:

I did drink more when I first came to college and ran into situations where I drank too much and didn't have close friends to protect me. This brought on a few situations where I woke up unsure of what happened the night before, and I really regretted these situations because I felt like I didn't totally autonomously make these decisions. (Tessa)

An intoxicated girl stumbling around a room is sloppy. These girls' bodies are treated like an object for someone to use. . . . Mark objectifies girls and uses them to satisfy his physical desires. His body is just a way to abuse others. (Ben)

I've seen many people make complete fools of themselves when drinking, mostly with situations that have occurred that they wish they could go back in time and change. I've even seen people that have gotten severely hurt because of alcohol or sexual relationships. Girls especially tend to become sloppy and vulnerable with alcohol, which makes it easy to become taken advantage of by men. (Sara)

Students frequently observed college men scoping out and making the moves on very drunk women:

Male students will also unfairly target the females who appear to be the most drunk since they are the easiest target in the attempt to have a random hookup or sex. (Scott)

A couple of the men were trying to get this very drunk girl to come home with them. She turned down a few, but eventually accepted one offer around 1:30 a.m. She then left with the man basically carrying her because she could not walk. Many women and men at the party repeated this behavior throughout the evening. (Sophie)

I observed two girls who became more open about their intention of finding a guy to hook up with that night. They started to dance with each other while standing on a table. This definitely drew a lot of attention, especially from the guys. High heels and too much alcohol led to one of the girls falling off the table. This type of attention is not positive and sends a message that if a girl has too much alcohol and loses control, she can become a target for all sorts of guys. (Austin)

Meet the Schemer

Of all student ethnographers, Eric offered the most in-depth account of a college man's hookup strategy by observing and interviewing his friend Dave on multiple occasions. I have decided to include nearly all of Eric's description because it offers such insight into the predatory behavior that many students observed during their fieldwork:

> I talked with Dave about this assignment and we had some good talks about his strategies and why he does what he does. . . . It took him a couple months to figure out a strategy that worked well for him. Once he figured out his tricks, he started going from girl to girl in rapid movements. I observed Dave over the course of three parties. . . . He ended up with a different girl each night. . . .

> When he gets to the party, Dave decides to pick targets or find targets he has been working on throughout the week. Many times he will start talking with a girl a week or two before he tries to hook up with her. He is extremely charming in these talks and tries to text the girls as much as possible. He gets into their friend zone, which makes hitting on them less awkward. He does not focus on one girl at the beginning. He keeps his options open and watches

how much some of the girls are drinking or picks out flaws in a girl, which takes her off of the target list. He is constantly drinking at the party, looking like he is getting pretty drunk. When I watched him closely though, I noticed he takes small sips often and is not consuming nearly as much alcohol as some of the girls and all the other guys. He keeps talking with girls that he previously targeted and starts flirting and hitting on them more and more as the night goes on. He occasionally makes a move. If a girl strongly rejects any moves, he leaves the girl alone and focuses on another. Once he finds a girl that shows signs of flirting back, he usually stays with that girl. He may then try to take her someplace quieter so they can talk alone. This is when he really starts flirting and making his moves. Many times these talks will lead to making out.

The first night, the breaking point for winning over the girl came after dancing. Grinding with a drunk girl can be a very sexual act and often can lead to making out on the dance floor. This soon led to Dave and his new girl leaving together. The second night I was observing Dave, they started kissing at this point and they soon left to go back to his room . . . . During the third night, Dave seemed to be having trouble sealing the deal so he played beer pong with a girl. This is a great place for sealing a deal because it gives Dave many chances to hug her and make moves if she makes a cup or they win. It also puts another beer in the girl's body, which may push her from being tipsy to drunk. After he lost his first pong game, he was in the clear and knew that she would come back with him that night.

I talked with Dave the day after each party. I brought up what I observed and talked to him about his strategy. The main thing he told me was that he had everything planned out in advance. Dave is a nice guy but when working towards hooking up with a girl, he is extremely nice. He initially seems really interested in the girl and makes her feel like she means something to him, but after the night is over, the girl usually feels used and hurt. After Dave hooks up with a girl he rarely keeps in touch with her. He got the nickname "Schemer" by having a reputation of hooking up with the drunkest girls at a party. This has worked fine except for one situation. Earlier in the year Dave was accused of taking advantage of a girl; they did not have sex according to Dave, but the girl felt used. Luckily for Dave, she did not report what happened. In his mind, he sees girls as challenges, and he likes to win. (Eric)

Eric's descriptions of Dave's strategies and his predatory behavior that targeted the women who appear the drunkest are deeply troubling on many levels. The very fact that Dave was happy to discuss (and perhaps boast) of his strategies to Eric suggests that Dave did not perceive his behavior as deviant, problematic, or shameful. After speaking to Eric in greater detail about Dave, I learned that his behavior was quite normalized within campus culture; Dave did not experience any negative social consequences due to his behavior. As far as Eric knew, none of the Schemer's friends criticized him or questioned him about his strategies and behavior.

I spoke to Eric about my concern that Dave may be a serial sexual offender on our campus.[7] During the semester that I read Eric's "Schemer" paper, I also read Olivia's paper in another class section, which included interviews she conducted with friends who had negative experiences with the very same "Schemer." These women described doing sexual favors or feeling sexually taken advantage of because they were drunk to incapacitation. They also described incidents of Dave's pinning them against walls or hallways and other aggressive controlling behaviors that sought to isolate them from others. It did not occur to any of these women to charge Dave with sexual harassment, sexual misconduct, or rape.[8] If my student ethnographers' frequent observations of men's predatory behavior are indicative of college parties throughout the United States, it means that such behavior has become normalized as part of the contemporary college masculine script. Of course, as we will see, not all college men conform to this dominant masculine social script.

Conclusion

This chapter has explored college students' party personas by analyzing sober ethnographers' observations of their peers at parties. They described what happens before, during, and after parties, and analyzed variations in social interactions within and between various social groups based on gender, race and ethnicity, and sexual orientation. Having gained insider accounts and analysis of these dynamics, we are ready in chapter 2 to explore students' motivations for their behavior. Why, according to our college ethnographers, do their peers act the way they do?

2

Why College Students Act the Way They Do

CONSIDERING TODAY'S PARTY norms and contemporary hookup culture, our question in this chapter is, Why *these* norms, and Why *now*? The student ethnographers' perspectives on why their peers act the way they do at parties, I discovered, can be grouped into two main categories: (1) college students act the way they feel they are "expected" to act as college men and women, and (2) college students' actions are greatly influenced by excessive alcohol.

Expectations for College Partying

First, most ethnographers observed that the majority of peers' behavior mimics and conforms to the media's story of sex, gender, and college culture, particularly acting wild and extreme at college parties, drinking excessively, having casual sex, and seeking to top friends' stories of sexual exploits. Students noted that, from the time they were in junior high or high school, popular culture and social media bombarded them with images of college party life and expectations about how they were supposed to act and who they were supposed to be:

> At the U frat party, I got the feeling that a lot of the activities going on were just what had to happen at a frat party. High school kids go into college with expectations about what college is going to be like, and then they fulfill those expectations. They know that they're expected to drink immense amounts of terrible beer, so they do. They know that frat boys are supposed to prey on girls and treat them like objects,

so they do. The girls know they are supposed to look a certain way, so they do everything in their power to look exactly like this. Women at the frat party were desperate for attention from these guys. Men had a lot of power over these girls, getting them to do whatever they wanted. The girls seemed proud if a guy grabbed her butt or said something demeaning to her like "you're such a slut." They seemed all right with it since it is normative for their culture to dress like a slut and act like a slut in front of everyone. (Mindy)

Our generation is influenced by Internet blogs, music, television shows, advertisements and movies. We are exposed to our favorite celebrities and our favorite characters behaving in ways that are demeaning to themselves, and for some reason we still idolize them. People act the way they do at parties because of the expectation. If you go to a party, you are expected by your peers to get drunk, play drinking games and dance, among other things. (Nina)

The dominant story about sex in college portrayed by popular culture, and reinforced by many peers, is that it is the time to enjoy casual sex with no strings attached and to experiment sexually with as many people as possible:

The people I was observing were acting the way they were because of all the models they have. Turn on MTV and there are multitudes of shows that portray America's youth as sex-starved partygoers. There has yet to be a show on MTV that shows people having fun without drinking and hooking up. Instead, MTV shows the kids who are not participating in this culture to typically be overweight, studious, not into the latest fashion, and only have one or two friends. Our culture gives people the idea that only young, beautiful, popular people go out and party, hook up, and never have any dire consequences. The media rarely portrays the after party affects: being hospitalized, getting an STI, or worse, getting sexually assaulted or raped. (Percy)

Our culture also tells us that you must have as many sexual partners as you possibly can before you find your future spouse. (Anthony)

As we have begun to see, many student ethnographers observed how peers' gestures, attitudes, and behaviors seemed to come straight from movies and TV shows:

At the party the women seemed exotic and willing and the men seemed overly sexual. It was like all of these people just got done watching *American Pie* or *Animal House* and were ready to act out their prescribed roles. (Mindy)

Our media, through movies, commercials, television shows, advertisements, music videos, etc., has ingrained what are appropriate behaviors for males and females in our heads so deeply that these behaviors are replicated unconsciously. Jasmine, for instance, was seemingly content with the time she was having with her friends through laughter and dance. Nevertheless, she and her female companions completely changed their behaviors when approached by a group of males. Wanting to please the males, they danced in a way that completely degraded their image, viewing this type of sensual dance as the image that a typical male desires. (Riley)

Ethnographers further acknowledge that college men's aggressive—even predatory—behavior at parties and women's acquiescence to such behavior simply mimics the popular culture's dominant story of gender norms:

The media plays a deadly role when it comes to determining who has the power in a social relationship. Most TV shows, movies, commercials, music, etc., show a female in the submissive role at a social scene. Their bodies are persistently dressed in an obedient way; thus the males take advantage. If the media were not so direct with the ways they depict men and women to act in a social scene, then I believe that many relationships would be very different. The social norms could shift from the media influence to legitimate personal preference. (Ian)

In almost all media advertisements, the man is depicted as very powerful and controlling while the woman is sexual and seductive. For example, think of the "Axe" commercials. These big strong men who are powerful and good looking are running away from a group of sexy women because they just want to please him, and be with him. These types of commercials put men on a pedestal. Men are shown as strong, independent, and powerful beings while the women are shown as fragile and dependent upon a man. (Collin)

The epitome of the media's portrayal of sexuality is present in shows like *Jersey Shore* (MTV). The behavior in these shows revolves around the run and gun lifestyle that many 20-somethings embrace. The shows portray sex as an easy to get, prevalent activity that is nothing more than the sum of the actions themselves. The outfits worn by women are skanky at best, and men are portrayed as strong, domineering individuals who basically prey on women. (Frank)

In many rap songs, artists describe women in a degrading manner and give men the power to do what they want with them. (Therese)

The popular culture's stories and images of how men and women relate to one another greatly influence students' assumptions of how they are "expected" to act. In the following pages, student ethnographers further reflect upon how the media constructs, celebrates, and eroticizes hyper-masculinity and hyper-femininity and sharply juxtaposes these constructs.

What Does It Mean to Be a College Male Today?

According to male ethnographers, college men navigate a highly competitive social scene with other male peers and are under great pressure to conform to narrow norms of masculine behavior. Below, I identify three such norms that stood out most clearly in my students' descriptions. First, masculinity involves being or at least acting heterosexual. Whenever a guy steps out of the normative masculine expectations, he is frequently "disciplined" through the insult of female names (e.g., "pussy" or "bitch") or with names that call into question his heterosexuality:

Males' appearances were very casual, which showed how it didn't matter really how males looked or cared how they looked. However, there were a few students who decided to be more outgoing in their appearance and go against what might be considered the norm. These particular students were subjected to being called "fags," "homos," or other derogatory names. (Scott)

Second, masculinity involves continual competition and aggression with other men, including one's good friends. Competing in beer pong, drinking others "under the table," having sex with more women than others, and even acting aggressively tends to increase one's status among male peers and often female peers as well:

I became aware of the amount of competition between males. Everything, whether it be a drinking game, dancing, or the amount of girls a guy talks to is a competition to men. There is an unbelievable amount of trash talking between individuals or even groups at parties. (Preston)

Third, proving one's masculinity involves being a sexually experienced "player" by boasting of sexual conquests that conspicuously lack emotional ties. Many ethnographers perceived that men's motivations for hooking up are not simply a desire for sex, but are also related to a desire for acceptance and social status:

Many guys fear being vulnerable. Therefore, they are aloof to some girls and talk up their "manliness" through much bravado and bragging. Some guys may want a relationship, but they are wary, cautious of being hurt by the girl: thus, they try to reduce her to more of a physical object than a human being. Many guys, however, just want sexual contact, which serves as a source of pleasure and bragging rights to friends. Therefore, many guys try to play the right moves to seduce a girl. Many guys talk about hoping the girl will be gone by morning, and this is not surprising. In order to seem dominating and powerful, he cannot be "whipped" by a girl. It is much easier to hook up than to deal with the emotional complexities of a relationship. (Alec)

For males, their goal is usually to hook up to build their own reputation and break away from the virgin/loser label. The concept of finding a girlfriend is rarely viewed; random hookups are far more common. Even when relationships are explored, you rarely see one that lasts for more than a few weeks—there are so many temptations all around you at parties and this is supposed to be the time to explore your sexuality. (Anthony)

There is rarely any attempt to build a long-term relationship—only an attempt to have a hookup and be done with the girl. Overall a male's main motivation for partying is to build his own reputation in the party scene. (Scott)

Students emphasize that acting stoic and dominant over women is key to the player mentality:

Either a man shows his manliness by exerting his sexual power over women or he is emasculated by his respect for women. (Blake)

Men find a sense of power and dominance over women by embodying the cultural characteristics of masculinity, including emotional disconnection in relationships, a sense of confidence and stoicism, and the objectification of female bodies. (Teagan)

Most of the men's behaviors were motivated by the need to prove their "manliness." I originally thought they were just motivated to hook up. However, even this seemed to stem from a deeper pressure to "prove themselves" to male peers and to women. I do not doubt that men wanted to hook up, but the way they went about it suggested that they were more interested in proving their dominance over women than actually having a sexual experience with them. (Adele)

Guys are terrified of being perceived to be weak or emotional, especially in front of other guys. Therefore, the guys spent much time trying to be powerful, dominant, and distant, and in the process, they often put women down. They labeled many character weaknesses as feminine. When someone said they did not want to get drunk that night, his guy friends quickly rebuked him saying, "Don't be such a girl." In the process of this, they clearly were demeaning women. (Tom)

Student ethnographers noted that the player mentality often results in a complete lack of concern for women's well-being when they can no longer be used as an object of pleasure. Riley recounts a story of Kelsey, a first-year student who declared to her friends that she was not going to drink because she didn't want to get sick and be hung over. Soon afterwards, Joe, an upper classman, offered her drinks:

Kelsey would have been seen as "not fun" and displeasing to the male whom she likes. For this reason, she began drinking and got extremely intoxicated, despite her knowledge that she might get sick later in the night. Kelsey and Joe ended up leaving and hailed a cab to go back to campus. I asked Ryan, Joe's friend, to text him to find out how the night ended for Kelsey. The two had gone back to Joe's house to hook up, and Joe had texted that he was "gonna get head from her." However, while at the house, Kelsey began to vomit, and the rest of the night was spent hugging the toilet. Joe had gone to bed and let her vomit the rest of the night on her own. Clearly, he had shown a liking for her the entire night, buying her drinks and making her laugh, so why the sudden change of heart? Joe was clearly only interested in her if there were going to be sexual rewards at the end of the night. Since he did not get what he wanted, he completely lost interest and showed total disregard for her well-being. (Riley)

What Does It Mean to Be a College Female Today?

Student ethnographers' analyses indicated that women, too, are expected to enact their feminine script, which is a blend of traditional and contemporary feminine norms and ideals. The resulting clash of norms sometimes creates conflict or at least tension in how college women should act, as Usher and Ludacris reveal when they want "a lady in the street but a freak in the bed."[1] The first criterion of the feminine ideal is to be thin:

Skinny girls dance with many boys. Boys probably see their bodies as perfection. He treated her body with respect. Other girls who were more overweight or not as pretty were ignored. Men did not interact with them. Most of these girls danced with their friends secretly hoping at least one boy would select her. (Therese)

It doesn't matter what a girl has unless she is skinny, tan, and wearing the right clothes. This is seemingly constantly at parties—the girls who are thicker tend not to get hit on as much as the super-skinny girls. (Lucy)

College male ethnographers also noted how popular culture's image of the thin sexy beauty ideal shapes male sexual desire:

Most professional models are white, skinny, sexy young girls. As a result, even as a man, I naturally think this is the ideal body or how the female body is supposed to be. This image forces me to automatically reject any other body type. (Collin)

Mark chose to approach the table of heavier girls and began to flirt with them. He may have chosen the heavier girls because he believed they would be easier to talk to, and that could lead to hooking up with one of them because they would be excited that this good-looking guy has noticed them. His friends' response was shallow: seeing Mark talking to the heavier girls, they approached the table and physically pulled him away. Seeing their friend speaking to "the less attractive girls" was unacceptable, and they did not want their friend's actions to reflect poorly upon themselves. (Ron)

The pressure to conform to this idealized thin body is intense; at stake is one's sense of attractiveness and social success with male and female peers.

Second, student ethnographers repeatedly described women as appearing passive, weak, fragile, submissive, and obedient. At least in the party context, there seems to be a return to traditional feminine characteristics:

> It is extremely frustrating to me to watch the way some of my female friends act in front of males. These strong, smart, independent girls take on such submissive roles, surrendering all power to guys and allow the men to take charge in most aspects of the relationship. It is extremely hard to not over-generalize, but I think this is definitely the case for all females, at least the college-aged ones. (Paul)

> Ultimately a man is supposed to be strong, courageous, aggressive and dominant. The woman is supposed to be submissive, a nurturer, sexy, and sleek. Obviously, these two descriptions significantly contrast leaving the impression that men are to dominate over women, ultimately holding more power. (Collin)

Third, college women are described as willing to embrace their expected role to appear and act as a sex object:

> Sexual objectification has resulted in women taking on that passive and sexually willing identity.... The women I observed seemed to present themselves, in dress as well as behavior, as trying to live up to the male fantasy. (Blake)

> In our culture women are generally portrayed as "sex objects." They appear in magazines and the general media scantily clothed or wearing very tight fitting clothing that shows every curve. Their facial expression is one of seduction and sexiness. Girls are exposed

to this at a young age and grow up believing that their self-worth is based on their ability to be seductive. Women are seen as objects to acquire—not as people. (Anna)

Women are seen as a body and therefore it's expected that what you need to win over guys is to show that body off because your personality and beauty aren't good enough without it. (Ilsa)

Student ethnographers' analyses demonstrate that it is not enough to appear like a sex object to gain attention. College women also enacted such a role to gain approval, frequently performing sexual activities like grinding, lap-dancing, and submitting to male requests for sexual favors:

It appeared as though females felt obliged to perform some type of sexual action with those who noticed them, which once again leads to the idea that females want to be seen as accepted by others. (Scott)

This socially constructed ideal woman is completely unrealistic, yet I observed women trying to accomplish this—not only as they all try to look the part, but they try to make up for parts they are lacking by behaving promiscuously. Many girls crave attention from guys and will behave and dress in any manner in which they can receive this attention, even if that includes exchanging sexual favors. Our culture is over-sexualized with its advertisements, movies, music, and media in general; the women I observed were trying to meet a certain image prescribed to them in order to pick up men. (Kelly)

Some students how college women internalized objectification to the degree that they were willing to "sell" their bodies for attention or male approval:

Sex sells in the media, so in a way, these women sell sex. They use their bodies in order to get what they want, almost as a sort of currency. (Carl)

While females appeared to feel the need to almost sell their bodies, males tended to both dress and act much more confidently, displaying an air of superiority in terms of the roles played in the hookup culture. (Dominic)

A good time in these women's opinion appeared to be selling their body to the guys in return for affection. (Maleah)

Many ethnographers how women passively went along with what men wanted sexually. Consider how the following descriptions suggest females' lack of agency over their sexual preferences and decisions:

It seems that the pursuer is seductive and the pursued (in these instances, freshmen) always seemed to just go with the plan. They were just willing and ready to do whatever they were confronted with. (Haley)

A man at the party walked up to this girl and grabbed her hand to dance with him. She did not even say anything back; she just walked with him to the dance floor. This also shows that some women feel less powerful. This can be caused by low self-esteem that they just want to please the male. (Cindy)

This theme of lack of sexual agency occurred most frequently in ethnographers' stories of severely intoxicated females. As I coded women students' papers semester after semester, I was struck by how many women revealed that they or their friends had endured "bad" sexual experiences when incapacitated. They described many incidents that met the campus definition of rape, but they never conceptualized such incidents as sexual assault. For instance, consider Colleen's account of her Saturday night. She began to observe her roommate Christina and other friends drink heavily for an hour and a half while pregaming at her place. After they arrived at the party, Colleen observed many men flirting with her drunk roommate:

Certain boys would talk extremely close to Christina's face as if they were telling her secrets. A lot of the time, boys wrapped their arms around her and sometimes they would slide their hand down her butt. I was sort of shocked when I did not see her move a boy's hand or get away from the situation. She simply allowed it to happen; I know that she would have not let something like this happen if she was sober. An hour or two later, everyone was about ready to head back to our residence hall and call it a night. However, one of the boys that was talking to Christina had something else in mind. Jackson kept pulling at Christina's hand and tried to drag her back into the house with him. She was still very nice and friendly, but she was obviously not trying to go back into the house with him. She finally got away from him and got into my car. Three minutes later, Christina got a text from Jackson that read, "Please come back here. I just want to talk to you." She responded, "I am sorry I can't. I am really tired and this is my only way back to the dorm. We can hang out another time." She fell asleep soon after we got back to our room and I thought that the night was over for us. Twenty minutes later, I heard our main door creak open. Wondering who was coming into our room at such an hour, I got out of my bed and opened my door. Much to my surprise, it was Jackson, who had weaseled into the dorm and into our room. He looked a little confused as to where Christina was, as he opened up two of our bedroom doors. Once he had figured out which room Christina was in, he walked in and shut the door behind him. I obviously could not follow him into her room and observe the two. However, I did get the full story in the morning from Christina herself. Jackson walked into her room, and sat down on her bed while she was sleeping. Christina kept reminding me that she was very drunk and she could tell that he was very drunk, but they continued talking for a while. Jackson began to talk to Christina about how much he liked her and wanted to be with her, even though they were never that great of friends. Even though Christina remembers having a gut feeling that something was not right, they started kissing at one point, and everything else happened so fast. They ended up having sex. She said that neither of them discussed or asked if they even wanted to have sex.

Christina said that she did not really know how to stop it. While Christina told me this story, she was crying and explaining that it was something she never would have done in a million years if she were sober. She also said that if she were sober and she was put in a situation like that, she would have known how to end the situation a lot quicker. It really upset her that she never even knew Jackson all that well, but now they had sex. I cannot say that I have never been in some similar situations as my friends have been in. (Colleen)

This story is as troubling as Eric's story of the Schemer in chapter 1, for many reasons. Colleen's story of Jackson entering a woman's dorm room when she is drunk and asleep appears to be quite normalized.[2] According to Colleen, she and other friends have had similar experiences. It is also clear that Christina did not react with frustration when Jackson came into her room and woke her up—even after she told him she wanted to sleep. Neither did she kick Jackson out of her room, even though he had clearly gone against her wishes. Her intoxication undermined her ability to "know how to stop" the sexual activity. Neither Colleen nor Christina raised the possibility that Jackson's behavior constituted sexual assault.[3]

This account is also disturbing because Colleen did not stop Jackson from going into Christina's room. Colleen presumably did not feel "entitled" to tell Jackson to get lost when he snuck into their suite after Christina had clearly told him she was choosing to go home. Once I had read her ethnography paper, I spoke with Colleen the first opportunity I had with her after class. As I expressed concern for her roommate and asked for more details about Jackson arriving at their suite, I asked her if she had considered stopping Jackson from entering Christina's room when she knew that Christina had decided to leave Jackson and go home to sleep. She responded that it wasn't "her place" to kick him out. This surprised me because I knew that, as a college student, I would have been alarmed if some drunk guy walked into our suite and was trying to get into my roommate's room. I would have gotten rid of him. I might possibly have reported him to campus police as well. While these opposite reactions might have been due to personality differences, I wondered if the ways we were socialized, and what we considered acceptable behavior, might also be powerful factors.

I asked Colleen how her roommate was doing, and she responded: "Not well at all." Christina continued to have crying spells, was upset about that night, and drank heavily when she partied. I asked whether Colleen and Christina had talked about whether the sexual activity that occurred that night met the university's definition of rape. I stated that her paper indicated that Christina had been very drunk, and I asked her if she had shown signs of incapacitation. Colleen responded that Christina would not want to "go there" and consider that she had been raped. I mentioned to Colleen that I was concerned about her roommate and thought it would help her to talk to a counselor about this experience. Colleen agreed, and mentioned that she would suggest this. I also asked her to tell her roommate that I would be happy to meet with her and talk confidentially as well. After several weeks, I met with Colleen again and asked how Christina was doing. After continuing to "not do well," she had started hooking up with Jackson every weekend. Colleen said: "It's like she can feel less icky or bad about

that night if she thinks she is in some kind of relationship with him."
I again expressed my concern for Christina and discussed possible posttraumatic symptoms she could be experiencing that could increase her
vulnerability to being in an abusive relationship with Jackson and further
experience revictimization. Colleen mentioned she would again broach
the subject of seeking counseling with her roommate.

What compels many women who enact these feminine norms connected to physical appearance, submissive behavior, and lack of agency
over their sexual decisions? The ethnographers speculated and elaborated
on three primary motivations. First, women long for male attention and
approval because their self-esteem and self-worth is intimately tied to
males' affirming their sexual attractiveness:

> Girls, too, hook up to boost their ego. I know girls who have sex
> because it makes them feel better about themselves. It makes them
> feel like they are worth something and that people actually do like
> them. (Elena)

> Katie's desperation to hook up with Mitch clearly shows how she
> places her empowerment in the physical approval of another man.
> She gets extremely drunk and "blacks out." She sometimes goes
> home with random guys. I think it's more than just wanting to have
> a random hookup or sexual encounter with someone. It is more
> about wanting to feel wanted by someone; it's nice to feel wanted
> and pretty. (Malena)

> The girl who was dancing on guys, girls, and walls as if she were an
> object was just ridiculous. I could tell she had little self-esteem and
> confidence because she was letting whoever dance on her. She didn't
> care what they were doing to her or how they looked; all she cared
> about was whether she was getting attention. It's not that females are
> particularly comfortable in the low-cut shirts and short skirts. It's that
> we feel we won't get noticed by any man, good or bad, unless we can
> attract them with a sexy look at first glance. I then think about the line
> of girls groin-to-groin putting on a show for the males, and again it is
> about the attention factor. I believe every girl has a belief that in the
> sea of hundreds of bad men, there is a decent one somewhere, and he
> may be at this party. (Maria)

Second, undergraduate women conform to party and hookup norms because social acceptance requires them to be viewed as fun and cool:

When I entered my freshman year, I quickly learned the rules of the college culture. Walking to parties was the excitement of the weekend. We adapted to parts of college to fit in with the others. Students go to parties, drink, talk, drink some more, kiss, and hook up or have sex with a random person. Because this is what is socially acceptable, it's what we do. We adapt and become "so college." (Therese)

We all have the desire to be accepted by our peers and it can be extremely difficult if we find ourselves on the outskirts. College can be a difficult time because it is our first real experience away from home and we are all trying to find our identity and unfortunately this can be a fragile time. We can become addicted to this feeling of being socially accepted and secure within a harsh society. (Tammy)

Hooking up is about how attractive the guy or girl is and who finds out about what you have done. It is all about peer recognition and how to climb the social ladder of college. I really care about what other people think of me. I don't want to be known as a "slut," but I don't want to be known as a "prude." Prudes get no attention from guys because the guys know it is not going anywhere. (Erin)

Third, college women conform because they think it is the only feasible way of having a chance at a relationship:

I love the idea of being committed to someone and sharing with them my love, care, and support. However, there are times when temptation gets the better of me, and I succumb to the attention of a guy. I have the mindset that "Maybe making out with him will help him realize he actually does have true, sincere feelings for me." Go ahead and ask me how many times that's been the case? Zero. (Paige)

Men more than women want to hook up. Most women will hook up, but they would much rather do something non-sexual because then it shows that the man is actually interested in a relationship. Women hook up with a guy in hopes it will evolve into something more. Women are constantly disappointed. (Erin)

My friends' outlook on sexuality is different than how they actually act when they go out on the weekends. All of my friends strive for good, healthy relationships. However, sometimes I think that they go about finding that strong relationship in an unhealthy manner. Some of my friends believe that, to find a boyfriend or girlfriend, they have to hook up with them consistently before they can actually start dating. Some of my friends think this is the only way to find a significant other. Some think that hooking up with a person means that the other person has strong feelings for them, even though this is rarely the case. (Colleen)

The Complicated Role of Alcohol: Causes and Effects of College Drinking

Many student ethnographers identified alcohol as playing a key role in contemporary hookup culture. As their observations and analyses reveal, a number of interrelated reasons help explain peers' excessive drinking and alcohol's various functions. First, echoing their comments about why their peers hook up, many ethnographers expressed that many peers drink to excess simply because their peers, fueled by media stereotypes, expect them to do so:

These people might also be wildly drunk, on a pursuit of what the media says a college weekend experience should be like. (Nolan)

I do understand that alcohol is used as a sedative in stressful situations but I feel that most times when people drink, they do so because they are expected by others to do so. People who don't drink seem out of place. Young adults drink because they are influenced by the conformity that rules so many people. If a whole dance club elected not to consume alcohol for a whole night, most people would not know what to do. (Ian)

Many ethnographers mentioned how socially awkward it was to be sober while doing observations at parties, with one student complaining, for example, that his friends "gave him hell" all evening for not drinking. Peer reactions ranged from puzzlement to outright hostility:

> I felt a disconnect between the more inebriated partygoers and myself. It is easy to see the role that group pressure plays in influencing people to drink. Being the only sober one in a house filled with my blissfully intoxicated friends did create a notable feeling of isolation. (Elliot)

> Being sober at a party is the worst. We were only there for about half of an hour pregaming at a house, and it felt like five hours. Everyone was extremely loud and ridiculously obnoxious. (Erin)

Second, ethnographers noticed that alcohol functions as a social lubricant: their peers drink excessively to escape feelings of insecurity and relieve social anxiety so they can interact more easily and become more outgoing:

> Alcohol is a way to break the ice. When people drink, they feel more relaxed, and more comfortable in otherwise awkward or unnerving situations. (Bailey)

> Everyone is insecure; the only real question is how insecure you are in relation to other people in attendance, and how much you have to drink before you forget the insecurities. (Ruth)

> People consume alcohol because they are uncomfortable with who they are in their sober state of being. If people had more self-worth, then they wouldn't need alcohol to help with their social experiences. (Ian)

> Guys find dating stressful. You ask somebody out when you're sober, and if they say no and reject you, you feel like crap and your friends give you hell. If you just get drunk and find someone to hook up with, you aren't letting anyone get to know the real you—the interaction is just physical. You then feel good about yourself (that you got someone to hook up with you) and you have something to tell your friends. (Greg)

> With alcohol in their systems, they were likely to avoid the feelings of rejection, embarrassment, hurt, or any other emotion of the sort

when flirting with, teasing, or talking to members of the opposite sex. (Britney)

A common observation made by ethnographers was that, at the beginning of a party, students tended to stick with their own friend groups; then, as they drank more and gained "liquid courage," they had an easier time socializing with others. Becoming intoxicated allowed them to go beyond their comfort zones and become "wild partiers" who enjoy flirting, grinding, and hooking up:

> When alcohol enters the bloodstream, inhibitions are lessened, so people are more likely to act in ways that would be considered abnormal for them. Whether that means being over-sexualized or just less worried about what people could say, alcohol clearly has its effects. (Carl)

> Alcohol is what allows people to slide their bodies up and down total strangers on the dance floor. Sally and Jane had been intent to arrive at the party intoxicated because it wouldn't be as easy to join the party atmosphere of sensuality without it.... Alcohol draws people into a very embodied sense of experiencing the party and this is key to understanding the behavior that comes afterward. (Max)

> Alcohol was key to breaking down the walls of awkwardness, pressure, desires, attractions, and relationships between men and women. Instead of putting time into developing a healthy sexual relationship or experience, men and women resorted to alcohol to form an instant bond where the two could engage in a pseudo-intimate and short moment of pleasurable connection. This type of behavior, reinforced as a sexual reality through media depictions and learning from siblings or friends, has become a norm for sexual relationships in high school, college, and beyond. (Teagan)

According to the ethnographers, a third reason many students drink heavily is to escape both the normal daily stresses of college life and more serious interpersonal and emotional problems:

> I know the temporary feeling of utter joy that alcohol gives you. The partiers felt as if they had no worries in the world. However, if you look deeper, you can tell that these feelings are merely temporary

for many people. The problems will reappear in the morning and could even be worse. This temporary happiness is actually pretty sad. Many people go to parties, and put on a happy facade but actually have something tearing at them on the inside. (Janet)

Parties offer a night of alcohol-induced stress relief and hookup fueled validation. I have never once attended a party with the intention of having a good time without a "bad time" in the back of my mind that I was trying to forget or ignore. Usually, it's the same for my friends. (Helen)

Perhaps they are drinking to forget, to escape reality for a little while because their life has turned into shambles. After my sexual assault, I continued going out and drinking with my friends because I did not want my assailant taking away that important social aspect in my life. But I was nowhere near happy or fulfilled, no matter how many beers I downed or how much I smiled and laughed with my friends. I seemed calm and collected and strong, even able to see the humor in some things. But on the inside I was a wreck who was completely out of touch with her feelings. But there is no way the person filling up my cup at the keg line had any idea there was anything wrong with me. I was just a girl at a party having a good time. (Cora)

Fourth, students become drunk because they perceive that intoxication excuses and frees them from accountability for their actions. In college it remains socially acceptable, as Jamie Foxx sings, to "blame it on the alcohol":

The people that I am observing are acting the way they are because they see alcohol as an excuse to do whatever they want. They think if they are drunk, no one will hold their actions against them, so they feel uninhibited by fear of conforming to social norms. For young women, it means being able to dress like a porn star and not feel like a whore, and make out with someone you just met and not be called a slut. It means being able to call or text friends, boyfriends, friends with benefits, or exes and tell them how you really feel without fearing that they will reject you. Even if they do, you can just say that you don't remember it in the morning. It gives women a certain type of freedom to express themselves. (Nora)

Alcohol is just an excuse to act in a way that you wouldn't normally act and not be held accountable. (Brandon)

My friend, whose 21st birthday we were celebrating, spent the entire evening absolutely intoxicated and did a laundry list of things only the drunk would perform, including being over-emotional and unable to hold a conversation for longer than a sentence or two. The following morning, he seemed to speak for everybody at the party with his Facebook status, coolly claiming "no responsibility for any of my actions last night." (Dominic)

Similarly, given students' belief that drinking relieves them of accountability or responsibility for sexual behavior, men who are or appear drunk typically can escape judgment that they "took advantage of someone" or acted sexually aggressive:

Guys commonly employ drunken hookups with girls that are drunk as well so as not look like they are taking advantage of girls since both partners are intoxicated. Men and women act the way they do under the influence of alcohol because our culture excuses them from judgment if their behavior is due to being drunk. (Dan)

I talked to a friend at the party about a random hookup that she had. I had warned her about the guy. He doesn't treat girls very well, he likes to talk to several girls at the same time, and his motto is, "Hit it and quit it." She disregarded my information and had sex with him last week in a bathroom at a party. She told me to read their texts the next day. She asked if he remembered having sex in the bathroom last night, and he said something along the lines of, "OMG, we had sex? I did not remember that. Wow." And she said, "I'm nervous because I'm not on birth control." He said, "Do you remember if I pulled out? Do you want to get Plan B just to be sure?" She said, "I think you pulled out before, but still it makes me nervous." He said, "If you wanna get Plan B, just let me know. I'll pay for it." She said, "Okay, I'll let you know." They haven't talked since. (Aunika)

Thus, college students appear to use (and abuse) alcohol for a number of reasons: they drink at parties because of media and peer expectations, to overcome social anxiety, to reduce stress, and to escape responsibility for their behavior.

The ethnographers also perceived that many hookups occur due to blackouts and incapacitation caused by drinking. Women frequently wrote about their own and friends' experiences of hooking up with random people and waking up the next morning wondering what happened. These hookups were unintended and usually unwanted, caused by severely impaired or completely incapacitated decision-making ability. They reported that these unwanted hookups lead to many negative psychological and social consequences:

> Alcohol completely drives hooking up at college. All of my worst decisions were made when I was tipsy or very drunk. Unfortunately, that is how it is: alcohol is in the center of the college experience. (Erin)

> I know from experience that when I do, I worry about it for the next week or so. If I do something really stupid when I am drinking, such as hooking up with someone I don't know, then I never forget it and worry about it. There have been times when I drink too much and do things that I normally would not do if I were sober. The things I do get me into trouble and make me feel really bad about myself, making me less confident and secure. (Anna)

Tim wrote about how his binge drinking and a drunken hookup resulted in a rape charge:

> I recall going to a bar with a group of friends and feeling like I was not having a good time because I was not drinking. My friends encouraged me to begin drinking by purchasing me five shots of tequila. After taking the shots, I proceeded to the dance floor where I met a girl. I ended up hooking up with this girl on the dance floor, and then she came back to my apartment afterward. A year after this night, the girl made accusations that I raped her. I spent an entire semester dealing with the legal side of a one-night stand. The after-effects were not at all worth one night of fun. This situation obviously led to major regrets for both parties. (Tim)

Conclusion

Students' observations and analyses of the social dynamics present in contemporary party and hookup culture reveal an unfortunate, perhaps cruel, irony connected to their college years: while college is generally perceived as a time of great freedom and self-discovery, the ethnographers' hypotheses about why college students act the way they do reveal great behavioral constraints for those who want to fit in. In other words, most students today who desire popularity and social status among friends and peers will encounter a distinctly narrow range of social norms. Opting to remain sober at a party, choosing "non-slutty" clothes as a female, expressing zero interest in casual sex, and trying to initiate honest, deep conversations at parties are all socially deviant decisions, for example, that risk social suicide or never being noticed or taken seriously in the first place.

Honoring the insider experiences and knowledge of student ethnographers in two chapters thus far, we have gained a valuable picture of social dynamics within party and hookup culture and also a number of explanations for why college students act the way they do. To deepen our understanding of the party and hookup culture, let us now proceed to the ethnographers' perceptions of power dynamics.

3

Power Dynamics at College Parties

DESCRIBING POWER DYNAMICS entails identifying which social groups have the most power to construct our sense of reality, influence social norms, and accomplish their own agenda. To provide a starting point for this part of the assignment, I suggested that a helpful approach for understanding types and manifestations of power would be to pay attention to how people's bodies are portrayed and treated. Specifically, I asked student ethnographers to observe the depiction and treatment of bodies according to race and ethnicity, sexual orientation, and gender, then to answer the following questions:

> What do the depictions of all of these bodies suggest about who has power at parties? You may have a very complicated answer as you try to figure out which social group has more power in the social scene: feel free to suggest the different ways in which different groups have power, if that is what you perceive.

This chapter will examine students' responses to these questions in conjunction with other research findings. While all students addressed gender—the depiction and treatment of men's versus women's bodies—many offered no observations and commentary at all pertaining to race and ethnicity or sexual orientation. As we consider their observations and analyses, and speculate on their omissions, we are again wise to acknowledge that race, heterosexism, sexism, and other biases undoubtedly influence their perceptions and judgments no differently than our own socialization influences ours.

Depictions of Power According to
Race and Ethnicity

Out of all ethnographers, 68% of students did not address whether bodies of varying race and ethnicity were depicted differently and did not analyze power dynamics related to this theme. Two percent of students reported that they could not answer the question owing to lack of diversity, 3% indicated that they observed no differences, and 27% observed differences among racial and ethnic groups. We cannot know why a high percentage of students failed to address questions of race and ethnicity every semester, but the truth probably involves a combination of white privilege, disinterest, discomfort, and lack of ethnic diversity observed at parties. If we compare Caucasian students' and ethnic minority students' responses separately, 70% of Caucasians did not answer this question compared to 50% of ethnic minority students.

As I coded the responses of ethnographers who perceived differences in the depiction of bodies according to race and ethnicity, common themes began to emerge. First, students frequently perceived that white bodies are often depicted as normal and/or ideal compared to African American bodies. Many believed that this gives white men, and secondarily white women, the most power in the room (and in society). With a few exceptions, students wrote nothing about Asian or Hispanic peers, and it is difficult to know whether these minorities were simply not present or whether ethnographers overlooked them. Many students began this section of their papers with analyses about the portrayal of certain ethnicities in society and not specifically about their party observations:

> In our society today the white man has the power. Today, a white masculine body is tall, has big muscles, tan skin complexion, and six-pack abs. (Jonathon)

> Most models are all Caucasian, which makes me think that this is the ideal way to look by people of all ethnic groups. It shows that Caucasians hold the power because they are already genetically and biologically closer to looking like the perfect person. Other ethnic groups try to get their skin lighter or their hair lighter or do whatever it takes for them to look the most like the ideal Caucasian shown in the media. (Colleen)

In contrast, many students perceived African American men and women as being depicted in demeaning ways:

> Black and white bodies are depicted differently in society. The black male body is depicted basically off what we see on TV and in music videos. The depiction of black males is seen as aggressive, uneducated, and only having one thing on their mind and that is sex. Also, black males are only concerned with materialistic things such as money. The depiction of black women is seen as very sexual. (Adaline)

> White bodies are depicted differently than black, Hispanic, Asian, and other ethnic group bodies. Racism is still a current issue within the world. Society views white people as a symbol of power. Stereotypes play a crucial role by altering the way people are viewed. Black people are viewed as poor and they all have guns hidden under their clothes. All Asians are brilliant. Hispanics are all illegal immigrants and only deserve to be outdoor workers in the U.S. These stereotypes take away people's real identity and have left the whites to have a sense of power when really we do not deserve it. (Eva)

> Black males are usually depicted as too aggressive to the point where they rape women and beat them. The white men have the "perfect" mixture between controlling and aggressive and charming and sweet. For the women though, I think black women are depicted as more outspoken and independent. They are portrayed as if they don't need a man to protect them. (Elena)

When they turned to describing the particular bodies at their college parties, ethnographers usually framed their responses in terms of clothing, noting almost unanimously that Caucasian and African American men dressed differently. White men tended to dress "preppier," whereas black men dressed in looser fitting clothes:

> Black males dress a lot differently. The typical "white boy" look is a graphic t-shirt to a polo, and the right size jeans, pants or khaki shorts. For black males, it seems that the baggier the better. (Ilsa)

> African American men came dressed in their casual best. Again layers were the theme to this predominantly black party. The black males had

on jeans, white tanks, fitted hats, t-shirts, do rags, jackets, and sneak-
ers. Every male had on this outfit give or take the fitted cap. (Melody)

There was less consensus about the depiction of women's bodies. A minority perceived that African American women dressed more provocatively
and appeared as though they took more time than white women to plan
their outfits:

> The way black women seem to dress also differs from that of the
> white women. Their outfits are more exposing and planned out.
> Many of the girls seem to be wearing leggings or tight jeans paired
> with cleavage baring, form fitting tops and heels. The girls are also
> wearing a considerable amount of makeup. (Krista)

> It seemed that the black females had a lot more variety in their outfits
> and put more thought into it. Their outfits also did not pull a person's
> eyes to one part of their anatomy. The white females tried to have the
> focus on their breasts, but the black females drew the attention to
> their whole bodies. (Melody)

The vast majority of ethnographers, however, perceived that women of all
ethnicities dressed more or less alike because they were all expected to
dress sexily and conform to certain beauty ideals:

> Although black girls tend to have bigger booties and white girls tend
> to have bigger breasts, it doesn't matter what a girl has unless she is
> skinny, tan, and wearing the right clothes. The girls that are thicker
> tend to not get hit on as much as the super-skinny girls. This does say
> something about power, meaning that the beautiful are more powerful.
> In today's society this is why people get plastic surgery or Botox. (Lucy)

> In judging the ways in which black and white female bodies are
> depicted, it seems to be about equivalent. Both are expected to wear
> clothes which accentuate the body parts that men like to see. (Cora)

Drawing on their analysis of the depiction of bodies, students perceived
that Caucasians (white men, followed by white women) had the most
power at college parties. Helen, who was examining the depiction of bodies in posters at the party, wrote:

> There was also only one image of an individual who was not white,
> and it instructed viewers to drink more, in light of those who are

sober in Africa. This suggests a dominance of white over blacks, and a nearly pitying attitude: we're good enough to drink, we have access to alcohol, and because you don't, we should not waste ours. Ultimately, the message that was sent about power in the parties I attended was that white men are in control, and that white women, while possibly doted on, are seen as sexual "tasks" and "goals" that could either be successful or failures. (Helen)

Marianne, who interviewed many of her friends and peers about power dynamics and groups on campus, found that most students perceived the following power structure on campus:

The Caucasian males are the head of the power, followed by white females, who are only slightly ahead of African American males. Following them are African American females followed by any person in the homosexual community and lastly any Asian or Hispanic person. It surprised me when I asked around that most of my friends put the power on [University A's] campus in that order. The last two groups, namely the homosexual and the Asian and Hispanic community, were the ones that I thought were the other way around. When I asked a few individuals, they told me to look at the clubs and societies around campus. The LGBTQ community is more supported here through their various clubs and organizations. After contemplating this, I could not help but agree.

Some ethnographers believed Caucasians had the most power because they constituted the majority:

The majority of the people at the party were white, and the males were running the show. (Mary)

At parties it is usually whoever is in the majority that has the power. It is in the body language. If there is a group of white males and females, and a couple of Asians walk in, there are bound to be racial slurs or innuendos directed at the minority. This happened especially at the house party because the few black people who were there were overwhelmed by white people, and you could sense that the white males were trying to show their dominance, as well as the black males proving they were able to be at the party. Usually the social group who has the most power is the race that has the majority of people present. (Jill)

> The absence of many minorities at white parties speaks volumes on what white girls think of black men's bodies and what white men think of black women's bodies. Maybe there is a separation of "black parties" and "white parties" because many blacks feel that they are on the lower end of a power structure. Many minorities may want to feel like they are on a level playing field with all their peers at a particular party. If they felt disadvantaged at a white person's party, they may prefer to be elsewhere. (Alec)

According to some ethnographers, the exception to this norm of Caucasians having the most power was the idea that power resides with talented male athletes regardless of their ethnicity. We will explore this perception in greater depth later in this chapter.

Depictions of Power According to Sexual Orientation

Similar to the low response rate concerning race and ethnicity, 47% of student ethnographers did not answer the question about the depiction of bodies according to sexual orientation. Sixteen percent explicitly mentioned they could not answer due to the lack of LGBTQ persons at the parties, 4% stated there were no differences in how bodies are depicted, and 33% of student ethnographers reported differences in body depictions between heterosexual and LGBTQ individuals. Among those who perceived differences in how bodies are depicted, several themes stand out. First, students perceived that their peers evaluate others' sexual orientation based on dress and behavior:

> In our society, heterosexual bodies are definitely portrayed in a different light than LGBTQ bodies. We tend to unconsciously characterize people into categories of heterosexual or homosexual just by their appearance. If a guy acted feminine at all, then he would automatically be questioned about whether he was homosexual. Heterosexual guys tend to have a more masculine appearance and tend to be freaked out by homosexual guys. Therefore,

they dress in ways that validate the fact that they are definitely heterosexual. (Max)

If a girl wore big baggy pants and a long big t-shirt, the majority of men and women would think it was out of character for girls and probably call her a "dyke." The same sort of attitude goes with hairstyles; girls are told long hair is beautiful and if they have short hair it is less feminine. (Tessa)

Students perceived that gender roles and portrayals of bodies are reversed in homosexual communities:

The gay male bodies are depicted sexually, while the lesbian bodies are shown to be more butch and "manly." The male bodies in the homosexual communities are used to sell products and to attract attention from people. (Kevin)

Lesbians are viewed as bigger girls with more muscles and fewer features of the ideal woman. This shows that roles change for lesbians and gays. (Jonathon)

Many ethnographers' comments reflected the belief that gay men's bodies—perceived as more feminine and flamboyant, non-masculine, and thinner and weaker than bodies of heterosexual men—are expected to conform to a particular beauty ideal similar to the measures held up for heterosexual women:

Gay bodies are depicted as sexy men with good style. Also, gay men usually have toned bodies and care about their appearance. (Mary)

Gay men's bodies seem to be fit but in the same way that a woman's body would be, such as muscle in the lower half of the body instead of the upper body. Also, gay men wear tighter clothes to show off their bodies, at least the ones I encountered. (Miley)

Heterosexual male bodies are depicted as strong, muscular, and big whereas homosexual male bodies are depicted as very slim and take on a more feminine image. (Elena)

Depictions of heterosexual and lesbian women's bodies were also contrasted explicitly by the ethnographers:

> Heterosexual women are depicted as slim, weak, and sexy whereas homosexual women are depicted as strong, powerful, and manlier. (Elena)

> Lesbian women are depicted as being "butch," or having guy qualities, which is completely opposite of the heterosexual female, who is dainty and beautiful. Lesbian women are usually depicted as having short haircuts and being muscular, as well as doing men's jobs. (Mary)

Students analyzing the depiction of bodies at parties perceived that, while sexual orientation was not always obvious simply by observing peers' outfits, there was definitely a tendency for homosexual men and women to conform to their stereotypes:

> The lesbian couple's attire wasn't really different from straight couples at the party; they dressed nice but definitely more casual than the other girls probably due to the fact that they had nobody to impress. (Marek)

> Lesbians are often depicted as "butch." On the other hand, I know some lesbians who are completely "girl" and one would not expect them to be lesbian. (Janet)

> It is commonly thought that women athletes seem to be more "dyke-ish" than the typical stereotype of a female. In my case, my teammates who are lesbian usually dress like a male when we hang out. They wear a bright colored polo, baggy jeans, a chain, nice basketball shoes, usually Jordan brand. They even wear men's boxers. When they start to try to look like men even more by dressing and acting like them, it puts them in an even scarier category for others who are not familiar with their lifestyle. Of course, not all of my teammates or other gay friends dress like males. Some of them are the "females" in the relationship and dress like the typical female would for a party. (Ellen)

> Of the two homosexual couples I observed, the gays were more effeminate and the lesbians more masculine. One of the boys was wearing a tight-fitting deep V-neck which many might call "queer" or "pansy."

The girls were not dressed in the cutesy cleavage-baring tops worn by other women at the party; rather simply in boyish jeans and form masking sweaters that could lead to the nickname "dyke" or "butch." (Krista)

Analyzing these depictions, ethnographers who acknowledged differences in portrayals of heterosexual and LGBTQ bodies perceived that white heterosexual men possess the most power. Students focused on heterosexuals' majority status and/or stereotypes that promote heterosexuality as the norm and thereby preserve long-held power:

The typical image of power is associated with being a heterosexual man; those who are homosexual are viewed as weak and not real men. (Scott)

By placing gay and lesbian groups outside the norm of what it means to be a man or a woman, heterosexual society can effectively establish their power over the homosexuals. (Krista)

Never would a homosexual person hold the power over a heterosexual person, not from what I saw at the parties I was at. They are a minority and that is the way it is. They are weak and so are their bodies. (Ben)

Power Analysis According to Gender

When asked to examine which social group has the most power at parties and whether bodies were depicted and treated differently based on gender, 3% of students did not respond, and all remaining ethnographers described power dynamics in one of the following three ways: 7% argued that women had more power than men; 66% thought that men were the most powerful social group; and 24% believed the answer is more complicated, attributing different forms of power to each gender or suggesting that power was based, among other things, on factors unrelated to gender.

Depictions of Power According to Gender
Women Have the Most Power

The first group of student ethnographers (7%) offered two main reasons that women—implied or described as attractive heterosexual females conforming to the narrow, highly sexualized beauty ideal—have more power than men at parties. First, by dressing deliberately to show off their best physical attributes (whether breasts, "ass," stomach, legs, or more), these women have the power to attract and arouse men. Some student ethnographers perceived that since attractive women's bodies were given more attention than men's bodies, and their bodies could arouse men, women had more power. A few student ethnographers argued that women also have more power since the success of a party depends on having attractive women attending the party: the greatest fear of men who host parties is that not enough "hot" women will show up and the party will turn into a "sausage fest." Such party failure brings about social ridicule, and one's social status "takes a serious hit."

This power and privilege of attractive women is especially obvious when they are admitted to parties or clubs free of charge while men, less attractive women, and women who dress more conservatively have to pay. Being able to gain attention and entice men sexually by using their bodies is believed to give such attractive women power and control over men because they know they have something men want—their bodies and the potential for sex. As defined by one ethnographer, power in these contexts is "the power to conjure strong desires in males":

> Women have a great deal of power over men. Girls know that by walking into a party in a short skirt that men will be looking at a certain part of their anatomical structure. Girls know that if they flirt with a guy, they can get what they want from him—say a few drinks, for example. Girls know that they can act in a way that gives them power over guys. (Michelle)

> Women who are proud of their bodies like to reveal them as much as possible. They dress like so on purpose to lead on guys and turn on their sexual appetites. Because males tend to be more visually stimulated, women can utilize the ability to use their bodies to get what they want from men. (Dan)

As described by student ethnographers, highly attractive women who are dressed the sexiest use the knowledge that "males are desperate for the chance to get with them" to have power and control over men as they "get interested guys to do what they want." "What they want" was described in these papers and during our discussions as having guys pay sole attention to them, flirt with and compliment them, show affection, get them alcohol, pursue them, and ideally compete with other men in the pursuit of a hookup. Women who enjoyed the attention of multiple men were perceived as most powerful since they could "string them along" until they decided on one at the end of the night.

The second reason that women have the power is that they can reject a man's sexual advances and determine whether a hookup happens. Being expected to initiate contact (including conversation, dancing, and hooking up) places men in a potentially vulnerable, awkward position of being rejected in public. Elaborating on this power of women, some ethnographers perceived that men simply want sex more than women do. Whereas "girls shoot down guys all the time," and attractive women could easily "score" any night they wished, men supposedly would never turn down the opportunity for sex. Women use this knowledge, according to one ethnographer, "as their own source of power":

> Guys want women. They aren't necessarily interested in impressing them always, but they want them. Since girls aren't the pursuers, they don't get turned down, which puts all the power in the hands of the females. The woman has final say in [whether] she is interested, if she will start a relationship with him, and if she will sleep with him. It's her choice and her choice alone. If a woman thinks the relationship is going too fast or is too sexual, she could back out at any moment. (Anthony)

> When you observe parties you can see how females have a certain control over males. Females tempt males and flirt with them in an attempt to establish control since they understand that males are dependent and desperate for a chance to get with them. You see instances where males will do favors and jobs for a female such as getting alcohol. Females control males because they understand that males are dependent on their bodies whereas females seem more content to not hook up. (Scott)

Men Have the Most Power

The next group of student ethnographers (66%) provided the following interrelated reasons for concluding that heterosexual men are more powerful than women at college parties: (1) depictions of men's versus women's bodies, (2) the prevalence of sexual objectification, (3) men's role as pursuers and sexual initiators, (4) a culture of male sexual entitlement, and (5) limited parameters for women's sexual agency.

In their analyses of the depiction of men's and women's bodies, students commonly mixed and blurred what they directly observed at parties with their own prior experience of gender expectations in popular culture. Whatever their source, however, gender messages are consistent: both in the media and at parties, men are depicted as strong, independent, courageous, aggressive, powerful, and dominant, whereas attractive women appear fragile, weak, thin, sexy, obedient, and submissive:

> Female bodies were depicted as delicate, small, and fragile. Many wore dresses or tops that were "off the shoulder," exposing the collarbone and making the girl look dainty. Girls often wore the least amount of fabric possible and their body language suggested that they did not want to take up much space. Girls would frequently squeeze together or slide past people inconspicuously, suggesting that they were small. Females are almost always depicted as skinny and small in comparison to strong men. This perpetuates our female stereotype of weakness and frailty, while allowing the hyper-masculine man to dominate our society. (Mindy)

> Women imprison themselves by trying to be in accordance with societal standards of what is sexy, which limits their wardrobe selection quite drastically. Women feel that their sources of power come from flaunting their body parts; for instance, girls at the party used their cleavage as a "distraction" to help them win a game of beer pong. They feel that the only way to gain power or attention is through flaunting how big their boobs are or how skinny they are or how great their butt looks. (Nora)

> Men have more power than women; our world today portrays women as weak and insecure and men as strong and confident. In American culture, women are constantly trying to make themselves look like totally different people and act like the perfect woman that every guy supposedly wants. When women do this, it makes men feel even more powerful than they did before. When women are insecure and depend on men all the time, it makes the man feel like he is strong and powerful. (Anna)

Some student ethnographers acknowledged a hierarchy of power and dominance among white heterosexual men, the most powerful being Division 1 athletes or those who conformed to the highly chiseled, tough, and stoic player ideal:

> Men who had athletic builds were on top of the social ladder by far. Many of these men appeared to feel entitled to the girls they chose. They were treated as strong, tough, invulnerable and impenetrable. Unlike the less athletic looking males whose bodies looked weak and "feminine" by comparison, these men's bodies were depicted as the best possible standard. Because of the highly glorified "jock" bodies, I believe that these physically attractive men had the most power at these parties. (Alec)

> Males tend, in the party setting and in everyday life, to have more of a pull in power than females do because of the tough, rugged, and hard-nosed type of people men are. Females tend to have a significant less amount of power than men do. This is because women as a majority are seen as compassionate, fearful, and scared. They also want to impress the guys with sexual appeal. (Tucker)

Second, ethnographers moved with ease from matter-of-fact observations about the depiction of bodies at parties to describe widespread sexual objectification. As noted in earlier chapters, many ethnographers recognized that women's value at parties depends largely, if not entirely, on the sexual attractiveness of their bodies, while men's bodies are not subject to the same kind of scrutiny and sexual objectification. This type of fragmentation, described by one college man as the "roots of social experiences in college culture," is in stark contrast to the completeness often attributed to men simply by virtue of their gender:

> Women are often broken down to body parts without faces. Men are usually depicted as a whole man—the whole package with face and the muscles. Right away this gives men a power over females. Women are seen as a body and therefore it's expected that what you need to win over guys is to show that body off because your personality and beauty aren't good enough without it. (Ilsa)

> The women spend great amounts of time trying to perfect their look and pick what is going to make them look best, while men

essentially sit back and watch. There is no pressure on men to fit a certain mold. Nobody expects me to wear anything in particular, and the expectation certainly would not be to wear anything revealing. It's as if, in the social scene, a man's body is completely ignored. It is rare at parties for there to be much emphasis on the male body. Because of this social construct, it makes sense that men are in power. (Harry)

While women's bodies are depicted as scantily clad—signifying their subservience and vulnerability—men's bodies are generally the most clothed, giving off an air of self-respect. (Nora)

The way bodies are depicted and treated is almost laughable. You have the women who wear clothing that barely covers any of their legs that are made to dance by bending over and grinding their hips into a random man's crotch. It's particularly sad when an overweight girl feels like this is the way all women should dress and attempt to dress the same way. They open themselves up to harsh judgments. The power stratification ends up this way: at the top are men who select the dance partner and get their crotch grinded on. The men who have the most power are the attractive and outgoing ones who are able to secure the attractive and outgoing women in the crowd. The less attractive men have relatively less power because all the attractive women are already snatched up, so they are often the ones who stand on the edge of the dance floor. Women have the least power in the group because of the way they are portrayed and made to dance. But the ones at the very bottom of the power stratification are the less attractive/outgoing ones. They don't even have the trivial power to attract male attention. (Isaac)

These student ethnographers recognized that beauty ideals exist for both men and women in the media, but whereas men's worth, attractiveness, and desirability are based on diverse characteristics that constitute men as more complete persons (physical appearance, athleticism, intelligence, personality, sense of humor, etc.), women's worth, attractiveness, and desirability are based on the extent to which they conform to a narrow, highly sexualized ideal of physical beauty:

Men are supposed to be strong, lean, and with good posture, while women are supposed to be thin, big-breasted, and beautiful.

However, only one of these depictions seems to hold true in society. It seems that all women are expected to uphold these strict standards for the "perfect body." However, some men are able to skirt these depictions using un-physical attributes. For example, I noticed one male who was not as physically fit or attractive was able to entice the women using his sense of humor. Further, men have been able to gain power through their status as opposed to their physical appearance. This is especially apparent with athletes. This is the opposite with women. A man wouldn't date a female just because of her athletic status or personality/humor. At the end of the day it always comes down to the female's physical appearance—thus showing that men are more dominant. (Emmie)

The men, overall, were casual with their dress, showing little thought in their outfits and were typically very modest with their bodies. I think this shows they don't need to use their bodies to get ahead, or get noticed, they are already in control. With the women, showing a good amount of their body indicates they need to use sexuality in order to receive attention or power. (Donna)

Men are given more privileges when it comes to their body image and the way they use their body than girls are. Men are judged less frequently in the way they dress, the sports they play, the hairstyles they choose, and the sexual acts they commit. (Tessa)

Given that women's social acceptance, social success, and (often) self-worth hinge so significantly on their physical appearance, they sometimes feel as if they have no choice but to compete with other women to have the "perfect" body. They will submit themselves to a host of disciplinary practices (working out excessively, eating less than other women, and spending lots of time and money on clothes and makeup) to attempt to be one of the most beautiful, sexiest women at parties, and therefore be sought after and pursued by men. In short, they embrace appearing and acting like a sex object in order to gain men's attention and approval and temporarily increase their sense of self-worth:

Generally, women's bodies were seen as an object, something to touch or something to ogle at. In order to be accepted, a lot of females I encountered catered to that by wearing more revealing clothing in order to better be appreciated by the men. (Carl)

The female dresses promiscuously in order to get the attention of the male. If the female were dominant in society, why would she strive so hard to get the attention of the male? The strong emphasis on body image and body parts leads into a casual approach to sexuality. When we separate the body parts of a woman and put them on prominent display, she no longer becomes a woman or individual, but becomes an anonymous pair of boobs or butt much like the *Playboy* models of male's sexual development. It then becomes easy for males to take advantage of females and assert their power. In turn, females feel that the attention of a male is an affirmation of their own self-worth. Thus, sex becomes a means of expressing male dominance and female self-worth, entirely severing any notions of intimacy or commitment. (Nora)

All women, regardless of status or race, were often regarded as sexual objects. I hear at least one group of guys referring to a woman as "the chick with big tits" or "that fine ass girl over there." Many drunken guys find it permissible to go up and grab a girl without her permission. I do not hear of reciprocated stories of women grabbing men, which leads me to conclude that men place themselves above girls by objectifying their bodies. My reasoning is this: nothing is more mine than my own body. If someone views my body as little more than a source of pleasure, I feel used and devalued. My body is part of me and attacks against my body are attacks against me. Thus, if guys find the purpose of girls is to use their bodies as a source of sexual pleasure, men must be in charge of that system. (Alec)

Due to the fact that women must become a sex figure in order to participate in the party scene, they are announcing to everyone that they are willing to be objectified. By becoming a sex object and seeing their goal as attracting men, they are empowering men. (Tammy)

These student ethnographers argue that because women "do all the work" at the beginning of parties to attract men, women are in an inferior position. They observe how men initially act relaxed and present themselves as superior while women strut around in an effort to attract men:

Men definitely had the power in how they presented themselves. The "I don't care" facade made it appear as if they considered themselves beyond everyone there. (Brandon)

It seems that the males have all the power. They just have to relax while the women come to them. Women really have to work at getting the attention of the men and keeping it. This could be really challenging and demeaning for women. (Patrick)

Another manifestation of men's power connected to sexual objectification was men's ability to reinforce the media's narrow sexualized beauty ideal and reward women who conform:

Throughout the house, there were pin-up posters of famous women or models in small swimsuits or with strategically placed objects, or skin-tight dresses, or soaking wet. These women covered the walls of the boys' rooms, the kitchen, and living room. The correlation between these women on the walls and the women who filled the rooms was quite obvious. The women at this party were obviously emulating the male ideal of what a woman is. It made it clear that men have more power in this way: men are able to create the ideal woman and get women to emulate that image. The actual woman becomes an object similar to the way the poster is an object. Men feel they have the right to use these women. (Mindy)

Women were catering to the fact that men like looking at scantily clad women. If they appealed to that, then maybe they would be lucky enough to spend a night with a guy. So clearly, men have the power, because they influence what women should or should not wear in order to better please males. Maybe as time goes on, things will not have to be a power struggle and people will just be able to treat each other's bodies with respect, but for now, it appears that males are dominating. (Carl)

Third, by recognizing men's active, decision-making roles related to hookups, ethnographers identified another reason for concluding that men possess the most power within college party and hookup culture. Specifically, student ethnographers noted that men had more power to pursue who they were interested in and determine the terms of sexual activity—with whom it occurs, what happens, when it happens, and where it happens. According to student ethnographers, the existence of a double standard regarding sexual activity casts men in the role of social actor who can do what he wants without being judged:

The media and our culture have given males an abundance of sexual dominance. If a woman is dressing sexy, she is being skanky. If a woman has a lot of sex, she is a whore or a slut. Males hardly receive any types of labels like this. Men have other nicknames like "player," with usually no negative connotation, at least among other males. The more girls a guy hooks up with, the "cooler" he is. (Paul)

When a guy hooks up he is considered to be "getting" something. What about when a girl hooks up? She isn't getting anything—she is giving it. (Ben)

These men players are rarely chastised or labeled, and are often praised and admired for their exploits. Women who engage in such an activity with even one male fear being labeled "whores" or "sluts." I believe that this discrepancy is grossly unfair, sexist, and reflects the "Madonna/Whore" complex that has run rampant throughout our human history. (Elliot)

Men, unlike college women who are frequently reduced to a sex object, were repeatedly perceived by student ethnographers as having greater freedom to act according to their wishes and "do what they want":

The male body was depicted as very strong and powerful, as the men simply did and said whatever they wanted. It was powerful in the sense that it felt they had the right to touch any other body, especially women. The female body was depicted as weak, as it allowed this touching without consent, and many females remained fairly reserved and passive throughout the night. (Kelly)

Men look at the female body and think of what they can do to it later in the evening behind closed doors. It gives the men some edge over the women, making the man more powerful in the relationship, because the woman is the symbol where the man is the one with the power to view the woman this way and act out viewing her as a sex symbol. (Georgia)

Another general theme at play for the men's actions is that there is almost no social norm for acceptable behavior. A man can be wild and crazy, or more reserved and it is seen as okay (although it is probably more acceptable to be wild, crazy, and excessively drunk at a party than more reserved). If a man acts wild and crazy at a party, men and women judge it as acting normal for a man. Conversely, if a man acts more reserved, he is judged as a good guy, or a nice guy. (Percy)

Students gave further evidence that men "do what they want" by commenting on their power to run the parties:

> For the most part, men appeared to be "running" the party, displaying an authority that no one had handed them. (Dominic)

> I don't imagine that all men were trying to get the women intoxicated but it was an interesting power dynamic that the men almost controlled what the women drank. It seems to me that these behaviors only happen in larger group settings, with many men desperate to display their power. (Marek)

Echoing the theme of men as the pursuers from chapter 1, this group of students perceived that men had more power because they are the initiators, making moves on women they are interested in, while women are usually consigned to the role of appearing attractive, flirting, and hoping to be pursued:

> Men have the power. At parties it seems that women dress up and show off their bodies to be as attractive as possible to men. Then it is up to the man to choose what woman he wants. (Paul)

> Men are the ones who can decide whether to take advantage of the sexual cues that women are giving them. They can choose whether to pay special attention to a girl's cleavage or not. Girls only expose and objectify themselves in those ways because they believe that's what men are looking for. They will act in the way that they believe will get them male attention, and if that means using their bodies, then they just feel that that is just how it is and has to be. So, in this respect, men wield some power over girls because what they are attracted to or not attracted to dictates how girls will act and what they will wear. (Julie)

> Females seem to be the inferior group when it comes to social settings. Males are the dominators and therefore select the female of their choice. The female responds with either allowing the male to dominate her or resisting his domination. (Dylan)

Fourth, students analyzing power differences based on gender also recognized that many college men manifest tremendous entitlement. It is not simply that men objectify women and hold idealized beauty standards for the women they wish to pursue; according to ethnographers, a dominant theme in conversations among men was what they would "do" to certain women if or when they could. Furthermore, men's audacious verbal expressions of entitlement extended to their actual physical interactions with the women at their parties:

> Female bodies are totally depicted as items, detached from personality, thoughts, or anything other than the body. . . . As we were passing this park on our way to the party, a guy did tell me: "I'm going to f**k a girl right on that dolphin tonight. It's going to happen." I have no idea if it happened or not, but the fact that he just proclaims it to everyone shows the objectification of women in the eyes of men. (Brandon)

> Guys will admit, on occasion, that their only intentions are to "get it in," or "get it on." If that's not a sign to treating girls like sexual tasks, I don't know what it is. (Helen)

Student ethnographers also frequently observed men treating women rudely and with disrespect—in ways that they would never treat their male peers:

> At the soccer house party, one of my friends asked for a drink and the guy responded, "Maybe if you didn't have such an ugly face, I'd give you a beer." His words reduced a strong, confident, straight-A student to simply a body. (Paul)

> Men thought it was acceptable to throw their beer in the air all over the females that were in front of them. This happened to me multiple times and guys just laughed and high-fived each other. One time, the guy that threw the most beer on me, actually came up to me and said, and I quote, "You look hotter when you're wet." However disgusting, I was not shocked by this expression. (Annie)

Student ethnographers also observed men at parties touching women when they pleased, which further signified entitlement:

> The female body is not nearly as respected as a male body because the female body is often touched or smacked, usually in a sexual manner. (Colleen)

The fact that a guy can go up to a girl and put his hand on her butt expecting her to like it or accept it is crazy. Also, the way men spoke to women gave me the impression that men felt powerful. (Preston)

Overall, the men behaved very aggressively and came on very strongly toward the women, as they felt they had the right to touch women whenever they pleased. (Kelly)

Perhaps the clearest manifestation of sexual entitlement was the occurrence of men boldly requesting sexual favors.[1] According to ethnographers, this occurred between acquaintances, hookup partners, and even dating couples:

The most frequent conversation I heard between couples at parties that dealt with sexuality was the man asking to go back to his room to have sex. Frequently throughout each night I would hear guys asking for sexual favors from their girlfriends with seemingly no objection from the woman in the relationship. The most appalling thing I observed was how women responded when asked for a sexual favor by their boyfriends. The girls had facial expressions and body language that seemed to weaken when the request came. On one occasion, the girl actually lowered her shoulders, took a really deep drawn out breath, and then led the way out of the house assumingly back to the dorms. It seemed that the women had no respect for their own bodies or for their own decision making. The men in the relationship were clearly making the decisions. Almost every time the guy asked for a sexual favor, the girl caved in. This only reinforces the behavior being exhibited by guys in the college culture. (Frank)

Student ethnographers also witnessed men getting noticeably frustrated at parties when their attempts to hook up with a woman fail and they get rejected. As Scott notes, some men will feel resentful about doing things for women and getting nothing in return and will seek power over women through coercion, getting them drunk, or physically overpowering them sexually. We have already seen that some college men discipline women who don't conform to certain cultural norms by ignoring or verbally ridiculing them; here we see that discipline is sometimes manifested physically as well:

Social power and respectability for males is so important and males therefore will degrade themselves to please females and be given a chance at hooking up. This is where males get into trouble since they feel like, if they obey women, they should get something in return. If they do not get any "rewards" for showing a certain female a good time, they will take matters into their own hands and sexually abuse them. This is an example of how physical power can be dominant. (Scott)

As elsewhere in student observations, entitlement is often a theme even when it's not explicitly named: men are due sexual rewards if they interact with women and show them a good time, and if women don't cooperate it is up to men to "take matters into their own hands" and "take" what they want. Furthermore, Scott's description of men as "degrading themselves" when they do things to please women reveals an underlying assumption that women are inferior since men "lower themselves" when seeking to please women. While it is clear from class discussions that many college men find this mindset reprehensible, it remains a theme that surfaces repeatedly in their ethnographies.

Fifth, ethnographers argue that men have more power by showing that women have more limited parameters of sexual agency. While men are expected to be the pursuers and sexual initiators, women are generally relegated to the role of deciding how they will respond. College women, far from possessing the agency to "do what they want," often feel like they face an immediate future with only two options: either embrace the status quo of parties and hookups in exchange for overall social acceptance, male attention, and the chance for a relationship, or refuse the status quo and pay the price of exclusion, loneliness, and irrelevance among those who matter. Of course, parties and hookups have their price, too. As we have seen, rules of the game for the first option include fierce competition with your female peers to be the sexiest, heavy consumption of alcohol, and conformity to the hookup script of emotionally detached sex. The uncompromising nature of some of these unwritten rules emerges in Rachel's reflections on power:

As a female, it does not make sense to attend college parties unless you are willing to embrace being a sex figure and be objectified. If you do not dress and act this way, you simply will look out of place and be overlooked or ignored, which defeats the very purpose of going to college parties. There are ways to use the power you do have; it is easy to manipulate men most of the time. They get so easily distracted sexually that it is not hard for a woman to get a man; then the man uses this power to turn around and demand certain actions from that woman. Life and relationships come down to finding a balance between the power you are given and your level of comfort using that power. A vagina has power over a straight guy—it always has.

In this context, a woman's power lies in dressing and behaving in such a way as to sexually arouse men so that she succeeds in "getting a man." And "getting a man," to be clear, means hooking up for the night or perhaps a series of nights. Crassly put, a woman's power is largely reduced to tempting men with the potential for sex and choosing who will use her vagina and who will not. As Rachel sees it, the task for women is finding a balance—appropriate to one's comfort level with tradeoffs—between using too much or too little of this "given" power. Rachel views herself as more or less achieving a decent balance, for hooking up gives her the temporary high of feeling affirmed and not being quite so alone:

> It is human nature to feel happy or a high from a relationship with another human. It gives one a feeling of knowing you're not alone. I get this same high; whether it's a cute comeback at the bar or a kiss from a staring kid at the end of the night. It does make you feel confident about yourself.

Rachel contrasts her own sense of balance with her friends' lack of balance in using their power. First, she describes her friend Kalynn:

> Kalynn is kind of a bigger girl who loves attention from guys. Kalynn loves to hook up with boys—she always has—and she loves to talk about it. Sometimes the way she talks she almost sounds obsessive. She especially loves to prey on freshmen. Kalynn really likes to exert that power and maybe it is because it makes her feel more powerful over another person especially when she goes after younger guys. Before a party night I find her in a random hallway making out with a guy. I laugh at her and she tells him she has to go and will see him at the bar.

After they have been at the bar for a while, Rachel realizes Kalynn has disappeared. Eventually, she spots her friend:

> Kalynn comes over looking like a hot mess with her knees scraped up. I shockingly asked her if she is okay as I tried not to laugh and

I asked her where she had been. She replied that she met some really cute guy (who was really a weird random guy) and they decided to go to the parking garage to hook up.

At this point, Rachel decides to leave the bar and "get Kalynn home before she does something stupid and dangerous." Interestingly, Rachel does not say that her friend already did something stupid and dangerous. According to Rachel, Kalynn's use of her female power is a bit too extreme because she frequently makes risky decisions that place her in danger.

In contrast, according to Rachel, her roommate Allie lacks balance in the other "extreme." Allie is not comfortable (or willing) to use her sexuality to play the game and to get a guy: "Allie is mild and very sweet and she has never done really anything with a guy, except kiss." Rachel perceives that Allie keeps clinging to an unrealistic hope that she can find a "nice" guy who will like her as she is and be interested in a relationship. Recounting the time Allie asked her to leave a party and drive to a bar where Allie had a "date with a soccer player," Rachel writes: "I knew how this was going to turn out for Allie with this guy, which wasn't well, but I told her we would go." When they got to the bar, Allie's face fell: "The guy she had come to see was in a very in-depth conversation with a girl who is very well known to put out and she wasn't even giving him a chance to look around even if he wanted to. Allie now felt stupid for being so hopeful that he was actually going to be a nice guy." Rachel perceives that Allie and others like her are unhappy because "they are not willing to put themselves out there."

Many ethnographers who concluded that men have the most power acknowledged that some college women enthusiastically embrace their role as sexual temptress and appear to take pleasure in this form of power. However, they expressed doubt that such women possess legitimate power to choose what they really desire:

While these women probably believe that they are acting the way that they want to, the truth is that society does not give them many possibilities to choose from. Either a woman gives in to the notion of the female as an objective sex tool or she acts like a prude. Even when a woman is dominant rather than passive in these interactions, I think that this still comes from fulfilling the desires of the male, and therefore signals the male's dominance. (Blake)

It seems that the females with the smallest, most revealing clothing seem to be the women of power, they are the leaders of the pack. Because they look more like the models and movie stars, they run the show. It seems at times they dictate what is considered "cool." However, I am not convinced the women of power have much power in the overall social situation. It is ironic for me to call them women of power because they are often the ones drunkenly walking home with someone they just met. In my opinion, power is nearly synonymous with control and these women are often being controlled by the situation, whether they realize it or not. They may feel in control of themselves, but how many of their actions really come from personal desires and how many are the result of conformity? (Milly)

While some women ethnographers in this group simply marvel at the irony of women's so-called power to sexually arouse men and have hookup sex—sex that frequently mimics porn sex, lacks concern for women's sexual pleasure, and involves harmful consequences—others express sadness, anger, and frustration at their peers' willingness to conform to disempowering norms:

I wish I could stand on a soapbox and proclaim to my female companions the harm in objectifying themselves. It's time for us girls to stop worrying about hair, nails, makeup, and short skirts. We would be less stressed if we actually approached males with our minds instead of our bodies. I feel this idea would give girls a better chance of finding true quality partners who leave us more fulfilled and happy. (Mara)

If women decided to value their sexual well-being as much as they value their physical bodies, I think many men would be forced to change the way they think about women. Many women think that they have power over men because they can get men to sleep with them. In reality, it is the men who have the power over women because the meaningless sex is exactly what the men want. Women have power, but they just need to use it in the right way. They have a lot of power sexually in that they are very attractive to men. However, if women just continue to give away their power for nothing in exchange, then their power is worthless. (Mindy)

Women must have higher expectations before men will change their expectations. Until women discover the value of self-respect, men will not discover the value in respecting. If women feel inferior in today's society, then they must step up and start breaking down the walls of male dominance. (Molly)

As much as these student ethnographers would like to change the culture, many do not perceive themselves as having the power to rewrite the rules of sexuality and relationships in a way that would make them more satisfied. From their perspective, it is discouraging that there is always a ready supply of women like Kalynn, whose need for a temporary ego boost trumps other considerations; like Rachel, whose pragmatism yields to a lifestyle of measured compromise; and like Allie, whose dwindling hope for a meaningful relationship (because she can never compete with women who are willing to have sex) convinces her to compromise and follow Rachel.

Gender and Power: The False Dichotomy of Male versus Female Power

The final group of ethnographers (24%) resisted the conclusion that one gender is clearly in a position of power over the other; instead, they reported that both men and women exercise different forms of power or that social factors unrelated to gender determined which individuals were most powerful at parties. Echoing other ethnographers' observations, these students described women's bodies as instruments of power and control, recognizing that sex is perceived as a commodity that men value more than women:

I also think that the female body can be very powerful in certain situations. If the girl looks good enough, some guys will do anything to get with that girl. This could mean being completely fake or trying too hard. Being highly attractive can be a great asset when going to college parties. I have been at parties that only charge guys and girls deemed not attractive to drink. The attractive girls are wanted so many times they do not have to pay to get in. (Mark)

Females understand and embrace just how much power they can wield when they use their bodies in certain ways. They know that this is a way that they can be somewhat dominant over men because they know that their bodies are something that they can control and can keep or give away to men as much or as little as they please. That is a lot of power to have simply in the way you look, dress, and carry yourself. (Julie)

Yet this group of ethnographers also recognizes that male power is operative as well for all the same reasons mentioned above. They express that men and women each use the power within their means to get what they want, whether that is sex, increased social status, attention, approval, being pursued, feeling wanted and valued, and/or a temporary ego boost:

I think that it is best that both men and women are a part of this power circle. The problem with it is that both men and women are able to exploit their respective positions of power to engage in acts that they believe to benefit themselves, even at the cost of harming others. (Ron)

Girls had to almost flaunt their bodies in order to get attention, whereas guys just kind of sat back and let the attention come to them. A guy is expected to make a move, and if he does, then all of the power is in the girl's hands from then on. She has options from there, assuming that the guy wants to hook up with her. She can either hookup with him with boundaries, hookup with him with no boundaries, or not hook up with him at all. (Cameron)

Attempting to identify power dynamics at parties, other ethnographers considered categories other than gender: the most powerful were the men and women who commanded the most positive attention and admiration. First and foremost, this included Division 1 male athletes. (University A did not have fraternities and sororities.) Of all social groups, being a talented male athlete guaranteed that one was instantly in the most powerful group, independent of one's race, looks, and wealth, especially for basketball players. If a basketball player was African American or unattractive by "normal" standards, his athlete status allowed him to soar above white good-looking men in regard to power and the ability to attract women and do what they want sexually. Consider the following:

The famous and celebrity-like status that the basketball players have on campus carries over to the party scene. The male basketball players have the most power because not only do women want to hook up with them, but men also want to drink a beer with them or smoke a cigarette with them. (Jill)

There were basketball players in attendance at the party. These men were tall, strong, and most were African American. Their size and social status helped depict the power that they had over the rest of the party that night. (Sara)

At one point in my conversation with a basketball player, a female student reached into the player's pants and fondled his genitals. I assume she thought no one could see it because of the way we were arranged near the bar, but my brother and I both noticed it about the same time the player did. He laughed in surprise and removed her hand from his pants. We all laughed pretty heartily, and she left clearly embarrassed. Jersey-chasers like this woman are fairly promi-nent. My guess is that she was looking for validation through sexual contact with someone with status, so she acted desperately on it by reaching down his pants. (Isaac)

Next, note how Rachel expresses ambivalence about her basketball "hookup guy." Obviously thrilled with the attention, she remains uncom-fortable with feeling out of control when she is with him:

There were several black male basketball players at the party. They were wearing what seemed to be their warm up sweats and a sweat-shirt but the girls still flocked to wherever they were. It was as if the girls danced a little raunchier and were more forward when they were there. Luckily, my hookup guy broke through and came right over to me to say hi and brought me a drink, and I just couldn't say no to the attention with all these girls eyeing his hand he kept on my hip. . . . When I came to the bar and the basketball player left all of those girls and came over to me, or when I just chill with him and the other guys on the team, it does make me feel powerful. I know there is the whole status thing even though I wish it wasn't there. It also makes you feel totally out of control because those guys will do anything to make sure they have the power in the situation and they are calling the shots. Status and who you are to the people around you is what gives you the power. (Rachel)

After male athletes, those with the most power were those who could stand out successfully in the crowd and be regarded by others as desirable.

For women, the measure is beauty. Although there are other factors for men, being attractive, outgoing, funny or wealthy each allows individuals to increase their power.

> The most attractive people have the most power at the party and it is the same in society. If you are not overly attractive, it is okay as long as you are powerful or wealthy. This is what the media teaches people from a very young age and people follow it unquestioningly. (Rene)

Research Findings on Power and Party Culture

In their analyses of power dynamics regarding race and ethnicity, sexual orientation, and gender, the majority of student ethnographers perceived that white heterosexual men are the most powerful social group at college parties. This perception is corroborated by much research on college party and sexual culture, including the work of Michael Kimmel,[2] Donna Freitas,[3] Mark Regnerus and Jeremy Ueker,[4] Kathleen Bogle,[5] and Laura Sessions Stepp.[6] In addition to their consensus about white heterosexual males having the most power to write and perpetuate the rules and norms of college parties, sex, and intimate relationships, these scholars recognize that an important shift in normative behavior has occurred, from dating and committed relationships to hookups. Consider how their accounts of college sexual culture in the following paragraphs resonate with the voices and perspectives of student ethnographers thus far in *College Hookup Culture and Christian Ethics*.

Michael Kimmel, especially interested in the impact of contemporary masculine socialization on college social and party culture, argues that college men today live and breathe in "Guyland," a social arena predicated on a mentality of male superiority and "bros before hos." Among men's significant preoccupations in "Guyland" is to enact and prove their masculinity to other men. College women, meanwhile, in order to gain social acceptance and approval in the party scene, must submit and conform to the bro-code rules that promote male superiority and narrowly construed roles for women.

In the following reflection on his own experience, Kimmel provides a telling account of how norms for masculinity and femininity as well as the range of social and sexual options have changed within just one generation:

> When I was a young man, there were more possibilities to swim against the current. Guyland was hardly the only arena. One could

be serious, sober, stable, and responsible, as readily as wild, bois-
terous, and predatory. One could be independent, an individual,
without being seen as a freak or loner. There were always other
cliques to join for support.... One of the greatest contradictions of
our era is that there is a super-abundance of choices now, far more
than ever before, and yet the range of those choices somehow feels
more constricted, and more constricting, than ever. The dramatic
increase in alternatives is accompanied by an equally dramatic cultural homogenization, a flattening of regional and local differences
with a single mainstream dominant culture prevailing.[7]

Donna Freitas's books on this topic—*Sex and the Soul* and *The End of Sex*—
similarly reveal a fully normalized gender hierarchy, manifest in theme
parties and accounts of actual sexual behavior, within today's hookup culture. Like Kimmel, Freitas reflects on changes that have occurred since she
was a college student:

In my personal experience in the early to mid-1990s the landscape
for navigating one's romantic and sexual life was much broader and
more diverse and included traditional dates and long-term romantic
relationships as well as hooking up. (There was also the possibility of opting out of all of it.) But even in the mid-1990s, hooking
up could still mean making out at a party and exchanging phone
numbers, with the thought of turning the make-out session into
an opportunity for a relationship. It didn't necessarily ride on the
notion of unattached intimacy both during and afterward, and it
wasn't an end in itself.[8]

Lending a unique perspective to this discussion, Mark Regnerus and
Jeremy Ueker draw on research to argue that college men in general prefer low-cost sex (sex in which little is expected in terms of effort, dating,
commitment, etc.), while college women prefer to have sex in a committed
relationship.[9] According to their argument, sexual and relational norms
on college campuses are greatly shaped and influenced by economic and
market principles. One significant factor to explain why hookups have
become the norm on college campuses may be related to current sex ratios
on college campuses. In 1947, there were twice as many men on campus
as women, but this gap decreased until 1980, at which point women began
to outnumber men in colleges. From 2005 to 2016, only 43% of the college

population has been male. As a consequence of changing demographics, men gained power to negotiate the terms and determine the norms
for sex.[10]

Regnerus and Ueker also examine the effects of the hookup culture's
increasing normativity on college campuses. Their research reveals that
women exhibit the following characteristics on campuses where they
comprise a higher proportion of the student body: they go on fewer dates,
express more negative appraisals of men on campus, hold more negative
views of their relationships, have a lower likelihood of having a boyfriend,
and receive less (in the way of relationship commitment) in exchange for
sex.[11] Laura Sessions Stepp's *Unhooked* also demonstrates negative repercussions of the shift from dating and relationships to casual sexual hookups. Specifically, involvement in hookup culture places girls' and young
women's self-worth and physical and mental health at great risk.[12] Finally,
note that similar conclusions are drawn by Kathleen Bogle in her book
Hooking Up; while hookup culture successfully serves college men's interest in casual sex, it does not meet the sexual, emotional, and relational
needs of college women.[13]

Immersing myself in similar questions about what's happening on college campuses, why certain behaviors are now normative, and what effects
particular lifestyle choices have on students' well-being, I found myself
thinking a lot about my own college experience and how much things
have changed. Significantly, Kimmel's and Freitas's personal accounts of
college life before hookup culture became normative align with my own
memories of being an undergraduate in the early 1990s. Compared to college students today, my peers and I enjoyed a far greater sense of freedom
in how we dressed, acted, and related to one another socially and sexually. It may sound foreign from today's vantage point, but college women's
sexual decisions did not make or break their social reputations: one could
choose to have casual sex, have sex in a relationship, sexually experiment
but not have sexual intercourse, or not sexually experiment at all and still
have an active social life and a great time in college. As a sorority member who attended sorority and fraternity parties regularly, I never observed
female peers shopping obsessively and extensively for the sexiest outfits,
and never heard of sorority sisters being so desperate for male attention
that they would perform sexual favors for male acquaintances. Of course,
masculinity and femininity norms, sexual objectification of women, and
the sexual double standard were alive and well in the 1990s, as in previous decades. Sexual violence was also a common phenomenon on college

campuses. Despite important commonalities, however, college students' pressure to conform to increasingly narrow sexual and gender norms, not to mention their actual behavioral interactions, are much different now than twenty years ago.[14]

To learn about contemporary gender inequality on college campuses, it is not necessary, of course, to read recent scholarship or conduct one's own research. For those of us outside of the party and hookup culture, simple conversations with students can be just as eye-opening. To conclude this chapter on power, consider the lessons we might glean from a class discussion that occurred one fall at University A.

Ashley, a soft-spoken student, was telling the class how she had been walking down her residence hall around noon when a guy grabbed her butt and said something sexual to her. After she responded, "Please don't do that," he called her a "bitch" and spread rumors about her being a "freeze." Her resistance, she explained to the class, led to her alienation from many peers in her hall. When I expressed surprise at her polite reaction and her use of the word "please" when requesting an end to sexual harassment, another student named Ellie responded with frustration that I and other women she knew my age (her therapist, aunts, etc.) "just don't get it" when it comes to interactions between college men and women. We assume "X, Y, and Z, which no longer exist." "X, Y, and Z," I discovered, refer to "forms of respect that women were once given, with regard to their bodies and their sexualities in the past." Elaborating further, Ellie emailed me the following later that day:

> It isn't that smart young women cannot tell guys off or hit them when they are treated in a demeaning way. It is just that those females are so stuck with the mindset that "Oh, that's just how boys are now" or "That's just the way it is." I myself do not believe that that is how boys *should* be, and this isn't the way it should be. If a boy demeaned me in that way, I can honestly say that I would tell him off right away (or even slap him if I felt insulted enough). It isn't right that males have that stupid power over females and that some females are so concerned that their reputations might be slightly tarnished in the process of standing up for what they believe.

Conclusion

While gains in gender equality have clearly occurred in many public arenas like athletics, politics, and the workforce, I am convinced through my own and others' research studies and years of class discussions that there has actually been a significant decline in gender equality when it comes to sex and in negotiating the terms of intimate relationships—at least on college campuses. My students' assessment, together with most researchers', is that white heterosexual men today have the most influence over the "rules" and norms of college party sexual culture, yet the following important points must be made clear as well: not all men in this social group actively endorse the status quo or benefit equally. Further, even if many do benefit socially from hookup norms, it does not necessarily follow that they personally would choose hookup culture as the dominant relational norm on their campus. It is also possible that such norms do not make them happy and fulfilled. My qualitative analysis of students' reflections on happiness in the next chapter—both their own happiness and their peers'—actually casts doubt on claims of Regnerus, Ueker, Bogle, and others that many college men are generally content and happy with casual sex and hookup norms. Delving further into these issues, chapter 4 explores whether hookups foster college students' well-being, happiness, and fulfillment.

4

Are College Students Happy in Contemporary Party and Hookup Culture?

IF SOMEONE HAD asked me as an undergraduate if I was happy at college parties, I am sure I would have answered (without hesitation) "yes!" To this day, I enjoy great memories of dancing, hanging out with friends, pursuing romantic interests, and drinking cheap beer to the point of a happy buzz. My experiences of parties also included post-party 7-Eleven nacho runs with friends in the middle of the night, our laughter as we recounted our evenings, and our bonding as we confided in one another. What was not to love? When deciding to include this question about happiness at college parties on my ethnography assignment, I did not expect that students' answers would be quite so complicated.

As a few students pointed out, even the best ethnographic descriptions of parties and the most educated guesses about peers' happiness and fulfillment could never produce definitive answers about something as subjective and complex as another's state of being. Nevertheless, generally trusting the perceptions and conclusions of 126 ethnographers about their peers' happiness, especially when they appear diligent with their observations and transparent with their thought processes, is entirely reasonable. The ethnographers are even more reliable when they decide to reveal their own and their close friends' experiences of happiness and fulfillment within party and hookup culture. Furthermore, my students' collective reflections have a ring of truth and authenticity that has resonated strongly among other students who have read drafts of this chapter in their classes. As with other chapters in this book,

I leave it for my readers to consider the following student reflections alongside their own knowledge and experience as they arrive at their own conclusions.

Happy?

Are students happy and fulfilled at college parties? Four perspectives emerged from ethnographers' analyses: first, 10% of ethnographers perceived that their peers are happy with contemporary party culture because they appeared happy and content. Specifically, partygoers are smiling, laughing, relaxed, free from daily stresses, and enjoying drinking, socializing, playing drinking games, flirting, dancing, and hooking up. This group of ethnographers typically perceived their peers as happy and fulfilled if they accomplished their goal of hooking up with someone by the end of the night:

> For the most part, the majority of people looked and acted happy and fulfilled. Just about everybody was dancing, drinking, playing games, listening to the music, or talking. People who see each other most days of the week are genuinely happy to see one another over the weekend and not have school hanging over their heads. Without the looming presence of school the next day, I saw students bare it all and truly unwind and be very happy. Some people I know who do not party have called the party scene an escape from reality. I would completely disagree with that. The fact is that right now this is the reality we live in. There is no escape—we are embracing it. Students only have so long to go to college; eventually, the real world will come and they do not want to feel as though they left anything on the table. (Bill)

> There are people who go out with the intention of meeting someone to hook up with. In the post-sexual gratifying experience, I'm sure they feel fulfilled, goal accomplished. Some people are really aware of their wants and needs and can handle a casual hookup. Those individuals must sense a separation between physical and emotional intimacy that allows them to filter through their different needs at different times. (I don't think you necessarily have to be "heartless" to be in this position, but you do have to be okay with basically using another person to fulfill physical needs.) (Lisa)

If I were to ask these people whether they felt happy or fulfilled, I would imagine their answers would all be relatively the same—yes. In today's materialistic me, me, me culture, it is very "fulfilling" (in the general sense) to do what feels good. (Sam)

These ethnographers also emphasized that students' outward display of happiness was driven by their high levels of intoxication, which made their evenings enjoyable:

The people I observed do appear to be happy and fulfilled. People get overly excited when they see someone they know, when their favorite song comes on the speakers, and when they win the drinking game they are playing. These emotions are probably just due to the alcohol. It is not the reactions of the same people on campus when similar situations occur. Girls who get out of a class and see their friends on campus do not normally squeal at the top of their lungs and take off running towards them. The manic behaviors seen at parties are a result of the alcohol. (Rene)

I think most people were happy. At the same time, I think that this was strongly alcohol induced. Based on how people were acting and talking, it was clear that most of the people were extremely drunk and acting how they wanted to. For example, there was a couple that was making out in the basement while they were dancing. The girl was wearing a short black skirt that had a tank top tucked into the skirt and heels. The guy was holding the girl around the waist and they were just making out right on the dance floor. It was as if the only thing that existed for them was the other person and they were happy. (Rachel)

By contrast, the remaining 90% of ethnographers considered evidence that some or most peers were not happy with college party culture, and suggested one of the following: 29% reported that some peers appeared happy with drinking and hooking up, while others appeared unhappy and dissatisfied; 33% perceived that partiers were momentarily happy—until the next morning or whenever they became sober; and 27% perceived that their peers were definitely unhappy and unfulfilled within the culture.[1] Ethnographers from these three groups who speculated about peers' private dissatisfaction expressed similar themes about why some or all of their peers might be unhappy.

First, partiers were observed clearly displaying dissatisfaction or other negative emotions during parties. Common observations included partiers looking "zoned out" with blank stares and lack of emotion, as well as drunken peers crying, throwing up, passing out, arguing with friends and their significant others, and getting into physical fights:

> The people who appeared to be truly enjoying themselves were those who did not know they were. In other words, those who blacked out seemed to be having the best time. While they were blacked out, they didn't have a care in the world. They were living in the present, which is a problem for most people. Those who did not black out appeared to have some sort of issue on their mind. I would hear people ask their friends how they look or if there was another party that was better than the one they were currently at. (Eric)

> Rarely is anyone at a party totally happy and fulfilled. Even people who come with large groups of friends still stand around awkwardly, half participating and half watching, as if they feel out of place despite hordes of people that they know. When you look around the room, it's almost as if everyone has something they'd like to say: "I'm lonely, I'm not doing well in my major, and I feel like my friends use me." But no one says anything: they just snap out of it, laugh at a joke they probably heard only half of, and take another sip from their Solo cup. (Helen)

> People attend [University A's] parties with the intention of getting drunk and hooking up, but inevitably they are disappointed by the parties and will drink more to try to make it more entertaining. Countless people walk away from parties mad that there wasn't enough alcohol, there wasn't the right type of alcohol, there were too many people, not enough people, complaining that it was busted by the police or that there was some sort of drama or fight with another student who was also on edge from something at the party. (Casper)

Second, many students observed that, while partiers looked and acted happy initially, many displayed their insecurities, worries, or unhappiness after they consumed too much alcohol or the alcohol wore off:

> The majority appeared to be happy on the outside but not fulfilled. Once people reached a certain point of drunkenness, the true

feelings began to emerge. Whether it was a previous fight with a boyfriend or seeing someone you've tried to avoid for months, alcohol has a way of resurfacing emotions, as well as hiding them. I know this from personal experiences. (Eva)

I went back to the room where I'd kept my coat to see a man sobbing with his male friends hugging him and repeating, "Fucking slut." The difference in dynamic between that room and the one immediately adjacent was enormous, and when I looked around the house later I saw the same scene repeated in numerous dark corners and private rooms. Not everyone at the party is happy. (Devon)

Third, ethnographers perceived that while partiers were momentarily happy with the instant gratification that alcohol and hookups offer, the next morning they typically felt dissatisfied and unhappy:

I think a lot of people do feel bad, or unhappy, or just like something isn't right after hooking up. (Ben)

In all that I have observed and experienced, no one is ever happy with a hookup the next morning, no matter how happy and content they seem when they are caught up in the moment. There is usually an overwhelming want to forget everything about the night prior, including removing pictures of themselves and the person they hooked up with and overall avoidance of the person. They do not want to discuss the night's occurrences and often laugh off those "mistakes." (Kelly)

The fun does not last when the night is over. Hangovers are never fun the next day. On many occasions, my friends have suffered the damages of drunk texting, such as starting arguments or embarrassing themselves. When people hook up I hear about all the regrets the next morning. All of these consequences lead me to believe that these people really are not happy and fulfilled with their lives. What happy and fulfilled person includes hangovers and drama and regrettable sex in his or her life? (Jaden)

Feelings of regret, embarrassment, and anxiety likewise surface repeatedly in ethnographers' personal reflections about themselves:

I have made mistakes while drinking and hooking up. I thought I was happy for the time being, but once I woke up in the morning and thought about my actions the night before, I was mortified. Looking back the next day or a few days later, I have regrets and questions as to why I did it. (Georgia)

In my personal experience, things done by in-the-moment impulses lead to a lack of happiness. During my sophomore year, I began to frequently do actions that gave me instant gratification but in the long run made me unhappy. Drinking large amounts of alcohol and then making out with random guys became a norm. While out drinking and partying the make out sessions made me happy and fulfilled my need to get some type of affection that I wanted while I was sober. But the next day, I always would regret hearing what I had done the previous night. It got to the point where people who I didn't recall came up to me and began conversations with me about my weekend actions. Party hookups equal instant gratification, which only equals immediate happiness. I have found that actual happiness and fulfillment comes from actual, intimate relationships. (Haley)

Finally, students regularly expressed that it's hard to really know whether their peers are happy because many students—themselves included—do not reveal even to their friends if they are disillusioned with the status quo of hooking up:

Many times we wake up to regret our actions the next morning. Even when we do regret our actions, it is easy to put on an air of happiness in order to simply fit in. (Tammy)

It seemed as if everyone was fulfilled and having a good time. I know from past experiences, though, that it isn't healthy and that my peers probably seemed happy but really are hurting inside. (Elena)

From my own hookup experiences, I would say that I have zero fulfillment the next day, but while it is happening, I feel happy and successful. For people who do not know me though, they cannot see the disappointment because to outsiders it is masked. I am always upset after the hookup, because while it's happening I have the feeling that it will lead to something more, like a relationship. This is never really the case though; once you are sober and wake up the next day, you just have the feeling of being used for physical pleasure, which never creates a happy satisfied attitude. (Olivia)

Dissatisfaction with Parties and Hookups

The vast majority of ethnographers believe their peers are privately dissatisfied and unhappy as a result of partying and hooking up. A minority of ethnographers emphasized the negative physical effects they and their peers experience, like being hung over the next day, contracting sexually transmitted infections, and being worried about unprotected sex and pregnancy:

> Because lots of freshmen were casually hooking up with each other, there was an outbreak of syphilis, which a basketball player contracted and spread to a bunch of girls. (Nikki)

> How do people feel mornings, days, and weeks after drinking and hooking up? The first thing that comes to my mind is the pregnancy issue. I think it scares people a lot, and makes them very unhappy about their decisions from the past. (Ben)

When Ben mentions "the pregnancy issue" and alludes to "decisions from the past," it is difficult to know if he is referring to abortion. It is striking that not a single ethnographer mentioned women having abortions as a result of drunken hookups. Perhaps this silence about abortion is due to the reality that college women are now taking Plan B (the morning-after pill) after unprotected drunken sex and so do not need abortions. Alternatively, the topic of choosing abortion after becoming pregnant from a drunken hookup may be taboo at this Catholic university; whenever I raised this issue in class discussions, students appeared uncomfortable and silent.

Nearly all ethnographers who perceived that peers were unhappy focused mainly on the negative psychological consequences that they and their friends experience after hookups. First, they report feeling like they had used someone or been used by someone, which creates regret:

> As for the hookups, I think the people are happy before and during the hookup, but they might have regrets the next day. From personal experience, you both feel good about it before and during, but by the end you may have doubts . . . you feel like you used the person—it's not very fulfilling after all is said and done. (Anthony)

> If I do something really stupid, such as hooking up with someone I don't know, then I never forget it and worry about it. There have

been times when I drank too much and did things that I normally would not do sober. The things I do get me into trouble and make me feel really bad about myself, making me less confident and secure. Regret is hard to live with for the rest of your life and can really damage someone's self-worth and respect. Many people will joke around and talk about the night they had with their friends. They make it sound like they don't care that they hooked up with someone they don't know but really they do. I think girls worry about it more than guys do in some cases. (Anna)

Second, students report feelings of emptiness, loneliness, or even a void in their lives that endures long past their hookup experiences:

Whether people admit it or not, no one wakes up from a random hookup and feels great about it. A lot of girls on [University A's] campus know I'm going into psychology and confide in me when they need to rant about mean guys or bad hookups. Such relationships are filled with regret from going further than they wanted to sexually and not having the emotional support they needed. Some friends came [to University A] as virgins with little or no sexual history and decided to have meaningless sex with the mentality that it's what everyone is "supposed to do" as a college student. The overwhelming result wasn't positive. Let's face it: people hook up for one thing and when that one thing is over, the void which they tried to fill simply comes back. (Nikki)

I feel that my opinions on the hookup culture are shared by most students [at University A]. When I go to a party, it is almost a challenge, or "game" to try and hook up with a girl at a party. Hooking up is fulfilling at the time and you feel proud of yourself, but in the morning (through personal experience) you feel regretful. After the excitement is over and your buzz wears off, you don't feel good about what you did. You feel emptier inside. You feel no sense of fulfillment or happiness. (Marek)

Part of my research was to ask my friends if they were happy with the hookup lifestyle, and their answer was that they did not like the lifestyle and wanted to get out. They also told me they have felt a sense of loneliness and emptiness at times. The reason for this feeling of emptiness is the fact there is no attachment because it meant nothing to either of the partners involved. They might have gotten their fulfillment that night, but they have nothing there in the days and weeks that follow. This feeling of emptiness is never fulfilled until there is an actual relationship, so by repeating this action they are just magnifying this feeling of emptiness and loneliness. During my experience in the hookup scene, I have never felt satisfied the next morning. I usually have no friendship with the person. This lack of connecting is why I don't feel satisfied the next morning, along with the weeks and months afterwards. (Jonathon)

Third and finally, ethnographers express that some or many peers, despite their dissatisfaction with hookup culture and a preference for a committed relationship, become ensnared in a repetitive cycle of hookups:

I know several people, myself included, who have woken up the next morning either to a reaction of "Oh, my gosh, I can't remember if we had sex" or to just an overwhelming depression. Finally, last year I was so depressed by drunken, meaningless hookups that I swore I would not touch anyone until it actually meant something. It made me much happier. I think having such a nonchalant attitude about sexuality leads to a lack of self-esteem and a lack of self-respect, which only perpetuates the cycle because you try to earn respect through sexual encounters. (Nora)

When people hook up with random people, it may be fulfilling at the time, but it leaves them feeling unwanted or used later when the alcohol isn't impairing their judgment. At breakfast, female friends talk about the hookups the night before and how they regretted them. However, my friends' feelings do not reflect their actions. After discussing how displeased they were, they were with someone new again the next weekend. (Paul)

Mitch was someone who more or less hooked up with a different girl each weekend, but he always told me of his strong desire for a committed girlfriend. Every time he hooked up with a girl, he got that momentary bit of relief, only to slip deeper into an unfulfilling habit of loneliness. (Teagan)

Longing for More Than the Casual Hookup

Alongside the majority of ethnographers' reflections on the negative physical and psychological consequences of hookups, another repeating theme was that they and their friends simply long for more than unattached sexual encounters. Some noted that while hookups are supposed to be about physical pleasure and zero emotions, this ideal rarely translates into reality. One person usually develops feelings, longs for a relationship that goes beyond "booty calls," and gets hurt:

> At least one person involved feels the effects of a hookup and is not able to just brush it off or have feelings of either regret or wishing it was more. (Kelly)

> Freshman year of college was a time when I had my random hookups. There was a boy that I was acquainted with and I hooked up with him the first weekend during orientation. At first, I didn't totally regret it. It was just kind of like "Oh, well, this is what happens in college, and I'm just having a good time." However, that eventually changed. I started to like him, but he made it very clear he didn't want a relationship because he wanted his freedom. I also only heard from him on the weekends to meet up at parties, and we both knew what would happen at the end of the night. This made me not feel so good about myself; I realized I was nothing important to him. After about two or three months of this "relationship" and him spending the night with me in my dorm room, I woke up one morning and was suddenly not attracted to him and wanted him out of my room. I think it was just me finally coming to my senses and sick of feeling upset when I wouldn't hear from him all week. (Malena)

> This momentary pleasure is completely absent of deeper feelings of intimacy and the deeper meanings of healthy and fulfilling relationships that people ultimately long for. Though many people looked happy, many also looked miserable. I witnessed females so drunk they could not stand up and had to be carried by their friends. I witnessed men who got into disputes and got kicked out of parties. These displays cannot be happiness. As human beings we always are longing for answers and longing for more and I just cannot see how desensitizing sex and sleeping with strangers can fulfill our being. (Jill)

A common perception among many women ethnographers was that women tended to develop feelings for their hookup partner and desire emotional connection and a relationship more than males did:

> My female friends who have had random hookups reflect on their bad nights. Not only did some not use protection, but many did not feel fulfilled in the moment. Many of the guys were forceful with the hookup and even in intoxicated moments, my girlfriends had bad feelings about their choices and decisions. Conversely, many male friends are incredibly satisfied with their hookup achievements. Most male friends say that they're sure the girls they hook up with do not expect anything and then two days later, the phone buzzes with the girls' numbers. (Maria)

> A male friend told me guys are pleased after the hookup, unless it was a dissatisfying hookup, meaning the girl did not do all that the guy wanted, or the girl stopped the guy from advancing. In that case, the guy is annoyed. Generally, the guy then expects to hook up with the girl the following weekend until he hooks up with a different girl who performs better than the [first one]. Once he grows tired of the new girl, he will return to the first girl. The guy really isn't dazed by the tangled web he's weaving—he's just focusing on his sexual desires. I've observed that girls, on the other hand, become emotionally invested and struggle to let go of their hookup partner because they are hopeful of a potential relationship. Obviously, they are not happy after weeks of hooking up. (Paige)

Women ethnographers perceived that more men than women are happy and satisfied with the current party status quo, but men's reflections challenge this view. The majority of male ethnographers did not express that they or their peers were fulfilled by drunken casual hookups. It is, perhaps, less socially acceptable for men to discuss dissatisfaction with hookups with friends, but given a more anonymous forum, they reveal a different story:

> I have experienced a "college hookup." It didn't take me long before I realized that it wasn't for me. Speaking personally, the desire to hook up serves to mask a desire for personal intimacy. (Elliot)

> I asked my friends how they felt about whether or not they were happy with their social life. The majority of them said they loved

to be college students doing whatever they wanted, whenever they wanted, and chasing girls in the process. Parties were a great time for them to release the steam built up from the week. Things changed for the worse when I brought up the word "fulfillment," though. As if there was a flip of a switch, my friends expressed that, although partying was fun and exciting, with new experiences occurring almost every weekend, there was nothing in their social life that really left them feeling fulfilled the following morning. They strongly expressed frustration with the difficulty of jumping the gap from hooking up to initiating a real relationship. The stories of the girls they *almost* had relationships with outnumbered the stories of actual relationships by a large margin. (Frank)

The people I observed are trying to find happiness but will never be fulfilled because they are looking for happiness in all the wrong places. I believe they are either unhappy with how they see themselves or are lonely so they search for a hookup to fill that void in life. I believe that once a person is truly happy with who they are, they will be able to look beyond the hookup culture and find a fulfilling long-term relationship. (Kevin)

Greater Happiness at College Parties: What Dynamics, if Any, Would You Change to Be Personally Happy at Parties?

When these ethnographers reflected on what, if any, changes in social dynamics they would make to be happier, only one expressed that he would not change anything. Interestingly, however, even his vote of confidence was not overwhelming: "For the most part, I enjoy all the parties I go to." (Spencer) Nearly all remaining ethnographers offered responses that fit into one or more of the following categories. They would: (1) change how females are expected to dress and act at parties; (2) change how males and females relate to one another; (3) be accepted for who they really are and be part of a college community that genuinely embraces diversity and inclusivity; (4) be freed from the norm of needing to drink to have a good time; and (5) be freed from the hookup norm and witness a return to dating and committed relationships as the social norm.

First, many students wished that college women would be more confident and feel free to dress and act however they wanted:

> The one social dynamic I would change about the party culture would be the competition between girls. Every girl who goes to parties prepares for hours, trying to make her hair perfect and her outfits just right, so she can look better than any other girl there. The main reason is so she doesn't feel insecure while she is talking to a boy. She can feel like his eyes are totally on her and he wants to be seen with her if she looks better than any other girl at the party. Unfortunately, the majority of boys at parties are always looking to do a little better, so the girl rarely has confidence, which just fuels the fire for her to try to look even better the next night or to drink more to increase her confidence and go after the boy anyway. If girls had to compete less, they would feel more relaxed at parties, dressing in more casual clothing and obsessing less over fading makeup. They would most likely drink a lot less at parties, leading to fewer regrets the next day over something they did or said. (Donna)

> If I could change any social dynamic at parties, I would change the way that girls are expected to dress and behave. Parties would be much more enjoyable if people were really getting to know the people based on who they really are, not who they are trying to be. I do not think any woman wants to walk around in revealing dresses, uncomfortable shoes, and pounds of makeup and hairspray. I do not think that any woman wants a man to be staring at her breasts, her butt, or her legs. I do not think any woman wants to grind on men, dance on bars, or run around yelling and screaming just to get attention. I feel that if we could change this social construct of the perfect woman, and diminish this need for an oversexualized society, we could begin to look at and value people for who they truly are. I do not think you could find any woman who wouldn't want to be loved for simply being who she truly is. (Kelly)

> If I could change one thing about how people interact at parties, I would hope that women would be more confident in themselves. I wish they did not have to get drunk and act "slutty" in order to talk

to men. I wish they did not have to change who they are in order for men to notice them. (Emmie)

Second, student ethnographers wanted a change in how men and women relate to one another: besides men treating women with more respect, they wanted peers to communicate honestly about what they really want regarding sex and relationships:

> If I could change any social dynamic, it would be to make every- one on a level playing field of mutual respect, inclusiveness, and interest in meeting people for the context of relationships or friend- ships. I would abolish hookup culture which I believe to be a subset of male-dominated culture because this culture is a result of many men wishing to avoid the intricacies of a relationship. Women would be treated as equals, people would not feel the need to con- form their behavior and looks to images of hyper-femininity or mas- culinity. Each individual person would be valued as a human being, not a source of pleasure. (Alec)

> I want girls to be confident and boys to be respectful. Girls can be seen as friends and not "slam pieces." Respect should flow through the room and perhaps boys and girls might find a relationship. (Therese)

> If I was with a lot of friends and there was not any drama like fight- ing, then I would say I had a good time. But in the past weeks and months the parties that I have attended were horrible. There was fighting, people were sloppy drunk, guys were disrespectful or high. If I could change anything about the social dynamics of a party, it would be drinking and how males acted, less alcohol, men not act- ing like pigs and grabbing a female's behind, or calling them names if they do not want to talk to them. Changing those dynamics would make me happier at a party. It is annoying that men believe that if a female dresses a certain way, they are allowed to act sexually towards her. Females should be allowed to dress however they want and not have to worry about a male sexually harassing her. (Melody)

> I wish men and women could share a disclaimer of their expectations with their partners before engaging in sexual activity so that the two parties can avoid confusion and unhappiness later. (Maria)

Third, students expressed a desire for greater diversity and inclusivity, predicting they would be happier if parties allowed people to be accepted for who they truly are:

> No one is being their real self anymore; society says you must be someone else and your true self is boring. (Tyler)

> The problem with party culture is that it is all about fitting in with norms, not about expressing your own identity. (Tammy)

> Even though people typically appear to have a good time at these parties, I think it is hard to actually do so. There are so many expectations of college students in the party scene. They have to look the right way, act the right way, drink the right way, and even hook up the right way. If someone does not conform to these societal norms and peer pressures, then they are in jeopardy of social rejection. It gets to be a little overwhelming. I think parties would be more fun if people really could just relax and forget about living up to some standard society has set. (Michelle)

> Overall, people go to parties and drink just because everyone around them is doing it, and we are not completely fulfilled. If there were one aspect that I would change it would be that we not degrade ourselves to have a false sense of happiness. We should act in ways that personally make us happy. (Scott)

> A social dynamic I would like to change about parties and the general population are the subtle glimpses of criticism people display towards people that may be different from them. In my experience of being bisexual, I have come across obvious crude judgments and "looks" or actions displayed by others that exhibit that I am weird because I am not like them. It is not just the subtle social judgments on the LGBTQ population, but the criticisms and closed-mindedness of young individuals toward anything different from them. (Tessa)

The fourth commonly identified wish for increasing personal happiness at parties involved eliminating the norm of excessive drinking. Drinking casually would allow better conversations, create more genuine connections among people, and be more fun:

> Why is it that we are so inclined to believe that it is desirable to drink gratuitously and hook up? These activities inevitably leave

more questions than answers. What happened last night? Who was that guy/girl? What was I thinking? Where is water and how do I get it into my body as quickly as possible? Do I need to vomit? Far be it for me to decry such activities as I have taken part in them enough. However, at best I received a night of catharsis in a carefree environment with a funny story. At worst I run the risk of hurting myself or someone else. (Kyle)

The social setting in college is too centered around binge drinking. Everyone is concerned with getting as drunk as possible each and every night. No one cares about the people they meet. It seems like the whole point to the college social scene is sexuality. (Derek)

I would limit the amount of alcohol. People can enjoy each other's company without being hammered. It's nice to have social beers, but they should be purely that. I think that we need to learn to engage each other in other ways than drinking. We are too reliant on it as an icebreaker. As a culture, we've entirely forgotten how to make friends, start conversations, or initiate relationships without the aid of alcohol. (Nora)

Why is alcohol so integral to the college party scene? Does it come from being afraid of each other? Are we really not bearable towards each other unless tequila shots are involved? Are college students so self-conscious and awkward that group interactions are impossible and scary without the aid of chemicals? (Elliot)

Fifth, similar to their desire to be freed from the norm of drinking, many students expressed that they would be happier if they were freed from the norm of hookups and could instead focus on developing and enjoying friendships:

If I had to choose one thing to change at parties, I would end the hookup culture. This makes the party atmosphere more about having fun, letting loose, and enjoying oneself and takes away the added pressure to find someone to hook up with. People will gain more self-worth because our culture would not be simply about physical attraction but also about creating an emotional bond with people. It seems to me that people who are in serious, committed, and trusting relationships are much happier than those who base their relationships solely on physical connections. (Tammy)

To make parties more fun, I would have less people and have those people be friends. There wouldn't be any pressure to act like a douche bag, and none of us would praise the degrading of the opposite sex. Plus, the girls wouldn't get itemized and the guys wouldn't be out to impress people. (Brandon)

I have been the most fulfilled and legitimately happy at parties when I'm just dancing with my friends rather than being drunk and looking to hook up. Partying with my friends provides me with memories that last and nothing to regret. (Rebecca)

Some ethnographers wished to end hookup culture because they were concerned that hookups would compromise future relationships and long-term happiness:

If I could change anything about the social dynamics of parties it would be the pregame attitude of, "I need to hook up with someone tonight." It's a sexually oriented idea that ultimately revels in temporary and unfulfilling happiness. This type of hookup attitude is dangerous to those who continue it as a way of life. For example, would this type of mentality carry over when students actually find someone they care about, and then the longing to find a fresh, new hookup ruins it? I believe a habit of hooking up could be more devastating to students' attitude about sexuality and relationships than they initially think. (Collin)

When women are objectified and degraded to the level of sexual objects, it is extremely detrimental. A woman who is used only for sex and competition can never feel truly secure inside. I believe it is within the party scene that many insecurities are instilled that later lead to divorce. Women and men are expected to fit into unemotional and sexual roles and these roles will always live within a person. This lack of emotional attachment and focus on sex leads to a lack of commitment in relationships later in life and ultimately, I believe, causes divorce and infidelity. Do people who are involved in the hookup culture in college have less fulfilling marriages in the future? Are they more likely to cheat or have self-esteem problems later in life? When will we finally figure out what we do today has such a strong effect on our lives tomorrow? (Tammy)

Many students in this category followed their critique of drunken hookups by expressing their desire for a culture that normalizes dating and romantic relationships:

> After recapping the night with the friends who helped me observe the parties, we all came to the same conclusion—what happened to good, old fashioned courting? When boys in high school would stop me in the hallway and ask if I wanted to go see a movie and grab some dinner on the weekend, they seemed to have more nerve than college boys. Once college started, boys quit wanting to date altogether. Between myself and my three friends, we had been asked out on a simple date less than a combined twenty times in our combined ten years of college. We all, however, had been texted by a guy asking to "pregame with him and his friends," or "hang out" at three in the morning on a Saturday night, or to come over and "watch a movie" while his roommates are in class. (Donna)

> In college, you meet someone through getting drunk and having a drunken make out, and something might come out of it the next day when you are sober and you look the other person up on Facebook. I wish it would be more socially acceptable to take things as slowly as I did with this one boy. It allowed both of us to really get to know each other before we got involved physically. I'm glad I really got to know him before I even kissed him; you don't really hear about that happening in college anymore. (Annika)

Some ethnographers expressed that they had no desire to hook up at all because they preferred being in committed relationships. Certain students even seemed to express surprise at how much happier they were in a relationship than when they were just focused on hooking up:

> A few months ago I met my current girlfriend and am so happy with her. I find it more fulfilling being with someone that you really like, and who likes you just the same back. I used to think that being in a relationship would be boring and get old after a while. However, I find myself to be much happier and fulfilled. (Marek)

Later in my freshman year, I started dating my current boyfriend. I found someone whom I respect and who respects me. When I was single, the guys I hooked up with didn't want anything but a hookup. My boyfriend wants to spend time with me, go places with me, and just be around me. When we go out to parties and bars he respects me and my body. I always go home happy and fulfilled because I know I am with someone who I truly care about. I waited and saved my virginity for someone I respect and love, but also for someone who respects and loves me for me, not my body. (Elena)

When I was 17 and in a relationship, I was exposed to a whole new dimension of happiness. Being loved and accepted for who I am was the most amazing feeling. Spending time with my boyfriend overwhelmed me with comfort and happiness. At [University A], I have not experienced any such feelings during or after hooking up with a guy. I believe holding hands, kissing, etc., should be meaningful acts of love, not things to do just because it feels good. This is the main reason I have never been satisfied after hooking up. The night means nothing. (Paige)

When I started the year, I focused on being with my friends, and if I happened to go home with a girl, that was an extra benefit. I then went into a five-month relationship in which my party habits changed a lot. I was more worried about giving my girlfriend attention and staying away from drunken girls. After I broke up with my girlfriend, I went back to my old roots and found myself hooking up with random girls again. I realized I was not as happy with random hookups as when I was with someone I liked for who she was. I soon found another girl who I was attracted to physically and emotionally and made her my top priority when I was out partying. I ended the year finding that being with someone I can connect with in and outside the party scene leaves me the happiest. (Mark)

Conclusion

When I first asked my students whether they and their peers were happy at college parties, I suspected that at least one social group with relatively high power and privilege would convey enthusiasm for the status quo. What I did not expect was that ethnographers across the spectrum of ordinary divides (race, gender, and sexual orientation) would privately express such strong and consistent discontent with party and hookup norms. I use "privately" because, while the vast majority of students were nearly unanimous expressing negative comments about hookups, I would have known much less about their emptiness, loneliness, pain, and disillusionment if left to glean impressions from class discussions and other "public" forums. Semester after semester, I noticed that the many students who were nonchalant or positive about hookups in class discussion would contradict their statements when given the opportunity for privacy in journals, papers, or emails. Similarly, in countless class discussions about intoxication and alcohol's connection to hookups, students found occasion for humor and laughter, saving negativity about "getting wasted" for another time.

The discrepancy between public and private personas occurs for many reasons. While "out of character" college student behavior can be explained in reference to societal expectations and the effects of alcohol (explored in chapter 2), another key reason is what social scientific researchers call *pluralistic ignorance*: conformity based on the widespread misperception that one's preferences concerning a particular behavior or practice are different from the beliefs of almost everyone else. Much research indicates that college students assume that their peers are happier and more comfortable with hookups and binge drinking than they themselves are. Consequently, many conform and eventually follow social norms that in reality few individuals privately favor. This in turn further entrenches current gender and sexual norms.[2]

Pluralistic ignorance is implicit in my own students' analyses. For instance, although the ethnographers frequently expressed a belief that "some" students were happy with hooking up and could easily separate physical gratification from their emotions, not a single ethnographer actually expressed being happy with typical hookups that involved a casual acquaintance or stranger. Out of the 126 ethnographers, only three male ethnographers expressed feeling happy after hooking up, and these occurred with a woman they already knew and liked:

> In some of my past hookups in college, I have felt happy. Waking up the next morning, sometimes I felt a small sense of regret, sometimes emptiness, depending on how shallow the hookup was. Other times I would wake up happy; this was usually if I hooked up with a girl I liked. (Nolan)

From my own experience, I know that if I am looking for a relationship and I have a night with the person that I want a relationship
with, I am usually very happy the next few days. I have had a few
encounters that did not mean much though and were not gratifying
the next day. Sometimes they made me feel bad about what I had
done. I am sure I have made some women mad in those encounters
as well. (Hudson)

I have hooked up, but never have I randomly or drunkenly hooked
up. It was with someone for whom I had feelings and with whom
I hoped something further would blossom. I was very happy afterwards. It was a way for me to express my feelings for that girl at
that moment. I know that all hookups aren't like this, but this is my
experience. (Ben)

Research confirms that pluralistic ignorance drives binge drinking and
hookup culture on U.S. college campuses, and also demonstrates that my
students are not alone in their dissatisfaction with the status quo. Studies
have regularly found that the majority of women, for example, experience a number of negative post-hookup emotions and effects, including
regret or disappointment, confusion, worry, stress, shame, depression,
decreased self-esteem, and/or post-traumatic stress disorder.[3] While some
researchers find that men report higher levels of positive emotions than
women post-hookup,[4] others have focused on the positive association
among men between hookups and higher levels of anxiety, psychological distress, and diminished well-being.[5] Furthermore, men (like women)
express the desire for emotional connection and intimacy and often have
similar hopes that a relationship may result from a hookup.[6]

As for the small minority of quantitative studies indicating that men
and/or women average more positive than negative emotions following a hookup, it is important not to leap to conclusions about overall or
long-term psychological well-being, happiness, and fulfillment. Take, for
instance, research of Owen et al., very commonly cited as evidence that
students respond positively to hookups.[7] In their 2010 study, undergraduates were asked if they experienced nine emotional reactions post-hookup,
and men reported higher levels of positive emotions than women: 50% of
men reported that hooking-up encounters were associated with positive
emotions, 26.0% reported negative emotions, and 24% reported a mix
of both emotions. As for women, 26% reported positive emotions after

hooking up, 49% reported negative emotions, and 25% reported a mix of emotions. Such findings hardly translate into an enthusiastic endorsement of hookups, since 50% of men and 74% of women experienced negative or ambivalent emotions following their experience.[8]

In Owen et al.'s 2011 study, students were asked to score (from 1 to 5) how they felt a day after a hookup: happy, desirable, adventuresome, pleased, excited, empty, confused, used, awkward, and/or disappointed.[9] As in their earlier study, men reported higher levels of positive emotions than did women. However, in this study, both men and women averaged more positive than negative feelings. One might conclude that this demonstrates college students benefit from typical drunken hookups. However, if we look specifically at the factors identified in this study that predict positive versus negative emotional reactions, we learn that, for both men and women, (1) positive emotional reactions were associated with hopes that the recent hookup might lead to a committed relationship, and (2) negative emotional reactions were positively associated with alcohol use, more depressive symptoms, and greater loneliness. Owen et al. also note that, among young adults who indicated more negative than positive emotions post-hookup, individuals reported more depressive symptoms and greater loneliness at the end of the semester if they engaged in penetrative hookups: "Something unique about hooking up influences young adults' depressive symptoms and feelings of loneliness."[10]

Even if we bracket the students who experienced negative or ambivalent emotions in these studies and only focus on those students who reported solely positive emotions, it is still difficult to ascertain how hookups affect these students' happiness and fulfillment. First, since the researchers do not offer a separate analysis of each positive emotion (feeling happy, desirable, adventuresome, pleased, and/or excited), it is impossible to know how many students actually felt happy as opposed to adventuresome or desirable, for example. Second, how might one know with confidence that these reactions even translate into a stable sense of well-being, happiness, and fulfillment? As many student ethnographers point out in reports included in this chapter, the positive emotions following a hookup can be momentary, and feelings about a hookup can change in the following weeks or months, especially if a committed relationship does not develop. Incidentally, Owen et al. agree: "Given that women were more likely to hope for their hooking up encounter to lead to a committed relationship, there may be other emotional reactions that transpire after this initial reaction."[11]

Third, it is unknown whether a survey participant's positive emotions are due to experiencing (1) the social benefits that one receives from the hookup, (2) a temporary self-esteem boost from being physically desired for an evening, (3) a deep affirmation of one's authentic self, (4) a meaningful connection to another person, or (5) some other reason altogether. Depending on reasons underlying the emotions, some positive emotions may be fleeting (most likely instances nos. 1 and 2) while others may be more lasting (most likely nos. 3 and 4).

In short, even in well-conducted, popularly-cited quantitative studies such as those published by Owen et al., a great many important questions remain unanswered, and sometimes the tidy lure of a tangible number (in this case, men reacting on average more positively to hookups than women) can mask real-life complexities (in this case how undergraduates perceive the impact of hookups on their well-being). While the methodology of ethnographic research might yield messy results by comparison, at least the realm of qualitative data forces us to slow down and resist, I hope, unintended research bias, oversimplification of our subject matter, and conclusions that are too easily misinterpreted.

What can we say with confidence? As evidenced by the majority of voices in this chapter, most men and women ethnographers long for more than what their college parties currently offer. Wary of the narrow rules that college students impose on each other to dress a certain way, drink a certain way, act a certain way, and hook up a certain way, they wish they could just relax, express what they really think, be who they really are, and simply enjoy being with one another. Both physically and emotionally, they long for the "realness" of knowing and being known deeply by others. For reasons we have explored, this vision appears daunting to college students active in contemporary party and hookup culture. The remaining chapters of this book intend to encourage and support the journeys of those who not only long for more but also are invested in making change happen. In the service of this larger mission, part II enlists the insights of another group of undergraduates (from a different university, referred to as University B) as they reflect theologically on the challenges of becoming "fully human" in the context of college culture and broader U.S. society. Part III develops a blueprint for university-wide cultural change.

PART II

Becoming Fully Human

5

Embracing Our Interdependence on God and Others

AS SUGGESTED IN MY INTRODUCTION, exploration of Johann Metz's *Poverty of Spirit* in the context of concerns raised in part I has resonated with a great many undergraduates who find themselves longing for more than their college culture is providing them.

As my students at University B delved into *Poverty of Spirit* and discussed what they found most insightful or challenging, many highlighted the way in which embracing poverty of spirit and becoming fully human involve grounding our core identity in our relationships with God and others. According to Metz, we do not each have a personal human *telos* to become a self-sufficient individual; rather, we are called to live our "yes" to God precisely through communion with God and others. Importantly, the first step in experiencing a union with God, self, and others is to recognize how deeply our sense of self and capacity to flourish depend on a network of relationships. According to Metz, Scripture clearly reminds us how our true, God-given selfhood emerges through our responses to and interactions with God, others, and the rest of creation:

> The history of religion in the Bible is the history of a people, and the individuals within it, becoming subjects in the presence of their God. "Subject" here does not mean the isolated individual, the monad, who only subsequently ascertains his or her coexistence with other subjects. Solidaristic-antagonistic and liberative-unsettling experiences with other subjects belong to the constitution of the religious subject right from the start. The histories of faith found in the Old and New Testaments are . . . histories of the dramatic constitution

of human beings as subjects—precisely through their relationship to God. The ways that this being a subject is defined have a
dynamic character: being called upon in the midst of danger; being
called forth from fear; exodus; conversion; lifting up their heads;
discipleship.[1]

Our own poverty of spirit begins first and foremost with an awareness that
we are not self-created, self-sufficient islands. Our very existence and flourishing depend on our divine creator and the complex webs of relationships
present in creation: "In poverty of spirit we learn to accept ourselves as
beings who do not belong to ourselves."[2] For Christians, it is always crucial to return to the example of Jesus, who embraces his dependence on
God, refuses the lure of egoism, and faithfully discerns God's desires for
his life:

> When we encounter Jesus Christ, we become sharply aware of our
> innate poverty as human beings. We see then the dire want of a
> person who lives on the bread of eternity, whose food is to do the
> will of God (cf. Jn. 4:54). Did not Jesus live in continual dependence
> on someone else?[3]

Cognitively, we might recognize that interdependence on others (and, for
theists, God) is necessary for survival, that the interdependent give-and-
take of healthy relationships is essential for a joyful and fulfilling life, and
that the rugged American individual who pulls himself up by his own
bootstraps is a false idol. Nevertheless, according to Metz we all experience a temptation to flee the neediness and vulnerability that accompany
our dependence on God and others. We do so by grounding our identity in
illusions of our own capacity for self-sufficiency:

> We can also dissemble our dependence on God, close in upon our-
> selves, 'take scandal' at our innate poverty. The temptation to do
> this is great. The radical indigence of our humanity has something
> repulsive about it. It devastates us, tears down self-created defenses
> and jars us out of the familiar, routine horizon of everyday life.[4]

According to Metz, we all experience this temptation to seize our divinity and cling to our own sense of security, rather than ground our sense
of identity and fundamental security in our relationships. To explore the

ways in which we are tempted to deny our interdependence on others, Metz refers to Jesus's temptations in the desert (Mt 4:1–11). Consider that Jesus, after fasting for forty days and forty nights, was tempted by Satan to seize his divinity and command stones to become loaves of bread: "You're hungry," Satan tells Jesus. "You need be hungry no longer. You can change all that with a miracle."[5] Yet as Metz reminds us, "Our needs are always beyond our capacities,"[6] and Satan's first temptation can thus be understood as the temptation for Jesus to flee from his human neediness as experienced in appetites, desires, and longings. Withstanding this temptation, Jesus accepts that being human entails the experience of desires and needs (physical, psychological, social, and spiritual) that frequently remain unsatisfied. Jesus accepts that we are not sufficient unto ourselves; our survival and flourishing is dependent on God and others. Metz argues:

> Satan tries to appeal to the divinity in Jesus, tempered with the gravity and grandeur of his humanity. As a matter of fact, Satan always tries to stress the spiritual strength of human beings and our divine character and has done this from the beginning. "You will be like God": that is Satan's slogan. It is *the* temptation the Evil One has set before us in countless variations, urging us to reject the truth about the humanity we have been given.[7]

Some students found the idea of Satan tempting humanity quaint or strange. They questioned how a narrative about the devil could be relevant to their lives. To reject a literal interpretation of Satan as an evil, active figure in our world, however, should not blind us to the possibility of Satan symbolizing the part of us that flees from our human finitude and resists our interdependence on God and others. For Metz, the important point remains either way: Jesus was tempted, just as we are, to escape the vulnerabilities of our human condition, and conversely any realistic hope for a "fully human" life.

This desire for self-sufficient security achieved through our own "divinity" (our individual strengths and well-established ego) also entices us to deny "the poverty of our provisional nature," the reality that we are creatures who cannot fully control the influences of the past, who exist in an ever-changing and impermanent present, and who cannot control our future. Metz argues that persons seek to avoid the poverty of their provisional nature in many ways. While some accumulate accomplishments, wealth, and power to master a sense of self-reliance and control over their present and future lives, others rely on spiritual strengths, establishing their superiority through a distortion of faith that provides religious truth to them alone. Our preoccupation with "being right," of course, leads ironically to vain self-reliance, disrupting healthy interdependence and driving wedges between ourselves, God, and others.

Obstacles to Embracing Interdependence

While my college students have often been drawn powerfully to Metz's Jesus, their attraction to poverty of spirit does not easily translate into a lived commitment. Why is this? My students have plenty to say about the obstacles they encounter in embracing all three components of poverty of spirit. As we will see, much of their difficulty comes from the ways they are tempted to establish their identity and self-worth. Not surprisingly, concern with social status figures mightily.

Self-Worth Based on Achievement

When asked each semester to reflect on poverty of spirit in the party scene, most students consistently avoided my narrow focus on the parties and instead reflected first on the general obstacles that arise from living in broader U.S. and college culture. The vast majority emphasized that the most powerful cultural influences in their lives (parents, school, peers, popular culture, social media, etc.) drove them to base their identity and self-worth mainly on individual achievements, materialism, and peer acceptance, all of which offer social status.

> Parents, professors, grad schools, and future employers all pressure me to succeed. I feel as though the content on my resume, the likes I get on Facebook, and the recognition of my achievements all sum up my value as a college student, as a human being. I am bombarded from every angle with messages saying that I'm not good enough and that I have to be better if I want to be successful. (Bella)

> You see why it is so hard? Every day I'm told to apply for this and compete at that. I'm told that my test scores are going to define me, that my grades are key to my future and my worth. (James)

As a way to delve deeper into the basis of undergraduates' self-esteem and worth, I asked students in my sexual ethics courses from 2012 to 2014 to estimate anonymously what percentage of their own self-worth and identity was based on their inherent value (meaning, for Christian students, the notion of being created with dignity in God's image and being loved by God), as opposed to their accomplishments and the ways they are perceived by others. On average, students reported that 86% of their self-worth/identity was based on accomplishments and peer acceptance. Interestingly, not a single student rated inherent human value more highly than accomplishments/social status. The very prospect that a person could base his or her worth on something other than achievements, materialism, and social status struck many students in class discussions as foreign, unrealistic, and even counterproductive for one's personal and social life. Most students had difficulty fathoming what this would be like.

Further, many questioned what would motivate them to study, compete, and improve themselves if they experienced self-worth simply on the basis of their inherent dignity and value. While some Christian students affirmed that they knew from religious services and religious education that their dignity and worth comes from being created in God's image, such conceptual beliefs had not effectively countered the dominant cultural influences that find value and self-worth elsewhere:

> In the world we live in, one is looked at as nothing without accomplishments. (Gabriella)

> The way kids are raised nowadays fosters so much competition and valuation of accomplishments that it is required we measure our worth in respect to our life's accomplishments. To let go of this and just find self-worth in one's relationship with God would likely cause social suicide for such a person. (Robert)

Students express that it is a struggle to experience positive, deeply held self-worth because the meaning of success is narrowly construed in our society as being nothing less than achieving the best, which requires hyper-competition and vigilant self-improvement in all areas of their lives:

> Embracing poverty of spirit is a hard thing to do, especially in our culture. Our culture is so focused on always being the best, which relates to having the most material goods, power, and wealth. "Being the best" relates to being extraordinarily successful. (Maddie)

> As a generation, we share a need to be all things to all people. I want to have the best article in the student paper every week, be the most

outrageous party animal every weekend, and have the most impressive resume for grad school. It's the structure we live in—that's how we become good capitalists, and we define our ability to do that by our outward successes. That's why we call college one big dick-measuring contest. College culture tells you that if you're not the best, then you shouldn't be satisfied. That's the definition of mediocrity and complacency. It is honestly an extremely scary concept to consider stepping outside of that rat race. By stepping out, I immediately lose a step on everyone who stays in the race. (Hunter)

According to these millennials, the need to outdo and "rise above" peers and "stand out from the crowd" was engrained early:

In our world today everyone is striving to be on top, to show the world in what ways he or she is better, more successful, and more powerful than his or her neighbor. From an early age, we learn to see value in success, money, and material things. We are taught that, if we want to succeed in life and achieve great things, we need to do more than our classmates, have better grades, have the greatest body, be the most athletic, be more creative, and never accept imperfection. We come home from school and we are expected to get 100% on our homework and tests. We must practice piano, flute, guitar, and all the other instruments so that we can become better and more talented than others. We go to sports practice after sports practice, lesson after lesson, so that we can get onto the varsity team or maybe receive a scholarship to play in college. (Lillian)

A dominant theme in undergraduates' reflections is that our society "is based on having clear winners and losers." Within this hyper-competitive, social Darwinian world, the stakes for almost everything become high. Winners are depicted as strong, fiercely independent, and sometimes even invincible. These individuals relentlessly outdo their competitors for the highest grades, attend the best graduate schools, achieve and distinguish themselves in their careers, and secure high salaries to accomplish the ultimate end goal of success: a lifestyle of financial security and enjoyment of materialistic possessions. Such career and financial success in turn secures respect, social status, admiration, and envy from their peers.

Echoing perceptions at University A, the 150 undergraduates at University B also acknowledge how they internalize the construal of success affirmed in popular culture and social media:

> Not to place the blame away from the students because they choose the paths they do, but one of the main reasons that we act how we do is the media. The praise that movie stars, professional athletes, and business gurus receive from our society is immense. This creates a want, especially for students entering the working world, for the same praise that these people receive, and also the same lifestyles these individuals live. We are constantly shown that social status is important. Be it the car you drive, the house you live in, or the toys someone possesses, a complete impression is made by people when they see you. This makes us want the best because we think that then we too can *be* the best. (Logan)

> Social media poses a great hindrance in regards to embracing poverty of spirit. I think that in seeing what others are doing at each moment in time affects us on a deep level even though it seems so superficial and shallow. We are conditioned, as a society, to compete with one another to be the best. Social media is an easy way to display our successes to a large group of people. Social media sites have such a profound impact on our daily lives, and we feel the need to post about our successes to make it look like we have a fulfilling life. This makes it difficult to discern whether or not we are truly leading a full life or just a shallow and unfulfilled life. Our Facebook, Instagram, and Twitter life may display a life full of activity, successes, and positive relationships while our actual life may consist of just the opposite. We can tailor our webpages to make it seem like we have the perfect life when in all reality we could be falling apart. This makes it difficult to embrace poverty of spirit because we constantly feel the need to prove that our life is full of joy instead of actually feeling joy and fulfillment. (April)

Students conveyed a sense that their survival is at stake:

> College students struggle to survive in society. We feel this pressure, as if it's gravity: forever pushing down and ever-present, to be the best in everything and that is the only way we can survive. . . . It is as though students and people in society are constantly pumping their

legs on a swing to only realize that they have to keep working and kicking their legs to stay at the top, yet they can never make a full rotation all the way around. It's hard to trust that if you stop pumping, someone might show up to keep pushing you if you've been swinging yourself for as long as you can remember. (Hazel)

Most college students are so busy with classes, extracurricular activities, and internships because we are socialized to believe that we need to accomplish more than everyone else in order to get jobs after we graduate. We want to become successful in our future careers, so that we can become wealthy and never have to worry about going hungry or not being able to afford medical care when we need it. (Nicole)

These undergraduates also acknowledge the embarrassment and judgment they experience when they "fail" to perform as well as their peers:

One of the greatest obstacles is the competitiveness on campus. It's hard because even though I might fully accept my shortcomings, other people don't. When I get a paper handed back to me with a lower grade on it than my friends'—a grade that I was fully expecting and accepting of—everyone looks down on me. They automatically draw the conclusion that you aren't as smart as they are, and you must feel so bad about yourself. Realistically, we all have our struggles, and maybe I wasn't able to prepare as well as they were because of a family emergency. It's just hard when I accept myself, only to have other people be unaccepting of me. (Josie)

Since the need for success is so intense and failure is such a shameful experience, some students note how their peers often resort to cheating to succeed or they put on a front of not caring or trying at all:

It is a common saying when students enter college that you can get good grades, have a social life, and sleep, but you only get to choose two of those three. One way to get around that adage is to fudge some lines of morality, and often that line is cheating. (David)

We have been raised to excel, to strive for perfection in our academics, and we go through extreme measures to attain those grades. We have classmates that cheat to avoid the embarrassment of not succeeding by the standards that have been set by our society. Students also pretend not to try—these are the people who spend hours slaving over their books and then, upon getting an unsatisfying grade, deny studying at all. The mindset is that, if you did not try, then you cannot fail. (Elise)

Students express a fear of uncertainty and the unknown because they perceive that failure is more likely without an exact plan for the future. Trying to exercise absolute control over one's future, however, is opposed to Metz's emphasis on being open to possibilities and personal growth, a tension captured well by Mackenzie:

Competition and pressure to perform exceptionally in terms of our worldly accomplishments leaves little room for poverty of our provisional nature as humans. Our whole life consists of plans: to get into college, to get good grades in college for graduate programs, to do community service, to be involved, to be an honors student, to decide a major, to decide the path we want our future to follow. How exactly can there be room for Metz's concept of our provisional nature when we are forced to decide upon a strict plan and stick to it in order to be a contributing member to society, to be a successful human being in societal terms?

Control over one's life and one's future emerge as a dominant desire that continually resurfaces throughout their reflections:

The reason people fight against having poverty of spirit so vehemently is because humans have a hard time giving up their sense of control. Humans want to feel like they are in control in every aspect of their lives. Essentially, they want to become like God. They want to be able to control their environment, control the situations that they are in—even going so far as to control other people. (Nicole)

Many students acknowledge that their priorities about how to spend their time and energy in the present are frequently determined by whether they think these activities will result in securing a successful future. They express how difficult it is for them to live in the present moment:

As I think about my life, I notice a reoccurring theme. I am always doing something in order to do something else. I studied incredibly hard in high school so that I would get into a good college. I am pushing myself to do really well in college so that I come out with a stellar GPA and great resume. I will use my success in college to get an amazing job so that I can make money. The wealth I accumulate will go into buying a nice house, a fancy car, a fantastic wardrobe, and entertainment. Some of it I will save in order to give to my children someday so that they may go to college and follow in this cycle of being successful and accumulating things. This life is very stressful if the only thing you do is try to be on top or in front of everybody else. I can only imagine 10 or 20 years from now what our culture will be like. More pressure. More stress. More children and adults with huge anxiety problems. (Maddie)

It is striking how clearly Maddie visualizes her own and her children's future and how resigned she is to her prospects—despite the fact that she foresees the future path as a stressful, pressure-filled, anxious one. Barely out of her teens, Maddie is resigned to working hard in a stressful, pressure-filled environment to be "on top" in order to make enough money to purchase or afford a lifestyle that symbolizes U.S. success. She also commits to passing on this way of being to her children even though she predicts that her children will be even more stressed and anxious than she is.

Furthermore, many students report that their hectic schedules and busyness gives them little time or energy to get to know themselves or God during college:

We are so wrapped up in our futures that we forget to think about what we are doing to better ourselves. We are so focused on having the perfect grades to get the perfect job. This makes it hard to embrace our fully human self because we don't ever take the time to get to know ourselves. (Annabelle)

Students' schedules are full of distractions that prevent them from hearing God's voice. Their days are filled from morning until night with classes, studies, work, campus organizations, sports, and social obligations. With this, they are on the go constantly, which can cause them to miss the voice of God. (Evelyn)

Students note that the mentality of grounding their identity and self-worth on successes and social status in their "day" lives manifests itself just as powerfully in the dynamics of college parties. The drive to compete to be the best and secure success just takes on different forms. Success now means drinking the most, having the most fun at parties, hooking up with someone highly attractive, acting the funniest or most outrageous for that particular night, or being able to tell the most extreme or most humorous hookup story the next morning. Many students describe how a lot of their peers are engaged in an unspoken competition to capture photographs that make them appear the best, most beautiful, or like the one who had the most fun that evening:

> This party atmosphere is all about selfishness. People are taking pictures probably just so they can put them on Facebook, or wherever, and show everyone how much fun they are having. There is this underlying competition to see whose picture can get the most "likes." (Caroline)

> When I posted pictures of the party on Facebook, why did I post them? To compete for a better life than someone else? To rub it in someone's face? To prove I am happy? (Penelope)

Competition to outdo others and be the best in order to feel good about oneself is suffused through party social interactions. In these students' descriptions of their bar and party scenes, men seek to outdo one another in all kinds of sports: drinking, beer pong, fights, and scoring the most hookups. Women compete with each other to appear the most attractive and sexy, secure the most attention, and hook up with the most desirable men. Both genders deliberately put down peers in an effort to look and feel better themselves. Tragically, it is these same pressures and dynamics of competition in their day lives from which students try to escape by drinking and partying.

Self-Worth Based on Wealth and Materialism

Students repeatedly note that Metz's *Poverty of Spirit* goes against the grain of the American dream of prosperity. According to my students, the very word *poverty* elicits negativity, fear, and repugnance:

> First of all, the term "poverty of spirit" is not attractive to anyone in our modern culture. Poverty is something that we try to eradicate; accumulating wealth is the goal for most people. (Naomi)

Students readily identified their attachment to materialism and wealth as a major obstacle to embracing poverty of spirit; what they have (and will have in their futures) forms their identities and self-worth and increases their self-esteem as much as "what they do":

> A main reason college students lack poverty of spirit is simply the way that society is hardwired today. In today's society you are taught from a young age that, in order to have a good life, you need money, a college degree, a lot of friends, the newest phones and electronics, etc. (Jack)

> We are taught that we are worth nothing without achievement, success, power, money. Many people have the idea that making lots of money and being successful leads to a fulfilling life. Well, in order to have a fulfilling life and become fully human like Metz's Jesus, we must change our mindset entirely from what today's society teaches us. It is not the success, achievements, and money that make you human but being fully human is determined by putting your worth in yourself as a child of God. (Paisley)

Students perceive that, in sharp contrast to accepting (as Jesus did) that experiences of neediness and unfulfilled desire are part of our human condition, societal norms and expectations keep us focused on instant self-gratification:

> Because of our society and the way that we were raised, college students are used to spending money in order to feel instant satisfaction. Feeling hungry? Buy some fast food. Bored? Buy a new video game. *Poverty of Spirit* calls for being happy without money, without worldly possessions and without that very need for instant satisfaction. Instead it comes with gratification on living simply and embracing the absence of belongings and attributes that cloud the spiritual mind. (Owen)

Revealing the level of their attachments to possessions, students describe how college students are "consumed by materialism" and how their possessions "become a part of them":

> Living in such a materialistic environment and mindset makes it hard for people not to be selfish and want what they do not have

rather than giving to others. We often focus on possessions and connect ourselves to what we have, such as our phones and computers. Materials have become a part of us, which takes over giving ourselves to others. (Brianna)

College students are fully rooted in their material possessions and their statuses within the social community. Just one glimpse around parties and bars and it is impossible to miss people glued to their cell phones, iPods, purses, and any other random item. These things pretty much define who we are. They are our artifacts that receive more attention than most people do. (Owen)

Because wealth is synonymous with success, college students perceive that most people prioritize money and possessions above all else:

In today's society, humans pride themselves on what they have. Cars, cell phones, money, clothes, electronics, the list goes on and on. Far too often we let these possessions take rule over our relationships with others. We become so fixated on these objects and let them rule our lives that in a sense we start worshiping these things. It's as if these objects become our own God in our lives. (Jack)

This sense that many of us succumb too easily to false idols is easily recognizable in Jesus's famous admonition against trying to serve two masters, God and mammon (Mt 6:24 and Lk 16:13). Not surprisingly, this is a common focus among Christian theologians through the centuries. Martin Luther, for instance, claims:

A god is that to which we look for all good and in which we find refuge in every time of need. To have a god is nothing other than to trust and believe him with our whole heart. As I have often said, the trust and faith of the heart alone make both God and an idol. If your faith and trust are right, then your God is the true God. On the other hand, if your trust is false and wrong, then you have not the true God. For these two belong together, faith and God. That to which your heart clings and entrusts itself is, I say, really your God.[8]

Our actual desires, motivations, and behaviors determine which god we worship, not simply the language we use to think and talk about God. College students repeatedly note that their most pressing desires are typically oriented around possessions, wealth, and social status rather than other nonmaterial values, other life priorities, and their relationship with God and others:

> We are often distracted and influenced by commercialism—owning nice cars, toys, etc. Commercialism promotes a life that is concerned with materialistic things that drive our focus away from God. (Aliyah)

> Our mind is always set on getting enough "money" to support ourselves and our family. It is very hard for us to put aside the material items in order to concentrate on what it takes to reach poverty of spirit. According to Metz, as long as the material objects are in our way we will never truly find ourselves. The material items will make up who we are instead. This is the opposite of what Metz wants for us. He wants us to find who we are through ourselves, not material items. (Thomas)

> We as college students struggle with viewing wealth, accomplishments and material things as having a higher status and pride ourselves on how much we have or do. It is a struggle for college students to focus on relationships with God and others rather than on their accomplishments or success. (Ellie)

In addition to giving them a false sense of security and self-sufficiency, students regard material possessions as essential to help them fit in and gain social acceptance. Being up on the latest trends boosts their confidence and provides a false sense of security when interacting with peers:

> Kids get to college and they see all the other stuff other kids have and they desire new materialistic items. It is a constant battle of who has what and who has this. People become fixated on gaining these possessions that they forget what truly makes life fulfilling and worthwhile. (Jack)

> Because these college students are in a time where they are trying to figure out who they are and what they want to do in their lives, they look at how other students are acting and what they have. This can lead to a feeling of need for more material goods in order to be like the other students in our society. (Connor)

Metz says we must become poor to ourselves and relinquish the material things that we base our worth upon. This is very hard for our age group because most college students are caught up in fitting in and having all of the right clothes, having money and having material things to help us feel secure. So much of fitting in today's society has to do with wearing the right clothes, going to the right parties, having good grades and prestigious accomplishments. The material things and social status has more importance than how we relate to others and what kinds of relationships we have with others. (Ellie)

While wealth and materialism help them secure acceptance and social status among peers, students note the irony that their attachment to possessions (especially technology) often interferes with their ability to connect with others and form deep relationships:

Materials take away from our relationship with God and draw us further away. They also get between others and ourselves because we are often distracted when materials are involved. We become selfish and vain. Related to our materialistic society, we also are so used to instant gratification and affection that we receive from others through technology and social media. Instead of focusing our time and energy on giving others affection, we concentrate on receiving. We live in a selfish society where we forget to think of others. (Brianna)

Everyone "needs" to have the latest and greatest gadget. Yes, technology is incredible and can be beneficial, but in this day and age, it is the downfall of genuine human interaction and communication. (Caroline)

Given the pervasive cultural norms of competition and being better than others, students also recognize that they do not tend to be content with simply fitting in. Technology, materialistic items, and drugs allow them to "seize their own divinity" to create the body and identity they desire and compete with others for higher social status:

The first obstacle that came to mind was the materialistic nature of our society. Growing up, we got to experience our own rat race of sorts. Everyone wanted to be the kid with the new basketball shoes

and the PS2 with all the coolest games. There was significant vari-
ance, of course, but many parents fed this beast by buying all sorts
of things for their kids. As we grew older, the toys simply got more
expensive. Popular media fed into this culture of needing *stuff* as
well. The more we watched TV, the more we were exposed to the
basic advertising message that without XYZ product, you weren't as
happy as you could be—you weren't fulfilled. (Christian)

Society is not letting us become anywhere near poor because of all
the technologies they are supplying us and telling us information
on how to better ourselves through our skin, looks, makeup, body
figure, hair, and wealth. These items teach us to be obsessed with
our materialistic possessions and to be self-centered. (Audrey)

The wish to look a different way causes people to abuse drugs to
inhibit appetite, or eat too much to achieve a better figure. Sometimes
it causes individuals to spend an absurd amount of money on themselves to change how God created them. (Zoey)

My qualitative analysis, then, reveals that students' materialism and desire
for wealth, similar to their attachment to individual achievements, pull
them away from grounding their identity in their interdependence on God
and others.

Metz's Critique of Modernity's Conceptions of Reason and Subjectivity

Students' identification of the cultural pressures that drive them to base
their identity and self-esteem primarily on achievements, materialism,
and social status powerfully substantiates Metz's theological critique of
society and contemporary Western Christianity. As I imagine the conversations that Metz might have with my students, I strongly suspect that
he would attribute today's cultural obstacles to poverty of spirit to the
Enlightenment's impact on modern society.

Metz affirms the Enlightenment vision of all persons freely becoming
responsible subjects who are treated as ends in themselves, and makes
it central to his theological project. However, he argues that the move in
modernity to sever rationality from religious and philosophical traditions
concerning the good life, along with the rise of modern capitalism, ironically resulted in a distorted form of "technical dominative" reason that

directly subverts the Enlightenment ideal. Among other problems, this form of reasoning encourages technological domination and control over nature (including humans) to maximize economic profit: "The model of domination has long since permeated everything; this revolution affects the whole societal construction of our reality, of our political and economic systems."[9] Drawing on Frankfurt School critical theorists, Metz further argues that the principle of exchange eventually became the sole principle and most trustworthy, rational authority governing political and social relations in trade, production, and consumption. Consequently, all ideas, attitudes, values, and practices that cannot be reduced to a unit of exchange become lost and no longer hold any persuasive authority in the economic and political governance of society: "Reason is reduced to technical, calculating reason, with vast areas of human experience (particularly in ethics and aesthetics) that had in earlier ages been taken to be subjects for rational reflection now rendered only matters of taste or whim."[10]

Reflecting on implications of this shift, Metz expresses well how this modern form of technical reason, oriented toward control over nature and the maximization of material wealth, normalizes a competitive dominative mentality that objectifies others as a means to satisfy one's interests. Such a mentality leads to an egoistic preoccupation with satisfying one's own desires—as we see so clearly in the hookup culture. As Metz argues, this norm of viewing and treating persons as a means to one's own end (which includes maximizing profits above valuing human well-being) absolutely undermines the Enlightenment and Christian ideals of all persons being treated as ends in themselves.

My students' sense that their worth is grounded in what they own and what they do further substantiates Metz's analysis of modern society. Our society, governed by technical reason and the exchange principle, fosters "a graceless form of humanity," says Metz, "strictly oriented to property, competition, and success." The pressure to project an individualized self who is strong, competitive, and fiercely independent of tradition and community is also consistent with Metz's account of the individualism of the modern subject. Since individual success is so basic to identity, competition for success in achieving wealth and social status typically trumps serious consideration of how one's choices affect the common good and the flourishing of one's community.

Ultimately, my students' combined reflections leave no doubt concerning the dominant thinking that pervades their lives and the extent to which elevation of ego, objectification of things and others, and post-Enlightenment principles of exchange and domination are woven into their economic and social realities, including both their academic/professional lives and their party lives. For our purposes here, the important upshot is that neoliberal capitalist values and attitudes (for example, self-sufficiency, invulnerability, a winner-take-all mentality, competition for financial success, preoccupation with power and control, and egoistic self-interest) powerfully undermine young adults' capacities to honor their interdependence with others and embrace poverty of spirit.

What Happened to Christian Values and Influences?

Since the majority of my students grew up Christian, readers may wonder why their identities were not formed more solidly and successfully on core Christian beliefs and values. As undergraduates in my classes have shown with remarkable consistency, a Christian upbringing does not represent a significant countercultural sway against the influences of peers, family, school, popular culture, social media, and so on. Not a single student who grew up in a Christian community expressed (even when encouraged to consider the issue explicitly) that his or her community criticized the status quo mentality of grounding self-worth in achievements, materialism, or social status. Not one student reported his or her religious community offering effective countercultural space in which to form a primary identity based on the notion that one is made in the image of God and is in relationship with God. While it is reasonable to ask whether my students were simply unreceptive to their community's actual, ongoing efforts to provide an effective countercultural narrative, social scientific research on U.S. Christianity suggests it is more likely that no such narrative was ever meaningfully articulated and sustained in their communities.[11] This missed opportunity corroborates Metz's own analysis of Western Christianity's reaction to the Enlightenment and its critique of religion.

Overall, the Catholic and Protestant congregations in my students' lives apparently did not articulate clearly and forcefully enough the dangers of developing identities based on success, achievements, wealth, and possessions; and they developed no meaningful critique of bourgeois society's construal of rationality and its dominant principle of exchange. Internalizing the broader culture's concept of the person as an individual, Christian communities have neglected to communicate that freedom understood as the satisfaction of individual desires is sharply opposed to the Christian faith. Christian freedom is the freedom to love and is a process of letting go of egoistic attachments that hinder our capacity to love fully God, others, and ourselves. According to Metz, Christianity needs to communicate effectively why its vision of a joyful, fulfilling life is more compelling and truthful than the bourgeois market narrative. Instead, in an effort to be attractive and "relevant" to modern persons (for whom religion is merely one activity among competing interests), many Christian churches uncritically adopted modern conceptions of rationality and subjectivity into their theology and practice. In doing so, Christianity became a social space that, in practice, actually prioritizes bourgeois virtues over Christian virtues:

> There is a widening split within the church between the messianic virtues of Christianity which are publicly proclaimed, prescribed, and believed in by the church (conversion and discipleship, love and acceptance of suffering) and the actual value-structures and goals of the bourgeois way of life (autonomy, property, stability, success). Underneath the priorities of the gospel, the priorities of the bourgeois life are being practiced.... The bourgeois virtues of stability, competitive struggle, and achievement obscure and overlay the merely believed-in messianic virtues of conversion, selfless and unconditional love for the "least of the brethren" and active compassion—virtues which cannot be practiced within relationships of exchange or barter; virtues for which one gets literally nothing in return, like the love which does not insist on recompense; virtues like loyalty, gratitude, friendliness, and grief.[12]

Has Christianity in Western Europe and the United States lost its potential to follow in the genuine footsteps of Jesus and act as a transformative social force in society? Metz repeatedly raises the concern that Christian communities in the wealthy Northern Hemisphere are social spaces in which Christians can profess mere *belief* in Christian virtues but actually are granted religious permission to practice bourgeois virtues and form their identities in ways that deeply oppose Christ's way of being in the world. Christianity thus functions as an "add-on" to one's primary identity, an add-on that prioritizes stability, competitive struggle, achievement, and materialism. Students' perspectives about bourgeois values trumping Christian virtues and their open admission that membership in a Christian community has had a negligible impact on their identity and self-worth substantiate Metz's critique of Christianity. For Metz, the practice of Christianity indeed functions too often as "a sort of ornamentation . . . for one's celebrations of bourgeois life"[13] or merely as a balm or opiate to buffer the harsh aspects of living in a competitive society governed by logic. In its offer of superficial comfort, Christianity helps the market by providing a stabilizing social force. This form of Christianity "either becomes increasingly abstract or impotent in broad regions of a person's life."[14] Most tragically, this form of Christianity fails to form authentic followers of Christ and offers no genuine consolation.

Furthermore, Metz's analysis of Christianity's marginalized role in shaping personal identity, values, and life priorities suggests why Christian students can assume multiple identities. Since Christianity functions as an add-on to an identity already formed primarily by a bourgeois worldview and values, it is easier to compartmentalize one's Christian or religious identity and move back and forth between a religious self who worships on Sunday or holidays, a competitive professional persona during week days, and a party persona in the evenings and on weekends. Such analysis also helps explain why many Christian students can smoothly retain their Christian identities while treating one another in dehumanizing ways in their social lives.

Effects of Competition on Interpersonal Relationships

Both Metz's theological critique of society and students' lived experiences indicate that pressures to succeed and social dynamics of exchange insidiously undermine our ability to recognize that we are interdependent beings who need supportive relationships to realize our fullest potential. Metz argues that the exchange principle has rendered two kinds of interpersonal relationships normative and most "reasonable" in our society. The first is an exchange between equals:

> This primary social practice in this regard is exchange, the context is the market, and thus the paradigmatic form of reason becomes the calculating reason that can assess and assign value in the market to different commodities, in relationship to quantifiable human needs. The paradigmatic relationship, the one that makes the most

sense and in terms of which normative claims can be formulated and gotten across in society, is the relationship of equals who enter into contractual relationships of exchange in the market.[15]

In this case of two equals, persons enter a contractual form of relationship in which both partners seek mutual benefit: " 'I support your interests; you support mine.' What makes them equivalent is called competence; their interests are oriented toward exchange, with the goal of mutual success and getting ahead."[16]

The second normative relationship occurs when some persons have more competence or power than others. In this case, the "superior" individuals, subtly or not, dominate the others and objectify them as a means to their own goals:

> This principle of subjugation has long since permeated the psychic foundations of our total sociocultural life. It has become the secret regulating principle of all interpersonal relationships . . . a poisoning of the inner nature of man himself [*sic*].[17]

These relationships based on the exchange principle, argues Metz, sharply oppose the kinds of relationships affirmed in the Judeo-Christian tradition and ultimately renders them suspect, irrational, nonsensical, and undesirable. Scripture consists of stories of persons being called to respond to God's love by loving and being in solidarity with others. Such love enables us to transcend the boundaries of our own egoistic perspective on reality and allows us to open ourselves in genuine encounters with others. Love defies the exchange principle, of course, for authentic love endures even when personal sacrifice is required or there is no hope for mutuality within the relationship. Solidarity with those who are marginalized or oppressed by unjust social structures also makes little sense in a world where one is taught to prioritize egocentric interests.

If Metz engaged my students in dialogue about party and hookup culture, he would undoubtedly lament the very same "exchange principles" at work. Hookup culture is indeed the logical result of the ubiquitous pressure of the exchange process permeating society. It is an obvious manifestation of the post-Enlightenment bourgeois norms we have inherited and perpetuated in the absence of a true countercultural anchor. While students express that ideals of individualism, competition, and self-sufficiency maximize undergraduates' prospects for success, they also acknowledge the negative effects of those ideals on relationships. Immersion in such a competitive mentality creates mistrust and a sense of wariness, motivating them to keep their guard up and appear as if everything is going well in their lives. Students frankly admit how "normal" it is to prioritize success and security over establishing intimate, supportive relationships with one another:

> The competitive nature of the college culture makes it hard to open up to one another. I mean, how are we supposed to have poverty of spirit and open up to someone when we're supposed to try and be better than them at everything? (James)

> Students are seeking personal security. This is an important characteristic, but it can blind them when not being careful of the full impact of their actions. They can grow disconnected from those that they should be dependent on. Only relying on ourselves divides us and keeps us out of communion with others. (Rosamond)

> I realized what a twisted society we exist in. We place emphasis on monetary values, popularity, academic success, etc., over all else, even our relationships with each other. I thought about all of the times I had let my grades and my own desire to succeed get in the way of a friendship. (Penelope)

In addition, prioritizing success over relationships often involves using others and exerting a power-over mentality to "step on others" to get ahead. Such a mentality is ubiquitous in popular culture and becomes an expected and acceptable attitude in their peer culture. Consider these representative quotes:

> We tend to praise people that seek control and power and know what they want in life and go after it. A lot of times this means stepping on others to get ahead. (Ella)

> We live in a society based as a whole on greed and power. Satan tempted Jesus with these exact things, and only when he denied using his skills to obtain these did he become human. Yet, our whole country is rooted on this idea of getting to the top and knocking down everyone below you so they can't get close. Not only is this present in jobs and our families; it translates to college campuses. (Faith)

This mentality corroborates Metz's blunt characterization of contemporary subjectivity:

> Man *is* by subjugating. All non-dominating human virtues such as gratitude and friendliness, the capacity for suffering and sympathy, grief and tenderness, recede into the background. They are deprived of social and cultural power or, at best, in a treacherous "division of labor" they are entrusted to women, who are deprived of power anyway in this dominating male culture. These non-dominating attitudes become undervalued also as unique kinds of knowledge. What dominates knowledge is subjugation . . . as a kind of taking possession.[18]

When Metz claims that "man *is* by subjugating," he means that a person's very sense of being a human subject is based on competitive superiority over others and upon the capacity to exercise power and will over others. Further, masculine identity is threatened when males express non-dominating characteristics that have been reconfigured as "feminine" and relegated to women. Fast-forward to our own time and place in the twenty-first century: my qualitative analysis of student reflections finds no detectable gender differences when it comes to obstacles to realizing poverty of spirit. While women might still be culturally expected to embody non-dominating characteristics in their interpersonal relationships, college women reported the same pressures as men to act strong, competitive, self-sufficient, and embrace a power-over dominating mentality in their academic lives. A significant cultural shift has thus taken place, and it now appears that no one can afford to embody Christian non-dominating virtues fully. As students indicate, expressing traditionally "feminine" characteristics (affirming relationality and interdependence, expressing a full range of emotions, and practicing non-dominating virtues) places both women and men at risk of being viewed as weak, less worthy of respect, and less likely to be successful. In fact, a strong cultural association between strength and individualistic self-sufficiency actually creates a sense of discomfort, shame, or denial about their need for supportive relationships in order to flourish and realize their full potential:

> Most people are trying their hardest to show that they can do everything on their own; assistance is synonymous with weakness. (Naomi)

Metz's last temptation is the All Powerful: humans want to be self-sufficient and never needy or fearful. This also includes total control of others and is based on fears of suffering, uncertainty, and vulnerability. This is extremely present within the individualistic society of America, but also among college students. (Addison)

Many people find it tough to be completely vulnerable. They are afraid of what might happen, not being able to know the unknown. So we seek control, strive to never be needy, and ignore our fears. We do what we can to be invulnerable. In reality, this is only an expression of insecurity and lack of trust. This is a result of how much society values individualism and not needing someone else. (Ella)

Despite the fact that they want to form genuinely supportive relationships with friends or a romantic partner, students repeatedly express discomfort with moving from the "secure" stance of being a self-sufficient individual to the insecurities of interdependence:

College students do not like to express that we can be weak and that we need support. We like to think of ourselves as invincible beings that can tackle the stress from school, demanding jobs, and a social life in a leisurely way. When there is something difficult that college students are struggling with, they find it difficult to ask for help because they do not want to feel inferior. (Meg)

Growing up in the upper-middle class white suburban demographic, my peers and I were raised to believe that we are independent individuals and to value individuals who are highly independent. However, if we want to accept our full humanity like Metz's Jesus, we must accept that we can't do anything on our own. To varying extents, we are dependent upon other people for our own well-being and they are dependent upon us for theirs. Whether it's academic success, career satisfaction or social needs, we often struggle to admit that we are interdependent on each other. I personally struggle with this element, because I have issues putting my trust in other individuals, let alone allowing my own well-being to be even partially in somebody else's hands. (Hunter)

Time-Consuming Relationships vs. "Reasonable" Hookups

Within this cultural context of market rationality, it becomes less mystifying why hookups have replaced dating and committed romantic relationships as the norm on college campuses. Metz would likely argue that, in a society governed by market logic, college hookups appear to be a more "reasonable" choice than a committed relationship. Hookups appear more reasonable than risking a relationship because they allow undergraduates to retain their strong self-sufficient image to others and themselves. Students who desire a relationship after hooking up are typically labeled "needy" or clingy, a shameful and embarrassing sign of weakness. Encountering these admissions and fears about romantic relationships in student reflections for the first time was shocking to me, because twenty years earlier, it was considered "normal" on my college campus to desire exciting experiences of falling in love and being in a romantic, exclusive relationship. How could social influences so quickly make youth and young adults ashamed of their most basic needs for genuine affirmation, emotional intimacy, and support?

Second, Metz would likely recognize that, under market logic and goals to maximize individual successes, hookups appear as the most "reasonable" choice in college because they are the most time-efficient way to get sexual and emotional needs for approval and acceptance met. Hooking up is just like scratching an itch or wolfing down a hamburger when hungry. In this respect, hooking up is multitasking at its best. Corroborating Metz's analysis, students' writings reflect this market logic. When pondering what is most attractive about party culture, students frequently identified with Jesus's first temptation in the desert to flee from his human neediness by seizing his divinity to turn stones to bread. A primary way they flee from their human neediness at college parties is to choose means that gratify their physical, psychological, and relational needs or desires, albeit momentarily and superficially. Students acknowledge that technology and social media have accustomed them to getting what they want instantly: by the click of a button, they can receive instant gratification for products, connection, and affection. Other popular "quick fixes" for instant gratification and stress relief, of course, are alcohol, drugs, and hookups:

Hookups are quick ways to get an animalistic need for sex fulfilled. (James)

The reason hookups remain the college norm is that they can be very pleasurable experiences and provide a simple high that is desired after a taxing day or week of school. Hookups allow for quick, simple, and fun experiences that are "just as ordered" for the busy college kid. The idea that someone can go out in pursuit of what they want and end up with it, even just for that night, is just perfect for many college students as it allows them to not worry about further engagements that would clutter their already busy schedules. (Jackson)

Hookups have become a source of relief for stressed-out college students that need some way to relax and forget their daily struggles. I think many college students have become so stressed out with their classes, job searching, and pursuit for friendships that they have begun to view the casual hookups on the weekends as a relief from all of that stress. It gives them a chance to finally let their hair down and have sex with a random stranger that they won't have to deal with back in their daily life. They do not want another person that will cause them stress during the school week, so they need to find someone that they can hook up with and forget about. (Ella)

College students are busy and very stressed. Hookups are said to be an easy pursuit to happiness, stress free, even a stress relief, and an activity that contributes to the independence that college students work towards. College students think about themselves as individuals in a society and desire to achieve goals only for themselves indirectly causing them to become self-centered. Hookups are all about consumption. People want something and they go out and get it to find happiness in a culture that encourages self-happiness and improvement mainly through easy and quick methods of satisfaction. (Samantha)

Investing emotional energy and time to get to know another person by dating or being in a relationship is viewed as too costly or distracting in their climb to the top:

How can you get further in life if you have all these other people you are invested in who are taking away the ability to strictly worry about bettering yourself? Our current society pushes individuals to get to the top, whether that be social status or job title; there is a desire to be the best possible and to get there alone so as to not share in the victory with anyone but yourself. (Sarah)

Even if college students aren't seeking their future life partners in college, they could still date, right? Well, dating is seen as a lot of work and time investment, a luxury that can't be afforded in our fast paced, uber-competitive society. (Elizabeth)

In the near future, will going to college parties be viewed as too time-consuming if the main objective is a hookup? Thanks to current technology, it takes only seconds for cell phone apps like YikYak and Tinder to access interested hookup partners in one's proximity:

Everyone has portable technology loaded with apps like Facebook, Snapchat, and Tinder, which allow them to be in constant contact with their peers. College students no longer need to form real, in-person relationships because they can just get to know someone through the screen. Technology puts distance, literally and figuratively, between two people so that they don't have to see the other person as a real person. When someone feels like they're just talking to a still-life picture, they can ignore all the feelings and emotions that belong to the person in that picture. That figurative distance between two people often carries over to real life. Even when physically together, hookup partners learn to . . . see the other as nothing more than their two-sentence Tinder bio, and this allows them to hook up without having any real feelings or getting attached. (Lillian)

Within this market-logic mindset, other people and relationships become encumbrances and burdens under the logic of the market because they siphon off time and energy from one's individual productivity. It might even appear foolish and irresponsible to fall in love and experience attachment and care for another person because it might require demands on one's time and compete with personal achievements. Hookups can also enable students to feel a sense of greater control over their lives. Relationships are inherently messy, and there is no way to control your own or your partner's feelings or the future of the relationship. For instance, what if you fall in love and get emotionally attached to another person, then have trouble imagining how your life could be as full and happy again? Such attachments will inevitably unsettle and challenge one's investment in being a "strong," self-sufficient, always-in-control individual.

Conclusion

After engaging in conversations with so many students about self-sufficient individualism and self-worth, I am deeply concerned that college students (and the rest of us) live in a social reality that not only undermines our capacity to form healthy relationships that celebrate our interdependence but also diminishes the rich scope and beauty of human experience and narrows the meaning of our existence. While such a way of being human might equip one with layers of self-protective armor and represent greater security in a harsh society, students' reflections and Metz's theological insights equally expose identifying happiness with self-sufficiency as a blatant lie. If being a "strong, self-sufficient individual" were the most essential variable for flourishing, college students today would be reporting unprecedented levels of happiness and fulfillment. Yet, as social scientific research indicates, college students overall (including the most talented and accomplished) are experiencing record levels of depression, anxiety, and loneliness. To further explore why this is the case, we turn in chapter 6 to students' reflections on the challenges of embracing the second dimension of poverty of spirit—love of self.

6

Self-Love

ACCEPTING OUR HUMAN CONDITION
AND UNIQUE CALLING

THE "SELF" WE are about to consider will take shape in the context of interpersonal relationships, which (as developed in chapter 5) represent an essential grounding for poverty of spirit and full humanity. To honor deep interdependence on God and one another, however, is not yet to love oneself. If, as Metz suggests, a "yes" to ourselves is simultaneously a "yes" to God and a "yes" to others, it is important to explore what "love of self" entails. Through his consideration of the full humanity of Jesus, Metz shows that authentic self-love has at least two components: (1) our willingness to accept compassionately the limitations and vulnerabilities of our human condition, and (2) the courage to discern and live out our unique calling and become our true selves.

Part I: Compassionately Accepting
Our Human Condition

As countless authors in diverse fields, genres, and spiritual traditions have acknowledged, we all have limitations, fears, and aspects of ourselves we dislike. The perennial question is what to do about this "shadow side," as Carl Jung called it. According to Metz, Jesus accepted not only his gifts and rich potentialities but also the physical, psychological, and spiritual shortcomings that constitute being an embodied, free human being. Because Metz understands the depths of our struggle to love and accept ourselves, he takes special care to highlight the importance of self-love within his account of poverty of spirit. For Metz, love of self requires both the willingness to grapple with who we are throughout our lives and the capacity for honesty with ourselves during the ongoing process of self-discovery. While most of us have no trouble accepting our gifts and relishing life's highs, we are regularly tempted to flee from the burdens and difficulties that we all experience. Usually we accomplish this with a profusion of masks and false selves. As Metz observes, however, the key to a fully human, joyful life is the ability to accept with compassion all—not just parts—of ourselves in this "painful experiment of living."[1] He argues: "We can try to run away from ourselves, from the burdens and difficulties of our lot.... On the other hand, we may withstand this temptation and lovingly accept the truth of our Being. For the moment we shall call this attitude 'self-love.'"[2]

In *Poverty of Spirit*, Jesus's second desert temptation represents this fundamental struggle to accept our human condition and love ourselves even in the midst of life's most difficult moments. Trembling on a pinnacle and overlooking a dark abyss, Jesus hears Satan say, "You need no longer put up with this frightening experience, this dangerous plight; you can command the angels to protect you from falling." According to Metz, "Satan's temptation calls upon Jesus to remain 'strong' like God, to stand within a protecting circle of angels, to hang on to his divinity (Phil 2:6)."[3] Instead of rejecting his humanity and taking refuge in his divinity, Jesus accepts that being fully human involves moments of encountering the abyss—experiencing rather than fleeing from fear, anxiety, sadness, lack of control, grief, pain, abandonment, hopelessness, despair, and all other forms of suffering that persons experience throughout their lives. Christ's acceptance of his humanity with its full range of emotions and vulnerabilities culminates in his experience of the crucifixion. Metz questions whether Christians are really comfortable imagining Jesus as a fully embodied human being and whether they truly acknowledge what Christ experienced during the passion and crucifixion:

> Christ, the sinless one, experienced the poverty of human existence more deeply and more excruciatingly than any other person could. He saw its many faces, including those shadowy aspects we never glimpse. In the poverty of passion, he had no consolation, no companion angels, no guiding star, no Abba in heaven. All he had was his own lonely heart, bravely facing its ordeal even as far as the cross (Phil. 2:8).... Everything was taken from him during the passion, even the love that drove him to the cross. No longer did he

savor his own love, no longer did he feel any spark of enthusiasm. His heart gave out and a feeling of utter helplessness came over him. Truly he emptied himself (Phil. 2:7). God's merciful hand no longer sustained him. God's countenance was hidden during the passion, and Christ gaped into the darkness of nothingness and abandonment where God was no longer present.[4]

It may be unsettling to imagine Jesus unable to feel God's presence in his final experience of the abyss. Metz deliberately presses his readers, however, to understand Jesus as fully vulnerable, as we are, particularly in light of his insistence that Christ's humanity saves us and "gives us the courage to be true to ourselves." Challenging his readers to imagine Jesus as both fully human and divine, Metz encourages them to encounter the mystery of the Incarnation—the reality that it is God who becomes human in Jesus Christ. Out of love for humanity, God willingly experienced vulnerability and powerlessness in order to overcome the separation between divine and human and make possible the experience of intimate union with us:

> What the devil really fears is the powerlessness of God in the humanity Christ has assumed. Satan fears the Trojan horse of an open human heart that will remain true to its native poverty, suffer the misery and the abandonment that is humanity's, and thus save humankind.[5] Satan's temptation is an assault on God's self-renunciation, an enticement to strength, security and spiritual abundance; for these things will obstruct God's saving approach to humanity in the dark robes of frailty and weakness.[6]

Especially after reading *Poverty of Spirit*, students in my classes who identified as Christian were able to better appreciate the implications of Jesus as fully human. Consider their reflections:

> My favorite focus throughout this reading was on the humanity of Jesus, and how by denying his divinity when tempted by Satan, we too can accept our humanity, even in the face of the greatest temptation. This hit me particularly well, because the night before I read this I read a few Bible verses that focused specifically on Jesus's humanity, one of them simply reading "Jesus wept." This particular side of Jesus' humanity struck me because of how in class we have been focusing on the ways that society restricts men from showing

their true emotions because it is not the "manly" thing to do. But here is Jesus, the person we Christians look up to most, and he is openly weeping. It is just a huge relief, especially for me, who has always been someone more prone to show his emotions, to see someone so influential being openly emotional. (Noah)

I've become desensitized to the power of the Incarnation and its deep implications for humanity. Understanding the Incarnation within Metz's framework gives me a great deal of comfort and relief. By becoming human, Jesus immersed himself in our misery and confusion that is the human condition, penetrating humanity's darkest depths. Jesus joined in our human struggle and felt a distance from God—standing there alone on the cross—just as many of us do; we reach out to God but feel nothing but the cold air. (Alexander)

Why does Metz claim that Satan's agenda to prevent the salvation of humankind rests on his ability to tempt Jesus to flee the poverty and vulnerability of his human condition and seize his "divinity"? As many students initially ask, why does Satan's greatest fear lie in Jesus's complete embrace of his humanity with all of its vulnerabilities, weakness, and suffering? Wouldn't Satan be more threatened by divine strength and power? Metz believes that Satan fears Jesus's full humanity (and our own potential to become fully human) because Jesus's embrace of poverty of spirit radically opens him (and us) to encounter God and others fully and experience the joy that such intimacy and communion brings. Such experience of union with God, others, and ourselves constitutes our wholeness, our salvation. In this experience of loving encounter with others (a topic to be explored more deeply in chapter 7), we experience our true selves and become radically receptive to God's transforming love and grace. Ultimately, this grace enables us to stand our ground when tempted to flee from the suffering that inevitably occurs when we embrace our unique calling and attempt to love ourselves, others, and God.

Undergraduates' Struggle to Accept All Aspects of Themselves

Metz is careful in *Poverty of Spirit* to develop the idea that a variety of ordinary daily experiences "point us toward the desert wastes of poverty."[7] What does Metz mean here, exactly? Physically, spiritually, psychologically, intellectually, and socially, we encounter external and internal limitations and vulnerabilities. The ethnographies and other written reflections of college students provide a view not just of the concrete modes of poverty they experience but also of the concrete modes of flight that so many embrace in response to their environment. As we will see, undergraduates are both attracted to and perplexed by Metz's emphasis on accepting all aspects of ourselves.

Judging by their written and oral responses, my students are deeply attracted to Metz's writings on self-acceptance and self-love. When writing about their struggles for self-acceptance, for example, they alluded to and identified with the following selection from *Poverty of Spirit*:

> Knowing the temptation that humanity itself is, knowing how readily we try to escape the harsh distress of the human situation, knowing how difficult it is for us to bear with ourselves and how quickly we feel betrayed by ourselves, knowing how difficult it is for us not to hate ourselves . . . we can then understand why God had to prescribe "self-love" as a virtue and one of the great commandments.[8]

Undergraduates recognize that U.S. culture and media are continually selling a very different perspective: the notion that we can defeat our limitations and imperfections and always "be better" than our current selves.

> As teenagers and young adults, the dominant message we are bombarded with via Internet, media, social networking, and advertising, is that we can "be better," look better, be more successful, and be more popular. We set the ideas as our goals and desire to achieve them in a state of neediness, seriously believing that by achieving them we will feel satisfaction. In reality, these "achievements" are short lived and leave us wanting more. When we fail to achieve these far-fetched goals, we are discontent and can even begin to hate ourselves and who we are. If we focus on perfecting ourselves to this important, ideal person, we begin to push ourselves away from who we really are; we are running from our true self. (Amelia)

> There is a deeply rooted belief in many of my friends that they are not enough. They believe that they are not smart enough, not pretty enough, not athletic enough, not wealthy enough. The list of "not enough" goes on and on. Metz begins his book by laying out that our

self-acceptance is the basic creed. When we do not accept ourselves as we are, we are also not accepting God. This is the biggest problem for college students today. There is much pressure, from outside sources telling us do more, to be more. (Taylor)

Unrelenting pressure to be the best and outdo their peers amply fuels their extreme perfectionism and severe self-criticism; and to the extent that these students' ideals and expectations are unrealistic, shame about their actual limitations and weaknesses undermines their ability to accept and love who they are:

Another obstacle we face is in accepting our weaknesses and limitations. So many college students try to run from imperfection and manipulate ourselves to perfection. We are so uncomfortable with struggle, limitations, pain, and failure and we see them as diseases that can be fixed by working harder or masking them with distractions and busying ourselves. Instead of accepting and embracing these parts of our humanity, we run from them. (Natalie)

Self-acceptance is one of the most important elements in embracing poverty of spirit and is the best form of loving oneself. However, it is extremely hard for college students to accept their imperfections and limitations because of the increasingly superficial, materialistic, and success-driven society around them. For example, because of the standard of beauty that the popular media provides, many college girls hate their appearances, and some use plastic surgery. It makes people unable to accept the truth of themselves, and they are driven by other people's attention. (Gina)

Party and Hookup Culture as Avoidance of the Abyss of Vulnerability

College students strongly identify with Metz's analysis of the desert temptation to flee from the "abyss" of our insecurities, vulnerable emotions, anxieties, despair, and other forms of suffering. Many also note that, just as Metz's Satan tempts Jesus to flee the abyss of suffering, contemporary party culture offers undergraduates a way to avoid their pain, fears, and vulnerabilities. Undergraduates perceive that drinking, drug use, and hooking up allow many partiers to escape daily stresses of college life, including academic worries and a host of personal, family, and relationship troubles. Echoing undergraduate ethnographers at University A, students at University B also perceive that alcohol and drugs can allow them to become very different people—the kind who revel in risky or outrageous behavior that attracts their peers' attention and grants higher social status:

> The majority of people at the bar are drinking enough to forget about the stress of the school week and to loosen up, be somebody other than themselves for the night and have fun interacting with friends and members of the opposite sex. (Ellie)

> I watch as the people around me lose inhibition, encourage each other to drink more, and abandon any sexual morals they had six hours ago. When people my age party they become different people. They aren't my down-the hall neighbor who volunteers at the Boys and Girls Club, or my best friend's boyfriend who loves to discuss education reform. They are twisted and morphed versions of themselves that thrive on making less-than-wise decisions and blaming it on alcohol the next day. Many college students use alcohol, partying, and sexual promiscuity to run away from the first tastes of a real, complicated life. We are all at an age where our decisions have real life implications, our actions can make or break opportunities for us, and our lives are becoming deeply our own in way that can be scary and lonely. As college students learn more about themselves and the mysterious complicated world they inhabit, the temptation to run away from themselves and this world becomes all the more tantalizing. (Aubrey)

Intoxicants help students take the edge off their inner critic by momentarily melting insecurities about not being attractive, sexy, or funny enough:

> As college students, we are bombarded by media that tells us we are not worth it until we buy this product or that item. We are told to doubt ourselves, our bodies, and our hearts. We always feel incomplete and there never seems to be anything that will complete us. In turn, college students turn to hookups and binge drinking as a form of release from the feeling of insecurity, self-consciousness, and powerlessness. (Kate)

Alcohol also allows them to escape their social anxieties about interacting with others and being sexual. A drunken state protects students from ridicule, rejection, and embarrassment because they know they will be judged less harshly for their actions if they are drunk. Alcohol even allows students to express a kind of "pseudo-vulnerability" that is socially sanctioned while still maintaining a sense of self-protected invulnerability:

> What they don't want is to be embarrassed or ashamed of themselves, so alcohol is a safety net, an excuse for potentially embarrassing moments. (Victoria)

> That one guy from my Spanish class (who has a girlfriend at another school) is grinding on that girl who works at the student center, and she is reciprocating the affection. That quiet girl that I always see at the library is dancing all-out off to one side. You would not expect to see such a quiet, withdrawn person move her body in such a bold way. I hear someone to my left exclaim, "I've always thought that you were beautiful!" and another yells through the music, "I accidentally slept with him last weekend," and yet another loudly states, "I am actually failing biology!" Drunken words are sober thoughts. They say what they mean, spilling their secrets to the ears of strangers that have become like close friends, in a relationship bound by alcohol. They dare to dance with all their effort, unafraid of the rejection that might accompany skills below the social norm. They are not competing; they are equally uncoordinated. They bond over their weaknesses, celebrating them as one would celebrate a success. (Elise)

In this "safer" state of pseudo-openness and pseudo-vulnerability, students seek acceptance, affirmation, and companionship as they enjoy the momentary sense of camaraderie that inebriation brings:

> Grinding, drinking, and hookups are part of a constant search of human beings for companionship. Often, alcohol inhibits our reasoning and our self-consciousness, and we feel we can more easily talk to people or hook up with them to find that companionship we so desire. We live in such a society of instant gratification that we don't want to put in the effort for the long term. (Emily)

"Socially lubricated" students search desperately for an escape, for some temporary companionship and acceptance on the dance floor;

they are trying distractedly to escape their own neediness whether in school or with friends or family or especially within themselves that natural human feeling of exclusion and disapproval and the deep sadness that results. (Brooklyn)

Overall, a clear consensus exists among my students that a lack of self-acceptance underlies the practice of excessive drinking:

Poverty of spirit involves accepting yourself for who you are and not wanting for things. Because most students usually drink alcohol with the intention of "loosening up," it means they are drinking to lose a bit of themselves. They want to become more outgoing or looser when they really probably could do the same thing if they just accepted themselves as Metz suggests to do. If they completely accepted their personality they may be less shy and be able to talk to others easier, or they may realize that they really don't want to talk to people in the party setting and would rather find more open and meaningful conversation elsewhere. (Kennedy)

Students are much too afraid to be vulnerable, and the fact that alcohol is required to reach a level near poverty of spirit shows that we are far from there. We are not living a fully human life. We are full of secrets. We work hard to stay in control. We disrespect our weaknesses, and we do not live a life with poverty of spirit. (Elise)

If people drink to get drunk, they are trying to rid the bad away, which could mean that they are not confident in how they look, overloaded with stress, depressed from some past experience, and have a negative state of mind. They reveal that they don't have enough confidence to accept and love themselves for who they are. Individuals that consume alcohol to an extent divulge into different characters that aren't themselves at all. Humans that truly self-accept and love themselves don't need to put a liquor confidence coat on because they can love themselves to their lowest point. (Audrey)

These reflections show that yet another aspect of the "abyss" students seek to avoid is the sense of emptiness in their lives. Echoing the ethnographers' analyses mentioned in part I, these students recognize that drinking, partying, and hooking up are attempts to fill a real void:

> Grinding, drinking excessive amounts of alcohol, hookups, and other activities are attempts to fill the emptiness present in the partiers' lives, and poor attempts at that. They make fruitless, half-assed attempts to fill that gap that all college students feel. However, this gap is only opened more. (Liam)

> We can also say no to ourselves by running from our emptiness and trying to fill ourselves with a false sense of satisfaction in a variety of ways. When college students choose partying and intoxication, we are choosing to run away from our real lives and our real selves by indulging in our own desires to make ourselves feel good briefly. (Aubrey)

> Alcohol is used many times as an attempt to fill in the longing and ache people have to be accepted. Hookups can be an attempt to fill that same void. That ache for something more and deeper doesn't go away, so people come back the next weekend to get another "patch" to cover their true desires a little bit longer. (Emma)

Meanings of Self-Acceptance

While students were drawn to Metz's focus on self-love and self-acceptance, they diverged in their reactions to his summons to accept limits and embrace suffering. Most wrestled at length with what it really means to accept things like pain and vulnerability, and whether persons are truly called to adopt Jesus's example. As students rightly surmise, Jesus's entire way of being in the world is countercultural because open acceptance of limitations and suffering places one at risk of appearing lazy, negative, or defeatist. Since overcoming suffering and defying limitations is associated with admiration and success in student culture, they question how such acceptance can be part of a joyful, fulfilling life. Wouldn't they get further in life and experience greater fulfillment if they pushed themselves to overcome limitations and avoid suffering as much as possible?

To untangle this, we need to clarify what Metz and other Christian thinkers mean by acceptance of limitations and suffering. There is a difference, of course, between honest and compassionate self-acceptance and acceptance of human violence and aggression, including unjust social structures (e.g., oppression, physical poverty, and marginalization). It is easy to dismiss Metz if his version of acceptance means that those suffering from physical poverty and injustice should passively accept and do nothing to resist or challenge structural evils. Fortunately, it is clear throughout Metz's writings that embracing poverty of spirit does not entail passively resigning oneself to suffering. Metz fiercely resists any version of Christianity that functions as an opiate to the poor and/or marginalized or anaesthetizes Christians from acknowledging the reality of evil and suffering. As we will explore in chapter 7, following Christ requires active resistance and transformation of unjust social structures and laws. Solidarity with those who suffer, a powerful commitment and calling, is neither weak nor defeatist.

When considering Metz's theology and other Christian writings on this theme, it is also clear that accepting limitations does not mean giving up on goals or quitting when challenges arise. A student struggling with demands of classes, for example, can embrace acceptance by becoming more compassionate and patient with herself as she seeks additional help and creates realistic goals that make sense in her context. Finally, self-acceptance does not mean being complacent and apathetic about character or personality traits that harm yourself or others. If you recognize a tendency to pursue your own wants and desires at the expense of others' wants and desires, acceptance does not mean affirming your selfishness as an inevitable character trait. Metz (and the Christian tradition overall) views the purpose of our lives as a journey in which we grow in our freedom to shed egoism as we love God, others, and ourselves more fully.

Finally, it is clear from Metz's theological writings that accepting suffering does not mean wallowing in negative emotions or painful experiences. Jesus did not seek out suffering, and he did not spend his life depressed, hopeless, or preoccupied with the negative aspects of life. Such a man would not have been an effective healer or leader, would not have attracted large crowds, and would not have inspired disciples to drop everything (notably their possessions and their prior identities and lives) and follow him. Metz's Jesus suffers precisely because he is an embodied human being who tackles rather than flees painful realities. Jesus experienced physical pain when assaulted, loneliness when abandoned by friends, sadness when betrayed, and anger when witnessing injustice, greed, and egoism.

Positively, self-acceptance involves being truthful and accurate about one's reality and who one is—one's gifts, limitations, and flaws. Students who found this liberating imagined Metz's Jesus encouraging them to develop their gifts to "accomplish new things and be as productive and capable as possible," but in a way that respects and works with their limitations:

> For a U.S. college student today, poverty of spirit would look like accepting that we cannot know and do everything. Often students are pulled in so many directions that they can either do them all poorly or choose a couple or a few to do really well. Finding this balance takes time and is not something that is easily perfected. Having a balanced college life is not what college students do because they are expected to do so much and become so much that it is overwhelming at times. For a college student to recognize what they cannot do is to recognize their humanity. But what would make them fully human is to embrace and accept their failings along with their successes. (Rosamond)

> When we find ourselves wishing we were different or someone else, we must stop ourselves and admit it is impossible to change ourselves at our core. Therefore, accepting ourselves as we are is literally the only option, unless we wish to waste time running from something that we can't run from. (Amelia)

> Embracing poverty of spirit is the act that allows us to become fully human. When we understand that we are truly poor, we recognize that we are vulnerable, imperfect, and sinners. When we see our own deficiencies we become open to accept love from others that fulfills us, and not from superficial success, achievements, and wealth. Poverty of spirit helps us comprehend that what is truly important in life is our relationships with others and in turn, our relationship with God. (Lillian)

Occasionally, students made the connection that accepting limits is essential for self-respect, as expressed by Amelia:

> Self-respect is when we choose to not talk poorly about our abilities, bodies, circumstances, or degrade ourselves but rather acknowledge we are good and valuable while still recognizing our limitations. We

recognize our physical, emotional, and intellectual limitations when we do not beat ourselves up over incompetency or failure and do not force or put tremendous pressure on ourselves to exceed our abilities.

Other students linked acceptance of limits with particular Christian virtues. In her fictional letter to her friend about her encounter with Metz's Jesus, Penelope connects Metz's affirmation of limits with the well-known serenity prayer:

> I asked "So how can I, as a modern college student, embrace poverty of spirit?" Jesus laughed. "Well," he said, "empathy, humility, joy, acceptance." "What kind of answer is that?" I was kind of irritated. But then he broke it down and told me about a prayer that his mom really liked called the serenity prayer. I had heard it before, but let me tell ya, it makes a lot more sense coming from him. It goes: "God, give me the serenity to accept the things I cannot change, the courage to change the things I can, and the wisdom to know the difference."

Many students associated Metz's acceptance of limits specifically with the Christian virtue of humility. Earlier in the course, they had discussed Christian ethicist Richard Gula's definition of humility as "the willingness to be who you are and do what you can." Humility, essential for a good, fulfilling life, can be understood as a mean "between the extremes of pride (acting as though I had no limits) and self-effacement (ignoring my real ability and accomplishments)."[9]

If being humble and accepting one's limits seem countercultural to undergraduates, the suggestion that they fully and intentionally experience (rather than resist or escape) negative emotions and suffering is an even harder sell. Does Metz really believe that suffering is an inevitable part of Jesus's becoming fully human, and are we really supposed to follow Jesus's example? Won't suffering consume and defeat us if we don't do everything in our power to resist its manifestations?

What's in It for Me?

College students who wrestle seriously with these ideas typically ask some version of the question, "What's in it for me?" Drawing on reflections from Metz, other spiritual writers, and undergraduates themselves, I offer two answers, each of which points unambiguously to prospects for a happier, more fulfilling life. It's good and wise to acknowledge and accept limitations because (1) it is ultimately futile and even more misery-producing to deny or otherwise flee our reality, and (2) doing so offers us the best opportunity to experience joyful, authentic, and fulfilling lives, even if this first appears counterintuitive.

The Futility of Escape Schemes

Many undergraduates in my classes have proven themselves capable of the same insight offered by spiritual writers three or four times their age. Regardless of their religious tradition, students who look honestly at their lived experiences recognize that it is impossible to escape limitations and suffering. Those who responded positively to Metz's idea of acceptance pointed out the futility of seeking perfection through technology, a stacked resume, and materialism—and when these fail, through brute will and sheer effort. They see through the illusion of the quest for self-perfection and recognize that they will always detect further imperfections and flaws in themselves, which breeds further dissatisfaction and suffering. This mentality of ignoring limits and constantly seeking to overcome them leads to an overscheduled or overly frantic lifestyle, and often results in unhealthy choices and behavioral patterns that harm themselves or others.

We should recall, too, the experience regularly recounted among undergraduates at both Universities A and B that the relief gained from fleeing limitations, insecurities, and personal problems is momentary and fleeting. Soon enough (usually the morning after partying), the emotions or problems they sought to flee return, usually with greater intensity:

> If people acted the way they did while drunk here—laughing, dancing and celebrating each other's presence—while sober, I would say that they were being fully human. However, when the buzz of alcohol wears away, and it will, people who had just met and had a great time together become strangers again, losing their connection. They become closed off once again. (Victoria)

> Being drunk for many people may break down some of those walls humans put up to protect themselves, but when you sober up the next morning those walls go back up. (Lauren)

We also know that students often resort to alcohol, drugs, and hookups to escape from their vulnerable emotions. Either the attempts to repress and dissociate from these emotions fail (as evidenced by the emotional drama, crying, and fights that students observe at parties), or students experience emotional numbness and complain of emptiness, boredom, and sense of a void. This way of being simply represents another form of suffering. Furthermore, spiritual thinkers and psychologists recognize that denying "negative" emotions connected with experiences of vulnerability and suffering limits the full range of life's positive emotions and possibly precludes any real experience of joy itself. Overall, then, repressing vulnerable emotions and suffering leads to a totally numbed-out existence.

College students also indicate that, as much as they and their peers may attempt to maintain control and avoid certain vulnerabilities and emotions, nothing actually shields them from mounting anxiety as long as they are courting perfection. Analyzing their papers, I was struck by how the majority of my students chose to elaborate upon Metz's suggestion that anxiety results from refusing to accept our limitations and from seeking to control that which cannot be controlled in their lives. Consider, for instance, the following reflections:

College students have become slaves of anxiety, from sources such as homework loads, employment, friendships, romantic relationships, family pressures, the fear of missing out, the fear of being left behind, and lack of sleep while they try to balance it all. (Laura)

College students must do their best to understand that constantly trying to obtain control over our own lives does not lead to a fully human life; it only leads to "crushing anxiety." (Aubrey)

My greatest obstacle and the obstacle of many of my college peers is that we have "become the slaves of anxiety." We are all scared of amounting to nothing, so much so, that we fill our voids with a "false sense of security." (Lillian)

To embrace poverty of the spirit as a college student means to accept our anxieties and quit running away from them through one way or another. (Landon)

The reality that so many students identified as being "a slave to anxiety" is not surprising given the vast psychological research on the dramatic increase in anxiety and other mental health disorders among undergraduates and across the U.S. population. Anxiety disorders are the most commonly diagnosed of mental health conditions, with more than 40 million Americans affected annually; furthermore, stress and anxiety are highly correlated with depression. The frequency and severity of stress, anxiety, depression, and suicide among college students has increased over the last fifteen to twenty years.[10] My students' reflections on the stressors that fuel their anxiety thus echo this broader social scientific research. Many undergraduates, already contending with relationship problems, academic pressures, self-esteem and body-image issues, financial concerns and post-graduation plans, have plenty of other factors weighing on them. These include an overall pressure to compete, please others, be the best, pursue only narrow versions of success, and conform to rigid social, sexual, and gender norms. It is little wonder that so many students experience a lack of social support, a sense of not belonging, debilitating loneliness, and worse.

In short, at least three unintended but interrelated consequences await most people who flee limitations and painful experiences: (1) the limits or problems people run from resurface in their lives with greater strength and intensity; (2) people resort to a variety of easily available numbing agents or addictive behaviors, all of which "catch up" with them eventually and exacerbate further suffering; and (3) people become defined and controlled by anxiety.

Prospects for Joy and Fulfillment

Besides the basic futility of placing hope for fulfillment in the status quo, a second, more positively stated reason to recommend the Christian tradition's acceptance of our limitations and suffering is that such acceptance is essential for lasting joy and fulfillment.[11] To begin, consider Kylie's imagined dialogue with Metz's Jesus as she explains why acceptance of limitations contributes to a more fulfilling life:

> KYLIE: "What's the reward of all this pain and suffering? What do we gain by giving up control and accepting ourselves, including our weaknesses?"

> JESUS: "Peace and a reprieve from anxiety are the big ones. Also by letting go and giving over our cares to God, we can have a fuller

existence and more openness to those around us. What I would really want to challenge you to do though is to accept everything about who you are. You need to accept that you have limitations and cannot do everything. You can only read so fast, you can only stay awake so many hours of the day, and you can only do so many things before you burst. Stop fighting so hard against limits and instead work with them to improve what you were given; you will find that it leads to a happier and less stressed you. You are currently a slave of anxiety; instead, accept your inherent poverty and experience the freedom of living and thriving in a human and God-centered life. What exactly that means for actual lifestyle changes in your life I will leave for you to figure out."

As for fostering our capacities to experience joy, Metz argues that we cannot construct, manufacture, or control joy. We may be able to tell ourselves and others that we are joyful if we narrow joy's meaning to the cessation of suffering, temporary satisfaction of momentary desires, and acts of hilarity fueled by intoxicants. However, a state of deprivation from pain and desire is actually far removed from the accounts of joy by Metz and other spiritual writers' accounts of joy. In *Theology of Joy*, Metz claims that we cannot experience joy unless we are willing to acknowledge and confront—not just with our minds but with our hearts and spirits—the suffering that pervades our world. For Metz, what threatens our capacity to experience joy and meaning is not actually the pain that inevitably occurs when moments of the abyss occur in our lives and others' lives. The threat is contemporary society's growing cultural taboo against the freedom to experience our own and others' suffering. In his reflections on joy, Metz pointedly asks:

> Are not our lives falling more and more under the control of an apathetic . . . unfeeling rationality? Does not the modern world suffer from an inbuilt suspicion of imagination, feeling, suffering and passion?[12]

If our priorities are dominated by concerns of exchange, profit, competition, and control, our very capacity to experience joy and play are threatened:

> In a society that is pervasively determined by this kind of scientific knowing, other ways in which human beings know and comport themselves—suffering, pain, mourning, but also joy and play—come into play in a functional and derivative way.[13]

In other words, in a society governed by technical rationality and the "bottom line," we will tend to experience suffering, mourning, joy, or play only insofar as they benefit us in clear, tangible, and instant ways. We will repress raw emotions or forms of joy or play that are viewed as pointless or simply not subject to our control or plans. Similarly, in *Theology of Joy*, David Steere argues that persons in contemporary society are experiencing a diminished capacity to experience both sadness and joy. Defining joy as "our basic response to love" and sadness as "our basic response to the loss of those we love," Steere admonishes us both to "enjoy" and to grieve our separation from one another in healthy ways. Further, he argues that our capacity to experience such emotions depends on the degree to which we feel permitted to experience them on both social and personal levels. If we live in a society that discourages us from expressing vulnerable emotions, we also tend to internalize these taboos and have difficulty permitting ourselves to experience these emotions.

Part II: Courageously Embracing Our Unique Calling

Metz emphasizes that a second essential component of self-love is discerning and pursuing our unique calling. This second theme subtly shifts our focus from theological anthropology to ethics—and engages undergraduates interested not just in the topic of themselves in general but also in particular perennial questions of who they want to become in relation to others and what they most want to do after graduation. How exactly do individuals discern and embrace a vocation that respects their unique gifts and reflects God's desires for their lives? As with "acceptance" discussed in part I, this is challenging, requiring both head and heart, and demanding real courage. Growing into our own authentic selfhood is difficult because (1) any effective discernment of purpose and vocation begins and ends with practices that most undergraduates have not "had the time" to cultivate very well, notably deep listening, solitude, meditation and/or contemplative prayer, and openness to learning from one's mistakes; (2) we are required to identify and shed masks and defense mechanisms that have served to shield us from risk and growth; and (3) our choice to honor our own uniqueness will frequently be at direct odds with expectations dictated by the status quo. How, then, might students discern their unique calling and vocation?

Purpose and Vocation

Vocation, says contemporary Quaker writer Parker Palmer, "does not come from a voice 'out there' calling me to become something I am not. It comes from a voice 'in here' calling me to be the person I was born to be, to fulfill the original selfhood given me at birth by God."[14] Expressing the same sentiment, Thomas Merton writes, "For me to be a saint means to be myself. Therefore the problem of sanctity and salvation is in fact the problem of finding out who I am and of discovering my true self."[15] "Sin," according to this vision, is the embrace—not always a conscious decision—of false selves, or "masks," as both Palmer and Merton explore so insightfully.

At this point, it is important to clarify that, for Metz and many other Christian theologians, God's will for our lives, our deepest desires, and the realization of our unique gifts are one and the same. The Christian journey is definitely not about sacrificing your deepest loves and joys in order to prove your obedience and faithfulness to a higher deity that demands senseless sacrifice or suffering. Palmer writes,

> Our deepest calling is to grow into our own authentic selfhood . . . As we do so, we will not only find the joy that every human being seeks—we will also find our path of authentic service in the world. Vocation begins . . . not in what the world needs (which is everything), but in the nature of the human self, in what brings the self joy, the deep joy of knowing that we are here on earth to be the gifts that God created.[16]

Following Christ in poverty of spirit, then, entails a willingness to be co-creators with God as we discern our calling and become our unique selves. Similarly, Merton's articulation of the meaning of vocation deeply resonates with Metz's *Poverty of Spirit*:

> Our vocation is not simply to be, but to work together with God in the creation of our own life, our own identity, our own destiny. We are free beings and sons [*sic*] of God. This means to say that we should not passively exist, but actively participate in His [*sic*] creative freedom, in our own lives, and in the lives of others, by choosing the truth. To put it better, we are even called to share with God the work of creating the truth of our identity. We can evade this responsibility by playing with masks, and this pleases us because it

can appear at times to be a free and creative way of living. It is quite easy, it seems to please everyone. But in the long run the cost and the sorrow come very high.[17]

Merton articulates the experiences of so many of us who experiment with different personas—personas that can completely eclipse our very identities for a time. The problem, as my college students repeatedly acknowledge in reflections about their identities and party culture, is that after a while, despite our mounting successes, wealth, and social and approval that result from adhering to the status quo, we experience an emptiness—like something is seriously missing in our lives—or we simply feel apathetic or miserable. According to diverse strands of Christian theology and spiritual traditions, it is as though God is whispering deep within our hearts, giving us the wisdom to identify our most life-giving choices and paths. As Merton writes:

> The seeds that are planted in my liberty at every moment, by God's will, are the seeds of my own identity, my own reality, my own happiness, my own sanctity. To refuse them is to refuse everything; it is the refusal of my own existence and being.[18]

Masks, Shadows, and Projection

According to spiritual writers in diverse religious traditions, when you ignore and repress your limits, suffering, and aspects of yourself you dislike, you are rejecting the reality of who you are. To jettison these parts of yourself is to exist as a divided self, projecting your idealized ego self (the aspects you like) and rejecting or repressing your shadow self (those aspects of yourself you dislike).

In their reflections, some students associated Metz's poverty of spirit and self-love with Parker Palmer's reflections on finding wholeness, meaning, and joy:

> Palmer and Metz are definitely two peas from the same pod. I feel like I just reread *Poverty of Spirit* but instead of the focus on Jesus, the main character is Palmer himself. Both say you need to accept who you are, understand your human limitations, live a life that fits with who God created you to be. (Addison)

Like Metz, Palmer emphasizes how essential it is to acknowledge and accept with compassion all aspects of oneself: "An inevitable though often ignored dimension of the quest for 'wholeness' is that we must embrace what we dislike or find shameful about ourselves as well as what we are confident and proud of."[19] Recommending that I assign Palmer's work in tandem with Metz for future classes because his writing clarifies Metz's concepts, some students identified Palmer as a contemporary who increasingly embraces poverty of spirit and experiences self-acceptance after much trial and error.

Cohering with undergraduates' reflections of U.S. cultural resistance to limits, Palmer acknowledges how his own socialization influenced him to resist such acceptance:

> Our problem as Americans—at least, among my race and gender— is that we resist the very idea of limits, regarding limits of all sorts as temporary and regrettable impositions on our lives. Our national myth is about the endless defiance of limits: opening the western frontier, breaking the speed of sound, dropping people on the moon, discovering "cyberspace" at the very moment when we have filled old-fashioned space with so much junk that we can barely move. We refuse to take no for an answer.[20]

Palmer assumed that he should be able to overcome limitations through sheer will and effort, and reacted negatively to his own failures. Ignoring his own limits landed him in a profession as a sociologist that was a bad fit for him. Intense unhappiness and depression ultimately forced him to reexamine his outlook on reality, shift priorities, and choose a new way of being in the world: "My true self dragged me, kicking and screaming toward honoring its nature and needs, forcing me to find a rightful place in the ecosystem of life."[21] As he became more and more comfortable with compassionately accepting aspects of himself he disliked, he began to experience fewer internal struggles: "To embrace weakness, liability, and darkness as part of who I am gives that part less sway over me, because all it ever wanted was to be acknowledged as part of my whole self."[22]

Palmer's experiences cohere with many spiritual writers' insight that "what you resist persists" and often grows even stronger. Franciscan spiritual writer Richard Rohr notes that the more you are attached to a certain identity, the more you will struggle with your shadow side: "The more you are attached to any persona ("stage mask" in Greek) whatsoever, bad or good, any chosen and preferred self-image, the more shadow self you will have."[23] Wholeness and healing occur throughout our lives when we can accept with compassion all parts of ourselves and experience life with an integrated heart, mind, and body:

> In order to finally surrender ourselves to healing, we have to have three spaces opened up within us—and all at the same time: our opinionated head, our closed-down heart, and our defensive and defended body. It takes major surgery and much of one's life to get head, heart and body to put down their defenses, their false programs for happiness and their many forms of resistance.[24]

Furthermore, many psychologists and spiritual writers alike find that when we reject our shadow self, we tend to project what we don't like about ourselves onto others, which often results in our harming others and damaging relationships. Often, such projection is not conscious; our irritation and criticism of others often reflects what we dislike or fear about ourselves. As Palmer states, "We must withdraw the negative projections we make on people and situations—projections that serve mainly to mask our fears about ourselves —and acknowledge and embrace our own liabilities and limits."[25] Similarly, Thomas Merton articulates how lack of self-acceptance poisons our relationships with others, even when we have good intentions of helping others:

> A man who is not at peace with himself necessarily projects his interior fighting into the society of those he lives with, and spreads a contagion of conflict all around him. Even when he tries to do good to others his efforts are hopeless, since he does not know how to do good to himself. In moments of wildest idealism he may take it into his head to make other people happy: and in doing so he will overwhelm them with his own unhappiness. He seeks to find himself somehow in the work of making others happy. Therefore he throws himself into the work. As a result he gets out of the work all that he put into it: his own confusion, his own disintegration, his own unhappiness.[26]

In contrast, compassionately accepting our own limitations and suffering allows us more easily to accept others' limits, failures, and weaknesses.

Experiencing genuine self-acceptance enables us to grow in our capacity and freedom to love God and others as they genuinely are. For Metz, love of self, God, and others are deeply intertwined—a subject that will be more fully developed in chapter 7.

Further Challenges to Becoming Unique Selves in a Sea of Conformity

As Jesus's life indicates, embracing poverty of spirit and one's unique calling frequently disrupts and calls into question dominant ideologies, taken-for-granted assumptions, and social norms. Consequently, those who embody poverty of spirit often face social disapproval, betrayal, loneliness, and other forms of suffering, including martyrdom. In *Poverty of Spirit*, Metz highlights how we all experience (as Jesus did) a fundamental temptation to sacrifice our unique selves in order to secure social validation and a life of relative comfort:

> "Be like the rest of humanity," whispers Satan, "feed on bread, wealth and worldly prestige—like the rest of us." It is a temptation put also to each of us: to renounce the poverty of our unique, mysterious personality, to do just what "everyone else" does. We are encouraged . . . to betray our mission, whatever its form, be it unswerving loyalty to another person, an undaunted love, the unyielding quest for the justice or the lonely call to duty. "Don't rock the boat. Why make a nuisance of yourself? Why not live from the daily bread of compromise? When in Rome do as the Romans—*vox populi, vox Dei!* You'll only be overruled and shouted down, without getting a word of thanks."[27]

In his writings on how to discover and become one's authentic self, Palmer addresses this temptation to conform and secure approval:

> As young people, we are surrounded by expectations that may have little to do with who we really are, expectations held by people who are not trying to discern our selfhood but to fit us into slots. In families, schools, workplace, and religions communities, we are trained away from true self toward images of acceptability; under social pressures like racism and sexism our original shape is deformed beyond recognition; and we ourselves, driven by fear, too often betray true self to gain the approval of others.[28]

In their reflections, students easily identify with this temptation "to renounce the poverty of our unique, mysterious personality, to do just what 'everyone else' does." Conforming to the unwritten status quo rules of popular and peer culture is tempting, they repeatedly note, because their identities and self-esteem are deeply affected by peer acceptance and social status:

> It is hard to accept poverty of spirit as a college student because we base so much of who we are on what other people will accept. (Kennedy)

> Friends and popularity still make up such a significant part of how college students view their own self-worth, and therefore many don't feel ready to venture away from the crowd, and stand alone on the path to which they are called. (Grace)

Echoing the undergraduate ethnographers quoted in part 1, these students perceive that the degree to which they conform to social and sexual norms at parties reveals that many peers are not accepting themselves as they truly are:

> Everyone was acting at the party how we are socialized to act, and by drinking excessively, most people are hiding who they are behind alcohol and hooking up. (Hannah)

> Heterosexual men and women's interactions do not ring true to the person inside. Our society has structured us to act a certain way, which often means putting on a façade. At parties, many people dress, act, drink, and do things to impress others, and Jesus would say we should not do this if it is leading us down a path that is not our own and is not our own desires. (Samantha)

> At parties, college students' "overconfidence" masks their true lack of confidence and dissatisfaction with their lives. Many of them did not actually want to be there and would have rather been catching up on sleep or having a genuine conversation with a pal, but were dragged along by friends. These reluctant people proceeded to get hammered to compensate for their annoyance with being there. Others had to be in attendance to be seen as fun, popular, sexy, and rebellious. How could they deny themselves that acceptance into

the "in" group? When we conform to "what everyone else does," we renounce the poverty of our uniqueness, and therefore are incapable of achieving genuine personal commitments or relationships because no one is honestly being themselves, but being just like everyone else. (Amelia)

Students perceive that they and their peers tend to conform to status quo norms out of fear of being judged as "less than," ridiculed, and/or alienated as an outcast:

Moving to college, most students don't know many people, and that can be a very scary thing. We don't know who we can trust or depend on, and we don't have that security of having someone that is there for you no matter what. In that situation, it is very hard to put yourself completely out there because we are afraid of being rejected. With that fear, we start to worry about how others see us. From social media, there is a lot of pressure on both men and women on how they should look and how you should act. It is hard for people to truly be themselves when they feel like they have standards that society expects them to live up to. (Lauren)

Social settings are a recipe for conformity. No one wants to stand out and be "that weird kid at the party." There is endless pressure to conform to your friend's ideals, or people that you want to be your friends. Trying to fit in means taking a look at the qualities you have to offer, and focusing on how you can best display this to a particular audience. (Lindsey)

Students' writings reveal that, while they project their strengths and a confident image of self-sufficient independence, they are paradoxically seeking to please others and gain their approval. This theme of caring more about pleasing others and fitting in than finding out who they truly are and expressing their uniqueness was dominant in both men's and women's reflections:

The biggest struggle that a college student comes across is trying to please everyone. From day one of your freshman year, you move into a big new place knowing a handful of people or less. Immediately, you want to be accepted and make friends. One desperately trying to fit in and find friends may change themselves in whatever way possible in order to please these new friends. In order to please others you may try changing yourself and hiding the things about yourself that you believe others won't accept. In hindsight, you may lose grasp on reality and the uniqueness of your being. (Gina)

Little by little, we might start to depart from who we truly are by basing or judging ourselves on what other people think or do. College is a time when many students are faced with new challenges that they have never had to tackle before. College students usually feel the need to be like everyone else and adapt themselves to the culture they are in. Because they are trying to figure out who they are and what they want to do in their lives, they look at how other students are acting and what they have. (Connor)

We have to be able to be comfortable with ourselves in order to be truly happy. This is a very hard concept for us in our culture because we are always striving to become better than others and try to please others instead of finding our true self. It is so easy for us to get caught up in trying to be someone that everyone else wants us to be instead of just being ourselves. Our peers are always telling us that we have to do this or be like that in order to fit in. When this is the case we are not listening to ourselves and are only striving to please the people around us. (Thomas)

In such reflections, students demonstrate how shallow popular culture's celebration of individualism and independence truly is. In their minds, they are expected to be fiercely independent and stand out from the crowd but only if such actions conform to societal conceptions of being the "best":

Rather than embracing our differences, society is trying to make it seem like everyone should look and act a certain way, along with being involved in certain activities in order to live a life that will make you happy and where everyone will always like you. (Melanie)

In our society today, there are so many expectations and standards that are thrown at us. We must make a certain amount of money to be considered part of a social class or, my least favorite, we must look a certain way to get things in life. We then all form our lives, ideas, and way of living to conform to these standards. (Molly)

I think that it's difficult in this society to really be yourself. Especially when there are images in the media telling young people how we are supposed to act. As 18- to 22-year-olds, we don't really know who we are or how we should act. These false images and pressures make it very difficult to learn who we are. Without learning who we are, we can never accept ourselves, which is one of the criteria for being fully human. (Nora)

Metz's Response to Conformity in Culture

How would Metz likely interact with today's college students in a dialogue about the just-discussed challenges of embracing their uniqueness rather than conforming to the status quo? I do not believe he would be surprised by the pressure students experience to conform to increasingly narrow and stringent social, sexual, and gender norms in college culture. Throughout his writings, Metz argues that our life's purpose of becoming free subjects who live out our unique calling is increasingly threatened by social structures like neoliberal economic globalization:

> Yet there is another social threat to identity that exists on the global level: the quiet disappearance of the subject; the death of the individual under the anonymous pressures and structures of a world that is engineered by an unfeeling rationality and that therefore breeds a weariness with identity and a loss of memory—putting the soul in a coma.[29]

Ironically, our task to become unique selves has become more threatened in contemporary society despite the fact that traditional authorities like religion, local cultural communities, and the like have less influence on person's and community's identities than in the past. Over the course of his career, Metz becomes increasingly sensitive and attentive to the extent to which a person's freedom to develop as a unique subject and realize his or her calling can be harmed or undermined by unjust social structures. He devotes much time to analyzing how wealthy Western nations' exploitation of poorer countries for profit creates such extreme suffering that many persons' capacities to become unique subjects is severely debilitated, if not destroyed:

> What I have in mind here is that suffering which makes people fall dumb in "worldly grief." This is a suffering that so breaks people down, so disfigures them, that it is as if they were "the son of no man." Who would dare contest the fact that there is

suffering like this, especially looking at the countries of the southern hemisphere? Who would deny the existence of this suffering, which one simply cannot "accept" in a Christian way, since it long ago destroyed any capacity to accept anything, and every way of being a subject? And who would dare deny that this is not a matter of some extreme individual cases, some extreme private affliction, but rather a situation of suffering that has collectively overshadowed whole peoples or groups? . . . It leads people to self-rejection and self-hatred. There is a suffering that forces whole peoples to lead a life without any affirmation, in which they can seek out affirmation at best in a bottle, and a simulated sense of identity.[30]

While situations of dire poverty may offer the clearest examples of the kind of suffering that can rob humanity's capacities for freedom and unique subjectivity, Metz's description of social groups experiencing self-rejection and self-hatred and seeking affirmation through alcohol or a simulated sense of identity (conformity to the status quo) easily applies to many college students' own analysis of their party behavior.

For Metz, our lived experiences of freedom, emancipation, justice, and happiness have become superficial and meaningless. For instance, what does freedom even mean to contemporary privileged persons? Metz argues that it unfortunately means the freedom to maximize self-gratification and freedom from care and concern for others:

Freedom ends up being the freedom to choose which entertainments will divert me from the world's suffering and the demand to do something about it. The great Enlightenment ideals dissolve into an apotheosis of banality.[31]

In short, Metz fears that we increasingly are being "incentivized" to repress our uniqueness and conform to norms that benefit not ourselves but the most powerful social and economic actors and institutions. Rather than living in a global society where the economy serves people, we instead submit to social practices that ultimately serve to maximize profit in a neoliberal capitalist economic system. Consider Metz's concern for humanity's prospects for flourishing as unique, fully human beings:

Left to itself the technological-economic planning of humanity's future will produce a completely adapted person, a human being whose dreams and imagination have been left behind, smothered in the functionality of technical mechanisms. The purely technological-economic planning of humanity's future seems in particular to prepare the way for the decline of that person who is nourished by the historical substance of his or her freedom, that is, by the power for what is different in the midst of conformity.[32]

Given these social pressures to conform, how can college students (and the rest of us) gain the courage and wisdom to diverge from the status quo, figure out what our unique callings and vocations are, and become the unique, authentic selves that God created us to be? Metz and other Christian thinkers would advise my students that two resources will greatly aid them in their journey toward becoming authentic selves: membership in a supportive community and a commitment to a spiritual practice that includes solitude. For Metz, the very purpose of Christianity is to offer persons membership in a community that is grounded in the dangerous liberating memories of Jesus Christ's way of being fully human through his ministry, passion, death, and resurrection. Such a community keeps alive freedoms that have been repressed in our society—the freedom to suffer, and the freedom to suffer others' suffering and respond in love.

Metz also emphasizes that Christianity should protect and encourage our freedom for solitude and contemplation in a society where "many seem hypnotized by work, by success, by planning, even down to the inmost recesses of their consciousness."[33] The purpose of prayer is to free us and give us some reflective space from the "mechanisms and prejudices of society, as well as the capacity for that selflessness which demands action in the interest of others, of 'the least of your brothers and sisters.'"[34] The challenge, of course, lies in giving ourselves the quiet space and time to discern our deepest desires and discover our true selves in the midst of living in a culture that subtly demands conformity despite its apparent celebrations of individuality and personal freedoms. Overall, with its obsession for proving worth by doing, Western culture is allergic to silence, solitude, contemplation, and trusting the deep wisdom and inner voice within ourselves—in other words, allergic to simply being. As Merton writes, solitude is essential for gaining a greater perspective that transcends the status quo and offers freedom from the status quo:

The need for true solitude is a complex and dangerous thing, but it is a real need. It is all the more real today when the collectivity tends more and more to swallow up the person in its shapeless and faceless mass. The temptation of our day is to equate "love" and "conformity"—passive subservience to the mass-mind or to the organization. . . . The great temptation of modern man is not physical solitude but immersion in the mass of other men, not escape to the mountains or the desert but escape into the great formless sea of irresponsibility which is the crowd. There is actually no more dangerous solitude than that of the man who is lost in a crowd.[35]

Simply noting the need for community and a consistent spiritual practice does not satisfactorily answer our fundamental question about how exactly students can distinguish their "true" selves from their false selves and become strong enough to diverge from group-think mentality and act in ways that increase joy and fulfillment. During my final semester at University A, I asked students in two sections of Christian sexual ethics to practice ten minutes of any form of prayer or meditation and ten minutes of a spiritual practice that focuses on a form of embodied meditation (walking meditation, Tai Chi, yoga, or QiGong) four times per week for six weeks at the beginning of the semester. Students wrote in a journal about their experiences each time they engaged in these exercises. Some students elected to continue with their spiritual practices and journal writing throughout the semester while others chose to stop and complete a different assignment. Although more data is needed to engage in qualitative analysis, two main themes emerged from students' experiences. First, most students shared in class and in their journals how much they struggled with simply giving up 20 minutes of their day for spiritual exercises. Some expressed resentment and even anger about having to do these practices when they had so much else to do that seemed far more important. One young man came to my office and asked desperately if he could read additional articles for each class rather than doing these practices. Second, those students who began to experience benefits and elected to practice the entire semester noticed that they felt calmer, more peaceful, more joyful, more grounded, and/or expressed increased appreciation of time spent in solitude. Many students also expressed that the kind of safe, nonjudgmental, confidential community they created in class over the course of the semester also fostered their discernment of what constitutes a fulfilling life. Student feedback on these activities signals the need, I believe, for more research on the impact of certain spiritual practices and types of community on undergraduates' spiritual growth, moral discernment, and overall well being.

Conclusion

In chapters 5 and 6, we discovered within Metz's first two aspects of poverty of spirit a potential for joy and fulfillment unavailable through the well worn paths of our culture's status quo. Chapter 7, where we round out Metz's vision, is no different. Despite the challenges connected with "love of God and neighbor" in college settings, the promise of a more "fully human" life appears to await those who learn to shed false selves, embrace the risks of neighbor-love, and pursue justice for others.

7

Neighbor-Love and Justice

WE NOW ARRIVE at the third and final component of poverty of spirit: the Christian call to love God fully and to love our neighbor as ourselves. Metz's theological writings on these themes throughout his career suggest that a fully human love, as exemplified by Christ, involves three interrelated commitments: (1) letting go of one's false, ego-driven self; (2) becoming vulnerable and authentic in our relationships; and (3) pursuing justice and solidarity for and among our neighbors both near and far.

Letting Go of One's False, Ego-Driven Self

In his reflections on neighbor-love, Metz seeks to raise our self-awareness about how we so frequently reduce other persons to our own limited and egoistic perspective. Addressing the implications of opening ourselves to encountering others in their full complexity, he states:

> Every genuine human encounter must be inspired by poverty of spirit. We must forget ourselves in order to let the other person approach us. We must be able to open up to the other person, to let that person's distinctive personality unfold—even though it often frightens us or repels us. We often keep the other person down, and only see what we want to see; thus we never really encounter the mysterious secret of their being, only ourselves.[1]

Because of our tendency to become wrapped up in our insecurities, needs, and desires, we do not open our eyes fully to others, seeing instead "what we want to see" and keeping "the other person down" in a conscious or subconscious attempt to bolster our self-esteem. Metz repeatedly uses terms like "self-abandonment," "forgetting ourselves," and "emptying ourselves" to refer to this process of letting go of our egoistic self, which focuses on how the other fulfills our needs and affects our self-image. To actually affirm our neighbor as a distinct other, we require epistemic humility, curiosity, and the courage to be challenged and transformed by another person. To the degree that we cultivate the practices of asking questions, listening with undivided attention, and tuning in to how our own needs and desires might be influencing our perceptions and reactions, we open ourselves to experiencing the mystery and joy that relationships with "neighbors" entail. Most important, letting go of our egoism allows us to transcend our preoccupation with how we and others perceive our worth.

Becoming Vulnerable and Authentic in Our Relationships

Love of neighbor requires a willingness to become vulnerable—to be affected, challenged, and transformed by our encounter with others. According to Metz, genuine love "dominates the whole human person, makes absolute claims upon us . . . and thus subverts all extra-human assurances of security. The true lover must be unprotected and give of himself or herself without reservation or question."[2] Elsewhere, Metz perceptively acknowledges how opening ourselves to the other's personality and reality can easily upset our own precarious sense of control and security, and how defense mechanisms often spring into action to help us avoid or deny what might frighten, repel, or simply inconvenience us. Consider these undergraduates' explanations of Metz's account of love and vulnerability:

> Genuine love, according to Metz, makes us poor. When love is really love, a person gives all of themselves, not a secret kept or blemish hidden, and is completely vulnerable to the other. They do not try to be someone they're not, make themselves look better, and do not worry what the other thinks because everything is on the table and there is nothing left to lose. If one person in a relationship is withholding a piece of their puzzle from the other, and the other person is more vulnerable or has less power, injustice can really flourish. It wouldn't take much for the less vulnerable person to use that to their advantage and hurt the other person—intentionally or unintentionally. (Emma)

> Poverty of spirit in the context of relationships and sex is having a
> spirit of humility and vulnerability. Being intimate with another per-
> son requires giving of yourself and allowing the other person (as well
> as yourself) to love you unconditionally despite your weaknesses.
> (Sarah)

As Emma notes, Metz is explicit that "every stirring of genuine love makes
us poor."[3] The description is apt, for we trade security for vulnerability
when we offer up our hearts to others. Genuine love shatters illusions
of security and absolute control over self and other. Specifically, our individual "I-self" shifts to an interdependent sense of self, as genuine love
moves us to take into account others' wants and needs. Pondering Metz's
descriptions of what it means to encounter and love another, my students
frequently wrestle with what it means to forget themselves and sacrifice
out of love for another in their daily lives. How can they discern when this
sacrifice fosters rather than threatens their sense of calling and authenticity? Based on her experiences, Natalie raises concerns about how this ideal
of sacrifice and selflessness can be destructive:

> I am a perfectionist and people-pleaser. I have a really hard time
> saying no to people. Part of that is because of how I was raised. My
> mom always taught me the importance of being self-less and put-
> ting the needs of others before myself. So, that's something that I've
> done since I've been little. There are times when people ask me to
> do things that I don't really see as valuable or worth my time and
> energy, but since someone asked me, I can't say no.

Natalie's version of selflessness—always placing the needs of others
before herself—is clearly not congruent with Metz's account of embracing
poverty of spirit and becoming fully human. Authentic self-love entails
embracing the poverty of one's uniqueness and realizing one's distinct
calling. In this instance, greater discernment about what forms of sacrifice
are called for and the purpose of sacrifice is essential. It is helpful to recall
that Christ's central commandment concerning love is not to love one's
neighbor *more* than oneself but *as* oneself. Thus, embracing poverty of
spirit does not sacrifice one's dignity, integrity, or calling to meet the needs
of others; followers of Christ need to distinguish between sacrificing one's
egoistic self (the self preoccupied with achievement and social status) and
sacrificing one's authentic self (the self that God calls us to become).

When imagining a conversation with Metz's Jesus about sacrificing out of love for one's neighbor, some students emphasized Metz's Jesus explaining the importance of discernment:

> Our mission is to take care of our neighbors. By devoting your life to this task of selflessly using your gifts and skills to help others, you are practicing poverty of spirit. By "selfless," I mean that you have no agenda for your own gain nor do you approach the task with bitterness. However, this is not meant to be self-neglect; causing harm to yourself is not a piece of poverty of spirit. (Metz's Jesus as imagined by Naomi)

> Another thing you can do to better embrace poverty of spirit is to further explore what it means to sacrifice yourself in your particular setting. When you volunteered abroad in South Africa, it was easy to give up yourself and live simply and for your neighbor instead of yourself. You were so happy in that place but now feel a little lost upon your return. Sacrificing yourself takes a different meaning here in America; you do not have to give up a job and go work at a soup kitchen or help kids as you did in South Africa for the rest of your life. There is importance in taking care of yourself and your own needs. It is also not required that you go off to another foreign country; it is possible to be giving of oneself in the U.S. You just need to find your own niche where you are able to give of yourself to others and also take care of yourself. You will be happy and fulfilled if you listen to what you know inside is truly you. (Metz's Jesus as imagined by Kennedy)

Pursuing Justice and Solidarity for and Among Our Neighbors

Another essential component of neighbor-love is a spirituality of "liberated freedom" characterized by its commitment to solidarity and justice.[4] Throughout his writings, Metz develops and radicalizes Karl Rahner's insight that, given the complexity and interconnectedness of our global reality, love of neighbor moves far beyond the context of selected individuals in familiar circles: working for justice in solidarity with others must occur without regard for others' proximity and social location. Also, discipleship for Metz is unapologetically political. Faith dictates that we be "willing to suffer others' suffering,"[5] "defying apathy as well as hatred,"[6] and bearing fruit as fully as possible "in an excessive, uncalculated partiality for the weak and the voiceless."[7] As John Downey notes, solidarity for Metz serves as a fundamental category of political theology that "responds in the real world" and "provides not just empathy or identity with the past but a chance to transform the future."[8] Metz expresses the intrinsic connection between faith and action: "It is of the very essence of Christian faith to be believed in such a way that is never just believed, but rather—in the messianic praxis of discipleship—enacted."[9]

Most fundamentally for Metz, meaningful engagement with the call for justice proceeds from the recognition that other persons' freedom to become fully human is just as sacred as one's own. Justice thus concretely means always treating the other as an end in himself or herself and never as "an instrument of self-assertion." Justice involves the commitment to protect our neighbors' dignity and rights, and foster their well-being and flourishing. Practically, this requires not only a commitment to justice in our interpersonal relationships but also a keen eye toward the myriad social-political struggles that occur in communities locally and globally. A justice that is fully mature includes the ability to examine critically and to comprehend the dynamics of structural causes of injustice. Emphasizing that we are as responsible for sins of omission as we are for sins of commission, Metz writes: "The Christian is not only responsible for what he does or fails to do, but also for what he allows to happen to others.... The person who does not act and withholds his decision can share in the guilt for everything which is left undone, unattempted, and undelivered."[10]

The Intrinsic Unity Between Love of Neighbor, Self, and God

For Metz, an intrinsic unity exists among love of God, love of neighbor, and love of self. Much is at stake, then, in our decision to open ourselves in love to other persons. To begin with, we realize our fullest potential and grow into our true selves through loving relationships with others:

> Failing to risk the poverty of encounters, we indulge in a new form of self-assertion and pay a price for it: loneliness. Because we did not risk the poverty of openness (cf. Mt. 10:39), our lives are not

graced with the warm fullness of human existence. We are left with only a shadow of our real self.[11]

Furthermore, when we open ourselves in love of neighbor, we brush up against and are transformed by the mystery of God's presence. In these graced moments, we experientially grasp unity existing between love for God, neighbor, and self:

> Poverty of spirit does not bring man from men to God by isolating these components into separate little packages: God—Me—Fellow men. (God can never be just one more reality alongside others.) It operates through the radical depths of human encounter itself. In total self-abandonment and full commitment to another we become completely poor, and the depths of infinite mystery open up to us from within this other person. In this order, we come before God. If we commit ourselves to this person without reservation, if we accept him and do not try to use him as an instrument of self-assertion, our human encounter occurs within the horizon of un-ending mystery. This openness to others can be enjoyed only in the poverty of self-abandonment; egoism destroys it.[12]

Many of my students who identify as Christian resonate with Metz's emphasis on this unity. For instance, Matthew explains this unity of God-self-others and its implications for our lives in the following way:

> You can see God through your friend, your classmate, your coworker, the stranger you just met at a bar, the custodian who works on your floor, etc. "The ones who see their neighbor see God." So basically life is not just about you; it doesn't revolve only around you. It is bigger than that. Life is more fulfilling when you put your egoistic self-interest aside and consider others' interests as well. If you are serving only your sense of self, you are missing out on the major piece of a satisfying life. As Metz states: "Our human neighbor now becomes a 'sacrament' of God's hidden presence among us, a mediator between God and humanity" (*Poverty of Spirit*, 32). When people forsake the people around them or love what they can get from others instead of loving the persons, they slowly become like the things they love—small, insignificant, and petty.

Furthermore, not only do we experience God's presence when we embrace poverty of spirit in our encounters with others, but also we express and mediate our love for God through our love of our neighbor. Metz draws on the Sermon on the Mount to illustrate how we experience Christ in our encounters with our neighbor:

> "Lord, when did we see you suffering?" And he answered them: "Truly, I say to you, whatever you have done for one of these little ones, you have done for me. Whatever you have not done for these little ones, you have not done for me" (Mt. 25).[13]

The way in which we express our love for God and realize a "yes" to God's invitation for relationship and communion, then, is through our love for others:

> God drew near to us as our brother and sister and our neighbor, as "one of these" (cf. Mt. 25:40–45). Our relationship with God is decided in our encounter with other human beings.... The only image of God is the face of our neighbor.... Every authentic religious act is directed toward the concreteness of God in our human neighbors and their world. There it finds its living fulfillment and its transcendent point of contact.... Love of neighbor, then, is not something different from love of God; it is merely the earthly side of the same coin.[14]

In these experiences of encountering and experiencing the unity of love for God, neighbor, and ourselves, Metz claims that we experience ourselves at our most whole, most joyful, most peaceful, and most fulfilled.

Challenges to Neighbor-Love in College Culture

Egoism

When asked whether their peers embrace poverty of spirit in the party scene, students identified ways in which such neighbor-love is both absent and present. Emphasizing the challenges of neighbor-love, the majority of students highlighted their own and their peers' tendency toward egoism and self-protection over the willingness to be authentic, vulnerable, and love others as ends in themselves. Most students singled out how cultural

pressures to succeed (explored in chapter 5) normalize self-centered preoccupation with their own desires:

> The biggest issue college students have with fully embracing pov-
> erty of spirit is letting go of their own egos. This becomes especially
> difficult due to the social pressures to achieve and conform to a
> certain look or behaviors. It is very difficult to let go of these feel-
> ings when your social status is based on your skills or your friends.
> When we are constantly submerged in this culture and we see every-
> body else participating in it, it is hard to believe that everyone else is
> doing something wrong when it comes to finding fulfillment. This
> warped sense of well-being has only been exaggerated by the use
> of Facebook, which only shows the happy things that other people
> want you to see. (Evan)

> We all know we should love our neighbors, but we're placed in this
> environment where competition underlies most of what we do. We
> get this idea that we need to be ahead in everything to be set up for
> the best job and the best future, so we get mixed messages. Are our
> classmates our friends, or our rivals for future opportunities? We're
> being told to love our neighbor as our self in the same cutthroat world
> where trust is so fragile. (Laura)

Some students also acknowledge the ironic connection between (1) self-
critical judgments and insecurities arising from the competitive pressure
to succeed, and (2) their tendency toward egoism and narcissism:

> We have created a culture where average is equivalent to the lesser
> and people have a belief that they are somehow above the average
> and more gifted than everyone else. This inflated sense of self and
> these egotistical views of the self, have made it difficult to be fully
> human today and to embrace poverty of spirit. (Lillian)

> Another barrier to experiencing poverty of spirit for people in our
> generation is the way we are taught to overvalue ourselves. In a well-
> intentioned attempt to battle low self-esteem and create confident
> youths, parents and teachers frequently told the kids of our genera-
> tion that they were special and that they could accomplish whatever
> they want to accomplish. While this isn't inherently bad, I told Metz's

Jesus about a book I read for a class titled *Narcissism Epidemic*. Very generally, the conclusion of the author is that our generation is more self-absorbed and overconfident about our ability to be self-reliant than any generation before us. (Christian)

Even service, which appears to be an obvious manifestation of neighbor-love, is often motivated by egoism and resume building:

I've learned to value getting into graduate school more than anything, and I value myself based on where I get in to graduate school. So now I'm sitting here thinking, "If I just have one more volunteer experience, my resume will be complete." Instead of looking for fulfillment and truly loving my neighbor, I'm satisfying myself with helping others really only to help myself. (Bella)

In high school, there was a general trend towards treating volunteering like a homework task to be accomplished. In order to maintain good standing with the organization, I had to complete X hours of volunteering per semester. The primary reason that I and others volunteered wasn't to genuinely help others in an act of selflessness, but to build our resumes for college applications. (Christian)

I am most baffled by the "save the world" attitude of so many of my peers—to help those in need, to travel the world in order to tell stories of refugees and feeding the starving children. Do not get me wrong, these are all great things. But the people who travel to foreign lands helping those in need are the same people I see being complete jerks here, to the people closest to them. I understand the necessity of helping those in need. However, should we not treat our loved ones and our true geographic neighbors with the love, care, and respect we give to strangers in need? If we travel across the world and help those in need, but cannot act in accordance of true humanity within our hometown, are our deeds truly rooted in goodness? Is it a genuine act of poverty of spirit, or is it a "see me do good deeds" act? (Lily)

Hectic schedules are another factor undermining students' willingness to be open and vulnerable to their neighbor's concrete reality. Students wrote, for example, about the implications of managing academics, extracurriculars, work, socializing, partying, and even their habit of multitasking—talking to friends while texting, tweeting, or checking Facebook:

> Look at the girls in that booth over there. None of them are looking at each other. They are so concerned with what is on their phones that they are denying themselves conversation with their friends. The relationships they have with each other go only skin deep. (Bella)

> A lot of us are so focused on getting good grades, doing well in our sporting competitions, and also having a social life that we forget that other people may need us to help them or just simply be there for them. I know that when I am stressed out about meeting a deadline or having the time to get everything done, I am so focused on my own problems that thinking about someone else's is just simply overwhelming. If there is a silent cry for help, it is difficult to separate ourselves from our own struggles to even notice. (Annie)

Many students also associate lack of neighbor-love at college with the expectations created by popular culture that the college years represent the only time in life to be selfish:

> College years are often looked at as a time to be wild and self-indulgent. Society often encourages students to experiment and do what makes them happy. The idea of making ourselves happy makes us selfish and gives us a sense of control that makes it difficult to become fully human. We self-indulge, believe we are powerful, and think we will live forever. We try too hard to find and assert ourselves, and we worry too much about our own happiness. (Aubrey)

> I think that one of the biggest struggles college students have with living fully human lives is the emphasis on having fun and being wild in college. The stress of living up to that college stereotype is holding college students back from being able to have healthy relationships. When we put so much emphasis on getting wild and having fun, we lose the ability to really communicate with other people to have healthy relationships. (Amy)

Given this construal of the college years, many undergraduates emphasize how normal it is to use other people as a means to get what they want:

> Western culture puts too much emphasis on self. Most students tend to use others as stepping stones to get to their goals. They are so focused only on their own achievement; they don't care about others. They seek others not because they want to get to know them, but in hope of benefiting themselves. Most sexual relationships I have seen so far are merely based on satisfying one's own sexual desire. Men go out with women who they don't even respect; they call them "bitches," but they automatically go into pleasing themselves when they get the chance. (Jackson)

> Those engaging in a college party environment are attempting to create an unrealistic fantasy of fun and pleasure. Typically, these desires are sexual in nature. The perception is alcohol enables individuals to "achieve" these ultimate fantasies to a certain degree—this causes people to request and expect others to fulfill their most desired wishes. (Wyatt)

A consensus emerges in their reflections that hookups are rooted in egoism:

> The hookup culture is based off of selfish wants. We want attention, affection, even sexual desire to hook up meaninglessly with another person. Based on Metz's description of being fully human, we are not embracing the act of becoming vulnerable or humbled through human experience. Instead, with the use of alcohol we are encouraging the displacement of vulnerability and treating others as means to our own ends. (John)

> Students are treating each other in a hookup as objects to be used for sexual pleasure and then tossed to the wayside. Many are only interacting with one another for this personal benefit, holding no respect—let alone love—towards the humanity and being of the other person. (Grace)

> A fulfilling relationship involves complete vulnerability and selflessness. In the hookup culture, people are only completing sexual acts with themselves in mind; the well-being of the partner is often not considered. (Layla)

Students point out that such egoism contrasts sharply with Metz's emphasis on a willingness to be vulnerable to and affected by our neighbor's concrete reality. Vulnerability, it turns out, is a second challenge identified by students considering obstacles to neighbor-love.

Risking Vulnerability

Vulnerability involves sharing our selves without apology or deception with others. Students recognize that revealing their authentic selves makes possible genuine intimacy, love, acceptance, and joy, yet many remain ambivalent about vulnerability on account of its riskiness. Overwhelmingly, students resonate with Metz's analysis of our tendency to shield ourselves from the vulnerability of revealing who we are. In an anonymous brainstorming exercise, I asked students to write their immediate thoughts and emotions after seeing the word *vulnerability*. Coding multiple classes' answers, I discovered that the ratio of negative to positive associations of the word was approximately two to one.[15]

Specifically, the word *vulnerability* elicited the following negative gut reactions: it terrifies students, making them feel weak, worried, overwhelmed, anxious, sad, exposed, alone, timid, embarrassed, self-conscious, doubtful, conflicted, shameful, and insecure. Students expressed how vulnerability is "a very scary goal," "not easy to achieve," and "not desirable on the surface"; that it takes them outside of their "comfort zone" and carries "potential for heartbreak." Vulnerability leaves you "with your guard down," "open to getting hurt," "with no self-protection or defense mechanisms," and in a "state of being taken advantage of, powerlessness, and having little control."

Two primary themes emerged in their reflections on *Poverty of Spirit* about why authenticity and vulnerability are so risky. First, students emphasize that being authentic involves feeling and expressing a full range of emotions, which is culturally associated with weakness. Such "weakness" undermines their efforts to project a strong, successful image and creates shame, embarrassment, and loss of social status:

> Emotions are seen as a weakness in society today, and kids have learned to play it cool. What they don't understand is that this has a crippling effect on their emotional well-being. As time goes on, they simply can't make themselves vulnerable in intimate relationships with other people, which prevents them from becoming fully human. (Jack)

We are raised to be competitive in school, in sports, in the job market, so we should also be competitive when it comes to emotions; being vulnerable does not fit well with that competition . . . if we open ourselves up to a romantic partner they may have a special kind of emotional hold over us. (Rosamond)

When surrounded by a status-minded social environment where weakness is discouraged, it is extremely hard to accept that it is okay to be vulnerable with others when it comes to feelings and relationships. Revealing these things will negatively impact our social standing. (Evan)

According to many men, expressing emotions needed for intimacy conflicts with expectations of masculinity:

We undercut our emotions and sensations at every turn in order to fulfill society's promotion of masculinity. Men cannot allow themselves to openly experience the emotions that we have. We are allowed to experience anger, lust, and happiness—all on different levels. But when emotions such as sadness creep into view, we must stifle them before they are shown. (Aiden)

I am of the firm belief that men are not inherently emotionless creatures. The emotionless face that men put on regularly is a creation of contemporary culture. Men's desire to be emotionless and to be strong forces them to portray themselves as something that they are not. . . . The constant emotional invisibility men create leads to intimacy problems. Men who are caught up hiding their emotions are unable to be themselves due to fear of exposure. (Garrett)

While we might assume that women experience greater permission to express emotions since "being emotional" has been a traditional feminine characteristic, college women reveal an increasing pressure to adopt the same stoic norms as men when it comes to expressing vulnerable emotions:

Our culture has pushed this identity on women to have a perfect body, be sexually inexperienced, but sexually adventurous, and not be too emotional and labeled clingy. (Abigail)

As women have become slightly more accepted into the executive portion of the business world, emotions have become more of a problem.

People have been affected by society to not foster their emotions. This affects hookup culture by making it an easy way for people to get what they need sexually and keep their usual method of not opening up and showing their emotions. (Zoey)

Students express that it is far easier to conform to hookup norms of being unattached, unemotional, and invulnerable than to risk ridicule and loss of social status.

Feelings bring the possibility of rejection and that is something everyone wants to avoid at all costs. If feelings are not involved, no one can get hurt. The biggest risk someone can take is to develop feelings and express them. With feelings and commitment thrown out the window and sexual expectations high, hookups are what students turn to. (Emma)

One of the most negative effects of hookup culture is the significant amount of emotional detachment that is arising in young people. This is because we are socialized to not want a relationship and to be the "cool girl" or "the ultimate bro" by casualizing sex and not wanting anything to do with attachment. With this mentality being such a huge part of this culture, young people are not learning how important relationships are in your life and how to be completely vulnerable with someone. (Brooklyn)

In regards to relationships and feelings, can we embrace poverty of spirit and accept the fact that we are vulnerable human beings and we have feelings? Oh no, absolutely do not show that you have feelings; you will get labeled as the crazy girl who is desperate to find a boyfriend. No, guys want the girls who have no emotions and enjoy the hookup culture just as much as they do. Those girls are the ones who have all the friends. But it's not just the guys who are going to talk about you if you show your emotions; the girls will too. Sometimes girls are even more relentless than guys by calling a girl psycho and saying she needs to take it down a couple notches and hide her crazy. Where in all of this are we able to let go and be totally vulnerable in relationships? (Kirsten)

Second, students emphasize that being authentic and vulnerable is risky because it opens up the possibility of getting hurt and/or rejected, and experiencing embarrassment and shame from such exposure. It is far easier to take refuge in alcohol and partying than to take the risks that a genuine encounter brings:

> Most people are frightened of rejection and being rejected while drunk is a lot less threatening than putting yourself out there and asking a person out while sober. When sober, you don't have an easy excuse for denying responsibility for your actions. (Ethan)

> Not many college students feel fulfilled during their college years when it comes to sexuality. There are far too many defenses, too many walls of isolation, too much "fakeness." People are afraid of being completely open to others. (Caleb)

> Instead of trusting that God made us perfectly and that who we are in our truest form is worth entrusting to others through genuine relationships, we instead, as Metz says, "fall prey to ceaseless experimentation," meaning we look to alcohol or brief sexual encounters as a means to form relationships. Time and time again, this method of avoiding vulnerability fails. Instead, it results in feelings of remorse, regret, and disgust. Yet, each Friday and Saturday night, college students fill bars and the party houses to repeat these shallow relationships instead of giving in to genuine human encounters. (Grace)

Many students also expressed a desire to fall in love and experience a committed relationship but were held back by the fear of appearing needy or getting hurt:

> Falling in true love is scary and exciting, and something college kids want to do but are afraid of. Overcoming the obstacle of completely taking down your brick wall piece by piece and letting another being in is one of the greatest feats. (Aliyah)

> Genuine love requires a deep sense of vulnerability and commitment, which can be truly terrifying for a person my age because we are so afraid of getting hurt. Being vulnerable in a way that truly makes us feel safe requires a sense of security that would take time to build: it definitely could not happen drunkenly in a couple of hours. By choosing to consistently hook up with people drunkenly and randomly, we run from true love that could make us more fully human and bring us so much more satisfaction. We trick ourselves into thinking that this

hooking up is somehow better for us, because it helps us gain experience, or satisfies us for a while, or because we have a sense of control over when, where, and how it happens. However, in the long run it leaves us feeling hollow and alone. (Aubrey)

Notably, students perceive that expressing any sign of vulnerability increases their chances of victimization and failure:

We as humans like to feel safe, and being vulnerable without a promise of the person reciprocating that vulnerability is scary. We are taught from a young age to be safe in our interactions, not giving others enough leverage to overpower us if they so choose.... Vulnerability doesn't partner with the idea behind the American Dream. If you are making yourself vulnerable, you are not pushing to the top. To show weakness is to display the ways to beat you. If I tell someone that I am insecure about something, they have that back-pocket knowledge to throw in my face should they ever need to. My weakness is their weapon. We do not like losing. We do not like being bullied. We do not like to be victims and want to protect ourselves. We hide our vulnerabilities, masking them from the world. (Elise)

This idea of wholeheartedly loving someone and being completely vulnerable to others is probably the most difficult for college students to grasp and follow through with in contemporary society. Many people are raised today with the idea that they are the only person who can fulfill their own needs. I know that I have a lot of trouble letting people in, and am very stubborn when it comes to asking for help. The idea of completely opening myself up to someone and letting them help me to fulfill my needs is completely terrifying, and I know that I am not the only one who feels this way. Many of us are scared. We are scared that we will be rejected, scared that we will be left with a broken heart, and scared that we will waste time on something that may not even work out in the end. (Annie)

Some students acknowledge that, faced with the prospects of personal rejection, emotional hurt, and social embarrassment, many strive for invulnerability by seeking power and control over others. In this respect, they resonate with Jesus' third temptation to desire power and control over others in relationships. A key fear is that if one does not gain power over the other, the other will gain power and domination over oneself, likely resulting in harm and loss of control. This fuels a "do-or-die" imperative where the ability to gain superiority is what matters above all else.

According to students' reflections, common ways men seek power over each other are by denigrating those who don't "man up." Consider the following representative reflections of men:

> Guys are frequently told to "man up" or "grow a pair" or "stop being a little B****" in response to the display of unaccepted emotions or struggles. (Daniel)

> In my time at University B, I've heard . . . hookups being justified with the words "Relax, it is college." This myth that college requires craziness and mayhem is pervasive throughout our and other campuses. Not partaking can be perceived as a sign of weakness or femininity, which is quickly and eagerly criticized. (Jordyn)

Echoing ethnographers' analyses in part I, students acknowledge that college men often seek power over women by dehumanizing them and pursuing their interests regardless of women's desires:

> Many of the man-to-man conversations that I've overheard about women do not treat them as equals, but instead as devices that are to be used once and thrown away. (Isabella)

According to students, women also seek power over men by using their sexual allure to "get men to do things for them." In a similar dynamic, many women seek power and control over other women by putting down or "disciplining" those who don't conform to unwritten social norms.

> Because of this fight for male attention, women treat other women as less than human as well. The amount of cattiness that goes on at parties or at bars is unbelievable, and women are actively trying to pull each other down instead of pushing each other up. (Isabella)

> When women call each other names, there is a state of jealousy. When women get jealous of someone they do not like, they use terms such as "bitch," "slut," "whore," etc. When women cannot

meet these standards, their self-esteem becomes significantly low and a woman can become depressed with herself. (Jessica)

As women, we ridicule each other and are constantly judging one another for our behavior, dress, makeup, and hair. (Brooklyn)

Given the harshness and competitive nature of their culture, it is not surprising when students reveal that key attributes of "traditional" masculinity—appearing invulnerable, in control, unemotional, and exhibiting a "couldn't care less" attitude—are increasingly embraced both by college men and women. Sadly, by prioritizing self-protection and invulnerability, students lose out on the prospect of a relationship in which they are affirmed and liked for who they truly are.

Desiring Authenticity and Vulnerability in College Culture

Within the social reality my students describe, it does seem quite foolish to be vulnerable, risk rejection, and take a chance on a loss of social status when you can simply be part of the crowd, adhere to hookup norms of no strings and no emotion, and reap the social benefits of doing what is expected of you as a college partier. And yet, in their anonymous brainstorming on vulnerability, many students also affirm and desire positive aspects of vulnerability: 51% of women and 34% of men included positive associations in their descriptions, indicating positive past experiences and a desire to embrace vulnerability in the future. The most common positive descriptions of vulnerability by students in this exercise included the following: vulnerability connotes openness, trust, honesty, joy, excitement, intimacy, true selfhood, comfort, mutual respect, equality, acceptance, relief, warmth, peace, excitement, genuineness, gratitude, and compassion.

Three reasons these students value vulnerability emerge in the brainstorming exercise and in their *Poverty of Spirit* theological reflections. First, they recognize that vulnerability is crucial in order to receive and offer genuine acceptance and affirmation:

Vulnerability is fundamentally necessary and risky behavior all humans should come to grips with. To be vulnerable is to ultimately gain and give acceptance. I'll admit it is scary when rejection becomes more probable than usual. But we ultimately want to experience it, living like there is no tomorrow and being real. (male student)[16]

Vulnerability—fulfilling! (If the other person is vulnerable as well), being completely open and honest. Expressing your true feelings and not holding back. (female student)

Second, vulnerability is essential to experience intimacy, connection, and love:

Vulnerability is when you are open and exposed in a way which can bring you closer to someone else. (male student)

Being vulnerable with a person means you really feel with them. You reveal your secrets and fears and emotions when being vulnerable. (female student)

I think of vulnerability as a necessary condition for intimacy. Being vulnerable to someone is something I only do to people close to me; extremely close to me. (male student)

Third, vulnerability is needed to experience a fulfilling relationship:

I give vulnerability lots of value and desire more. This weekend I met a guy, and I credit what has become of that relationship to vulnerability. Excited for more. So real. So raw. It's scary but with great risk comes great reward. (female student)

Vulnerability is something that is key to being in a good relationship. Without vulnerability it is impossible to be comfortable. (male student)

To me, vulnerability is not something we should strive against but rather a goal. Ideally I would like the strength to be vulnerable, particularly in a romantic (and eventually marital) relationship. (female student)

Embracing Neighbor-Love in College Culture

While most students focused on the challenges they face to embody neighbor-love, a minority of students also highlighted positive ways they and their peers implicitly embraced poverty of spirit and neighbor-love in

their social reality. Certain students expressed enthusiasm about embodying poverty of spirit at college parties—it all came down to the intentions
of the partiers. Three repeating themes of neighbor-love appeared in their
reflections. First, while students had much to say about the college partiers
who were intent on getting drunk and hooking up, they also acknowledged
that some groups were more focused on simply having a fun night out
enjoying their friends and drinking casually or not at all. Some perceived
these groups as having the most fun and likely experiencing a taste of the
self-neighbor-God communion that Metz celebrates:

> Some are embracing poverty of spirit. There are the people who are
> there who are not drinking. In most cases these people are there
> for their friends and just to have a good time. These people are not
> rowdy and seem to be having a great time. By not drinking, they are
> not running away from their imperfections, and by being there for
> their friends, they are being caring. (Landon)

> There are some people in this bar who are simply here to have a
> good time and use this as a venue for spending time with friends.
> These people are modestly observing their alcohol consumption,
> and are treating others with respect. (David)

> A good number of the people talking around the bar and dancing on
> the dance floor are embracing poverty of spirit and living life as fully
> human in this moment. Poverty of spirit doesn't mean totally giving
> up things that make you happy like parties. For example, a group of
> friends were dancing together and really seemed to be having a good
> time and enjoying each other's company. They invited others to join
> them. They really weren't drunk; maybe they'd had a drink or two. But
> if something went wrong they could easily function as needed. I see
> contentedness. None of them were trying to be someone they're not.
> (Ashley)

Some students also identified groups of friends engaging in genuine conversation and bar rituals as embracing poverty of spirit:

> Look at that group in the back of the bar. It appears to be a couple
> roommates and a recent alum catching up. As far as I can tell, they
> are seriously engaged in the conversation and are being supportive
> of the guy on the left who, by the sounds of it, just got fired from his

job. Isn't that the sort of conversation that Metz calls for? Everyone in that group has offered something—a couch to crash on, a lead on another job, all sorts of things. (Christian)

With Jesus by my side at the bar we observe and discuss what is happening around us. To our left we see a table of friends talking and having what looks to be a great conversation. They are mellow, composed, but enjoying a few drinks and enjoying each other's company. When I asked if he thought they were living a fully human life and embracing the poverty of spirit, he nodded his head, "Yes. The table is engaging in good conversation and enjoying time with their brothers and sisters." Jesus would argue that they are fully human because they are living in communion with one another and while the communion might be at a bar instead of a church, the relationships they are forming are healthy. (Savannah)

I turned to Jesus and asked him my second question. His response was: "I see a mix of those embracing and abandoning poverty of spirit. Those playing beer pong on the far side of the room, as unaware of it as they may be, are embracing poverty of spirit. Both sides are providing humor, companionship, and conversation to create a relationship with each other. Whether either team wins or loses in the game they're playing, they accept the outcome without complaint and carry on." (Benjamin)

Second, students clearly found evidence of poverty of spirit and love of neighbor in those partiers who made sacrifices to benefit others. They pointed out those who acted as a designated driver or helped drunk friends when they got sick or needed help getting home safely:

Those who chose not to drink (or not to drink excessively) sacrificed fulfilling a desire for popularity in order to be more aware and helpful to others. The person who took the keys from a drunk and the woman with the sick friend in the bathroom are two examples. These are the ones who embrace their identity and do not allow others to form them in a negative way in order to fit in. (Matthew)

By this point in the night, Brianna, sitting with the group of people to our right, spots a girl who is in one of her classes. By the way she is walking and talking, it is clear that she is not okay. Brianna asks her friends if one could help her bring her classmate back to her apartment. Without hesitation, someone stands up and agrees to help her. Both of them put an arm around the classmate and leave the bar to safely bring her home. I turn to Jesus and ask if they are embracing poverty of spirit. Jesus states they are living out their poverty of spirit. They have put aside their own wishes and desires in order to help someone they hardly know. (Savannah)

Third, although less commonly noted, some students perceived that not all of their peers sought a hookup by the end of the night: they identified couples who acted like they were in a healthy relationship as expressing neighbor-love. They acted comfortable with being themselves around each other and enjoyed mingling with their friends:

The people who are out there just to have fun and maybe meet someone new are open to new people and experiences and displaying some of the poverty of spirit qualities. All dancing at the bars is not bad considering how many couples have met at this bar, my brother and his girlfriend included. He was able to let his guard down as Metz suggests we do when experiencing true love, a trait that displays a true poverty of spirit. (Kennedy)

Motioning toward the students dancing, I ask Jesus whether he thinks they are embracing poverty of spirit and living a fully human life. Jesus points to a guy and a girl, "They're dating," he says. This seems to make quite a difference to Jesus. "They are living a fully human life because they are in love, and this is a fun night out for them. They go on real dates, they trust each other, and right now they are out having fun with their friends," Jesus explains. Neither the girl nor her boyfriend appear to be heavily intoxicated, which further proves his point that you must be coherent in order to fully embrace life. (Josie)

In their reflections, some students even drew on their own experiences of being in a satisfying, committed relationship in college, indicating that it is socially feasible to risk vulnerability and love in a poverty-of-spirit kind of way:

I like that in my relationship I am completely comfortable with opening myself up and allowing myself to be completely vulnerable.

I do not have to change who I am in my relationship and actually understand more about myself through this relationship. Love is the mutual dependence on each other and yet the maintenance of staying an independent person. Love is having a person to be with through all the hard times and all the good times. I have felt completely happy and fulfilled. Falling in love has only made me a stronger and better person. (Sophia)

To me, love is selfless and to be in love is to concern yourself with the chaos of someone else's life. Loving someone is accepting them for all they are, chaos and all. Of course, fights and arguments suck, but they help you grow and understand how to compromise and how to be in a real relationship. (Jacob)

Most students go into college thinking that hooking up is what you do in college, but I have noticed that people begin to change their minds. Relationships and love seem to be what people really want deep inside. I have at least found this to be true for myself. I am currently in a serious/romantic relationship because I find it much more fulfilling than anything else. (Mason)

I came into college hoping I wouldn't fall in love. I feel like college relationships either really work out or end terribly so I thought I would save myself from challenges by just hooking up with lots of guys. After a semester, I was pretty bored so I decided to focus on my friends and schoolwork. Later in college, I fell in love. All of my previous relationships have been fun and easy because everything was on my terms and I usually ended things before it got really serious. I didn't want to be vulnerable because I was afraid I'd get hurt. Now I'm in a serious relationship, filled with love. (Rosamond)

Conclusion

Throughout chapters 5 to 7, students' insightful analyses of the challenges to become fully human mirror contradictions and ironies in contemporary U.S. culture. A popular cliché is that college is supposedly *the* time for self-discovery and finding oneself, yet many students express that they are too distracted pursuing present and future success and social status to take time to reflect on themselves and who they really want to be. Furthermore, according to my students' perceptions, popular culture and broader U.S. culture celebrates individualism and "owning who you are," but only if your brand of individuality conforms to a narrowly construed version of success based on proof of one's superior talents and acquisition of material wealth. Although the discourse of proclaiming individuals' right to freedom of self-determination is central to U.S. cultural identity, these college students reveal that they are rewarded for certain forms of expression (aggressive competition, repression of vulnerable emotions, invulnerable superficiality), and are at risk for social exclusion if they engage in other forms of expressions that interrupt status quo assumptions and norms. Anxiety over individualistic survival and successes leads to risk-averse behavior and narrows their vision of a fulfilling life for themselves, others, and communities. In short, students reveal that what constitutes success and fulfillment for mainstream U.S. culture directly contradicts Jesus' way of being fully human in his embrace of poverty of spirit.

Of course, fear of being vulnerable, relational, and authentic is not a novel phenomenon. Generations of college students have experienced social and sexual competition and suffered through heartbreak and betrayals. My sense from my own and others' research, however, is that millennials as a whole find revealing who they truly are and risking vulnerability in their pursuit of intimacy more terrifying than previous U.S. generations in the twentieth century. I suspect that a primary cause of this is the fundamental fear that vulnerability to being hurt and betrayed represents failure, which has become the greatest social taboo of all:

> The United States is such an individualistic culture; we are raised to believe that we can sink or swim, but it totally depends on us. So, we are all fighting for success. However, what we are forgetting is that—in this fight to define ourselves in college and feel prepared to be successful in the real world—we are letting our relationships falter. We are not allowing ourselves to completely open up and be vulnerable to others because we are too scared of failing. (Annie)

> As I leave the bar that night, I feel at war with myself. All I have to do to embrace poverty of spirit and become fully human is accept who I am, let go of the fact that I am not divine and need God's help, forget about other people's opinions of myself, and use my gifts and talents for others to enjoy. Easy, right? WRONG. Very wrong. This type of life seems unrealistic because of the society in which we live. We are taught to compete against the world from birth. Our parents try to raise us "the right" way in order to get us farther ahead in life.

They want us to succeed right away and not experience any failures. Without experiencing failure, we cannot learn. We cannot learn to accept the fact that we are human and will make mistakes. (Melanie)

Furthermore, particularly in class discussions on vulnerability, students articulate how technology ratchets up their fears of vulnerability, failure, and shame since their personal lives are made public in ways that no other generation has experienced. Within seconds, thanks to social media, everyone can witness the embarrassing details of a drunken night out, failures, breakups, and rejections. There is a lot more at stake to taking risks than ever before. It is no wonder that, within college culture, so many seek to escape these anxieties by chasing instant highs from alcohol, drugs, and casual hookups, only to feel the return of emptiness and loneliness the next day. It is these cultural crises in authenticity, vulnerability, and relationality that are at the root of the rise and perpetuation of hookup culture as the social norm on today's college campuses.

Students' frank accounts of risking vulnerability and authenticity in relationships are invaluable because they reveal the complexity present in college students' experience of freedom and moral agency. Students reveal they are conscious of the cultural pressures that impinge on their ability to become authentic, vulnerable, and relational selves. Yet, simultaneously, they recognize instances when they flout such pressures, courageously act "real," and love others as Metz's fully human Jesus would do. Their ability to offer insightful critiques of dominant cultural attitudes and norms indicates that their ideas, beliefs, attitudes, and behavior have not been completely colonized by popular culture and influential forms of media. In other words, while it takes effort to question dominant values that we so easily "breathe in" and internalize, my students' reflections demonstrate that it is possible to depart from the crowd and follow in Jesus' way of becoming fully human.

In summary, chapter 7 has challenged us to begin thinking more about the need to protect our neighbors' dignity and rights, to foster their flourishing, and to expand our circles of compassion from immediate interpersonal relationships to larger and larger communities. Yet readers may have noticed that Metz's third component of neighbor-love—justice—is absent in students' accounts of poverty of spirit and of neighbor-love in college culture. This omission is not surprising since Metz only developed this theme in his later writings. The word *justice* only appears once in *Poverty of Spirit*. Exploring what it means to treat oneself and others justly in college party culture is the very subject of part III. While chapter 8 examines justice in the context of college partying, sex, and relationships, chapters 9 and 10 consider major obstacles to sexual justice on college campuses—sexual assault, its traumatic effects, and the role university communities play in either exacerbating or alleviating the traumatization of sexual assault survivors. Finally, chapter 11 fleshes out three commitments needed to create a sexually just culture on college campuses, and envisions how undergraduates can collaborate with administrators, faculty, and staff to effect cultural transformation.

PART III

Sexual Justice

A Call to Action

8

Justly Relating to Self and Others in College Culture

OUR FOCUS IN chapter 8 turns to examining what constitutes justice in the arena of college culture. When it comes to college partying, social interactions, sexuality, and relationships, what does justice look like, and what do undergraduates deserve? As with earlier chapters, college students themselves offer individual and collective voices that are extraordinarily insightful. In this chapter, I focus on contemporary Christian ethicist Margaret Farley, whose coherence with Metz and connection with my students has made her a valuable voice in my ethics classes for many years. As we will see, there is a disconnect among many students who, while often passionate advocates of justice in other contexts, continue to hook up and tolerate injustice in their embodied sex lives. Why is this the case?

Margaret Farley's Account of Just Sex

Deeply resonant with the theology of Metz in *Poverty of Spirit* is the work of Christian ethicist Margaret Farley, whose contemporary vision of just sex challenges the college students who read her work *Just Love* in my classes. For Farley, justice entails the ethical principle that requires "persons and groups of persons" to affirm one another "according to their concrete reality."[1] She acknowledges the diversity among persons and the fact that our knowledge of persons is in flux owing to ever-changing historical and social contexts and new interpretations of reality. Yet Farley thinks it is possible to arrive at an inductive understanding of the shared concrete reality of all persons. She claims that two shared features of persons' concrete reality—autonomy and relationality—ground our obligation to respect all persons as ends in themselves. First, human freedom enables us to make autonomous choices and to determine for ourselves "our ends and our loves."[2] I am convinced that Metz would agree with Farley's conception of autonomy as the capacity "to determine the meaning of our own lives and, within limits, our destiny."[3]

A second feature of everyone's concrete reality is our inherent sociability and need for others in order to realize our own potential and grow in our capacity to know and love God, self, and others. These two shared capacities of freedom and relationality are intrinsically interconnected. As Farley insists: "We cannot grow in freedom except in some nurturing relationships; and freedom ultimately is for the sake of relationships—the loves, the relationships we finally choose to identify with in our deepest selves."[4] And so we must attend with special care to our own and others' interpersonal needs and vulnerabilities.

Yet affirming the other's reality also involves the deeply personal work of discovering their unique characteristics and context. This coheres with Metz's rich descriptions of what it means to encounter another person as a distinct other. Moreover, when discerning how to relate to each other justly, Farley argues that it is essential to know the person well enough to judge whether our interactions are positively contributing to that person's growth, and that our capacities for freedom and relationality enable us to transcend ourselves (and our egos): "We are who we are not only because we can to some degree determine ourselves to be so by our freedom but because we are transcendent of ourselves through our capacities to know and to love."[5]

Our actions must not only affirm the other's concrete reality but must honor our own as well. Our interactions are not just if they violate or diminish our authentic sense of who we are: "A love will not be true or just if there is an affirmation of the beloved that involves destruction of the one who loves. I do not refer to a justifiable 'laying down of one's life' for the beloved, but rather to a letting oneself be destroyed as a person because of the way in which one loves another."[6] Farley thus leads us to the important distinction between sacrifice arising in accordance with one's authentic self, and the all too common sacrifice that disregards human dignity, violates one's true self, and distorts one's sense of life's purpose. Given our tendency toward self-deception and sometimes even self-destruction, we must learn to be on guard against sacrifices contrary to the spirit of Christ.

When considering what it means to affirm the concrete reality of the other or our self in the context of sexuality and relationships, Farley claims that it is ethically insufficient to focus on determining a particular sexual act as morally good or just in the abstract. She begins instead with questions like these: "When is sexual expression appropriate, morally good and just, in a relationship of any kind? With what kinds of motives, under what sorts or circumstances, in what forms of relationships, do we render our sexual selves to one another in ways that are good, true, right and just?"[7]

Farley has been extremely helpful in expanding the minds and moral imaginations of my students. Best of all, perhaps, students consistently have been empowered by Farley's framework for inquiry and especially by her seven specific norms for discerning whether sexual expression is just, each of which is grounded in respect for autonomy and/or relationality. First, one must do no unjust harm—meaning any action that violates persons as ends in themselves and instead treats them as a means to further our own interests. Farley urges us to consider not just physical, psychological, spiritual, or relational harm, but also more subtle forms like the "failure to support, to assist, to care for, to honor, in ways that are required by reason of context and relationship."[8] Given that our sexuality and embodiment render us vulnerable, we need to take extra care with ourselves and the other when engaging in sexual activity.

Second, free consent to sexual activity is essential in order to relate to others as ends in themselves and respect their capacity for self-determination. Free consent requires the assurance that each person's capacity for autonomous decision making is fully intact and is not undermined, for example, by alcohol or drugs. Free consent also entails the absence of forms of coercion and manipulation that can be based simply on a lie or false promise.

Farley's remaining five norms speak to our own and others' capacities and needs for relationship. The third norm is mutuality: respect for persons as ends requires that *both* partners actively and receptively express themselves sexually, emotionally, and relationally. Farley argues that underlying this value and norm of mutuality is a view of sexual desire as a desire that goes beyond pleasure alone and includes a sense of connection. Fourth, an equality of power is an essential condition to avoid harm and make possible free consent and mutuality. While equality is seldom perfect, the balance of power needs to be close enough for each partner to respect both self and other as ends. Fifth, some level of commitment toward one's partner's well-being is required to ensure that norms of no unjust harm, free consent, mutuality, and equality are honored. Having sex with multiple partners can be ethically problematic because one risks violating the norms of free consent and mutuality and treating others as a means to addressing one's own agenda. While Farley acknowledges the possibility that a brief sexual encounter could offer some form of relationality or value to an individual if the norms of free consent, no unjust harm, equality, and mutuality are met, she argues that such value remains limited. In order for sex to foster love, union, and holistic growth, a deeper sense of commitment is needed. Sixth, for just sexual expression to flourish, it needs to be fruitful, to impact others positively. While fruitfulness has often been interpreted to mean procreation and raising children, Farley suggests other ways that a couple's intimate relationship can positively impact others. For instance, the kind of intimate love a couple enjoys can fuel their energy and passion to give to others at work and in their community. A couple's faithfulness and joy in one another can also strengthen other couples' hope and commitment in sustaining and deepening their relationships. The seventh and final norm is advocacy for social justice, an active commitment to create a society where all people are affirmed in their unique contexts as sexual and relational beings and are treated as ends in themselves—subjects, not objects. Social justice also involves an obligation to take into account the common good of one's community and make sure that one's own sexual decisions do not threaten others' health or well-being.[9]

Applying Farley's Norms to College Students: Examining Equal and Mutual Sex in Greater Depth

These seven norms constitute valuable criteria for analyzing the dynamics of hookups and the broader hookup culture within a framework of justice. Farley's work has challenged my students on a personal level to articulate which criteria are negotiable and which are nonnegotiable in their own sexual and relational lives. Farley's account of just sex also aids students in brainstorming which norms ought to be upheld by all members of their college community to create a safe and just campus culture.

In class discussions over the past six years, certain key topics and points of consensus have emerged as students have analyzed Farley's account and sought to apply it to their own contexts. I have found in my last three Christian sexual ethics seminars that class discussions have been more thorough and productive when students first completed an anonymous online survey that asked them to describe equal mutual sex and unequal nonmutual sex.

Question 1: What would equal mutual sex be like?

First, in equal mutual sex, both partners would desire sex, feel comfortable communicating what they do and do not desire, and freely consent to the sexual activity that takes place:

> Equal mutual sex would look like both the girl and the guy consenting to sex and both of them being happy during the entire experience. They would both be able to voice their opinion and one person would not be dominating over the other. Also, if either of them wanted to stop at any point they would be able to and the other would not be opposed to it. (female student)

> Equal mutual sex would include clear communication and checking in on each other all the way through ("Is this okay?" "Should I keep going?" "What should I do next?"). This is desirable because you can make sure you experience exactly what you desire and how far you want to go. (female student)

Underlying equal mutual sex is a basic respect for each other, which results in an equal balance in power and results in respect for each other's sexual boundaries. No one would feel pressure to do things that made them uncomfortable and both partners could feel positive afterwards:

> Equal mutual sex is about understanding and respecting boundaries that both parties establish ahead of time—not dehumanizing or making individuals feel uncomfortable or inferior in any way, shape, or form. Overall there is just a mutual understanding, which allows both parties to be intimate with each other, yet not cross any boundaries or force any sort of sexual behavior. (male student)

> Equal mutual sex would be the best kind of sex there could be. If there were no double standards, no forced . . . sex, and no need to try to be the dominant one in sexual encounters, the sex could be really good and could result in much better consequences/emotions afterward. (female student)

Second, equal mutual sex would involve both partners caring about the other's sexual pleasure and overall experience:

> Mutual sex would be sex where both partners are intent on not only finding their own pleasure but bringing pleasure to their partner. There is an emotional and conscious understanding that neither partner has preeminence in the experience but that it is meant to be shared completely. This sex can be desirable to help their partner discover his or her best possible sexual experience. (male student)

> Equal mutual sex would occur between two people who desire to please each other sexually, not out of desperation, fear, obligation, or own self-interest, but out of selfless desire to contribute to the pleasure and joy of the other person. (female student)

Third, equal mutual sex occurs when both partners share a common understanding regarding their feelings for each other and the meaning sex has for them. Most students assumed that some emotional connection is needed for this kind of sex. They would mutually like or love each other to the degree that they feel comfortable experiencing intimacy and vulnerability:

> For totally equal mutual sex to happen, the two partners need to be exactly in the same frame of mind in regards to each other and what the sex means for them. I think it could be amazing, it is just totally dependent on the people involved and their openness regarding feelings, emotions, and motives. (female student)

> Equal mutual sex would be the result of a mutual love, affection, and respect between the parties. This would mean both parties are allowed to be entirely vulnerable with one another without the fear of reproach. This sex would truly be "making love" and not seek for individual, but mutual pleasure through love and devotion to the other that results in the most pleasurable experience possible. (female student)

Question 2: What would unequal, nonmutual sex be like?

Not surprisingly, both men and women describe unequal, nonmutual sex as unwanted or less desired by one party. First, unequal sex ranges from rape to sexually coercive tactics to a sense of pressure experienced by one person to please the other due to fear or hope for a relationship:

> People have to do things that they are uncomfortable doing. (male student)

> Unequal sex is either unwanted, unwarranted, rushed, or really in some way off balance of what it could be between two people. (female student)

Second, unequal, nonmutual sex involves one person having more power over the other. The more powerful person expresses little or no vulnerability, controls what happens during sex, and is intent on his or her own sexual pleasure:

> Unequal, nonmutual sex would be bound or disordered by desperation, fear, obligation or self-interest. It would lack vulnerability of both partners or would take advantage of the vulnerability of partners. It would be centered upon personal fulfillment and designed to "get" something from another person. (female student)

> This would be when one person forces or significantly pressures someone into engaging in a sexual activity. Many times dominance of one individual is displayed over the other. This may include one individual dehumanizing the other person. This type of sex can be very undesirable for the person who does not feel comfortable with it, but it can make the person who is forcing this type of activity feel very superior and dominant in a sexual way. (male student)

Third, according to both genders, sex is nonmutual and unequal if the partners are not "on the same page" concerning their intentions and desires for sex:

> Unequal sex can also be an instance where one participant is more invested physically while the other is more invested emotionally. If one person really likes the other person and has sex with them because of their feelings while the other person solely wants a no-strings-attached sexual encounter, they are engaging in unequal sex. (male student)

Fourth, both genders frequently associated unequal, nonmutual sex as occurring most often in the hookup context, although some acknowledged it also takes place in exclusive relationships:

> Nonmutual sex is when sexual activity occurs when one of the partners does not desire the activity to happen. This happens in hookups with acquaintances or random people. Many feel like they can't or shouldn't say no in hopes that the sexual activity might lead to a relationship and that the male partner might want to extend the hookup into a long-term relationship. It can be degrading and cause many issues of self-esteem and self-confidence as well as feeling vulnerable or weak. (male student)

> Unequal sex is all about pleasing only one person (often the male) and there is no respect between sexual partners. You just get the job done and there is no connection, because God forbid that someone "catch feelings" during a drunken hookup because it's just sex, and nothing else. It's not desirable or arousing, despite what society tells us. (female student)

After they explored what equal mutual sex and its opposite entails, I asked my students to analyze Farley's account of just sex. Specifically, did they agree that all seven norms are necessary for just sex? Could they identify additional norms that are essential for just sex? In every sexual ethics class in which I have assigned Farley's *Just Love*, the vast majority of students came to a consensus in discussions and anonymous reflections that sex cannot be just if Farley's first four norms—no unjust harm, free consent, mutuality, and equality—are violated or absent. As we will see, students debate whether commitment is essential for just sex. Four topics repeatedly surfaced in students' journal reflections and class discussions on Farley's work: (1) Can hookups be just?; (2) Is equal mutual sex desirable and/or prevalent in college (and U.S.) culture?; (3) Is just sex boring?; and (4) What kind of sex do college students actually desire? The rest of the chapter takes up these issues.

Can Hookups Be Just?

After analyzing Farley's account of just sex, one of the questions students are most interested in discussing is whether hookups can be considered just sex. To access their perspectives, I assigned a reflection paper on this question: "Can hookups be just? Why or why not? Explain your reasoning." Second, I asked students to respond anonymously to a survey question: "If you were to have a drunken hookup (including vaginal, oral, or anal sex) with an acquaintance or someone you just met that night, is it likely or unlikely that such sexual activity would be equal and mutual sex?" I wanted my students not only to engage the question abstractly but also to imagine themselves in this context and reflect on whether their hookups would likely be just.

A minority of students (18% of women and 27% of men) responded that hookups could be just if two dominant criteria were present. First, for a hookup to be just, free consent, equality, mutuality, and no unjust harm were essential:

> Yes, if they treat each other as equals with respect, no pressure, feel comfortable and safe, feel more than just a physical connection, no harm, free consent, mutuality. (female student)

> Yes, if mutuality is achieved and the hookup is not driven by lots of alcohol or social pressure and no harm is done. (male student)

When mentioning these norms, students spent the most time focusing on what conditions were needed to ensure free consent. The four most commonly cited conditions were: (1) partners would need to be sober or not "too intoxicated" to consent; (2) both partners would communicate and mutually agree about what will happen in the hookup sexually; (3) both partners would share the same expectation that no romantic relationship will result from the hookup; and (4) both partners would not be motivated to hook up due to social pressure or pressure to please the other person.

Second, many students expressed that lack of regret and feeling positive afterward is a relevant factor when determining whether a hookup is just:

> As long as you are being true to yourself and the other person, then a hookup is fine. This idea, of course, is almost never present in a hookup because most hookups take place after overconsumption of alcohol has taken place, which negates the chances of you being true to yourself or the other person involved. (male student)

Yes, if you know 100% that both will feel good and happy afterwards. (male student)

Students frequently noted that just sex is most likely to occur when one's sober self feels positive about the prospect of hooking up and anticipates positive rather than negative emotions afterward.

Interestingly, students who perceived that hookups could be just were divided about whether a just hookup would involve feelings and emotions:

A hookup, under the right conditions, could be just if the two people who do not know each other very well want to engage in a physical, spiritual, and emotional connection with another person and keep the best interests for their selves and each other at heart. (male student)

Yes, a hookup could be just if it's mutual and they can completely leave out emotion, then one will not be more vulnerable than the other. (female student)

When asked to imagine themselves experiencing a drunken hookup in the anonymous survey, a minority of students (30% of men and 11% of women) perceived that their drunken hookup would likely be equal and mutual. An additional 13% of women responded that whether or not a hookup is just depends on certain circumstances.

Most men in this group expressed that their hookup would be just because they are confident that they have self-control over their sexual desires when drunk and/or they want sex to be mutually pleasurable and would not force women to do unwanted sexual activities:

This is a tough situation for me to imagine for myself, but I think that even the drunken version of myself would value equality and mutuality. I think that I do a good job of controlling myself, even under the influence. (male student)

Other men in this group qualify their positive response by acknowledging that it is hard to tell whether sex is equal and mutual when there is alcohol or a lack of communication involved:

If I were in that situation, I think it is likely to be mutual, but sometimes it can be hard to tell without talking about it. (male student)

Although I would like to think that any hookup I would have would be mutual, it is impossible to read another person's mind well while drunk. It is also harder if the person is a stranger and finding the emotional connection that can add to sex would not happen. (male student)

Women who believed their drunken hookup would likely be equal and mutual perceived themselves as having strong boundaries and refusing to engage in unwanted sexual activities:

I think that it likely would be, but that's just because I have no problem saying no to something I don't want to do. I worry for those girls who are so easily influenced by men and want to feel accepted so badly that they would do anything, even blame themselves for unwanted sexual experiences. (female student)

Similarly, 13% of women responded that whether or not their drunken hookup would be just depends on the following conditions being met: (1) that both partners are not "too" drunk; (2) that the woman clearly communicates her desires and boundaries; and (3) that the man respects her desires and boundaries:

In today's society, it is easy to say that equal and mutual sex would be unlikely. However, in all of my cases, I have been lucky enough to have been with guys that respected me and what I wanted. They never did anything I wasn't comfortable with. So the sexual activity was mutual and equal. (female student)

It depends how drunk you are and who you are with. If you didn't know them and were both pretty drunk, I think it could turn into unequal sex. (female student)

In contrast to those who affirmed the possibility of a just hookup, the majority of students (81% of women and 68% of men)[10] perceived that hookups in reality fail to be just. When imagining themselves in a drunken hookup context, 67% of men and 74% of women perceived that it was very unlikely that their drunken hookup would be equal and mutual. Analysis of students' responses revealed four specific reasons they believe such hookups fail to be just. First, this group of students doubts it is possible for mutual respect, equality, free consent, and mutuality to be present in a hookup. They point out that the vast majority of hookups occur between two drunk people. Alcohol makes it impossible to tell whether the other person can meaningfully consent to the hookup, and being drunk often undermines decision-making that coheres with one's comfort level:

> A lack of sobriety leads to someone being taken advantage of, even if consent was given prior to drunkenness. Things may come up that were not consented to prior to sobriety that one would feel horrible about later. (female student)

> It is highly unlikely that a drunken hookup could be considered equal and mutual. First off, the fact that both I and the woman would be intoxicated makes it very difficult for us to truly articulate our motivations for the hookup. I feel that a casual hookup could potentially meet the definition of an equal and mutual sexual experience under the right circumstances, but once alcohol is thrown into the mix it becomes extremely difficult to meet the definition. (male student)

Second, in addition to being drunk, hookup partners do not know each other well, which makes them less motivated or comfortable with communication:

> In hookups, there can be confusion and blurred lines when it comes to mutuality and equality and respect for each person's humanity. It is not common for hookup partners to really talk about what they want, what they need, and how they are feeling about the situation. (female student)

> It is very unlikely that this would be mutual sex because often hookups occur when people do not have the strongest feeling for each other. This causes people to just go through the motions of sex which in our day and age is getting the guy to his finishing point and then it ends . . . not caring for the girl's pleasure. (female student)

> The fact that there is no deeper emotional connection between us would mean that the sex is unlikely to be equal and mutual as we would be unlikely to communicate effectively with each other. (male student)

Some men were explicit that since hookup partners don't really know or feel anything for their partner, there is little incentive or sense of obligation to strive for equality and mutuality in a hookup. The lack of a prior relationship with one's hookup partner combined with a lack of negative consequences after unequal, nonmutual sex also fuels exploitation of the other person:

> In a hookup, the sexual activity would be extremely skewed in terms of mutual sex. The possibility of negative ramifications resulting from nonmutual sex are so low that one person is almost always going to take advantage of another person because there was no sort of prior relationship. I think both parties do not really owe each other anything, which poses a great risk for unequal sex. (male student)

Third, students argue that hookups are unjust because the very point of a hookup is to prioritize and elevate one's own agenda. The other person therefore undeniably becomes a means (whether for sexual satisfaction, a boost in self-esteem or ego, or increased social status), never only an end. Hookups are clearly not about affirming the other person or about being affirmed for who you are:

> During hookups, you are not being yourself and fostering growth within yourself, you are doing the opposite because you are with someone who you don't know and someone who you cannot be fully vulnerable with. Many times during a one-time hookup, a person is self-conscious and uncomfortable. In contrast, when you are having sex with someone who is of significance to you, you are able to be yourself and not worry about fulfilling expectations and impressing the other person. (female student)

> When you engage in a drunken hookup, it is generally about fulfilling your own sexual desire. (male student)

Echoing the undergraduate ethnographers' analyses of their college party scene, students at University B repeated the common theme that hookup sex is mostly nonmutual "guy" sex: it's usually focused on women satisfying men's sexual preferences and desires:

> Most sex in the hookup culture is dominated by the male and is "male sex." (female student)

> Drunken hookups are usually not equal and mutual. I think they are more than likely benefiting the man. The girl wants to prove that she is willing to do anything for the guy and usually guys don't care much about the girl's pleasure if they are being pleasured. (female student)

Many women express that they often feel pressure to please the male to avoid a bad reputation or negative labels like being labeled a "prude" or a "bitch":

> In terms of sexuality, many women feel as though they cannot say no to males, or they don't want to make the male feel bad if they are uncomfortable with a situation. I think that women may also perform certain sexual acts, for example a blow job, even if they don't want to because they don't want to be labeled as stiff and they want their partner to be happy with the experience so they don't get a bad reputation. A lot of times I think it can be easier for women to just be submissive and let the male do whatever [he] please[s] even if [she] may be uncomfortable. (female student)

> It is unlikely that hookups will be equal and mutual. My most recent hookups have been with a person who I try to please. My greatest concern is making the other person feel as good as possible and not caring if I receive anything. A perfect example is something I said while hooking up with someone: "Can't tonight just be all about you?" It was my way of trying not to have sex but still pleasing the other person. (female student)

> If the hookup was with an acquaintance or someone I had just met, it would definitely not be equal and mutual, especially if I was drunk. I think I would have felt very pressured to "put out" or else risk being labeled a prude, a tease, or risk flat-out being raped. (female student)

Social science research on hookups confirms most students' assessments that hookup sex is unjust because it frequently lacks equality, mutuality, and/or free consent, and that it is fundamentally about using another person as a means for one's own benefit. Studies consistently indicate that many women experience disrespect by hookup partners and perceive that their male partners treat them like a sex object to be used and discarded.[11] Women's accounts that hookup sex tends to be nonmutual, focusing on male pleasure, also finds much support in the literature.[12] Much research indicates that sexual mutuality is expected in relationships but not hook-ups, owing to a sexual double standard in which men are praised for sexual promiscuity while women who pursue hookups are denigrated. Armstrong et al. state:

> A challenge to the contemporary sexual double standard would mean defending the position that young women and men are equally entitled to sexual activity, sexual pleasure, and sexual respect in hookups as well as relationships. To achieve this, the attitudes and practices of both men and women need to be confronted. Men should be challenged to treat even first hookup partners as gener-ously as the women they hook up with treat them.[13]

Fourth, many students express in their anonymous responses that it is highly unlikely, if not impossible, that equal mutual sex will occur while hooking up because the party and hookup culture is predicated on a funda-mental inequality between the genders. Students express that social pres-sure to conform to current masculine and feminine norms makes it easy to treat others and themselves unjustly. Being emotional, getting attached to someone, or not having sex all undermine masculinity:

> As a male, I say our sense of self is unjustly hindered. We undercut our emotions and sensations at every turn in order to fulfill society's promotion of masculinity. Men cannot allow themselves to openly experience the emotions that we were gifted with. We are allowed to experience anger, lust, and happiness—all on different levels. But when emotions such as sadness creep into view, we must stifle them before they are shown. (male student)

> Men are seen as emotionless statues who want nothing but to have dominating sex with just about any woman they can find. I feel like men treat themselves unjustly because they are constantly being questioned about their manhood by nearly everyone, including themselves. (male student)

> I cannot help but feel that men have denied the emotional part of their personality to such an extent that women have been affected negatively. One of the root causes of disrespectful treatment of women lies within the insecurities of men. When men want to appear particularly virile, they tend to be somewhat reclusive and standoffish.

This extends to all parts of their lives, including their relationships with women. When men cannot conceive of being vulnerable they do not enjoy the idea of having a close and committed relationship. This inevitably leads to men trying to fulfill their sexual desires in casual sexual encounters that have the propensity to harm women physically and psychologically. If Christian colleges wish to instill a mindset of respect toward women there should be a focus on telling men that it is acceptable to emote a little bit. (male student)

A common theme among women is that they likewise dismiss their authentic selves and/or desires and tolerate unjust treatment in order to conform to the dominant, sexy, feminine, beauty ideals that promote self-objectification:

Women have such a hard time expressing themselves sexually on their own terms because they are in constant fear of not impressing the men and not being seen as desirable. We are giving men the right to treat us as sexual creatures. (female student)

Women are embracing as well as internalizing their role as sex objects. If women are treating themselves as sex objects, they are selling themselves short as human beings. Until men and women can both be secure in their own sexuality without basing it solely on cultural expectations, sex and relationships will continue to have unjust characteristics. (female student)

Many women comment on how being immersed in this culture that privileges male sexual pleasure erodes women's self-esteem:

If someone is repeatedly acting in a way that makes them feel uncomfortable just for the pleasure of another human being, it can eat away at them and make them feel like an object and not a human. The ultimate way someone can act unjustly, whether it is sexually or in day-to-day actions, is to be untrue to themselves. When someone is untrue to himself or herself, they are following the crowds, stereotypes, and trends pretending to be someone they are not. (female student)

Hookup culture does affect a person's ability to reach fulfillment because all that rejection really takes a toll on a person's self-esteem.

For example, if a girl hooks up with multiple guys without receiving love or care from them, she will begin to feel like she doesn't deserve those things. I have literally seen this happen. Her self-worth stoops so low she thinks all she has to offer is her body. It is sad; I hate this culture. (female student)

Furthermore, since both men and women are competing to meet the masculine or sexy feminine ideal, they treat others unjustly by putting them down and ridiculing them so they appear better than their competition:

Men struggle with being called sissies if they are not having sex. (male student)

Guys face the fear of being labeled a "pussy" by his friends and the fear of being labeled a "pussy" plays a huge role in the construction of his relationships. In relationships, a guy's friends can prove to be his worst enemies at times. (male student)

Women ridicule each other for our sexual behaviors and are constantly judging one another for our actions, dress, makeup, and even hair. (female student)

When women call each other names, there is a state of jealousy. When women get jealous of someone they do not like they use terms such as "bitch," "slut," "whore," etc. When women cannot meet these standards, their self-esteem becomes significantly low and they can become depressed with themselves. (female student)

Such masculine and feminine norms reinforce inequality among college men and women in the sexual social sphere:

Mutuality and equality cannot survive in this culture that emphasizes such power imbalances between genders. Hookups are meant to be a one-time deal, and there is definitely no concern for the wholeness of the other person. (female student)

Hookup culture is doing nothing but degrading men's views of women and women's views of themselves. My female friends desire relationships so they go out in search of a boyfriend. They end up hooking up with a guy and are disappointed when they don't get a call or a text back. Eventually this lack of response becomes normal and they begin to not expect anything to come from these hookups. They start to feel like hooking up is supposed to be like this and at least the guy wants them in that moment. They think that moment is all that they are worth. Hookup culture is a vicious, endless cycle. Once a person is caught up in it they have a very difficult time getting out. Intimacy becomes near impossible because they are so used to rejection they are unable to open up to anyone, even if someone down the road genuinely cares for them. (female student)

As noted in chapter 3, much research corroborates these students' perceptions that hookups tend to be unequal, nonmutual, and often nonconsensual because of the power dynamics of party and hookup culture that perpetuate gender inequality.

Is Equal Mutual Sex Desirable and Prevalent in College (and U.S.) Culture?

When students were asked to describe equal mutual sex, unequal nonmutual sex, and drunken hookups, a dominant theme that emerged among both men and women is that unequal nonmutual sex is the norm among their generation. Exploring the cultural factors that fuel their behavior, men reported the following:

Mutual equal sex is when both people give themselves fully and both sides are on a level playing field. I feel like this is what we all seek naturally, but some cultural messages are toxic for our expectations, which clouds our intentions. This results in unequal sex. (male student)

Unequal, nonmutual sex is not preferable, but it occurs when harmful messages are ground into our minds. These harmful messages value dominance over equality and are found in the porn industry. (male student)

I have noticed that very few relationships in my age group are based on equality. I think that most of the time we see that one party dominates the relationship and the other party is submissive. The main reason behind the phenomenon is that either one or both parties have not fully developed their identity so they don't know what their values and priorities are. (male student)

Women, who similarly conveyed the prevalence of unequal, nonmutual sex among college students, were much more likely to reflect further about the extent to which equal mutual sex is even possible or attainable:

> To me, equal mutual sex is unimaginable. It's totally desirable, but to me, this is something untouchable and almost unattainable. I hope that's it real, but I don't know if it is. (female student)

> Equal mutual sex would be where both the man and woman want to pleasure one another and they're willing to give themselves completely to the other person. This also means completely trusting the other person, and therefore not being nervous or ashamed or self-conscious of anything. I think it's something that's desirable, but people don't know that it's out there and that it is possible to have. (female student)

> I think a lot of people find equal mutual sex to be unattainable, but upon attaining it in my own relationship, I would never want anything else ever again. (female student)

Women also express that, in such a competitive social reality, many women are willing to trade sexual pleasure and satisfaction for temporary companionship, approval, and affection:

> Of course unequal, nonmutual sex isn't as desirable as equal sex, but it's tough because I'm sure it occurs more often between people in our age group. Why? People want love. People want acceptance. People want sex. People want companionship. But they can't have it all, so some things have to give. And sometimes sex is that thing. (female student)

> Nonmutual sex occurs when the sex is all about one person. It is meant to make them feel the most pleasure and the other person is often disregarded as just a tool in the sex. I think that this kind of sex is very undesirable because this kind of sex more times than not favors men. Being a woman, this is not desirable for me. This kind of sex would be anal sex; it would be getting the guy to orgasm but not

the girl. I think this kind of sex occurs more frequently than mutual sex and it is sad because one person always loses out. (female student)

Although more research is needed to determine the prevalence of equal mutual sex among college students, my students' reflections suggest that it remains relatively rare—at least in the hookup scene.

Is Just Sex Boring?

After apparent gains in gender equality over the past decades (in the workforce, education, politics, collegiate sports, etc.), why have so many students settled for a social reality where equal mutual sex appears to be the exception? We have explored a number of reasons for undergraduates' sexual choices throughout this book, and now we might add another: Could there be a widespread notion that equal mutual sex is boring? I still remember the first time a student raised this question. My class was fleshing out what it would actually mean to have sex in an equal mutual context when a student named Sara asked: "But . . . wouldn't that kind of sex be boring? Would it really be arousing?" Silence filled the room for a moment and then other students began nodding their heads and agreeing.

While students struggled to articulate what exactly made just sex boring, there was a sense that "spicing up" sex involved a dynamic of domination/submission. I then wrote a claim on the whiteboard: "Our culture ethicizes equality but eroticizes inequality." I asked students to write an anonymous reflection about cultural ideas, factors, and social practices that either support or dispute this claim. It turned out that no one in my class sections disputed the idea that our culture eroticizes inequality and violence. Some pointed out that even the colloquial terms they use to refer to sex imply domination, aggression, and violence. As one woman wrote, "The terms 'screw,' 'fuck,' 'bang,' 'do,' and 'nail' are all used by young people when referring to the physical act of sexual intercourse. Although each detail on its own does not seem powerful, the overall combination is strikingly significant."

Among cultural influences that eroticize and normalize sexual inequality, domination, and violence, students mentioned pornography most frequently in their journal reflections and in class discussions. Students preparing for their upcoming group research presentation on porn pointed out that the majority of online heterosexual porn is characterized as gonzo porn, a form of aggressive and violent body-punishing sex that degrades and humiliates women.[14] Viewing porn has consistently been associated with problems including poorer sexual functioning, relationship dissatisfaction, religious and spiritual concerns, increased negative emotions (e.g., shame, guilt, and loneliness), aggression, occupational problems, legal problems, and sexual deviancy.[15] Research indicates that online porn greatly influences teens and young adults' sexual expectations, patterns of arousal, sexual preferences, and sexual behavior. Consumption of porn affects the kind of sex that teenagers and young adults desire and experience. For instance, consuming porn is also associated with higher rates of risky sexual behavior and anal sex. Viewing pornography has been associated with (1) a decreased interest in relational sexual intimacy; (2) an increase in egocentric sexual practices aimed at personal pleasure and with little regard to the pleasure of the engaging partner; (3) an increase in the belief that sexual satisfaction can be obtained without affection or emotional attachment; and (4) an increase in the belief that relationships are sexually confining.[16] It is worth noting that the very same beliefs, attitudes, and practices constantly appear in students' analyses of hookup culture.

My students' attribution of our cultural eroticization of sexual inequality, domination, and violence is corroborated by many studies linking pornography use to an increase in the acceptance of rape myths.[17] Rape myths consist of attitudes and beliefs that function to deny the problem of sexual violence, justify male sexual aggression against women, and blame victims for sexual assault. Common rape myths include the following: (1) women incite men to be sexually aggressive by what they wear or how they act; (2) women are "teases" who want to be coerced into sex; (3) rape occurs spontaneously because men, once aroused, cannot control their impulses and pass a point of "no return;" and (4) if a woman really did not want the sexual assault to occur, she could have fought off her attacker. Rape myth acceptance can also include adversarial sexual beliefs and an underlying hostile attitude toward women that fosters a sense of easily being slighted by women or viewing them as "teases" who either "secretly" want to be coerced into sex, or else "deserve" it.[18]

Men, after watching a coercive sex scene, were more likely to espouse rape myths. Women who view violent pornography, with its coupling of intercourse and aggression, also have distorted views about rape including increased victim blame and decreased assignment of responsibility to male sexual assault perpetrators.[19] For men, porn use also led to an increased desensitization toward violence against women, and increased motivation to act aggressively toward women. Porn consumption frequently functions like a drug in which consumers need more domination/violence (spicier forbidden themes) in sex to get aroused and experience an orgasm.[20] Porn use has consistently been identified as a risk factor for sexual assault; men who frequently view pornography report a stronger behavioral intent to rape.[21]

Of course, college students (and the rest of us) do not need to watch porn to "breathe in" the eroticization of inequality in sex; inevitable exposure to advertising images, pop culture, music, TV, movies, social media, and romance novels also eroticize inequality and domination. From 2003 to 2012, I asked the students in my courses to bring in a picture from a magazine that appeared erotic. We were all struck by the lack of diversity in the images they collected: nearly always they portrayed either a thin, scantily clad, and well-endowed woman with a "come hither" look or a domination/subordination theme between men and women. The most common image students brought to class semester after semester was the Dolce & Gabbana ad of four men standing over a prone woman. This ad and many others like it clearly intimates and eroticizes domination and violence toward women.

In my classes, students also watched and discussed the video Dreamworlds 3, which analyzes how heterosexual male pornographic imagination constructs the dominant story of masculinity and femininity that pervades our media and commercial culture. Producer Sut Jhally argues that music videos relentlessly and powerfully repeat this pornographic story, encouraging us to "think of women as being defined only through their sexuality and that sexuality [is] to be at the service of men's desires."[22] Jhally notes: "Examining the stories that music videos tell us about both male and female sexuality, about what is considered normal . . . gives us a way to think about how the culture in general teaches us to be men and women."[23]

In their writings and class discussions, students frequently mentioned how works of popular fiction, especially romance novels or series like Twilight and 50 Shades of Grey, are premised on female protagonists in love and attracted to men who are physically violent during sex and/or men who are constantly in danger of losing control and even killing them. These books exemplify and normalize popular eroticization of inequality and violence for young girls and suburban moms alike. As one student wrote, "Popular culture thrives on stories like Fifty Shades of Grey, in which Anastasia Steele is physically beaten—to her overwhelming satisfaction—during sexual intercourse." According to many scholars, the degree of inequality and sexual violence eroticized in novels, movies, and porn has increased over the last twenty years as pornographic images and themes have become so mainstream that even children's advertising, clothing, and toys have become increasingly sexualized.[24] Constructing a pornographic sexual narrative of the erotic that links sexual pleasure and arousal to the dynamic of domination and submission creates a culture in which sexual violence and other forms of harm are normalized. Eroticizing inequality reinforces unjust traditional gender stereotypes, and makes them appear normal and natural.

The Eroticization of Unequal Sex in Western Culture

The social construction of the erotic as unequal, dominating, and violent sex is not a recent phenomenon, of course, so blame cannot rest simply with the global porn industry and the widespread dissemination of pornified media images on the Internet. Since at least ancient Greece and Rome, Western culture has eroticized inequality and the domination and subordination dynamic in sex. The construction of masculinity has been deeply rooted in being the active, dominant actor while norms of femininity have relegated women to the passive, subordinate role in sex. Cristina Traina notes that inequality in sexuality has not only been normalized but also "moralized" as right and good:

> In the West sexuality has been the field upon which socially approved, gendered relationships of domination and subordination have been enacted, reinforced, and symbolized. For nearly all of recorded Western history, inequality was a central criterion for the morality of sexual relationships. Western culture sexualized power; sex was always already about domination and submission; and domination and submission were always already gendered. The logical consequence is that in traditional Western sexual culture domination has been essential to male sexual arousal and satisfaction; penetrative domination and receptive submission have been undisputed elements of sexual relations.... Sex has been defined in reference to dominant males' arousal and satisfaction patterns.[25]

Students' responses and porn research clearly indicate that the domination/subordination dynamic continues to be a key aspect for many men's sexual arousal. The reality that many women are experiencing hookup sex rather than their version of the most arousing and pleasurable kind of sex (equal, mutual, emotionally connected sex) indicates that sex—at least the sex frequently occurring in hookups and celebrated in popular culture—continues to be defined "in reference to dominant males' arousal and satisfaction patterns."

Furthermore, the eroticizing of inequality and violence manifests itself in racism throughout U.S. history. As a way to better understand this history, my students study Foucault's philosophy of power, Kelly Brown Douglas's scholarship on racism and sexuality, Miguel De la Torre's analysis of patriarchy and Western colonialism, and Marvin Ellison's writings on erotic justice.[26] Particularly valuable is their analysis of the ways that narratives of sexuality, gender, race, and class are constructed by dominant social groups to justify their own privileges and power.

Foucault argues that the most effective forms of social power and domination operating in modern society do not originate from a centralized force that employs direct coercion and oppression (i.e., a government and/or political leader), but function in productive and disciplinary ways. Foucault views the history of human cultures as a struggle between social groups vying for domination. At stake in this struggle for domination is the power to construct the dominant story about the "truth" of reality and humanity (power as productive), and by extension the "truth" or dominant story about social groups' sexuality and bodies. Foucault argues that controlling a person's or social group's perception of their sexuality and bodies is a particularly effective way of affecting their self-concept and self-esteem, and in turn their agency and self-realization. He analyzes how the body is constructed and how subjects are formed by the stories of dominant social groups throughout different historical periods. He calls these stories "power-knowledge discourses." Discourses are "ways of constituting knowledge, [and] together with the social practices . . . are more than ways of thinking and producing meaning. They constitute the 'nature' of the body, unconscious and conscious mind and emotional life of the subjects they seek to govern."[27] These dominant discourses are disseminated through a variety of social institutions (i.e., education, religion, law, and politics). Since these discourses create ideals and norms, power functions in a disciplinary way. As Kelly Brown Douglas notes:

> Power . . . exercises constraints over the body and conscience of individuals. It compels people to behave in certain ways. It obliges them to adhere to certain societal and personal standards, that is, norms,

rules, regulations, values, and more. This kind of power rewards those who do adhere to these standards by integrating them into the mainstream of society. It grants them at least the opportunity to secure all the rights and privileges of the "bourgeois." Those who are judged as nonconforming do not merit inclusion into society's mainstream. Instead, they are ostracized, alienated, marginalized, and even punished through legal and extralegal methods.[28]

Drawing on Foucault's account of power and sexuality, Douglas argues similarly that one of the most effective ways to disempower and denigrate a social group's collective identity is to attack or denigrate their sexuality and bodies:

> Power can be exerted over a people through careful regulation of their bodies, their perceptions of their bodies, and their reproductive capacities. Such regulation and hence exercise of power can be achieved through the conscientious deployment of sexuality, manipulating how persons view their sexuality, primarily through discourse.... An attack upon people's sexuality becomes important, then, because sexuality implies one's very humanity. It involves a person's self-image, specifically the way an individual defines her or his femininity or masculinity and the way a person regards her or his physiognomy.[29]

Historically, for instance, elite whites in the United States created a dominant narrative about the differences between white and black sexuality and bodies. Denigrating and demonizing black persons' sexuality and bodies legitimized slavery and subsequent social and economic oppression of African Americans. Variations of this dehumanizing narrative and resulting stereotypes still pervade dominant U.S. culture.[30] For instance, *Dreamworlds 3* analyzes the dominant story in music videos about African Americans. Hip-hop videos depict black women's sexuality and bodies as objects in the service of men's desires, as prostitutes and strippers, those whose bodies can be bought and controlled by men. As viewers watch clips of Nelly's *Tip Drill* video, Sut Jhally narrates, "Women's bodies are there to solely please men and be under their control, to be bought and sold like so many pieces of meat. Here a woman's body is used to swipe a credit card and indeed the term 'tip drill' signifies women who will allow man after man to have sex with her for money."[31] Furthermore, music videos perpetuate the same racist stereotypes of black men constructed by whites since slavery: "Black men in mainstream rap and hip-hop videos are largely presented as violent, savage, criminal, and drunken thugs interested in molesting and insulting any female that happens to be around."[32] Jhally cautions his viewers:

> We have to remember that these representations do not reflect the reality of African-American masculinity but how someone has chosen to represent it at this point in history. As such, they constituted the most racist set of images found in decades in American media and resemble most closely D. W. Griffith's 1915 white supremacist film *The Birth of a Nation* where blacks are portrayed as irresponsible, drunken buffoons and as out of control, lust-filled rapists of white women.[33]

Dreamworlds challenges us to ask why media corporations (run mostly by wealthy white males) choose to portray black masculinity and black femininity (and femininity overall) in such denigrating, dehumanizing ways. Who benefits most from these images—economically, politically, and socially?

In the same spirit, Miguel De La Torre analyzes how, since colonialism, white wealthy heterosexual males have constructed a dominant narrative about "real men" that has functioned to legitimize their privileges while casting all other social groups (such as women, men of color, and LGBTQ persons) as less than human and inferior. As De La Torre notes: "The construction of race and its eroticization is so woven into white America's identity that it has become normalized in the way many whites have been taught by their culture to see bodies of color."[34]

Another obvious contemporary example of the eroticization of racial inequality is the porn industry, which brazenly perpetuates historical dehumanizing stereotypes of black male and female sexuality and bodies, and legally profits from the vicious sexual abuse of female black bodies. As Gail Dines notes, while extremely blatant examples of racist images that denigrate and dehumanize African Americans in the mainstream media have become less acceptable, the porn industry "gets away with a level of racism that is breathtaking in its contempt and loathing of people of color."[35]

Similarly, Christian ethicist Marvin Ellison insightfully captures how easy it is for both men and women to internalize the eroticization of inequality (found in racism, sexism, and classism) and experience domination/subordination and actual injustice as pleasurable:

> The moral problematic about sexuality in this culture is that racist patriarchy annexes body pleasure and attaches it to injustice. Many people find themselves erotically aroused only by dominant/subordinate power relations. They accept these patterns as normative and entirely natural.[36]

Ellison argues that, to the extent that men and women experience domination and subordination as sexually pleasurable, they more easily internalize injustice at a bodily and psychological level and accept their own or others' oppression:

> If we fail to see how patriarchal eroticism has electrified injustice and made it titillating, we will not grasp why so many people manage to rest comfortably with oppression, their own and that of others. Why is it that people not only tolerate injustice, but do so with smiles on their faces? Could it be that injustice corrupts at the body level and, therefore, at the core of our personhood?[37]

Foucault's, Douglas's, and De la Torre's analysis of power and Ellison's insight that we feel, internalize and replicate power inequalities in and through our bodies may help to shed light on why so many college men and women can perpetuate injustices in their sexual, embodied party lives and do so "with smiles on their faces," while they simultaneously value equality and justice in other areas of their lives.

What Kind of Sex Do College Students Actually Desire?

Given these cultural factors that create and tragically reduce our social imaginary of the erotic to domination/subordination sex, Sara's frank and courageous question about whether equal and mutual "ethical" sex would be boring challenges students to examine more deeply what kind of sex they actually desire and find arousing. As a way to generate honest responses to Sara's question, my classes decided the best strategy would be to construct an anonymous survey that all three sections of my course would complete. After brainstorming, students decided to include the following three questions:

1. Do you think equal mutual sex is desirable and arousing, or alternatively undesirable and boring? Explain your reasoning.
2. Do you think unequal, nonmutual sex is desirable and arousing, or alternatively undesirable and boring? Explain your reasoning.
3. In what context do you think you are most likely to have the most pleasurable sexual experience? (a) sex in a hookup with an acquaintance/stranger; (b) sex in a hookup with repeat hookup partner; (c) sex in a hookup with a friend; (d) sex in a relationship during the first three months; (e) sex in a committed relationship of four or more months; and (f) sex in marriage.

In response to the first question, 42% of men expressed that equal mutual sex is desirable and arousing:

> This sex would be the most desirable sex, and I can personally say that it is more arousing and desirable than hookup sex. Equal and mutual sex is when you truly care about the person that you are with and are able to open up to them. You are able to express yourself and be true to yourself which in turn allows you to be true to the other person. (male student)

> Equal mutual sex happens when both partners are concerned about each other's experience and there is good communication during sex. It is most likely to happen when both partners take their time and don't rush. It also helps to show affection after the act instead of immediately stopping. This kind of sex is desirable because it serves to foster intimacy between partners and reaffirms that they can be vulnerable around one another and trust each other. (male student)

> The obstacles to mutual sex start largely before we get to the bed. I am picturing an ideal world where, rather than males needing to persuade females to have sex with them (and females deciding whether or not to "give it up") two people engage in coitus because they have a connection and want to be more intimate with each other. In my world there could still be "hookups" but there would be no such thing as making a sexy-time with somebody you didn't genuinely care about or WERE NOT ATTRACTED TO ON A PERSONAL LEVEL.

I shout because that sounds like a utopia and it shouldn't be that hard to achieve—two people who have a genuine connection and attraction to each other's personalities wanting to explore their relationship by having an intimate physical, emotional, and spiritual experience together. (male student)

According to this group of men, mutual desire, intimacy, care for the other, and/or emotional connection create the most desirable and arousing sexual experience. Another group of men (25%) responded that both equal mutual sex and unequal, nonmutual sex can be desirable and arousing:

Equal and mutual sex would be an act between two people who are both completely invested in the act they are doing together. Both parties of the sexual encounter would both be fully gratified and fulfilled from the encounter and would not be left with any remorse or disappointment after having sex. This type of sex is very desirable, especially in a committed relationship. The word *arousing* to me has more of a physical connotation, so this kind of sex seems a little less arousing than unequal nonmutual sex—mostly because it focuses on the mental and emotional connection between two people just as much as the physical pleasure. (male student)

Some men are turned on by a woman that is powerful or a woman that is submissive. While these can be bad things if a man tries to overpower a woman who doesn't want to be submissive, it can work if they talk about it and figure out what is the most pleasurable for them. (male student)

The rest of the men (33%) did not answer the question and instead simply described equal mutual sex. It is thus difficult to attain a clear understanding of men's desires and experience of arousal in the context of equal mutual sex. The 33% who did not answer the question may have avoided it because they felt uncomfortable acknowledging to others or themselves that equal mutual sex did not seem arousing or desirable. Alternatively, they could simply have not read the question carefully. Research affirming a positive relationship between men's exposure to the eroticization of inequality found in porn and other mainstream media and their desires and preferences for these sexual behaviors suggests that many men experience ambivalent desires when it comes to just sex.

As for women, 100% affirmed that equal mutual sex is desirable and arousing and preferred this kind of sex, describing it as the "most awesome," "best," and "most pleasurable" sex they could experience. They offered one or more of the following reasons why this kind of sex is most desirable: (1) when both persons want to have sex and mutually participate, the sex is more satisfying and pleasurable; (2) mutual sexual pleasure is more desirable and arousing than sex that focuses on the satisfaction of one partner; (3) the emotional connection and shared vulnerability present in equal, mutual sex create the most desirable and arousing kind of sex; (4) feeling known and loved for who you are makes equal mutual sex the most desirable, arousing, and pleasurable:

> Equal mutual sex would be incredibly desirable and arousing. There would be an equal level of commitment which would result in total vulnerability with one another. (female student)

> In equal mutual sex, both sides know that the other really wants to have sex. They know this because they asked each other before they reached the bed. They have mutual interest for each other. They have seen each other naked many times before and they not only extremely like the other's body but their personality and everything else about them makes them happy. They hold each other's hands. They kiss each other. They touch each other in a loving way. This kind of sex is desirable because it makes one feel secure. It makes both people feel like they are wanted not only in physical ways but in emotional ways also. There is no pressure and worry in the kind of performance that the other wants from the other. They are both comfortable and do what they want to please the other and themselves. (female student)

> Mutual sex would be between two people who love and care about each other and are willing to give themselves fully to one another. Mutual sex shares a deeper connection emotionally, which makes the sex more desirable and arousing. (female student)

> I think that equal mutual sex would result in a very pleasurable orgasm because you are in love with the person and are not just focused on the physical aspect of things and performing well. I think it is very desirable and arousing, because you have more than just a physical connection; you also connect on other levels and

feel comfortable with each other outside of that moment. (female student)

A key theme in their reflections is that feeling mutual trust, emotional connection, and/or love allows you to enjoy and take pleasure in the sexual experience because you feel less pressure and are less concerned about your sexual performance and doing what is expected:

> Equal sex would give you one of the most secure feelings. If both people are just focused on the other person and loving that one person, he/she would feel so loved that they would not be worried about body image, performance, or any of that extra stuff. (female student)

> Well, I know what equal mutual sex is like, and it's very exciting. There are no pressures to meet standards or make sure that you are satisfying the other person so you can keep them around, it's much more open and more fun that way. (female student)

> Equal mutual sex is a very desirable and arousing form of sex. It occurs when two people develop a trust and respect for both themselves and their partner and together choose to share the most vulnerable intimate aspect of their being with them. As scary as being vulnerable is, it is also thrilling. Risks are thrilling and therefore, risking oneself in sex with another person would be exciting. (female student)

> I have had a lot of experience with sex, in a long-term relationship, before a relationship started, in long-term hookups (fuck-buddies), and in one-night stands. Sex with a person that you know, who has the same desire for you that you have for them, and you both have a desire for a long term relationship is the best sex I've experienced. There is no worry about the after-effects. You aren't worried about who they are going to tell or anything else. (female student)

Even those women in the minority group of students who affirmed that hookups could be just elaborated that just hookups were nevertheless not as good as the sex that takes place in a relationship:

> It is likely that hookups can be mutual, but it's just that it's not the most pleasurable for both people, and there isn't that complete

trust there—it's more for the "action" and getting the quick pleasure without having the feelings involved. (female student)

The sexual activity in my hookups were mutual and equal. But they
are not as good as being in a relationship, because relationships
bring intimacy and so many more intense emotions. Hookups are
just physical, even if they are equal and mutual. (female student)

While some women expressed that their own experiences leave no doubt
that equal mutual sex is most desirable, others expressed dissatisfaction
that their sexual experiences thus far have only consisted of unequal,
nonmutual sex:

Equal mutual sex is wanted and desired by both parties. There is
a mutual respect and selflessness. This would bring the ultimate,
satisfying sex. I would prefer this sex over hookup sex. But I do not
know how to love myself . . . and that makes this kind of sex unat-
tainable. (female student)

What I have been experiencing—drunk hookup sex with someone
I rarely talk to during the day—is unequal, nonmutual sex. At the
moment it feels great; however, it requires a lot of work and usually
leads to embarrassment the next day or even week. However, I still
end up engaging in this cycle. (female student)

Similarly, students' answers to the second question about whether
unequal, nonmutual sex is desirable and/or arousing revealed stark
gender differences. While 25% of men did not answer the question
directly, 42% expressed that unequal, nonmutual sex is undesirable or
not preferable:

I have experienced unequal, nonmutual sex. It sucks. Despite the
injustice and inequality it brings to the relationship, it is hard to
relate to somebody when you don't see them as your equal or they
don't see you as their equal. Even in a nonsexual relationship, it
would be unsatisfying. The idea of somebody being greater than
me makes me uncomfortable and feel inferior; it is not a pleasant
feeling to feel inferior. The idea of feeling superior to somebody is
lonely, that might be worse. To be quite honest, it's a total boner-
killer. (male student)

Undesirable, because I do not think sex would be good if both members were not into it. I think that sex would be so much better if both sides were all in. On top of that, the consequences of such actions would dampen the spirits of the event. (male student)

I feel that today's society recognizes that unequal, nonmutual sexual experiences may have some detriments, but overall it seems to accept them and still views them as acceptable. I myself find these types of sex to be very undesirable. (male student)

The remaining 33% of men affirmed that unequal, nonmutual sex can be desirable and/or arousing:

This type of sex can be very undesirable for the person who does not feel comfortable with it, but it can make the person who is forcing this type of activity feel very superior and dominant in a sexual/erotic way. (male student)

In general, this type of sex is undesirable because it leaves one party wanting and has so much potential to have negative effects on relationships. But there could be instances where unequal sex is sought because a partner wants to focus on the other. This experience could be desirable if you wanted to show your partner a good time at the expense of your own pleasure, or vice versa. (male student)

Nonmutual sex is just the action of sex instead of the true intimate feelings that come from mutual sex. It can be arousing for the time being as clearly there is the physical attraction between the two people but there is not the real connection that makes the sex fulfilling. (male student)

In contrast to men's varied responses, 100% of women respondents viewed unequal, nonmutual sex as undesirable and the degree of their negativity was more intense. They described the experience of unequal sex as aggressive, violent, terrifying, demeaning, painful, denigrating, and humiliating:

Awful. Terrifying. Literally my worst nightmare. I don't even want to try and fully imagine it because I think that it could be scarring. Undesirable does not even begin to depict the total violation I would feel if sex was forced upon me. It would be the most helpless, damaging, and destroying thing that could ever happen. Life would never be the same, and I'm sure years of therapy later I would still hold a strong distrust for a lot of males. (female student)

Such sex results in regret, remorse, a loss of control, loss of self-esteem and self-confidence, and damage to one's capacity for sexual arousal:

I don't think nonmutual sex is desirable. It can be degrading and cause many issues of self-esteem and self-confidence as well as feeling vulnerable and weak. When the other person does not want to participate in the sexual act, they are not going to be aroused, which makes the forced experience even more unpleasant. (female student)

I would never want to experience this kind of sex. It seems as though women are degraded and used as objects in this kind of sex. Their feelings don't matter; they are more of a prop than anything else. It would not be very arousing because I wouldn't feel as though I was wanted. I would feel like an object with no feelings rather than a human being who has wants and needs. I would feel used and abused. All that this kind of sex would entail is the physical parts. There would be no real love, no real affection in it. It would all be physical. As a female, the physical part of sex is great, but the connection between partners is what makes or breaks it. All women want is to feel loved and wanted. (female student)

Nonmutual sex would be one person choosing the sexual activity and only satisfying his/her needs without regard for the other person. The person not in control is not having his/her needs met, so he/she is less involved. This type of sex is undesirable. Nobody wants to be doing something they don't like/want to do in any aspect of their lives. (female student)

As for whether unequal, nonmutual sex is arousing, 10 percent of women reported that unequal, nonmutual sex can seem exciting or arousing initially, but tends to become boring or painful and creates dissatisfaction and unhappiness:

Unequal, nonmutual sex usually happens in a context where one or both of the people involved are intoxicated and consent is questionable. This is done between two people who only care about the act itself and not the person they are doing it with. One of them just wants to relieve some sexual tension and they don't care about the boundaries of the other person. I don't think that this type of sex is desirable. While it can be arousing, it's not something that brings happiness. (female student)

Unequal, nonmutual sex would involve one partner (or both) using the other to gain their own sexual pleasure, and then after it's done going back to not actually caring about the other person or what they want. I think this type of sex can seem desirable at first; the idea of sexual pleasure with no strings attached can seem very appealing. However, after the experience has happened, I know through both personal experience and the experiences of friends that you feel worse than you did before. In unequal sex, one person is using the other as a device to gain their own pleasure, and figuring out you've been used is not a good spot to be in. (female student)

The rest of the women (90%) emphasized that unequal, nonmutual sex was definitely not arousing:

I think unequal, nonmutual sex would be undesirable and boring. In this type of sex, one partner is sexually satisfied and the other is not. I see this type of sex as distancing individuals from one another because they are not vulnerable with one another and are not considering the other individual. (female student)

Unequal sex does not celebrate both people's pleasure. This would not be arousing because most of the time the woman's orgasm doesn't matter in unequal sex. (female student)

The theme of unequal, nonmutual sex being boring appeared in their responses as well:

Unequal, nonmutual sex is undesirable and boring because one person is not involved or at least not as involved. If one person is less involved, sex becomes awkward or boring or uncomfortable. No one likes to feel unequal. (female student)

Unequal sex feels like a chore if you are in the subservient position. This sort of sex is not desirable and can be boring since it feels more like work than a pleasurable experience. For example, it is not fun for a female to give a guy a hand job or blow job and receive little in return. I do not know what it would be like to be the dominant party, but I imagine it is better. Nonetheless, I think both parties would enjoy the sex better if it was mutual. (female student)

Lastly, both men's and women's responses to the third question about which relational context promotes the most pleasurable sex reveals that neither gender views hookup sex as the most promising context. As table 8.1 indicates, 92.3% of men and 98.1% of women perceived that the most pleasurable sex would likely occur in a relationship, with most respondents (76.9% of men and 92.2% of women) specifically identifying a committed relationship of four months or more. These results are consistent with students' anonymous responses from 2006 to 2011 at University A. Every semester, the vast majority of students identified marriage or a committed relationship of four months or more as the most likely context in which they would experience the most pleasurable sex.

In sum, students' responses to three major questions about sexual desire, arousal, and pleasure reveal that the majority of my students view the prospect of equal mutual sex and/or sex occurring in relationships as most desirable and arousing. While 33% of men and 10% of women report that unequal, nonmutual sex can be arousing, all women and at least 42% of men expressed that they preferred equal mutual sex over unequal, non-mutual sex. As table 8.1 indicates, the vast majority of students indicate that the most pleasurable sex does not occur in drunken hookups but,

Table 8.1 In what context do you think you are most likely to have the most pleasurable sexual experience?

Context	Male Response Percentage	Female Response Percentage
Sex in a hookup with an acquaintance/ stranger	0	2.0
Sex in a hookup with repeat hookup partner (you don't hang out except for a hookup)	0	0
Sex in a hookup with a friend	7.7	0
Sex in a relationship during the first three months	15.4	5.9
Sex in a committed relationship of four or more months	69.2	35.3
Sex in marriage	7.7	56.9

rather, in relationships in which feelings and mutual "liking" or love are likely present.

Given the small survey sampling number (70), we cannot assume that these students' views, preferences, and desires are representative of the broader college population. I could find no research studies that directly asked students about whether hookups are just, what kind of sex is the norm among their generation, or about their sexual desires and preferences for equal mutual sex and unequal, nonmutual sex. However, much research corroborates key themes in students' responses. To begin, the research cited earlier about the disrespect women encounter in hookups, the tendency for hookups to be nonmutual and focused on male sexual pleasure, and the high rates of unwanted sex and sexual violence that occur disproportionately in hookups support my students' perceptions that hookups are unjust in reality and that equal mutual sex in hookups is the exception rather than the norm in their generation.

Furthermore, in light of research on the effects of porn and other sexually explicit materials on the desires and behavior of college men and women, it is far from surprising that the majority of my college students' sexual fantasies contain the theme of unequal power dynamics and that 33% of men and 10% of women report that unequal/domination sex can be sexually arousing. In some respects, it is even surprising that so many college students in the anonymous survey explicitly prefer sexual activity that occurs in a relationship that involves physical and emotional connection. This preference directly conflicts with all the images and messages of sexually explicit media and suggests that, while the eroticization of inequality heavily influences undergraduates, it does not fully determine their experiences of sexual desires, arousal, preferences, or behavior.

Many studies also corroborate my students' preference for sex that occurs in a relationship context. For instance, in a study of 681 emerging adults, 63% of college-aged men and 83% of college-aged women preferred a romantic relationship as opposed to an uncommitted sexual relationship.[38] Similarly, Garcia and Reiber found that while 89% of young men and women reported that physical gratification was important, 54% reported desiring emotional gratification and 51% reported a desire to initiate a romantic relationship; there were no gender differences in the responses.[39] Furthermore, students' perceptions that the most pleasurable sexual experiences are more likely to occur in a relationship marked by emotional expression and connection rather than a hookup coheres with decades of research revealing that sexual desire, pleasure, and sexual satisfaction increase for both men and women when they are involved in a longer term, more established relationship in which emotional connection and intimacy exists. Kleinplatz found that emotional intimacy was a key factor in experiencing high levels of sexual desire.[40] In another study, Higgins et al. found that involvement in an exclusive dating relationship was associated with both physiological and psychological sexual satisfaction.[41] In yet another study, by Armstrong et al., women reported more orgasms in relationships than in hookups.[42] This study found that romantic interest, affection, and commitment enhance orgasm and sexual enjoyment for women: "Women reported they most frequently had orgasms when they were with a caring sexual partner: he was concerned with her pleasure, willing to take time and perform the practices that worked, and she could communicate about what felt good.... These conditions were much more likely to be met in relationships than hookups."[43]

Conclusion

Why do so many students who hook up perpetuate and tolerate injustice in their embodied sexual lives, when they are often passionate advocates of justice in other contexts? Semester after semester, students raised my awareness of this inconsistency whenever they mentioned certain peers who were actively involved in social justice organizations and who also actively participated in drunken hookups or treated their romantic partner unjustly. Feedback from students indicates that critical dialogue with scholars like Margaret Farley and the introspection I have encouraged have helped many undergraduates confront destructive dynamics in their lives and make choices that promote their holistic well-being.

Students' responses in this chapter rule out the possibility that the majority choose unjust sex because it is what they find most desirable, arousing, and sexually pleasurable. Their reflections strongly indicate that a disconnect exists between the desires of a majority of my students for equal, mutual, emotionally connected sex and the kind of hookup sex they are actually experiencing. Such private dissatisfaction with the sex that occurs in hookups is corroborated by extensive research on pluralistic ignorance (explained in chapter 4) at work in the perpetuation of hookup culture.

This chapter has explored how students may tolerate unjust sexual and gender norms and perpetuate injustice in their sexual lives due to the "toxic messages" found in the ubiquitous eroticization of sexual inequality throughout our culture. Such eroticization of power-over interactions deeply affects their sexual expectations, sexual desires, arousal patterns, and sexual behaviors. Marvin Ellison's insight that persons internalize injustice deeply at a bodily level helps explain why so many college students may pursue social justice advocacy during college while simultaneously tolerating sexual disrespect and injustice in hookups or in their relationships.

However, while the cultural eroticization of inequality, domination, and violence deeply influences college students (and the rest of us), the anonymous survey findings that all women and at least 42% of men prefer equal and mutual sex also suggest that their desires and actual experiences of sex are influenced, but not entirely co-opted, by cultural influences that sexualize and eroticize inequality and violence. Additionally, research findings that many college students are privately dissatisfied with hookup culture offer hope that college students can create a new status quo in which abstinence or equal, consensual, mutual sex is the accepted social norm on college campuses. College students have effectively created and led national social justice movements, impacting global realities. Why would they not be equipped to lead a social justice movement to create sexually just college campuses?

Before exploring how to make such a possibility a reality on college campuses, we need to understand a major obstacle to sexual justice—the high prevalence of sexual assault, its traumatic effects, and the role university communities play in either exacerbating or alleviating the traumatization of sexual assault survivors. These are the subjects of chapters 9 and 10.

9

Understanding the Complexities of Sexual Assault and Its Traumatic Effects

ANALYZING THE FULL range of unjust social and sexual cultural dynamics on college campuses is highly complex and beyond the scope of this volume. Such injustices are rooted partly in sexism, racism, heterosexism, and classism. This chapter focuses on the particular injustice of sexual violence because it emerged as a dominant theme in the reflections on party and hookup culture by students at both University A and University B. If we hope to create a just sexual culture in which all college students are respected and treated as ends in themselves, we first need to confront honestly the reality of sexual violence on college campuses. Drawing on both student perspectives and important research studies, this chapter first examines why sexual violence is so prevalent on college campuses and then identifies risk factors that increase the likelihood of such behavior. Chapter 9 concludes by exploring the traumatic effects of sexual assault on victim-survivors.

The Prevalence of Sexual Violence

Studies over the last thirty years have identified high rates of sexual assault on college campuses. Understood by the White House Task Force on Sexual Assault as actual or attempted sexual contact with another person without that person's consent, sexual assault includes unwanted sexual advances and touching, as well as rape, which is defined as "penetration, no matter how slight, of (1) the vagina or anus of a person by any body part of another person or by an object, or (2) the mouth of a person by a sex organ of another person, without that person's consent."[1] In the 2015 Association of American Universities (AAU) study of 150,072 college students at twenty-seven universities, 26.1% of women seniors, 29.5% of TGQN (transgender, genderqueer or nonconforming, questioning, or not listed) seniors, and 6.3% of senior males reported being victims of sexual assault involving completed penetration or unwanted sexual touching as a result of physical force or incapacitation.[2] Similarly, in the 2007 National Institute of Justice's Campus Sexual Assault Study, 26.1% of the senior women reported having experienced attempted or completed sexual assault since entering college, with 6.9% experiencing physically forced sexual assault and 16.0% experiencing incapacitated sexual assault.[3] Of college men, 3.7% reported being victims of completed sexual assault since entering college. Of this group of men, 90.2% were victims of incapacitated sexual assault. The vast majority of sexual assault cases involve a perpetrator who is an acquaintance, classmate, friend, or ex-boyfriend.[4]

In over twelve years of class discussions about sexual assault on college campuses, few undergraduates have expressed surprise at the research statistics concerning the high prevalence of sexual assault on college campuses. A majority of students have either experienced sexual assault or know a sexual assault survivor. Such familiarity with sexual assault coheres with broader research studies. In a 2011 study, 64.5% of undergraduates reported knowing one or more women who were a victim of sexual assault, and over half (52.4%) reported knowing one or more men who perpetrated at least one of the types of sexual assault.[5]

College Students' Perspectives on the Prevalence of Sexual Violence

To access student perspectives about why sexual violence is so prevalent on college campuses, I engaged in two projects. First, I read students' private responses to this question in my sexual ethics courses from 2003 to 2012. Second, I identified repeating ideas and themes from over 200 interviews of students at University A who also responded to this question for a video project students and I engaged in from 2009 to 2011.[6] Three dominant themes emerged from analyzing these two sets of data.

First, students emphasized that masculinity today encourages, normalizes, and justifies sexual aggression and violence. Countless cultural and media images and attitudes associate masculinity with superiority and dominance, which results in a sense of entitlement related to what one desires:

> Young men see on television women getting raped, and the music industry where you hear some rappers talking about "fucking bitches and smacking hoes." Obviously, this has some kind of influence on the young men, and some men believe that they have this kind of control over females which can cause rape. (male student)

> These men who commit sexual assault have a lack of respect for women's desires and wishes. They feel that they are the highest in the hierarchy and no one will or would stop them. (male student)

Many students emphasize that the combination of masculine entitlement with the hookup script, men's high sex drive, and desensitization to violence fuel the high prevalence of sexual assault:

> It's not a coincidence that 1 in 4 college women are raped. College-aged men seem to have a very strong desire for sex. Not only do they desire sex but they are so exposed to violence in the media. In fact it is the "in" thing to enjoy violent movies, video games, TV shows, etc. (female student)

> In shows and movies, college life is portrayed as everybody looking to hook up. A guy thinks that a girl talking to him a lot is looking to hook up with him. This leads to him taking it too far, and he doesn't take no for an answer. He thinks the girl has passed the point of no return, and so he just ends up forcing the girl. (female student)

In addition, students perceive that masculinity is associated with being sexually experienced with many different women. Such pressure to have sex and be able to share stories of their sexual escapades motivates men to do whatever it takes to have sex, including zeroing in on very drunk or incapacitated women or forcing sex:

> There is so much pressure on men to have sex in college. They think that they have to have sex to earn respect of other men. We are told, basically, if you don't sleep with tons of different girls in college, there is something wrong with you. (male student)

I believe a main reason for men's hostility is the pressure society places on individuals. Until society changes its ways of pressuring individuals, and portraying emotions in a negative and unrealistic way, men will always have that need for power and violence and continue to commit such terrible acts. (male student)

Second, students perceive that women are too trusting of their peers and wrongly assume acquaintances will respect their wishes when they are drunk and partying:

When girls get too drunk, they can black out and some men will take advantage of this. (male student)

One out of 4 college women are raped because being in a new place, the risk is much greater. You constantly have to be on the lookout. When women get drunk, when anyone gets drunk, their ability to make decisions is severely lessened. They may think they can trust the guy, but a lot of the time it's the exact opposite. Women become even more vulnerable than they already are when they are under the influence. (male student)

College women will get real drunk easily and go home with a friend or a random person they just met and don't know very well. They are often just trying to meet new people and they are assuming they are decent people who will not take advantage of them. (male student)

Third, students perceive that the prevalence of sexual assault is connected to lack of reporting and the lack of serious consequences and sanctions for sexual assault at universities and in the legal system. Students are aware that a woman is highly unlikely to report the assault—especially if she was intoxicated. Most women are afraid of the social ramifications of reporting the assault:

College women are meant to simply accept sexual abuse as the norm and come to terms with the fact that they will probably not get much support, as women who experience it don't regularly mention it for fear that they will not be believed. (female student)

Rape happens in college because it can. It shouldn't, but it does. Rape could be stopped by harsher punishments for rapists and more knowledge of it happening. (female student)

Some male college students believe that they can get away with it and not get caught. A male college student who sexually harasses a female student thinks that there will be no consequences for his actions, and unfortunately in most cases, there may not be. (male student)

We should have stricter laws. Anyone who is found guilty of raping someone must serve time in prison. Women who have been sexually assaulted should be treated respectfully by the legal system and not made to look like the guilty ones. I feel that if more women had the emotional support of others when they were abused, they would more likely report the crimes committed against them. This, in turn, would deter some men from being violent towards women. (male student)

Thus, three themes emerge as dominant in students' reflections: (1) masculine scripts normalize sexual violence; (2) women have a false sense of security among peers and become even more vulnerable to assault when drunk; and (3) the lack of serious consequences fuels the high prevalence of sexual assault. Let us now examine how research corroborates my students' perceptions and offers additional insight in understanding the phenomenon of sexual violence.

Risk Factors for Sexual Victimization and Perpetration

Researchers have identified two key risk factors that significantly increase the likelihood of sexual victimization, the first of which is consuming alcohol.[7] Studies indicate that in 72 to 81% of cases in which a male rapes a female college student, the female is intoxicated.[8] Another study finds that women who drink frequently and heavily are eight times more likely to be raped.[9] Since alcohol negatively affects cognitive and motor skills and capacity to analyze complex stimuli, it significantly decreases women's ability to resist sexual assault.[10] Furthermore, when alcohol is involved, the victim is more likely to be blamed for the sexual assault. In surveys of incarcerated rapists and college students, both regarded the rapist as less responsible if he was intoxicated. On the other hand, if the woman was intoxicated, she was regarded by both groups as *more* responsible for the rape.[11]

The second most significant risk factor for sexual assault is casual sex. Research indicates that negative sexual experiences, coercive sex, and sexual assault are more likely to occur in the context of uncommitted sexual encounters than in committed or exclusive dating relationships.[12] In one study, 25% of women reported at least one sexual victimization during their first year of college, and hookup behavior was found to increase risk for sexual victimization; 78% of unwanted penetrative sex (including oral, vaginal, and anal) took place while hooking up.[13]

The prevalence of sexual violence in college, of course, does not occur in a vacuum; it mirrors the epidemic of sexual violence in the United States and worldwide: 25% of women and 16% of men have been sexually abused as children,[14] and 17.6% of women and 3% of men were raped at some point in their lifetime.[15] According to the World Health Organization, recent global prevalence figures indicate that 35% of women worldwide have experienced either intimate partner violence or non-partner sexual violence in their lifetime.[16]

As for sexual perpetration, research studies consistently find that most sexual offenders on college campuses, as well as worldwide, are male. In a comprehensive study of U.S. rape survivors, 98% of female rape survivors reported a male perpetrator and 93% of male rape survivors reported a male perpetrator.[17] Research studies since 1987 have found that 14 to 57% of college men report committing behavior consistent with the definition of sexual assault and 6 to 25.4% of college men reported attempting or completing rape perpetration during college.[18] In the most comprehensive study to date, 795 men were asked to complete a survey on sexual behavior twice per year during their four years of college. Of these, 30% reported acts of sexual coercion or assault. Of those who committed one act, 68% reoffended during the four-year timeframe; 42% offended at two time points, 22% at three time points, 14% at four time points, and 23% at five or more time points. In total, 33% of single offenders and 55% of repeat offenders had also committed an offense before college.[19] Similarly, 6 to 14.9% of college men in other studies report committing acts that are legally defined as rape.[20]

Studies consistently find that sexual assault usually involves premeditation, planning, and deliberate sexual assault tactics, which are defined as behaviors used by a perpetrator to increase the chance of coercing potential victims into sexual intercourse and to decrease the chance that she/he will report him/her for his/her behavior.[21] Researchers have identified three primary tactics: (1) verbal coercion, (2) physical incapacitation due to alcohol or drugs, and (3) force. In Zinzow's study, of the 33% men who committed sexual assault, 13% were in the verbal coercion group, 16% were classified in the incapacitation group, and 5% were classified in the forcible group.[22] Many in the incapacitation group also used verbal coercion tactics and many in the forcible group also used incapacitation and verbal coercion tactics. Altogether, 88% used incapacitation tactics.[23]

Many perpetrators intentionally take advantage of the cultural norm that using alcohol is an excuse or free pass for their sexually aggressive behaviors, knowing they will be judged less harshly if they are or appear drunk. Sexual assault perpetrators are skilled in identifying likely victims and testing prospective victims' boundaries. According to Lisak, who studied undetected college male rapists, perpetrators typically plan and premeditate their attacks, using sophisticated strategies to groom their victims and to isolate them physically.[24] Many deliberately rely on alcohol as their primary sexual assault weapon to make their victims less able to resist attacks.[25] They also use psychological weapons—power, control, manipulation, and threats—and back these up with physical force when necessary. Perpetrators can also be incredibly cunning in their attempts to lower the chances of victims' reporting the assaults, confusing victims they rape by sending flowers the next day, for example, or asking them out on dates. In fact, owing to complex factors involved in traumatization, some victims who have been sexually assaulted form relationships with their rapists and are thus at risk of further assault.

Researchers have identified a cluster of personality and risk factors that increase the likelihood of perpetrating sexual assault. First, college men who perpetrate sexual assault endorse a hyper-masculine identity to a greater degree than nonperpetrating college males.[26] Hyper-masculinity includes sexist attitudes of viewing women as objects, affirming male dominance attitudes, and endorsing the belief that sexual conquest is key to masculinity. A second risk factor is high endorsement of rape myth acceptance (a concept explained in chapter 8). Third, sexual perpetrators report higher levels of sexual preoccupation than peers who are not sexual perpetrators. They show a greater than average interest in sex, greater than average sexual activity, and greater than average sexual arousal when watching aggressive and nonconsenting sexual scenarios.[27] Fourth, pornography use has been identified as a risk factor for sexual assault. Frequent porn consumption for men has led to an increase in acceptance of rape myths, desensitization toward violence against women, and increased motivation to act aggressively toward women for sexual aggression, assault, and rape.[28] Fifth, college rapists exhibit poor empathy and emotional constriction, which makes it possible for them to reduce victims to an object of sexual conquest and experience gratification even while hurting others.[29]

Sexual assault and rape perpetrators also report lower levels of tender-mindedness, warmth, positive emotions, and altruism. Some researchers find that college rapists frequently exhibit other antisocial and psychopathic traits like extreme hostility and anger.

A sixth risk factor for sexual violence includes male peer support and social norms that encourage the sexual conquest mentality and that view sexual aggression as acceptable.[30] College rapists are often part of sexually violent all-male subcultures that normalize sexual conquests through violent pornography and deem explicit images of rape to be acceptable, non-criminal, and the sign of male virility.[31] Male friends of rapists in this group commonly take cellphone pictures and videos of their rapes, because they perceive aggressive sex to be part of late-night drinking antics. Two longitudinal studies indicate that fraternity men are three times more likely to commit sexual assault than other college men.[32]

The reality that these factors—endorsement of hyper-masculinity, acceptance of rape myths, greater arousal at aggressive sex, frequent porn use, low empathy, and male peer support—increase college men's likelihood of perpetration also strongly demonstrates that sexual assault is a culturally learned behavior, and that there is a cognitive component to sexual assault. As Kathryn Ryan notes, "A man must be able to think about the possibility of sexual force and aggression before he willingly uses it, even if this 'preparation' is only in fantasy form."[33]

When seeking to confront and respond to the reality that college sexual perpetrators exist on every college campus, it is tempting to focus solely on Lisak's findings that 6% of college men are repeat, undetected rapists and are responsible for the majority of sexual assaults. One could jump to the highly attractive conclusion that only 6% are the "bad guys" while 94% of college men are the "good guys." This is an attractive narrative for all members on campus. College men are happy to consider themselves as part of the majority of good guys, and college women experience greater security and confidence, and the sense that they can detect whether someone is a "bad guy." Some faculty are equally prone to accepting such black-and-white narratives. In my own experiences seeking to educate a campus community on sexual violence, I have often found that faculty members can be the most resistant to acknowledging the reality of predatory behavior among students, for it is psychologically uncomfortable to consider the possibility that the men they teach and with whom they form mentoring relationships are capable of callously disregarding their peers' bodily integrity. To assume that the male students they know and like are "good guys" also reduces the obligation to learn and teach about the complex cultural factors that contribute to this sexual assault epidemic. Finally, this narrative benefits administrators and staff because it narrows the scope of the problem and solution to identifying and expelling the undetected rapists.

Yet research studies and college students' own reflections throughout this book reveal that this narrative is simplistic and dangerous because it compromises the campus community's effectiveness in responding to sexual violence. While undetected rapists exist on college campuses, they are not the only type of sexual assault perpetrators. As noted above, many studies indicate that the percentage of college men who acknowledge committing sexual assault is higher than the 6% in Lisak's study. This simplistic narrative also ignores how normalized the tactic of preying on incapacitated peers has become. My students at both universities indicate how viewing drunken people as targets or conquests, and treating hookup partners as a means to one's own ends, is part of the accepted social fabric of party culture. Within this context, it is very possible to be perceived as a well-liked "good guy" on campus, view yourself as a caring, respectable individual, and still sexually assault an incapacitated peer. Research corroborates my students' perceptions. In one study, 35% said their friends approved of getting a woman drunk to have sex with her, 20% had friends who had gotten a woman drunk or high in order to have sex with her, and 15% acknowledged having committed some form of alcohol-related sexual coercion.[34]

Matt's story makes this all too clear. During a group discussion one day on hookup culture, I had noticed that Matt, normally outspoken and gregarious, was not speaking a word. After class, he asked if I had time to talk. We went outside and sat on a bench on a beautiful, sunny afternoon. Alluding to the well-known "Schemer" (described in chapter 1), he touched on his own hookup history and said, "The Schemer is nothing compared to me." Devoid of emotion, and without bragging, Matt related how he had it all down to a science and could "pretty much get almost any woman on campus" to hook up. He talked about the thrill of the chase, the high that accompanied every conquest, and his inevitable let-down and post-hookup emptiness. The previous summer, he actually "fell for a girl in D.C.," and they planned to remain together even though they went to different schools in different states. Back on his own campus, however, he succumbed to the familiar lure. Feeling guilty but unable to escape this cycle, he had decided to break up with the woman rather than continue cheating on her.

Matt paused significantly before relaying his much more disturbing confession. The previous year at a party, "there was this gorgeous woman" named Caitlin who was "completely wasted." Even though he had never talked with her before, Matt was his charming, flirtatious, manipulative self. He told me that he kept having the same thought over and over: "This is my only chance to hook up with her—she'd never hookup with me sober—this is my only chance." Matt told me he took Caitlin upstairs to a bathroom and took off her clothes. She was like a doll who couldn't hold herself upright, he continued, so he propped her up on the toilet and kept holding her up to have sex with her. Matt's description of his assault was excruciating, and I fought back the urge to ask him to stop talking.[35]

Matt shared that, after raping Caitlin, he was horrified at what he had done. He fled the bathroom, found his friend Brad, and said, "We've got to get out of here—I did something stupid—we've got to get out of here." He saw Caitlin, blurry-eyed and crying, with another woman as he and Brad left the party, and on their drive home, Matt admitted to Brad that he had raped her, repeating over and over how stupid he had been. Matt told me that Brad never brought up the evening's events again. Worried about Caitlin reporting him to the police, Matt called his older brother and dad and told them what he did. His older brother told him to not tell anyone and to forget about it, and his dad became angry at Caitlin, calling her a slut and a whore. She never should have gotten so drunk, flirted, and danced with him. He assured Matt that he had done nothing wrong. Matt continued to feel uneasy, wondering whether the campus police might show up, but nothing happened: no campus police, apparently no rumors, no perceivable negative social consequences at all. Matt remained one of the most popular, even adored guys on campus. He had no problem getting women to hook up with him weekend after weekend, yet he still felt guilty about Caitlin.

At the end of his story, Matt apologized for "putting this heavy thing" on me and said he had no one else to talk to about the experience. I knew Matt identified as Catholic, and I mentioned that in the Christian tradition when a person is sincerely sorry for hurting someone, he/she makes reparations. Matt was not willing to report himself to campus authorities because he wanted to avoid suspension or worse. I asked whether he had apologized to Caitlin, and whether there was still some form of restorative justice that might occur, perhaps (at the very least) reimbursement for the counseling or tutoring she required following the rape. Matt shook his head and responded,

"She won't talk to me." A few weeks after the rape, he approached and began speaking to her, but the look in her eyes was pure terror and panic. She ran away and consistently avoided him. I suggested to Matt that he think about other forms of reparation not directly related to Caitlin. Several weeks later, he asked whether I would share his story if I ever published anything on the hookup culture. "I want to get across how easy it is to rape someone when you're in the partying mindset," he said. Matt also signed up to be a peer mentor for a program on hookup culture and sexual violence I was sponsoring the next fall for first-year students.[36] Matt remembered his own freshman orientation when peer mentors had talked about rape, and he had written it off, thinking "I'm not a rapist—I would never rape someone."

Matt and I continued to have conversations about sexuality and relationships throughout his years at University A, and he expressed always feeling a serious low following a hookup. I challenged him to consider how his current hookup habits might be hurting his chances for what he said he wanted most in life, namely "a nice, happy marriage" and "lots of kids." Matt said he was excited about being an awesome dad and husband, especially since his own father had repeatedly cheated on his mom, and Matt knew how much it had hurt her. He wanted to be faithful and loyal to his future wife, but admitted he was worried about being able to follow through, especially since his infidelity had already sabotaged a relationship with a woman he really loved.

Despite his concerns about how his hookup habits might affect his future, Matt continued to drink, party, and hook up regularly throughout his time in college. Matt perceived himself as genuinely caring about others, and he told me he never had violent, forced sex with anyone again. Nevertheless, he was still regularly hooking up and having sex with drunk women. To the extent that these women were incapacitated and nonconsenting, he was a repeat rapist on our campus. And yet, Matt does not fit into Lisak's description of undetected rapists who lack empathy and savor the power they derive from incapacitating victims. Matt was a kind and supportive friend to many women and men on campus, and was widely perceived as a "good guy" among his peers.

Insights from Trauma Studies: Effects of Sexual Assault on Victim-Survivors

Implicit in the all-too-common assumption in the United States that sexual assault is not that serious is the belief that sexual assault victims, especially if they are psychologically healthy, can "get over" unpleasant or unwanted sexual experiences and just "move on." This tragic misrepresentation could not be further from the truth, for sexual assault constitutes a severe traumatic experience that negatively affects survivors' physical and psychological health,[37] identity development, relationships and social functioning, and academic and work performance, as it likely did for Caitlin. Sexual assault can result in serious short-term and long-term negative health consequences.

Physical injuries resulting from the assault often require medical care and frequently involve bruises, black eyes, cuts, scratches, swelling, or chipped teeth.[38] Potential pregnancy for women and STIs (sexually transmitted infections) can also result, which can adversely affect their sexual and reproductive health. According to the American Association of University Women, 40% or more of sexual assault incidents involve transmission of a sexually transmitted disease.[39] Sexual assault is also associated with gynecological problems including pelvic pain, excessive menstrual bleeding, urinary problems, and sexual dysfunction. Furthermore, sexual assault survivors are also at greater risk for developing eating disorders, chronic physical conditions, chronic pain, and lower generalized health than survivors of other crimes and women with no sexual victimization history.[40]

Sexual assault is traumatic. Trauma, a state of being overwhelmed both physically and psychologically, involves the experience of terror, loss of control, and utter helplessness during a stressful event that threatens one's physical and/or psychological integrity. Consider the following two traumatic accounts of rape by survivors at University A:[41]

So we (a fellow student athlete and I) left the party and got in his car, and he turned down the street and turned left instead of going right towards University A. He pulled over and started to kiss me and I kissed him back, and I was okay with kissing him. He was like "well, let's just get into the back seat," and I said "okay." We climbed in the back and I kept kissing him and then he reached up and locked the doors. I said, "Okay, you know, I don't think that this is the best idea. I'm just going to go home; can we go home now?" And he said something like, "No, I want to have sex with you." I said, "No I'm not having sex with you right now. No, absolutely not," and that's when he kind of like pushed me down on the seat. A lot of people will say to me, "Why didn't you punch him or

kick him or something like that?" And you know, it was like temporary paralysis—I completely froze. I kept telling him, "No," and he
kept telling me, "Shut the fuck up." Literally he kept saying it over
and over again, "Be quiet, be quiet, no, no shut up, shut up." I just
froze. I just didn't know what to do. I was watching the situation.
I didn't feel like I was in my body. That's when he proceeded to rip
my pants off, and forced himself inside of me. At one point he even
got up and held my mouth, and I kept moving my mouth because
he was trying to put his penis into my mouth, and I was holding it
shut, and he just kept forcing it into my mouth. After about 15 minutes, a campus police car drove past the car. He was on top of me
basically and he must have seen it, so he jumped off me and threw
me my jeans and said, "Put those on." He climbed in the front seat,
and I unlocked the doors and started running. I ran all the way back
to my dorm room, sobbing and in shock. (Kari)

Derrick kept pouring me drinks, just like he had done the previous
weekend. Suddenly things got very fuzzy, and we were kissing. I could
hardly even keep my eyes open. I remember someone yelling "get a
room!" and suddenly we were headed toward his. I didn't like him
like that, and had even told his roommate, a friend of mine, as much
when he seemed to not be picking up on my previous rejections, but
I was suddenly so tired that I welcomed the opportunity to get away
from the noise of the party. All of a sudden, I was naked. I cannot
for the life of me remember how it happened, but I know he did it.
I would have never taken my clothes off. He was lying next to me
with his pants off, and he grabbed my hand and made me touch his
penis. I instantly pulled it away, thinking he would pick up on the
hint. I started to get very groggy and before I knew it, he was finger-
ing me. Then I passed out. I don't know how long I was out for, but
I awoke to an intense pain. I tried saying "Ow" as loud as I could in
my drowsy state, and I looked down to see him biting my breasts. I
pushed his head away, and he continued to finger me. I passed out
again. I awoke to the pain of his biting again, and again I pushed his
head away. I told him to stop. I saw him holding himself, attempting to have sex with me. I said as loud and as clearly as I could, "No,
Derrick, I don't want to have sex." He ignored me. I must have said it
five times, verbatim. But he didn't listen. I felt an extreme pressure,
but before I could tell him to stop again, I passed out once more. I was

in and out of consciousness for the rest of the time, so it's unclear to me what exactly happened after that or how much time had passed. I was helpless. I couldn't move, couldn't push him away, and couldn't understand what was going on. I'd never been that sleepy. To this day, I regret not taking a drug test at the hospital. I've always wondered if he put something in my drink. When he finally stopped, I began to cry. (Kristin)

In these instances of rape, the women experienced shock and betrayal when an acquaintance suddenly turned on them and sexually assaulted them. Kari's common experience of a "freeze" response to sexual assault, and Kristin's incapacitation and passing in and out of consciousness created a deep sense of helplessness and loss of control.

The especially sinister side of trauma is that, even when the event has ended, it has only begun to shatter one's core assumptions about oneself and one's relations to others in the world; and that process continues long term, often over a lifetime. Sexual assault destroys a sense of self-protection, personal security, and safety in a world that has lost all predictability. Since a traumatic event overwhelms a person's capacity to "take in" and process the experience physiologically and psychologically, one of the most effective defense mechanisms that enables survival is dissociation. Dissociation refers to separating and splitting off elements of the traumatic experience—emotions, thoughts, sensation, location, time, and meaning—into shattered fragments that defy conscious integration. Kari's experience of not feeling like she was in her body and was simply watching the event is a clear example of dissociation.

Many sexual assault survivors continue to re-experience the assault memories as though the original sexual assault event were presently occurring. Subsequently, they develop a host of physiological, affective, cognitive, and behavioral responses now identified as posttraumatic stress disorder (PTSD) symptoms. Between 17 and 65% of women with a history of sexual assault develop posttraumatic stress disorder.[42] Researchers identify four main clusters of such symptoms.[43] First, survivors re-experience the traumatic sexual assault in the form of intrusive thoughts, flashbacks, nightmares, and intense bodily or emotional sensations. Re-experiencing the traumatic event causes survivors to alternate between persistent forms of hyper-arousal and avoidance—the second cluster of PTSD symptoms. Hyper-arousal involves reacting to the slightest stimuli as if everything in one's environment represented potential danger. Irritability, restlessness, difficulty concentrating, and difficulty sleeping are also common signs. In their attempts to ward off hyper-arousal, trauma survivors avoid all reminders associated with the traumatic event and trauma-induced feelings by experiencing emotional numbing, withdrawal, and detachment from emotions and physical sensations. When detachment does not occur, trauma survivors frequently resort to numbing agents like alcohol and drugs. For this reason, survivors are at greater risk of abusing alcohol and drugs, engaging in binge drinking, and developing dependency than nonsurvivors. Approximately 13 to 49% of survivors become dependent on alcohol, and 28 to 61% use other substances.[44] Some survivors also resort to forms of autonomic arousal, like self-mutilation, impulsive risk-taking, or compulsive sexual behavior, which offers temporary relief from unbearable emotions. It is thus not uncommon for sexual assault survivors to drink heavily, hook up, and engage in risky sexual behavior. While their peers may perceive such behaviors as "proof" that the survivor is a "slut" and that her allegation of prior assault was a lie, such behavior can actually be a posttraumatic reaction to the assault.

Closely related to forms of autonomic arousal, the third posttraumatic stress symptom is a tendency to reenact the trauma by repetitively reliving or recreating a past trauma in their present lives.[45] The most common forms of reenactment are acting self-destructively (self-injurious behaviors, hyper-sexuality, walking alone in unsafe areas), harming others, or experiencing sexual re-victimization (repeated sexual assault or becoming involved in repetitive abusive relationships). Women who have been sexually victimized are up to twice as likely as nonvictims to be sexually assaulted within four months.[46] Risk factors for sexual revictimization include lack of acknowledgment of previous victimizations, posttraumatic symptoms, self-blame, avoidance coping, problem drinking, and risky sexual behaviors.[47] PTSD symptomatology also lowers survivors' ability to recognize signs of danger and avoid or escape threatening situations.[48]

The fourth and final PTSD cluster of symptoms includes increased negative affect and overly negative thoughts and assumptions about oneself or the world. Trauma research indicates that sexual assault survivors are also at great risk for developing major depression and anxiety. According to research studies, 73 to 82% experienced fear and anxiety following an assault, 13 to 51% of survivors experienced depression, and 12 to 40% developed generalized anxiety.[49] Depression, anxiety, and other PTSD symptoms can negatively impact one's ability to engage in coping with the assault and engage in effective problem solving.[50]

The traumatic experience of sexual assault also negatively impacts adolescents' and young adults' identity development and self-esteem. Survivors' negative views of themselves are due in part to the shame they experience at the loss of control and the inability to defend themselves during the assault. Influenced by pervasive cultural rape myths that blame sexual assault victims rather than perpetrators for the assaults, most survivors' immediate reaction is to criticize and blame themselves, especially when the perpetrator is a college peer, acquaintance, or friend. Such self-blame further increases negative self-cognitions, PTSD symptoms, and depression.[51] For instance, consider Lily's and Megan's immediate reaction of self-blame and failure to conceptualize what occurred as rape:[52]

> After the sexual assault, I went up to our dorm room, and I got in my roommate's bed, and I was physically shaking her and screaming and crying. All I kept saying was, "It's not my fault, it's not my fault. I can't handle this. I can't handle this. I want to kill myself. I want to kill myself." Those were the only things I kept saying over and over again. When I woke up the next day, I was trying to figure out what had happened, and I just spent those whole 24–48 hours blaming myself and thinking what I could have done to avoid this situation. I put all the blame on myself and it wasn't until an RA—a male RA—said to me, "Well, are you going to press charges?" and I said, "Why would I do that?" I just did not understand, and that's when I first started to realize that, "No, I did not ask for this and this was not my fault." I still never used the word "rape." (Lily)

> After the sexual assault I immediately called myself a slut, a whore, and was extremely angry at myself. I decided that I had been a slut, but that's what I got for my choice of getting drunk. I had to face the facts, and I decided to be a big girl and just "move on." For an entire week, I hardly thought about it, and in the few moments I did think about it, I just called myself a slut and felt completely guilty, but then pushed it from my mind. However, at the end of the week I went on a retreat. I began to think about the night, and began to sob and beg God for forgiveness. I pulled a friend aside with the intention of telling her my darkest sin, and asking if she thought I should go to confession for it. But as the story spilled out of me, I blurted out the phrase "and I told him 'no sex' twice but . . ." and it hit me. I realized from her reaction and my own what had honestly happened. She told

me that it wasn't my fault and that what had happened to me was wrong. But neither of us used the "R" word. (Megan)

Notice the clear interconnections between self-blame, negative thoughts about oneself, and shame in their experiences. Taking into consideration undergraduates' reflections in part II about the connections among self-control, self-esteem, and being a "winner," we understand how shame increases when one experiences loss of control and the ability to protect oneself. Furthermore, posttraumatic stress symptoms, depression, anxiety, and abuse of alcohol and drugs for self-numbing further assault one's sense of self and identity, one's sense of agency and self-control, and basic trust in others: "All the structures of the self—the image of the body, the internalized images of others, and the values and ideals that lend a sense of coherence and purpose—are invaded and systematically broken down."[53] The disintegration of one's perception of self, others, and the world disrupts one's normal pattern of physiological, psychological, cognitive, and social functioning. Sexual assault survivors' subsequent physiological and psychological distress can negatively affect their ability to socialize and can harm valuable relationships with family, friends, peers, and romantic partners. As a way to cope with fear and lack of safety, survivors frequently withdraw socially, especially if they encounter unsupportive, dismissive, and otherwise negative social reactions when disclosing the assault.

In addition, owing to the negative impact that a traumatic event and subsequent PTSD, anxiety, and depression have on concentration, cognitive abilities, and motivation, sexual assault negatively affects survivors' process of learning and academic performance. This impacts their future career and graduate education opportunities.[54] Research demonstrates that sexual assault survivors' grade point averages (GPAs) frequently decrease after an assault as they struggle academically, drop classes, and find they cannot carry a normal course load. Survivors often miss classes owing to their need to withdraw socially to feel safer, avoid the perpetrator, and avoid negative social reactions from peers or friends. In a research study of 750 first-year college women, 40% of women reported rape or sexual assault during their teen years prior to college. Twenty-four percent experienced sexual victimization in their first year of college, and another almost 20% were raped or sexually assaulted during their second semester of college. Those with prior teen sexual-victimization experiences tended to enter college with lower GPAs and receive lower grades during their first year of college than did nonvictimized women students. Women sexually assaulted during their first year of college tended to have lower GPAs by the end of the year than nonsurvivors. The more assault experiences survivors experienced, the greater the negative impact on academic performance.[55]

Sexual assault also predicts greater risk of transferring or dropping out of college.[56] Research indicates that sexual violence is a more important predictor of leaving college than traditional predictors of academic performance (such as standardized test scores). Female students at the greatest risk of leaving were those who reported victimization prior to college and revictimization in college. One study, for instance, indicates that only 56% of those who experienced more than one sexual assault graduated (compared to 85% of those who reported no sexual violence).[57] Many survivors leave school because it is too traumatizing to encounter their perpetrators on campus or face friends or peers who react unsupportively. Others drop out for financial reasons: it is simply too costly to pay for tutoring or repeat classes that they failed or had to drop as a result of their traumatic experience.

We are right to describe the effects of sexual assault on survivors as utterly devastating, and yet the picture is still incomplete if we ignore the fact that a community's (and society's) unsupportive responses to trauma too often exacerbate the survivors' degree of traumatization.

According to trauma researchers, the broader cultural, social, and political context in which trauma occurs either facilitates or impedes individuals' capacity to cope with the traumatic event and experience healing and recovery:

> Traumatic experience needs to be conceptualized in terms of a dynamic, two-way interaction between the victimized individual and the surrounding society, evolving over time, and not only as a relatively static, circumscribable entity to be located and addressed within the individual psychology of those affected.... Post-traumatic symptoms are not just a private and individual problem but also an indictment of the social contexts which produced them.[58]

Such insight into the significant role that social, cultural, and political factors play in the degree of posttraumatic stress has been overlooked in Western culture. Historically, Western societies have blamed posttraumatic stress following a traumatic event on the psychological/biological vulnerabilities and/or moral weaknesses of the individual. What lies behind our societal impulse to blame traumatized individuals for their suffering? Van

der Kolk suggests that doing otherwise threatens the nonvictims' sense of
security, self-control, and sense of agency over their lives:

> Society becomes resentful about having its illusions of safety and
> predictability ruffled by people who remind them of how fragile
> security can be.... [Society's reactions] are primarily the results of
> conservative impulses in the service of maintaining the beliefs that
> the world is essentially just, that "good" people are in charge of their
> lives, and that bad things only happen to "bad" people.[59]

In her analysis of traumatic events that are due to human design (apart-
heid, genocides, war, and sexual violence), trauma theorist Judith Herman
points out that bystanders are inevitably caught up in a conflict between
perpetrators and victims:

> It is morally impossible to remain neutral in this conflict. The
> bystander is forced to take sides. It is very tempting to take the side
> of the perpetrator. All the perpetrator asks is that the bystander do
> nothing. He [or she] appeals to the universal desire to see, hear, and
> speak no evil. The victim, on the contrary, asks the bystander to
> share the burden of pain. The victim demands action, engagement,
> and remembering.... In order to escape accountability ... the per-
> petrator does everything in his power to promote forgetting. Secrecy
> and silence are the perpetrator's first line of defense. If secrecy fails,
> the perpetrator attacks the credibility of his victim. If he cannot
> silence her absolutely, he tries to make sure that no one listens.[60]

Herman argues that, unless bystanders are in a social context that publicly
denounces the trauma and supports victims, most people side with the
perpetrator by engaging in collective denial and silence or by "forgetting"
about the particular atrocity.

Let us now turn to chapter 10 and examine the ways in which university
communities frequently exacerbate sexual assault survivors' traumatization. Secondary victimization, a useful concept for understanding the full
impact of sexual assault, is explored in more detail next.

Secondary Victimization

THE COMMUNITY'S ROLE IN TRAUMATIZATION

RECENT RESEARCH ON UNIVERSITIES' communal response to disclosures of sexual assault is consistent with the cultural dynamic that denies and minimizes the reality of sexual assault, blames survivors, and ultimately sides with perpetrators. The reality that approximately 2% of incapacitated sexual assault survivors and 13% of forcible rape survivors report to campus or local law enforcement itself signals a lack of adequate support for survivors of sexual assault.[1] Such lack of reporting mirrors broader U.S. society, where rape remains the least reported violent crime, and where fewer than 10% of rape cases reported to police result in criminal charges against a defendant.[2] Research demonstrates that survivors' reasons for not reporting sexual assault are connected to many cultural and legal factors that deny or trivialize sexual assault, stigmatize and blame survivors for their sexual assault, and foster harassment and retaliation against sexual assault survivors. Such negative and unsupportive social reactions from friends, peers, family, faculty, staff, administrators, and authorities constitute another layer of traumatization, which is referred to as *secondary victimization*.

This chapter will look specifically at the responses to sexual assault allegations among survivors' college peers and also the decisions of those in positions of authority within university institutions. Concluding with theological reflection on secondary victimization, we gain clarity not only about "other people's" roles in the ongoing traumatization of sexual assault survivors, but our own collusion with perpetrators (the obvious "bad guys") as long as we shun activism in favor of the more comfortable status quo.

College Peers' Responses to Survivors' Allegations of Sexual Assault

The ways that college peers respond to survivors' allegations of sexual assault—disbelief, denial, trivialization, blame, alienation, stigmatization, and retaliation—emerge most clearly against the backdrop of four reasons that survivors typically do not report sexual assault. The first main reason survivors do not report sexual assault is that they are confused and uncertain about how to understand their unwanted sexual experiences; many do not immediately (or sometimes ever) acknowledge what occurred to be sexual assault or rape. Our society's tendency to deny the prevalence of sexual violence, and also the reality that most sexual violence is committed by a familiar person, make it difficult for college students to name sexual assault for what it is and feel they have a right to stand up for themselves. Popular conceptions of sexual assault and rape are frequently limited to scenarios where strangers attack victims and employ physical force, not the kind of awkward act that occurs when one is too incapacitated to consent and the perpetrator is an acquaintance or trusted friend. Consequently, undergraduates who experience forcible rape by a stranger are far more likely to acknowledge the event as rape and report it than students who experience the vast majority of assaults on campus—incapacitated sexual assault by a known assailant (an acquaintance, friend, or romantic partner).[3] In these instances of sexual violence, survivors frequently conceptualize their experience as an event that involved a miscommunication or was an instance of bad sex. In Cleere's 2013 study, 61% of college women reported at least one experience that objectively met the definition of a sexual assault. Of these women, 75% failed to acknowledge their experience as sexual assault.[4]

Frequently, college students will confide in a close friend after the assault in an attempt to understand what happened and to receive help and support. Unfortunately, friends frequently convey disbelief at survivors' accounts of sexual assault, trivialize what occurred during the sexual assault, and/or ask questions or make statements that imply that the survivor was partially to blame. Such reactions that deny or trivialize the assault also discourage survivors from acknowledging that they were assaulted and from reporting the assault to the authorities. Failure to acknowledge sexual assault frequently results in many long-term negative health consequences. Survivors who do not conceptualize their experiences as assault are less likely to seek medical assistance and are left to deal on their own with physical injuries, potential STIs, and/or unintended pregnancies. They are also less likely to seek counseling, depriving them of support and education about negative psychological symptoms (PTSD, anxiety, and depression). Lack of counseling also means that there is no one to help them identify maladaptive coping behaviors and educate them on trauma survivors' compulsion to reenact trauma. Such unacknowledged victims are particularly at risk for substance-use disorders, which may exacerbate post-assault PTSD and major depressive symptoms.[5] Moreover, such lack of support increases survivors' risk of sexual revictimization. Failure to acknowledge assault creates psychological barriers and emotional responses that undermine sexually assertive behavior, which increases risk for subsequent revictimization.[6] Unacknowledged victims are significantly more likely to report continuing their relationship with the assailant after the assault, which also increases their chances of revictimization.

A second main reason that survivors do not report or acknowledge sexual assault is the negative social stigma placed on victimization. As many college students note in their private reflections, no one wants to acknowledge to themselves or others that they have been sexually victimized: to be a victim in our culture expresses weakness and vulnerability, which can be deeply shameful. Consequently, survivors often employ defense mechanisms such as denial or minimization of the assault and its negative effects. Collective denial and silence surrounding male sexual victimization can make it even more challenging for male survivors to acknowledge victimization and its negative consequences. Besides frequently experiencing intense fear and a "freeze" response that temporarily paralyzes them while being assaulted, along with shame at not being able to fight off their attacker, males fear that they will be blamed for not being "man enough" to prevent assault.[7] Fear that others will suspect them of being gay is also common.[8] Research indicates that fears about maintaining confidentiality and concerns about "shame, guilt, embarrassment, not wanting friends and family to know about the rape or sexual assault" was a greater barrier for male than for female victims.[9]

Third, survivors avoid reporting sexual assault due to cultural attitudes that discourage belief in survivors' accounts and even shift blame to the survivors themselves. Rape myths and other victim-blaming attitudes definitely existed at University A. When asked why sexual violence was so prevalent, students repeatedly reported that the prevalence is due to masculine expectations and a lack of serious consequences for an assault. And yet, when asked how to reduce sexual assault, the vast majority focused on changing the behavior of women (who they presumed were most likely to be assaulted) rather than the men (who they presumed to be the perpetrators). Women and men alike reiterated common rape myths that men cannot control themselves sexually and that women "ask for" rape by the way they dress, drink, and flirt. Many students partially or completely blamed women for assault due to what they wear:

> The ability to go wherever we want, dress however we want, and "hook up" whenever we can is definitely not handled well by some females, and they may find themselves in a compromising position they did not expect. (female student)

> I recognize a female's right to wear whatever she may please, but perhaps more dangerous and possibly hostile situations require more conservative attire. Hence, if one eliminates the cause of temptation, one can avoid undesirable consequences. (male student)

Women are also blamed for drinking too much and for being too trusting that male peers will respect their boundaries and bodies:

> College women will get drunk easily and go home with a friend or a random person they just met and don't know very well. They are often just trying to meet new people and assume they are decent persons who would not take advantage of them. A lot of times the girls bring the rape upon themselves by doing stupid stuff to put them in a bad situation. (male student)

> Girls need to try to not put themselves in situations where they can be taken advantage of, and not be stupid and drink so much that it impairs their judgment and awareness. (female student)

> If two adults fueled by alcohol hook up and have anonymous sex, then both parties are partly responsible. I feel bad for the girls who are legitimately raped. It's a horrible experience, one that I have encountered myself, but at the same time I took responsibility for getting too drunk and the consequences which come along with those actions. (female student)

Notice how the focus is on blaming women for "placing themselves in compromising positions by drinking" rather than a focus on the predatory mentality and behavior of undergraduate perpetrators. This signals how normalized it is to prey on the most vulnerable, incapacitated partiers.

Women were also blamed for assault if they engaged in any kind of flirtatious or sexual behavior, or chose to be alone with a man. The underlying assumption is that such behavior communicates consent for sex and obligation to have sex (according to the man's wishes):

> I don't feel that it is only the guys that are making this happen. Not to say that any girl WANTS to be raped; rather, girls tend to lead guys on. They wear revealing clothing, act in a flirtatious way . . . this can get girls in trouble. (female student)

> Sometimes rape can be derived from women leading males on and then the males wanting more. Ways of preventing rape is to hang out in groups so rape cannot occur. (male student)

> Alcohol gets involved and all lose their inhibitions and true sense of tact. The man's primal nature takes over. He becomes what society says he should be and the woman dances like a sex goddess. It is both of their faults for allowing themselves to reach that point. Even when a girl finally says no, often everything she is doing still says yes. The man takes what control he believes he is supposed to take and the woman feels taken advantage of. They are both taken advantage of. (female student)

In their suggestions of how to prevent and reduce sexual assault, students again focus on women's behavior, their need to stay in groups at parties, and to be more cautious:

> A way to lower the number of sexual assaults is to have a conference for freshman women and tell them not to trust anyone unless you know them really well and to still be really careful and not to let themselves get in that kind of situation. Always stay with a group of friends or have pepper spray and don't be afraid to use it. (male student)

> People need to take the proper precautions—make sure they have their drink with them at all times, have friends with them whom they trust, and most importantly, that they do NOT go into a room or isolated place where an act of violence would go unnoticed. (male student)

Many women know how to prevent rape. Such actions are to walk in a group, always to be cautious of what is going on around you, never take a drink that you didn't see being poured, never go to a room with a guy you really don't know, etc. Women just have to be aware and know that anything is possible. (female student)

I feel women need to protect themselves better and stay away from certain situations that can get out of hand. (Don't get me wrong, I'm not blaming the women in this case.) (male student)

If college women actually followed my undergraduates' advice, they would have to follow these rules:

1. Do not have more than one or two drinks when you are with other people.
2. If you do drink at parties, do not lose sight of your beverage in case you're targeted for a date rape drug.
3. Only wear conservative clothes when you go out.
4. Never flirt, dance, or engage in any sexual behavior—even kissing—with a male because others will say you led the guy on and were implicitly saying yes to sex.
5. Always stay surrounded by friends. If you're alone and sexually assaulted, others will say you put yourself in a compromising position.

Note, of course, that all these rules are in direct conflict with key social and party norms for college women. If a college woman actually did follow all of my students' advice in order to avoid being blamed for rape, imagine how her peers would react to her strategies for prioritizing safety. She would likely gain a reputation of not only being prudish but also being paranoid or mentally unstable and would become a social pariah. Women would not view her as "fun" or popular and would be concerned that her negative reputation would affect their own social status. Few college men would likely be interested in her conservative dress and behavior, not to mention her refusal to be alone with them. Ultimately, my students' well-meaning advice actually reveals how vulnerable women really are, not just to sexual victimization but also to being blamed for it.

Negative social reactions conveying disbelief or blame typically fuel fears of stigmatization, social ridicule, loss of social status, and rejection by friends and social groups. And as research demonstrates, negative social reactions also exacerbate survivors' sense of self-blame.[10]

Increased self-blame in turn can have a devastating impact on survivors' psychological state, placing them further at risk for increased PTSD symptoms, major depressive disorder, and substance abuse.[11] Self-blame is also manifest in many survivors' decision not to report assault out of a desire to protect known assailants from consequences and not ruin the perpetrator's life. In light of the reality that many sexual assault survivors' own academic performance suffers and that they drop out of college while perpetrators remain and graduate, such concern for the perpetrators' well-being over the survivors' well-being speaks volumes about how deeply survivors can internalize our society's victim-blaming attitudes.

During my nine years at University A, I marveled at how the same narrative on my campus played out each time a sexual assault survivor broke the mold of silence, filed a report, and pursued a disciplinary hearing. Consistent with Judith Herman's insight that bystanders usually side with perpetrators, the vast majority of college students on the campus adamantly refused to believe each survivor and publicly sided with the alleged perpetrator. Individual details about each woman[12] who reported an assault never mattered; year after year, each woman was placed under scrutiny, and rumors of her drinking, notorious lies, sexual past, and/or "bitchy" behavior spread like wildfire. All the survivors I became aware of were discredited as untrustworthy, manipulative, vengeful, and/or mentally unstable. When a survivor reported a forcible sexual assault, many students cast doubt on the allegation, making comments like, "everyone who knows the guy knows he's not capable of assault." When both students had been drinking and the woman became incapacitated, students echoed common rape myths.

Absolutely every survivor I met or learned about was blamed for her assault. Especially heartbreaking was how the survivors I knew lost most or all of their friends. Some friends expressed outright that they did not believe the survivor, and one friend of a survivor was later raped by the same perpetrator she had so staunchly defended. Others withdrew from the survivor somewhat apologetically, stating that the negative social ramifications of being perceived as her friend were too high. Still other friends gradually distanced themselves because they could not understand or handle listening to the survivor talk about the assault or witness her flashbacks. Consequently, at the very moment when such survivors are struggling with sexual assault and its effects, and are in most need of support and validation, they are frequently betrayed by even their closest friends and social groups. Consider, for instance, Kristin's experience:

Over the next few months, my friends slowly began to alienate me. They stopped inviting me places, stopped pretending to care about what I was going through, and eventually, stopped talking to me altogether. In text messages, Sarah and Audrey told me they were not going to be witnesses for me anymore in my University hearing. It was stressing them out too much, they said; they didn't want to be a part of it. Brenda, who had also been raped by Derrick and planned to do a joint trial with me, also told me that she was no longer going to go through with it. I felt like the burden of all the women Derrick had raped was on my shoulders. I was abandoned by everyone and expected to just take care of it on my own.[13]

Fourth and finally, survivors often avoid pursuing justice because they fear retaliation from the perpetrator, his social group, and even an entire campus community. Such harassment occurs especially if the accused student is a valued athlete. Kristin continues:

Things with my old friends only got harder. They called me a slut on Facebook, said that anyone could win a University hearing as long as they had a box of tissues by their side; they told people my rape kit came back "negative," a misconception I will never understand. Rob, my old best friend, would stare me down every chance he could, and Sarah and Audrey, my roommates, made my life a living hell. I would go to parties and people would yell at me and say things that weren't true. One student in particular went out of his way to shake his head at me every time he saw me around campus. I was miserable. Somehow I was the bad guy, even though I felt like I was the only one doing the right thing. I contemplated transferring schools almost every single day.

Research studies and journalistic investigations demonstrate that sexual assault survivors' experiences of negative peer responses in college, in the military, and in local communities are commonplace. Such negative social reactions increase PTSD symptoms, feelings of inadequacy, self-deprecation, distress, anxiety, depression, shame, self-blame, problem drinking, and poor physical health.[14] In their study, Relyea and Ullman examined the impact on survivors' recovery of two different negative social reactions—unsupportive acknowledgment and actively turning against the survivor. Of survivors, 94% experienced unsupportive acknowledgment while 78% experienced persons actively turning against them. The latter indicated greater levels of potentially harmful behavior or thinking: social withdrawal, increased self-blame, and decreased sexual assertiveness. Survivors who received acknowledgment of their assault but were not supported experienced increased depression and PTSD.

Universities' Institutional Responses to Sexual Assault

Research also indicates that trusted authorities (administrators, staff, faculty, campus security, state police, prosecutors, and judges) have frequently exacerbated the suffering of many college sexual assault survivors,[15] specifically by asking questions that expressed doubt, trivialized the assault, or implied that the survivor was to blame for the assault. Since it is important to understand how universities tend to respond to sexual assault allegations without adequate federal regulations and enforcement of regulations, I primarily focus in this chapter on universities' responses prior to the Obama administration's efforts from 2011 to 2016 to address the sexual assault crisis on college campuses. (In chapter 11, I will discuss the Obama administration's guidelines for universities to effectively respond to and prevent campus sexual assault.)

Prior to federal changes in Title IX regulations, many survivors found that university authorities advised them to protect their reputations by not disclosing the assault to others, not filing a campus or police report, and not pursuing a disciplinary hearing.[16] For instance, university officials told a survivor that the police would not likely investigate the incident, that the university's internal discipline process would be harmful to her, and that she should stay focused on her schoolwork and mental health rather than press charges.[17] Survivors who persisted in filing a campus report frequently had to wait months (in some cases, years) to learn whether their university had decided to investigate their allegation; the process was delayed and obfuscated even more if the accused student was a valued campus athlete.[18] After such delay, university officials often informed a survivor that they had chosen not to investigate or pursue a disciplinary hearing owing to a lack of evidence. As recently as 2014, a Senate survey found that 41% of schools had not conducted a single sexual assault investigation in the past five years. Remarkably, as of 2012, more than 20% of schools gave their athletic department oversight on cases involving student athletes.[19] Consequently, because of these policies, survivors nationwide struggled with uncertainty and lack of resolution while perpetrators remained on campus. The knowledge that they could encounter their perpetrator at any moment frequently increases survivors' PTSD symptoms, anxiety, and depression. Fears or actual experiences of retaliation from the perpetrator or his friends also escalates symptoms.[20]

Those universities that did pursue a disciplinary hearing often employed procedures that elevated survivors' psychological distress and revictimized the survivor.[21] Disciplinary committee members frequently questioned survivors about their sexual past, what they were wearing, whether they flirted with the accused prior to the assault, and whether they screamed or physically fought against the attacker. Such questions are rooted in rape myths and insufficient knowledge about physiological responses to trauma. For instance, the question about screaming or physically resisting the assailant is based on the rape myth that a person who does not want to have sex will scream and physically resist his or her assailant. Such an assumption is unreasonable because a key response to a traumatic event is often a "freeze" reaction. Many sexual assault victims report that they literally could not move during the assault. Procedures often dictate that survivors need to be present while the accused victim and witnesses challenge their credibility and integrity. According to the National Center for Higher Education Risk Management (NCHERM) consulting group, such a process discourages survivors from filing reports and participating in judicial hearings.[22]

Furthermore, since judicial boards prior to 2012 used the "clear and convincing evidence standard," many accused students were found not responsible for sexual assault—a devastating judgment for survivors. The "clear and convincing evidence standard," a higher standard than is typically used in civil lawsuits, requires that the evidence used during the trial must be substantially more likely to be true than not.[23] When "clear and convincing" was the standard used by judicial boards, many board members viewed unwanted sex that occurred when a victim was drinking and incapacitated as a "gray area" or a "he said/she said" situation that failed to meet the legal standard.

Even when accused students were found responsible for rape and other forms of sexual assault, the vast majority of college perpetrators still faced no serious consequences. In a 2010 year-long investigation of campus disciplinary processes concerning sexual assault, the Center of Public Integrity found that 75 to 90% of disciplinary actions given by schools that report statistics to the Justice Department's Office on Violence Against Women consisted of minor sanctions like reprimands, counseling, writing a letter of apology, or a research paper on sexual violence: "The database shows that colleges rarely expel culpable students in these cases—even though the Justice Department encourages its campus grant recipients to train judicial panels to hand down 'appropriate sanctions, such as expulsion.'"[24]

A 2011 *Chicago Tribune* investigation of six midwestern universities tracked 171 alleged campus sex crimes reported by students and investigated by police over the previous five years; of the twelve accused perpetrators arrested, only four were convicted. The rate of arrests and convictions in these college sexual assault cases is well below the average reported nationally. As the *Tribune* article concluded, "The trend leaves untold numbers of college women feeling betrayed and vulnerable, believing that their allegations are not taken seriously."[25] In a 2014 *Huffington Post* investigation of sexual assault cases at nearly three dozen colleges and universities, students found responsible for sexual assault were expelled in only 30% of cases. Additionally, after examining 2011–2013 data from 125 schools who receive Department of Justice federal grants to address rape, the *Post* found that between 13 and 30% of students were expelled.[26] Universities' unsupportive policies and procedures, frequent findings of "not responsible," and/or minimal sanctions for sexual assault (allowing students found responsible for sexual assault to remain on campus) culminate in a profound sense of institutional betrayal, which in turn intensifies survivors' posttraumatic symptoms.[27] In a study of 349 female college students, 68% reported at least one unwanted sexual experience. Of the women who reported any unwanted sexual experiences, many (46%) also reported experiencing at least one form of institutional betrayal.[28]

With survivors thus deprived of a safe and supportive environment essential to recovery from traumatization, it is no surprise that such a high percentage of survivors drop out of college while their assailants graduate. The prospect of encountering their assailant on campus exacerbates PTSD and other disorder symptoms, and the layers of secondary victimization interfere with their capacity to learn and succeed academically. Thus the decision to allow students found responsible for rape to remain on campus results in survivors dropping out or transferring.

Tragically, secondary victimization caused by negative social reactions and universities' institutional betrayal increases survivors' risk of suicidal ideation and suicide.[29] When asked eighteen months after her rape to describe its effects on her life, Kari's response highlights the impact of her college community's unsupportive responses and betrayal:

The loneliness, the isolation that I felt—that has caused severe depression. I've tried a ton of different medicines. I still see a therapist at least once a week, so I would say the flashbacks, the depression; I mean I've had suicidal thoughts.... The majority of the first couple of months I really felt like I didn't want to live anymore. It got really bad. I was having flashbacks, and I think it just kind of hit me that day, and I was just like, I don't want to do this anymore, I don't want to do this anymore. I didn't see any reason to continue. I really didn't. And I think about it now, and I think about, oh that was selfish of me, but I really just didn't want to do it anymore. I have major trust issues with anyone. It's hard for me to see the good in people. It's hard for me to not feel like they are going to betray me because I just felt like so many people betrayed me.[30]

Kari's peers, friends, and athletic team not only rejected her and spread rumors about her after the assault but also harassed and retaliated against her when her perpetrator—a popular athlete—was suspended after being found responsible for rape. With the exception of a therapist, counselor, several professors, and a few survivors on campus, Kari encountered negative social reactions from peers, administrators, and staff, experienced many delays in the disciplinary hearing, and was even pressured to drop her allegation and negotiate with her offender. Having witnessed Kari's depression and anxiety throughout this excruciating process, I remained concerned about whether she would survive. I am relieved that she did; Kari is now a professional who helps others seek justice.

Not all college students are as fortunate as Kari. Lizzy Seebring, a first-year student at St. Mary's College, committed suicide September 10, 2010—ten days after she reported that a Notre Dame football player sexually assaulted her in his dorm room. After reporting the assault to Notre Dame campus police, she received text messages from one of the football player's friends: "Don't do anything you would regret," and "Messing with Notre Dame football is a bad idea." During the next nine days that Lizzy was alive, the police did not interview the football player, and Lizzy was intimidated by their texts and overwhelmed by her decision to report the assault and "go up against" the entire Notre Dame football establishment. She worried about "betraying Notre Dame"—an institution she had grown up revering—but she also worried that dropping her allegation could harm other women who might be victimized by the same player.[31]

Negative rumors about Lizzy circulated after her death. When the football player was finally interviewed five days after Lizzy's death, he told the police that she was the aggressor, and that he stopped her from initiating sexual activity. Rumors circulated that the player was wrongly accused by an aggressive young woman who had made up prior stories of assault for attention. Some also used her history of being diagnosed with anxiety to discredit her and blame her assault on her psychological condition. Many sought to attribute her suicide to her history of anxiety rather than the traumatic impact of the assault and the community's negative response. Lizzy's therapist responded that Lizzy's anxiety did not make her a high risk for suicide. She pointed out that sexual assault, however, is linked with suicide. Melinda Henneberger, a journalist who interviewed Notre Dame students, faculty, and staff in fall of 2010, discovered that many students were not alarmed by Lizzy's assault nor concerned with Notre Dame's handling of the assault. A female student expressed to Henneberger that she felt the Seeberg case "received more national attention than anyone here found necessary."[32] The student believed Lizzy's allegations. However, she stated:

> What drew my attention is she was depressed and was in some psychological distress prior to the event—and that she wasn't raped. It was a disrespectful and wrong action, but I was more drawn to the fact that this wasn't something new. Ultimately, I didn't get worked up or outraged or upset about it.[33]

Trey Malone's story is similar to Lizzy's. Trey was a student at Amherst College when he was raped in September, 2011. Trey reported the assault to Amherst administration. Less than a year later, in June, 2012, Trey committed suicide by jumping off a bridge in Tampa Bay.[34] In the letter he left behind, Trey emphasized how Amherst did not provide adequate support for him and how society fails to take seriously the crime of sexual violence and instead blames the victims of sexual assault:

> The sexual assault was too much. There was no adequate form of preparation available for that and no repair afterwards. What began as an earnest effort to help on the part of Amherst, became an emotionless hand washing. In those places I should've received help, I saw none. I suppose there are many possible reasons for this. But in the end, I'm still here and so too is that night. I hold no ill will, nor do I place an iota of blame upon my family. I blame a society

that remains unwilling to address sexual assault and rape. One that pays some object form of lip service to the idea of sexual crimes while working its hardest to marginalize its victims.[35]

Trey also included statistics about sexual assault in his note, making sure that everyone reading his letter would know how common it is and how frequently victims of sexual assault are blamed because people believe rape myths. His suicide called attention to how a lack of social support increases a sexual assault victim's suffering and can result in suicide.

Kari's suicidal ideation and struggle to survive, and Lizzy's and Trey's suicides after experiencing their communities' secondary victimization are far from rare. Studies indicate that between 11–18% of college students seriously consider attempting suicide and 2.8% of students attempt suicide. Approximately 7.5 per 100,000 students commit suicide each year.[36] Of these students, it is impossible to know how frequently sexual assault plays a role, but I do not doubt that improvements in our responses to sexual assault survivors would significantly reduce these figures.

Theological Reflection on Sexual Assault and the Community's Response to Survivors

Johann Metz's theological framework can shed light on the dynamics of college sexual violence, and a return to his theology is helpful as we prepare for the constructive phase of this book's final chapter: the creation of sexually just campus cultures. It's crucial, before moving on, to acknowledge a depth of connection that we don't easily notice among the "players" in the scenarios we have been exploring: instead of a clear separation between bad guys and good guys, the divide between sexual perpetrators, on the one hand, and the friends, peers, college administrators, faculty, and staff who fail to support survivors, on the other, is a more complicated continuum. Metz's uncomfortable but important gift is to illuminate our own tendency as "good guys" to collude with perpetrators rather than support survivors. Consider from Metz's theological perspective the choices and behaviors of members of a community impacted by sexual violence.

Perpetrators

The wake of destruction left by perpetrators of sexual assault as they embrace the very opposite of poverty of spirit is the easiest to identify.

Poverty of spirit entails a genuine openness to encountering another person as a distinct other, which in turn opens up the possibility of being rejected and hurt. Being naked and sexually active with another person in the context of encounter intensifies our vulnerability and relationality, as well as our awareness of the prospect of suffering. Instead of experiencing such vulnerability and relationality, sexual assault is all about pursuing one's own desires for sexual satisfaction, superiority, power, and control over another, and about obliterating the subjectivity and desire of the other. The decision to have sex with a person who is incapacitated functions similarly, and is another way to escape the vulnerability that might otherwise occur with a partner who is fully aware of and actively engaged in the sexual encounter. In each instance, the perpetrator's own egoistic desires for sexual satisfaction, power, control, and invulnerability are all that matters. Finally, as students' earlier reflections indicate, social pressure to have frequent sex and boast about it to prove one's masculinity and gain social acceptance motivates both predatory and incapacitated sexual assault. Perpetrators flee the poverty of uniqueness each time they endorse pervasive sexist beliefs, rape myths, and dominant cultural messages that associate masculinity with frequent sex, domination, superiority, aggression, and sexual prowess.

Bystanders

The unsupportive or hostile responses of bystanders to sexual assault survivors and their tendency to side with the perpetrator are sharply opposed to Christ's embrace of poverty of spirit. University members' collective denial of the scope of sexual violence and their decisions to side with the perpetrator are grounded in our collective denial of cruelty and evil in our midst. It remains far easier for everyone to either blame the victim for dressing too immodestly, getting drunk, and acting flirtatiously, or to attribute the assault to sexual miscommunication than to confront the reality that a significant percentage of students on college campuses sexually assault their peers.

Confronting this reality, by contrast, creates extreme cognitive dissonance. How can a student believe that her friend is capable of the cruelty described by the survivor? Likewise, it is threatening to faculty and staff to acknowledge the prospect that students they mentor, teach, and genuinely like are capable of such dehumanizing and predatory behavior. I have witnessed faculty members bending over backwards to advocate for accused students or to help them get course credit even when they were suspended midway through the semester. It is far easier to believe an accused student's story of innocence than to believe that she or he is capable of cruelty.

Believing survivors' accounts of sexual assault also brings us face to face with our own vulnerability to acts of evil, harm, trauma, and suffering. Such awareness that we, too, could become victimized threatens our illusions of security, self-control, and our cherished conviction that the world is fundamentally just. Such disbelief of the survivor and blame-the-victim tendencies represent our preference to flee from the abyss of suffering and choose the illusion of power and control over one's reality rather than experiencing the vulnerability and pain that occurs through empathetic connection and support of survivors.

Furthermore, bystanders' decisions to side with perpetrators stem from a tendency to conform to the status quo and renounce the poverty of uniqueness in order to maintain their own social status. If a student challenged his or her friend accused of rape, that student's relationship with both the alleged rapist and the alleged rapist's friend group would almost certainly be ruined. Going a step further, if he or she were to question and challenge the norms of what constitutes college fun—drinking to get drunk, demonstrating masculinity through wild antics, tallying drunken hookups (the list goes on)—that person would risk loss of reputation, social isolation, and utter rejection.

University administrators' systemic failure to implement best practices aimed at encouraging reporting and preventing sexual assault, supporting survivors, and holding perpetrators accountable is also about fleeing vulnerability and seizing power and control over their university's image. Prior to the 2011 Office of Civil Rights Dear Colleague Letter and subsequent changes in federal regulation concerning universities' responses to sexual assault,[37] fear of negative publicity meant that few universities were motivated to find out the truth about the prevalence and complex reality of sexual assault on their campuses or to create a campus culture that supported survivors. If a university were to do the "right thing" and conduct campus climate surveys to understand the scope of sexual assault and alter policies to support survivors, its public record of assault would create the impression that the university had higher rates of sexual assault than its peer institutions. Negative publicity and its impact on recruitment kept many universities from creating a supportive environment for survivors to come forward and report sexual assault. It was far easier for many university staff to follow the status quo and carry out their bosses' orders (such as discouraging survivors from reporting and pursuing a disciplinary hearing) than to stand up and challenge an unjust system and risk critique or job loss.

Changing policies and procedures to ensure due process rights not only for perpetrators but also for victims and choosing serious sanctions like expulsion could also harm a university's reputation and make the institution vulnerable to lawsuits and financial losses. Suspending and expelling highly valued athletes could also result in negative repercussions. Having a reputation of expelling athletes for rape and sexual assault could make it more difficult for university coaches and athletic directors to recruit top talent. When we consider all these complex dynamics that lead friends, peers, administrators, faculty, and staff to side with perpetrators rather than sexual assault survivors, we understand that the problem of sexual assault is not simply about a few bad guys (the 6% of college men who are repeat rapists). Nor is progress made by lumping all college men into the "bad guy" category and characterizing all college women as good. As innumerable survivors' stories attest, college women may not commit sexual assault as frequently as men, but they can exacerbate survivors' traumatization by their cruelty and betrayal.

Every member of a campus community, then, faces temptations to flee poverty of spirit and abandon the challenge of becoming fully human. We are all would-be accomplices sometimes, by: (1) wanting to flee neediness, vulnerability, and the abyss of suffering; (2) prioritizing egoistic self-interest, power, and control; and (3) renouncing the poverty of uniqueness by following the crowd. For both individuals and entire communities, yielding to these temptations culminates in a tragic failure to love neighbor as self and God, and to experience what truly constitutes our joy and fulfillment—communion of God, self, and others. Through Metz's theological lens, we learn that embracing poverty of spirit in our response to sexual assault consists of (1) encountering the abyss by acknowledging our weaknesses, vulnerabilities, and limitations; (2) relating to others as ends in themselves; and (3) embracing our unique selves and challenging injustices. At stake in our response to sexual violence is a fundamental choice to embrace our interdependence and love others and God.

Metz would say that we can only be fulfilled by loving others—particularly such vulnerable others as survivors of sexual assault. Although this chapter may tempt us toward despair and cynicism by its hard look at our collective tendencies to deny the reality and trauma of sexual assault and side with perpetrators over victims, it is possible for members of a campus community to work together to create a culture where sexual assault is no longer tolerated, survivors are supported, and each person is treated as an end in him/herself. Fortunately, alongside the many discouraging stories we can tell, there have also been instances that remind us of our capacity for compassion, truth-telling, altruism, courage, and commitment to work for communal transformation and justice. The next and final chapter will identify three particular commitments needed to create a college culture of justice that honors persons' dignity, bodily integrity, and deepest desires for relationships.

Moving forward, we must not think that accountability for change rests primarily with a single constituency on college campuses—college administrators, for example—nor even among a broader circle led by outspoken faculty or student activists. Key players should include as many faculty, students, and staff as possible (counselors, coaches, campus security, residential life, etc.) collaborating to promote and protect students' well-being; local religious leaders transforming church culture to be a stronger counterculture of justice-making; media leaders changing how they depict men and women, sex and relationships, and life in general for adolescents and young adults; parents modeling responsible behavior and having honest discussions about alcohol and relationships with their high school and college aged children; and so on. In the end, of course, accountability cannot simply end with a list of "others," no matter how extensive. No longer permitting ourselves to turn away from the injustices we perceive, accountability rests from here on out with you and me as well.

11

Creating a Sexually Just Campus Culture

TOGETHER, THE VOICES of college students and the findings of social scientific research indicate the immense challenges we face in creating a sexually just culture in which all persons are respected as ends in themselves. These challenges are rooted in and fueled by systemic injustices (e.g., sexism, racism, heterosexism) and social structures (e.g., neoliberal capitalism, the legal system, educational systems) that are much bigger than any single well-meaning person. Yet even these big problems are not insurmountable. Our collective responsibility is to name and challenge unjust narratives of sexuality and gender and to alter unjust norms through our daily actions. For those of us attending or employed by universities, our first task is to envision what a sexually just university campus culture would look like and consider how all members of a campus community can make this vision a reality.

Spurred by students who questioned the validity of traditional scholarship on hookup culture, my journey through qualitative analyses of party ethnographies and students' theological reflections has taught me much about students' complex lived realities. Synthesizing what I have learned from listening to my students year after year, from social scientific research, and from recent social movements by undergraduate activists nationwide, I propose in this chapter that creating a sexually just college culture should begin with three essential commitments: (1) an endorsement of an affirmative sexual consent policy; (2) an embrace of a culture of zero tolerance for sexual violence; and (3) a conscious, collective decision among undergraduates to free one another from the constrictive sexual, gender, and social norms of typical party and hookup culture.

Endorsing an Affirmative Sexual Consent Standard

There needs to be cause to say "Are you okay with this?" for someone to proceed. So, I think a lot of times people don't make that step. And people aren't in the right mind to consent or to stop and that's why drunken hookups are so dangerous.

UNIVERSITY A FEMALE STUDENT, 2011 interview

A hopeful sign that a future in which communicating and respecting one another's sexual desires and boundaries is culturally normative has appeared in the recent social movement to prevent sexual violence and enhance student safety by implementing an affirmative sexual consent policy on college campuses. The 2014 California Senate Bill 967, which requires its institutions of higher education to adopt an affirmative consent standard, defines *affirmative consent* as:

> affirmative, conscious, and voluntary agreement to engage in sexual activity. It is the responsibility of each person involved in the sexual activity to ensure that he or she has the affirmative consent of the other or others to engage in the sexual activity. Lack of protest or resistance does not mean consent, nor does silence mean consent. Affirmative consent must be ongoing throughout a sexual activity and can be revoked at any time. The existence of a dating relationship between the persons involved, or the fact of past sexual relations between them, should never by itself be assumed to be an indicator of consent.[1]

Partners can signal affirmative consent for sexual activity either verbally or through positive nonverbal gestures and cues. According to these expectations for consent, it should be clear and unambiguous to both parties that their desire to participate in a sexual activity is mutual. As Jaclyn Friedman explains:

> Sexual consent isn't like a light switch, which can be either "on," or "off." It's not like there's this one thing called "sex" you can consent to anyhow. "Sex" is an evolving series of actions and interactions. You have to have the enthusiastic consent of your partner for all of them.[2]

As of 2015, at least 1,500 universities had adopted some version of an affirmative consent standard for their campuses,[3] and thus far California, New York, Illinois, Connecticut, and New Jersey have passed legislation requiring all institutions of higher education to do so. In California, affirmative consent legislation even extends to high schools. Twenty additional states are considering statewide affirmative consent policies or have cities hoping for city-wide policies for their colleges and universities.[4]

This trend constitutes exciting, meaningful progress, particularly insofar as new consent policies create a cultural shift away from a "no means no" consent framework, which arose as a response to entrenched gender expectations. These cultural expectations relegated men to being sexual initiators and persuading (or pressuring) women to have sex. They also consigned women to being gatekeepers who say "no" to unwanted sexual advances. This cultural expectation that men are to persist despite women's initial refusal and reluctance often undermined the effectiveness of the campaign to have women's "no" be respected as a legitimate refusal. The "no means no" approach to consent is also ineffective because women often experience a freeze reaction to unwanted sexual advances that prevents them from verbally or physically refusing sex. A 2011 study, for instance, found that 42% of women who experienced unwanted sexual advances froze and expressed no verbal communication or physical resistance.[5] In contrast, the affirmative consent motto "yes means yes" fosters a different perspective and set of expectations in its view of both partners being active and responsible in sexual decision-making and its emphasis that communication and affirmative consent is needed prior to pursuing differing levels of sexual activity. For instance, rather than viewing aggressive, nonconsensual sex as a mistake resulting from innocent, drunken miscommunication, the affirmative consent framework expects that persons will not drink alcohol if they are at risk of making decisions that harm others, and it expects that persons will clearly communicate about sexual desires. As Melanie Boyd notes, affirmative consent is simply an "accurate description of what we do when we are having sex that is not abusive or coerced: We seek confirmation that our partner is a willing participant."[6] Ultimately the concept of affirmative consent rests on the basic assumption that bodies are not generally available for sexual penetration. As Michelle Anderson explains:

> If people's bodies are generally available to be sexually penetrated, then one should be able to penetrate someone else at any time,

unless that person communicates an objection to being penetrated. If, by contrast, people's bodies are not generally available to be sexually penetrated, one should not be able to penetrate someone without that person's affirmative permission. Affirmative consent thus rejects the argument that mere submission or acqiescnece is sufficient for consent. It is a mechanism to maximize sexual autonomy.[7]

Critics of affirmative consent sometimes argue that requiring partners to receive verbal or nonverbal consent to sex does not resolve potential ambiguity inherent in nonverbal communication. Claiming that innocent men could be expelled under an affirmative consent policy, critics on social media argue that a man could innocently interpret a woman enthusiastically consenting while she, in fact, does not want to have sex. Yet research indicates that young men do recognize and understand subtle verbal and nonverbal ways of communicating sexual refusal.[8] Those who oppose adopting an affirmative consent standard also complain that affirmative consent is excessively detrimental to "the mood" and the spontaneity that characterize good sex. Such claims may appear compelling to undergraduates, since my students' reflections suggest that their generation remains highly uncomfortable with sexual communication and the vulnerability it entails. Such momentary uneasiness, however, is a small price to pay compared to the common experiences of dissatisfying sex or the profound suffering of sexual assault that results from lack of communication and consent.

With all of this in mind, faculty, student affairs staff, and student groups need to offer academic spaces and other forums on campus for students to discuss and ask questions about how to communicate about sexuality, be assertive about their sexual boundaries, and obtain affirmative consent. Fortunately, many universities are beginning to utilize diverse approaches to promote affirmative consent, ranging from Facebook messages, to required first-year orientation meetings, to classes and workshops addressing sexual respect and healthy relationships.[9] Many organizations and college student groups are seeking to change cultural discomfort about sexual communication and asking for consent by embracing media campaigns like "Consent is Sexy," and creating projects and videos that promote sexual communication and affirmative consent.[10] For instance, Men Can Stop Rape, a nonprofit that seeks to redefine masculinity and male strength to create a culture of nonviolence, utilizes "The Strength

Campaign" to educate and promote affirmative consent among adolescent and young adult men.[11]

It is still too early to determine the extent to which affirmative consent policies and programs are motivating students to adopt a cultural drinking norm that is different from drinking to get drunk and incapacitated. Under the affirmative consent standard, a student wishing to avoid charges of sexual assault and potential expulsion needs to limit his or her sex partners to those who are sober or who have only consumed an amount of alcohol that has obviously not affected their cognitive abilities to consent. Without shifting the cultural norm of drinking, of course, affirmative consent will never become a normative practice, since conscious and voluntary agreement to engage in sexual activity cannot be given if one's partner is incapacitated. As the student reflections revealed in part II, the desire to have drunken sex rather than sober sex is due partially to fears of vulnerability and the desire to escape accountability and moral judgment from one's peers. If students become comfortable with sexual communication and seeking consent, and if they stop judging their peers about sexual decisions that do not cause harm to others, a future is possible in which undergraduates find sober, mutually consensual sex more desirable, satisfying, and pleasurable than drunken hookup sex.

Creating a Culture of Zero Tolerance for Sexual Assault

Throughout my years at University A, I was inspired periodically by the efforts of young men on campus who went out of their way to renounce sexual assault publicly and sought to transform their peer culture to one of sexual respect. The words and actions of two students will suffice to introduce what is needed for a culture of zero tolerance.

During my first year of teaching, after my students had written their perspectives on reducing sexual violence on our campus, I received their permission to make an appointment with the provost during finals week to discuss their ideas and provide him with a copy of their reflections. As class ended, Mark, a popular senior who had been a likeable class clown, asked me whether he could attend the meeting. Not sure of his motives, and a little concerned about the effect his presence might have on the meeting, I nevertheless honored his right to discuss class findings with the administration. At the beginning of our meeting, he informed the provost that sexual violence was a huge problem on our campus: three of his closest friends had been raped in the four years he had been a student, and he was furious about how University A had failed his friends. As a professor with training in sexual ethics, I was prepared to convey a number of important points, but the provost's eyes remained glued on Mark, and he directed his questions to Mark rather than me. As the meeting ended, I handed the provost my students' reflections, and three weeks later I received a request to attend meetings on sexual violence throughout the summer. The provost wanted to set up an advocate group for sexual assault survivors and a hotline to be ready by mid-August. While the provost might have arrived at his decision without a conversation with Mark, I couldn't help but wonder whether a male student's perspective and anger about the university's failure to address the scope of sexual violence had a more profound impact on the provost than the perspective of various female professors who had been raising these issues for many years.

A second person who made a lasting impression was an easygoing junior who participated in a DVD project I undertook for three years to interview University A students on hookup culture, sexual violence, and sexual justice. During his video interview, Jake mentioned that he had organized some events called "Men's Rally for Respect," which involved recruiting male athletes and other men to speak about their respect for women as they renounced campus sexual assault. I asked what had motivated him to create and organize these events. Jake responded:

I won't accept it—sexual violence—as the reality that we live in. There's a statistic [that] 1 in 4 college women are raped; they are victims of sexual violence, and I don't know how anyone can accept that. Even if the statistic is 1 in 10, that's still way too many. I remember after I heard the statistic, I would count 1, 2, 3, 4, and there would be one of my friends and I would go, "Oh, my God" . . . 1, 2, 3 . . . "Oh, there's another friend!" That's so negative. That's not a reality that I want. And so the Men's Rally for Respect was kind of a goal to get men to realize this because we felt as though sexual violence is stereotypically a women's issue. I think that women have been better educated than men, so we want to reach out to men and say, "Hey, this is not a women's issue, this is a people's issue. This is something that affects all of us." And it was called Men Rally *for* Respect because we didn't just want to be *against* sexual assault, we wanted to be *for* something, so we're *for* respect. What that meant was we are encouraging men to say, "Hey, this is a problem, we don't want to accept this as the reality."

During his interview, Jake identified several ways he sought to live out his respect for women each day. Besides talking "a lot" about sex and intimacy with his girlfriend and making sure they were on the same page with their decisions, he found it important to challenge friends and acquaintances whenever they made comments that were offensive and derisive toward women. For example, if someone said, "I got raped by that test," he would draw attention to the trivialization of sexual violence unintentionally conveyed by those words. There is an art to commanding peers' respect and maintaining one's likeability as one challenges unjust norms. Jake was able to advocate for sexual respect and greater justice without sacrificing his masculine image, respect, or popularity.

Fortunately, students like Mark and Jake who embrace countercultural commitments to a healthier campus climate are not alone in their decision to devote time and energy to issues of sexuality and justice. For instance, between 2009 and 2011, over two hundred students at University A volunteered, along with Jake, to be interviewed and share their honest perspectives on hookups, sexual violence, and sexual justice for my DVD project. When I sought to train students to watch and discuss this DVD with groups of first-year students, sixty to ninety juniors and seniors volunteered extensive time and energy every fall to become trained as "peer leaders for sexual justice." Elsewhere, at universities including Yale, Amherst, Dickinson, Swarthmore, Dartmouth, UC Berkeley, and Princeton, student activists have utilized protests and other strategies to pressure their colleges to respond more deliberately and emphatically to sexual violence. Students have demanded more transparent policies and procedures on campus sexual assault, expulsion of students found guilty of violating campus conduct standards, and creation of more effective support systems (including academic support) for survivors. According to Dr. Angus Johnston, eighteen examples of student activism concerning sexism and sexual assault occurred in the fall of 2014 alone.[12]

Building on local achievements at particular colleges and universities, activists can also now see the fruits of their labors in a variety of larger initiatives, including the formation of national websites such as "Know Your IX," which educates students about their civil rights when sexually assaulted; the Department of Education's investigation of colleges and universities over Title IX sexual assault violations;[13] legislative victories such as the drafting of congressional bills; and work being done on numerous state-level committees. Most notably, perhaps, the national movement to end sexual violence on college campuses found a powerful ally in the Obama administration's White House Task Force to Protect Students from Sexual Assault. From 2014 to 2016, the White House made unprecedented progress in raising awareness of campus sexual assault, funding and disseminating research on best practices to prevent and respond to sexual assault. If the Trump administration and subsequent administrations pursue the initiatives of this White House Task Force and continue to enforce the revised Title IX regulations, I believe we will be in the best possible position to create a cultural environment in which sexual assault is no longer tolerated on college campuses.[14]

How, specifically, shall we proceed to establish a culture of zero tolerance? I propose that colleges and universities adopt the following five practices: (1) education to all campus members about sexual assault (with a special focus on the relationship between alcohol and sexual assault), affirmative consent, and sexual violence prevention; (2) transparent university policies and procedures on sexual assault; (3) mobilization of a supportive community for survivors to reduce traumatization and foster their recovery; (4) bystander intervention training for undergraduates to prevent sexual assaults; and (5) implementation of consistent and serious sanctions for sexual assault.

The White House Task Force report *Not Alone: The First Report of the White House Task Force to Protect Students from Sexual Assault* and the related NotAlone.gov website are tremendous starting points, the latter being perhaps the best place to access resources for both students and schools. Perusing its information and links, one easily identifies the interweaving and recurrence of at least the first four practices listed above. Under the student tab, for example, is the vitally important topic of bystander intervention. Following the question "How Can I Help as a Bystander?" leads to the "It's On Us" public awareness and bystander intervention campaign to equip every man and woman across our nation to prevent sexual violence. During the first year of this campaign, many universities joined the "It's On Us" movement, and students at over 300 schools hosted more than 650 "It's On Us" events.[15] Many were also trained in bystander intervention through programs like Bringing in the Bystander, Green Dot, and the Men's Project.

How and why does bystander intervention work? First, the very presence of a bystander makes a completed rape 44% less likely.[16] Studies indicate that bystander training dispels rape myths and increases partici-pants' willingness to intervene and prevent assault. Undergraduates are also most likely to intervene if they feel confident about their skills, believe they can effectively help, and perceive that their peers also want to help and intervene. Since students tend to underestimate other peers' willing-ness to intervene, using a social norms approach (educating students that the majority of their peers favor intervention) is critical to bystander train-ing programs.[17]

Among major recommendations of the Task Force is the action step for institutions to develop "better school disciplinary systems," although the report remains tentative about specifics. Because serious sanctions for sex-ual assault, as I include in my fifth condition for a healthy culture of zero tolerance, have remained contested in some circles, the Justice Department acknowledged the need in 2014 to "begin assessing different models for investigating and adjudicating campus sexual assault cases with an eye toward identifying best practices."[18] Those practices must include serious, consistent sanctions for sexual assault.[19] When I asked my students: "What is the most just sanction if a student is found responsible for sexual assault involving any form of penetration?," the vast majority recommended expul-sion. Even Matt, the student mentioned in chapter 9 who committed rape, argued in class discussions that expulsion was the most just sanction. Here is a sampling of my students' individualized responses:

> I think the only way to completely prevent rape is to go with an all-out, zero tolerance policy toward rapists. (male student)

> University A needs to be very clear in the policy on campus that all sexual offenders will be severely dealt with, and that sexual assault of any kind will not be tolerated. This would mean a complete change in the attitude of this campus. Instead of shying away from the subject and hiding the real facts, campus police and officials need to make the occurrences known and deal with the offenders in a swift manner. There shouldn't be any question or thought as to getting off with a small penalty. (female student)

> Justice should be expulsion from the university because it's not the university's role to rehabilitate the rapist. (male student)

> The only way to prevent or lessen rape on campus is by giving out severe punishments to males or females who have committed

the crime. To be honest, in cases where a male knowingly takes advantage of a woman and rapes her, I think a good punishment would be for him to be treated back the same way by an inmate in prison. I think the man should be raped by another man so he will get a sense of the pain he caused a woman. I think that kind of punishment would dramatically decrease rape on campus. (male student)

Being raped is an extremely traumatic, life-altering experience. At the least, the perpetrator should be expelled and criminal charges should be leveled against the rapist, if the victim so chooses. Most importantly, we should change the system so that the victim does not feel like she is being repeatedly raped by every officer, judge, and lawyer she meets so that rape can be prosecuted more often and hopefully crime decreases. Right now women aren't reporting it because they don't think they can. I never prosecuted the guy who raped me because I was basically told I had no right to do so: wrong place, wrong time = my fault. So I said nothing. (female student)

To foster debate in class, I drew on arguments against expulsion that were being made at that time by certain University A administrators. Since the mission of the university was educational and eighteen to twenty-two-year-olds were still in a crucial developmental phase (with their frontal lobes not fully developed, etc.), sanctions should focus on educating students found responsible for sexual assault and universities should give them a second chance to learn from their mistakes. Not a single student found this rationale compelling. Students in multiple sections of the course pointed out that eighteen to twenty-two-year-olds face serious consequences for drunken driving, physical assaults, and murder within the criminal justice system. Society also considers them mature and responsible enough to vote and go to war. Why would universities not hold college students accountable for sexual assault and have serious sanctions in place? Other students emphasized that their generation was motivated most by consequences: if no severe negative consequences exist for sexual assault, it is highly likely that sexual assault will continue to occur and college campuses will remain unsafe. Students were also skeptical of the prospect that those found responsible for sexual assault would be rehabilitated by their university's educational efforts and second-chance philosophy and actually stop committing sexual assault. Such skepticism, it turns out, is entirely appropriate, for there remains a lack of evidence that college campuses can effectively rehabilitate sex offenders.[20]

Recently, universities including Yale, Duke, Vassar, Dartmouth, Princeton, the University of Iowa, the University of North Carolina-Chapel Hill, and Northwestern University have revised their sexual assault policies to include expulsion as a strongly recommended or likely sanction for rape.[21] They are recognizing what my students years ago found obvious: expulsion is essential to prevent assault, create a culture of zero tolerance for sexual violence, and ensure the safety of the community to the best of our ability. While progress has been made, the 2016 report "Addressing Gender-Based Violence on College Campuses" continues to identify a need for campuses to improve offender accountability.[22]

Freeing One Another from Dominant Sexual, Social Norms

A third central component of creating a sexually just culture should include the commitment to unseat hookup culture as the dominant social, sexual, and relational norm and instead promote a range of socially viable options such as dating and committed relationships on campus. Throughout their reflections, students at Universities A and B express that in a happier and/ or more just culture, they would be freed of the narrow sexual, gendered, and relational norms of party and hookup culture. Recall, in chapter 4, University A students expressing that they would be personally happier at parties if women could dress more comfortably, if men and women interacted as equals and did not conform to traditional gender norms, if they felt accepted for who they are, and if they were freed from the expectation to drink heavily and hook up. Consistent with this, the vast majority of students at University B expressed both that hookups fail to be just sex and that the most equal, mutual, and pleasurable sex is far more likely to take place in relationships than in casual hookups.

Furthermore, in over two hundred interviews in which students from University A were asked to describe a sexually just college culture, dominant themes were that students would not be expected to hook up and they would not objectify each other as they do in hookup culture; instead, they would know each other when getting involved sexually:

> There wouldn't be an expectation of a hookup necessarily. So we wouldn't pressure ourselves, we wouldn't pressure our friends to be

sexual and the desire to be sexual would be from one's self and not from an external force. (male student)

People who are active in the hookup culture tend to objectify other people and also themselves. Thinking that it's okay for people to be treated like that—that totally needs to be removed. It would be great if sex wasn't something that happened after you've had a large amount of alcohol. If you are talking to someone and just hanging out and you really are getting to know them and you like them, the sex is going to be way more pleasurable and you know you are going to be more excited by it than if you hooked up with somebody. So I would say a sexually just campus culture would involve no alcohol and that people would know each other. (female student)

I think a sexually just campus would have people look at each other not so much in lust but in a way of friendship. Hookup culture lacks friendship. People have friends with benefits but I think it is kind of like—you know people, you have sex with them, you let them go. It is not like you know anything deeper about them—other than how their bodies look obviously. I think that a sexually just campus would be a place where you would get to know the insides of people—what goes on beneath the skin. How do people think of you? What challenges them? What doesn't challenge them? What do they take for granted? What do they like? You know those are the things you don't really get to know about people when you just hook up with someone. A sexually just culture would be about accepting other people based on who they are. (male student)

I would love to see the dating scene come back, the ability for me to ask a girl out on a date and not feel this huge social pressure like "What do I do?" and all of this stuff. And kind of having all these expectations whereas it used to be that people could just ask people on a date and be like "Oh, okay." We need a little romance. (male student)

In class discussions throughout my years of teaching Christian sexual ethics, many students have expressed curiosity and interest in the very idea of dating (as long as it doesn't adopt the overt sexism associated with dating in the fifties). Students consistently express that they wish dating could be viewed more casually in their culture; men in my courses have repeatedly mentioned that they would likely be perceived as a creepy stalker if they were to ask a woman to have lunch in the student cafeteria, whereas they would be considered normal if they simply had drunken sex with her at a party. How, when, and why, they wonder, did college culture become this way?

Throughout my years of teaching and learning from students about sexuality, gender, and justice, I have come to the conclusion that the cultural shift most needed to achieve a sexually just, genuinely inclusive culture is the abandonment of a taboo, judgmental approach to sexuality and the embrace of a justice and fulfillment approach.[23] College students and adolescents need to recognize that putting others down either for not having sex or for having sex (by calling women "prudes" or "sluts," for example, and abstinent men "gay") is an egoistic and cruel attempt to feel superior and bolster their own struggling self-esteem and social status. Judging persons' character on their sexual decisions fuels the sexual double standard and also encourages excessive drinking in order to escape or mitigate sexual judgment. As students note, they are judged "less harshly" if they are drunk and sex "just happened" than if they are sober and consciously decide to have sex. In a climate of safe and open dialogue about personal and communal flourishing and justice, however, young adults are encouraged to make and "own" their decisions. Characterizing certain sexual acts like hookups as "bad" and "impure" (and thus taboo) only shuts down youth and young adults and invites shame and silence. Instead of operating from an all-knowing and judgmental stance, religious traditions might focus their energies on sharing their rich and distinctive theological and spiritual resources to encourage critical deconstruction of dehumanizing, reductive narratives of sex, relationships, success, and happiness. Religious communities can use their resources to engage in open dialogue with youth and young adults about their social reality and struggles to foster wise discernment about one's authentic self, life's purpose, fulfillment, and justice for themselves and their communities.

Rather than preoccupying (or entertaining) ourselves with judgmental gossip about persons' sexual actions, we need to reorient ourselves to focus on what really matters most in life. I believe sexual and gender justice advocate John Stoltenberg points us in the right direction:

What matters is the center inside yourself—and how you live, and how you treat people, and what you can contribute as you pass

through life on this earth, and how honestly you love, and how carefully you make choices. Those are the things that really matter.[24]

While Stoltenberg most likely has never encountered Metz's account of
full humanity, his emphasis on authenticity, love, relationships, and other-
centeredness embodies the poverty of spirit I have found so important to
identify, celebrate, and encourage in the pages of this book.

Conclusion

The task of *College Hookup Culture and Christian Ethics* has been to place
undergraduates' own accounts of their social realty in dialogue with
Christian theology and ethics, to imagine alternative future realities, and
to recognize individuals and groups already achieving great things in our
midst. Understanding, imagining, and recognizing are relatively easy, however, and no amount of excellent observation, analysis, and argumentation
can take the place of what we might call the real work that awaits us now.
My hope is that these eleven chapters will foster empathy for those who
suffer from party and hookup norms, and will serve, in the next chapter of
our lived commitments, as a call to action. As my students and undergraduate activists everywhere have demonstrated, many are already implicitly
embracing poverty of spirit by devoting their creativity, time, and energy
to creating healthier, happier, and more justice-filled campuses. We may
draw hope and inspiration, too, from scholars like Johann Metz, whose
theological anthropology and reflections on poverty of spirit light our own
path to full humanity; Margaret Farley, whose insistence on affirming each
other's "concrete realities" and whose seven moral norms for just sexual
expression give us an initial blueprint for creating a sexually just culture;
and the numerous social scientists (including my student ethnographers)
whose mutually corroborative work paves our way to new understandings,
ongoing inquiry, and powerful collaboration in the service of justice.

Research Methodology

The 126 undergraduate ethnography papers used in part I were generated from an assignment I gave for my Christian sexual ethics seminar and were collected during five academic terms (Summer 2010, Spring 2011, Summer 2011, Fall 2011, and Summer 2012). I kept only the papers written by undergraduates who signed a consent form granting permission to use their written work anonymously for the purposes of teaching and research. I received Institutional Review Board approval to analyze this data.[1] Undergraduate ethnographers chose their field research sites and attended college parties at a variety of private and public universities in seven states. They also had the freedom to utilize a variety of methods for their data collection. While all ethnographers engaged in participant observation, many chose to interview strangers, acquaintances, and/or friends at parties. Some ethnographers observed and interviewed friends intensively prior to, during, and the morning after parties, while others utilized text messages to obtain information about their peers' perceptions, desires, and behaviors.

After collecting the data, I employed Carl Auerbach and Louise Silverstein's grounded theory of qualitative analysis. Methodologically, this approach consists of five steps when interpreting transcribed interviews: (1) highlight the relevant text from the transcribed interviews; (2) identify repeating ideas in the relevant text; (3) organize repeating ideas into themes; (4) organize the themes into more abstract ideas called theoretical constructs; and (5) organize the theoretical constructs into a theoretical narrative that summarizes what one has learned about initial research concerns.[2]

There are several issues I wish to address regarding the trustworthiness of the data, the justifiability of my qualitative analysis, and its transferability regarding other populations. First, I utilized a convenience sample of students enrolled in my sexual ethics course. Since the course fulfilled both an upper-level theology requirement and a gender studies requirement, it attracted a diverse set of majors from arts and sciences, social sciences, and business. According to students' self-reports on the first day of the course, their primary motivation was to satisfy these two course requirements. Throughout each semester, students possessed a diverse range of beliefs and attitudes regarding sex, gender, relationships, religion, and ethics. As for gender and ethnic diversity among the research sample, 56% were female and 44% were male; 92% were Caucasian, 6% African American, and 2% Asian American. The lack of ethnic diversity in my sample reflected the broader population of this university. Classes generally reflected the religious composition of the student body: the majority were raised Christian, although these students were diverse in regard to beliefs, practices, and stance concerning whether they currently identified as Christian.

Since undergraduate ethnographers were assigned a grade for their ethnography paper, readers may question whether the power differential between the students and their professor compromised the trustworthiness of the data. Did students feel comfortable being honest about party descriptions and their perspectives, or did they offer responses that they surmised would resonate with the professor's ideas and views? I am confident, for the following reasons, that the vast majority of students' papers represented honest observations and sincere reflections:

1. My goal for this assignment was to have college students describe and analyze party culture as accurately as possible, then to encourage students later in the semester to compare their findings with social scientific research on college sexual culture. To ensure academic freedom, I assured students that grades would be based on the precision and depth of their descriptions and analyses and not upon their personal views or contextual factors of their descriptions and analysis. Furthermore, this assignment was situated within the broader context of my ordinary pedagogical commitments. The highest pedagogical priority in my courses is to honor students' academic freedom and create a respectful space where students can express their views honestly without fear of reprisal. I seek to ensure academic freedom by grading all major assignments blindly and pledging transparency with respect to final grading, which is based on a cumulative percentage. I do not raise or reduce a grade based on my subjective assessment of students' engagement with the materials or their class behavior. On anonymous midterm and final course evaluations of my Christian sexual ethics seminar, students have consistently agreed with the following statement: "I trust that I can be myself and express what I really think without being concerned that this could negatively affect my grade."

2. During the semesters that I collected this assignment I strongly encouraged self-reflexivity in students' roles as ethnographers and pressed students to reflect critically on the accuracy of their ethnographic observations and analysis. In small groups, they discussed specific questions like the following: How accurately did they capture what was happening at the college parties they attended? Did the fact that the assignment was graded and part of a theological ethics course compromise their

ability to be honest in their party descriptions and analyses? What, if anything, did they leave out of their descriptions and analyses? When assessing the pedagogical value of all readings and assignments at the end of the course, students were also asked to reflect again on the value of this assignment and to assess, in hindsight, whether they had been frank in their descriptions and analyses. Students consistently expressed feeling comfortable about being honest in their observations and perspectives. They also consistently recommended the assignment for future classes, ranking it as one of the most pedagogically effective, thought-provoking assignments of the course.

In regard to the justifiability of my qualitative analysis, I utilized many steps to ensure that my interpretations of repeated themes and theoretical constructs were grounded in the data itself and not an imposition of my own biases and perspectives. Along with most qualitative researchers, I reject the idea that it is possible for a researcher to interpret data with complete objectivity, as if unaffected by one's own subjective stance and cultural influences. The art of successful qualitative research requires one to be self-reflexive, profoundly aware of how subjectivity and biases may be influencing the process of interpretation. Immersing myself in this data intensively from 2012 to 2014, I sought to read and process the data on distinct but interrelated levels. On one level, I was aware that as a white heterosexual female ethics professor, mother, spouse, and person with particular values, passions, and hopes, I was responding uniquely to ethnographers' perspectives and descriptions. I kept notes of my reactions and ideas to study when I sought later to engage in my own theological and ethical analysis of this culture. On a more immediate level, my overriding objective was to capture as accurately as possible these undergraduate ethnographers' experiences and analyses of their social reality. Thus, I regarded it as essential to consult undergraduates throughout the process of coding and analysis. Besides my own qualitative coding, I hired two students (one white female and one white male undergraduate from a different university, neither of whom took my sexual ethics course) to code portions of the relevant text (de-identified) and identify repeating ideas and themes. In addition to discussing our coding outlines of repeating ideas and themes, I asked them to critique later drafts of my first four chapters in part I. Their primary task was to identify any ideas or themes not adequately grounded in the data that could represent an imposition of my own biases and concerns.

Moreover, in order to ensure that my qualitative analysis represented as accurately as possible undergraduate ethnographers' collective account of their social reality, I embraced a stance of epistemic humility throughout my two years of coding and analysis and asked for feedback from students in my sexual ethics courses from 2010 to 2012. During every semester that I read ethnography assignments, I took notes on repeating ideas, themes, and particular quotations and checked with students on which ideas were representative of their college party culture and which appeared as exaggerations. When classes came to a consensus that a particular description of a party behavior or sexual act was extreme and not representative of typical college parties, I deleted it. During the fall of 2011, I also asked students to read a conference paper I was presenting at the American Academy of Religion on gender dynamics of college party and hookup culture. Their assignment was to identify party behavior descriptions, ideas, quotations, and analyses that failed to represent accurately their own perceptions of college party culture. During two sections of my Summer 2012 course, I engaged in a final member check. Students critically evaluated an initial draft of my qualitative analysis of the first 55 ethnographies I had collected. This draft included the topics addressed in chapters 1–4 of this book.

It is important to clarify that I did not delete voices from students who were in the minority in terms of race or sexual orientation. I was only interested in deleting descriptions of party behavior that appeared "extreme" or sensationalistic to a class of college students. For instance, several students witnessed some particular acts of sex that occurred publicly. When classes of students came to a consensus that these kind of behaviors did not frequently occur publicly at parties, I deleted those descriptions.

However, given the lack of ethnic diversity among my students and the larger student body at University A, it is crucial to acknowledge that my ethnographers' accounts of party culture and my students' assessment of which party descriptions are representative of typical party culture predominantly reflect the perspective of Caucasian students—the majority of whom also gave the impression that they were heterosexual from comments made in their papers about their interest in the opposite sex.[3] Thus, the understanding of college party culture emerging from the ethnographies could possibly have been much different or more varied if the student body had been more diverse in regard to race, ethnicity, and sexual orientation.

Throughout the process of qualitative analysis, I sought to demonstrate the justifiability of my analysis through transparency, clarity, and coherence. While qualitative researchers do not claim that their analysis of data constitutes the only valid interpretation, they do seek to make clear and transparent how they justifiably arrived at their analysis. I have therefore kept a careful audit trail, saving each stage of coding, including my and other coders' outlines of themes and repeating ideas. I have also saved documents of each ethnographer's response to particular questions as a means of achieving transparency with regard to how I identified themes and percentages.

Lastly, readers might question whether the perspectives of ethnographers attending a midwestern Catholic liberal arts university cohere with the broader experiences and perspectives of college students in the United States. The data may have differed if I had expanded my sample to include undergraduate ethnographers attending public, private secular, and evangelical colleges and universities from diverse geographical locations. My study, however, involving undergraduates at a single university, never had such a broad scope in mind. Intending to be exploratory, it simply investigates one group of undergraduates' sober ethnographic descriptions and analyses of college party culture in midwestern and southern states. I sought to discover general patterns that emerge from an in-depth qualitative analysis of this particular group of undergraduates. I leave it to my readers to render their own judgments about whether they recognize their own, their friends', or family members' experiences and struggles within my account of contemporary college party and hookup culture and the broader American cultural trends that influence us all. Thus far, feedback I have received from college students during lectures on my research findings in Wisconsin, Minnesota, and Missouri (from 2012 to 2014) strongly indicates that my descriptions and analyses resonate with a broader population of college students' experiences and perceptions of college party dynamics.

Notes

1. To protect students' confidentiality, all names and other identifying features throughout this work have been changed. As necessary, I made slight edits to avoid confusion and awkwardness that occurred occasionally in students' writing.

2. See Justin R. Garcia et al., "Sexual Hookup Culture: A Review," *Review of General Psychology* 16, no. 2 (June 2012): 161–76.

3. Ibid.

4. When I received a 2009 grant to organize a program on hookup culture for first-year college students, I asked my students for ideas. Their emphatic advice was the following: "The last thing you want to do is bring in an adult speaker. They will *not* listen to some adult." Their counsel led me to collaborate with students at my university to create a video of college students sharing their honest perspectives about hookup culture, the relationship between hookups and sexual violence, and how to create a more just sexual culture.

5. As noted throughout part I, many ethnographers wrote about witnessing or learning about unwanted sexual experiences that clearly or potentially met the definition of sexual assault. Many ethnographers observed men seeking to hook up with very drunk women who showed signs of incapacitation. To the extent that these women were incapacitated, these college men were committing sexual assault. Ethical issues thus emerged about ethnographers' and my ethical obligations about how to respond to these situations. Discussing these situations with my students was also complicated because many ethnographers did not conceptualize these instances as sexual assault. During this time period (2010–2012) when I assigned this paper, many students viewed instances of one student's pursuing a very drunk/incapacitated student as a "gray area" and some were highly resistant to naming such sexual experiences as assault. In the fall of 2010, University A had just changed its sexual misconduct policy to make explicit that

having sex with someone who cannot consent due to alcohol or drug incapacitation constitutes sexual assault. However, most students were unaware of this
revised policy. The concept of bystander intervention was also new on our campus, and the administration was in the initial stages of training some students,
faculty, and staff. If I were to assign this party ethnography paper again in my
classes, I would address bystander-intervention strategies with my students so
they were equipped to identify warning signs and prevent sexual assault.

6. Research studies indicate that between 60 and 80% of North American college
students have reported hooking up. See Garcia et al., "Sexual Hookup Culture,"
161–76. Lisa Wade's research indicates that one third of college students opt
out of hooking up in their first year of college. Lisa Wade, "Sex on Campus isn't
What You Think: What 101 Student Journals Taught Me," *The Guardian*, August
23, 2016.

7. Sophomores and juniors also took this survey at the same time. Results show
47.7% of sophomore and 45.7% of junior women reported hooking up once
or more during their first year; 55.7% of sophomore and 53.6% of junior men
reported hooking up once or more during their first year. This study had a sta-
tistically relevant response rate; 43% of first-years and sophomores and 42% of
juniors completed the entire survey.

8. I used Carl Auerbach and Louise Silverstein's method of qualitative analysis. See
Carl Auerbach and Louise Silverstein, *Qualitative Data: An Introduction to Coding
and Analysis* (New York: New York University Press, 2003).

9. I received IRB approval from this Midwestern university to collect and analyse
my students' written work, provided that I delete names and all identifying information of students. The IRB determined that the data met the criteria for the
Exempt from Review category under Federal Regulation 45CFR46.

10. I collected only the papers written by undergraduates who signed a consent
form granting permission to use their written work anonymously for the purposes of teaching and research. Students were asked to sign a form granting
or withholding permission at the end of the semester, with the understanding
that I would not know who gave permission until the semester had ended and
grades were submitted. As for gender and ethnic diversity among the research
sample, 56% were female and 44% were male. 92% were Caucasian, 6% African
American, and 2% Asian American. The lack of ethnic diversity in my sample
reflected the broader population of this university. The ethnographers' names
have been changed to pseudonyms and reflect each ethnographer's gender.

11. Please see the appendix for further reasons.

12. It is important to clarify that I did not delete voices from students who were in
the minority in terms of race or sexual orientation. I was interested in deleting
descriptions of party behavior that appeared "extreme" or sensationalistic to an
entire class of college students. For instance, several students witnessed some
particular acts of sex that occurred publicly. Since various classes of students

came to a consensus that these kinds of behaviors did not frequently occur publicly at parties, I deleted those descriptions.

13. By the time I had written chapter drafts, the female undergraduate had graduated and did not have time to read and offer feedback.

14. Since I did not want to invade my students' privacy, I did not ask students to disclose their sexual orientation or economic class. On consent forms granting or denying me permission to use their written work for educational or research purposes, students only disclosed their gender and racial identity. Thus, my study cannot analyze the effects of sexual orientation or class on students' involvement in party culture.

15. In *Poverty of Spirit*, Metz uses "becoming human" when describing what it means to reach one's full potential and become the persons God created us to be. Because this language has frequently invited confusion among my students, who often insist that they are already biologically human regardless of whether they embrace poverty of spirit, I have found "full humanity" and "fully human" (a normative concept in Christian ethics) more useful for conveying Metz's account of the challenges we face to become the persons God created us to be.

16. Metz's theological framework in *Poverty of Spirit* is undoubtedly influenced by Karl Rahner's theology of the fundamental option.

17. In this chapter, I do not offer a full account of Metz's interpretation of God, creation, the Incarnation, the meaning of Christ's death and resurrection, or salvation. Instead, I am exploring what insights *Poverty of Spirit* offers readers as they reflect theologically on college party and hookup culture and as we discern more broadly which values and priorities in our lives foster genuine joy and fulfillment. See Johann Baptist Metz, *Poverty of Spirit* (New York: Paulist Press, 1998).

18. Prior to reading *Poverty of Spirit*, students had engaged the work of Kelly Brown Douglas on the intersections between racism and sexuality. They had examined unjust racist stereotyping historically and in contemporary society. See Kelly Brown Douglas, *Sexuality and the Black Church: A Womanist Perspective*, (Maryknoll: Orbis Books, 1999). I chose to depict Metz's Jesus as African American to see if students would explore how racist dynamics at college parties undermine poverty of spirit and full humanity. Only a few students mentioned Metz's Jesus's ethnicity in their reflections or acknowledged that white students might not be as open toward or accepting of Metz's Jesus owing to his race in their imagined scenarios of college parties.

19. I collected only the papers written by undergraduates who signed a consent form granting permission to use their written work anonymously for the purposes of teaching and research. In order to protect confidentiality and anonymity, I used pseudonyms.

20. I mention the difference between Division I and Division III athletics because my study of hookup culture in both settings leads me to suspect that, for complicated reasons, the degree of dehumanization present in hookup culture and

the prevalence of sexual assault are higher on campuses that offer Division I athletics. More research on the impact of athletics on party and hookup culture is needed.

21. I did not collect information on University B students' sexual orientation.

22. Donna Freitas, *Sex and the Soul: Juggling Sexuality, Spirituality, Romance, and Religion on America's College Campuses* (Oxford: Oxford University Press, 2008).

23. Christian Scharen and Aana Marie Vigen, *Ethnography as Christian Theology and Ethics* (London: Continuum, 2011).

24. Reflection becomes "critical reflection," I believe, when accompanied by epistemic humility, acknowledgment of the need for community feedback, and a willingness to have one's own interpretations of knowledge gained from experience be challenged by other sources of knowledge (academic disciplines and religious traditions). This is important because it reminds us that even critical reflection, valuable as this is, should never be considered infallible. Owing to our tendency toward bias and self-deception (understood theologically as aspects of sin), no source of human knowledge (our interpretation of scripture, theological tradition, and academic disciplines) can be perfect.

25. Charles Taylor, "Modern Social Imaginaries," *Public Culture* 14, no. 1 (2002): 91–124.

CHAPTER 1

1. According to the perceptions of the ethnographers, the vast majority of college students at the parties they attended acted as heterosexuals, and the ethnographers only rarely identified LGBTQ students or concerns; with the exception of the section explicitly on sexual orientation, my qualitative analysis of college party behavior focuses on heterosexual college party culture.

2. It is unclear if this was because no Hispanics or Asians attended the party or that students were more interested in observing the dynamics among Caucasians and African Americans.

3. Kelly Brown Douglas, *Sexuality and the Black Church*.

4. For more insight on developmental processes that may influence students to self-segregate, see Beverly Daniel Tatum, *"Why Are All the Black Kids Sitting Together in the Cafeteria?" And Other Conversations about Race*, (New York: Basic Books, 1997).

5. In addition to these four comments, two ethnographers attribute minorities' lower power status to racial dynamics. (See chapter 3 for their comments.)

6. G. A. Garcia et al., "When Parties Become Racialized: Deconstructing Racially Themed Parties," *Journal of Student Affairs Research and Practice* 48, no. 1 (2011): 11–16; V. Dave Poteat and Lisa B. Spanierman, "Modern Racism Attitudes Among White Students: The Role of Dominance and Authoritarianism and the

Mediating Effects of Racial Color-Blindness," *Journal of Social Psychology* 152, no. 6 (2012): 769.

7. Eric's description of the Schemer deeply troubled me, but it did not at all surprise me. During my career, many students had shared with me stories about being raped by male peers who had already allegedly raped up to four other women on campus. Campus policies at that time only allowed for the filing of reports of sexual assault by victims. While there was nothing I could do in terms of reporting my concerns about Dave to campus police, I did make an appointment with the provost to discuss repeat offenders on our campus. During this meeting, I gave the provost a summary of Eric's descriptions of the Schemer and Olivia's descriptions of her friends' negative sexual experiences with Dave. (I protected the confidentiality of my students and also had received their written consent to use their writings for research and educational purposes.)

8. I spoke to Olivia about my concern that she was describing situations that met the campus definition of sexual assault, and I asked her to talk to her friends who had had these experiences with Dave. I also expressed a willingness to talk to her friends if they wished to do so. No one was willing to publicly disclose these incidents.

CHAPTER 2

1. This verse is from the song "Yeah!" by Usher and Ludacris.
2. Between 2011 and 2013, several other female students wrote in their journals about having a man show up and go into a roommate's room after she had become drunk, gone home, and fell asleep. Other students wrote about friends' or their own experiences of being sexually assaulted when they were passed out at a party.
3. Such silence about whether this experience constituted sexual assault could be partially due to the fact that the campus sexual misconduct policy had just been changed during the 2010–11 academic year to clarify that having sex with someone who cannot consent due to alcohol or drug incapacitation constitutes sexual assault.

CHAPTER 3

1. See also ethnographers' observations of sexual favors in the analysis of contemporary feminine norms in chapter 2.
2. Michael S. Kimmel, *Guyland: The Perilous World Where Boys Become Men* (New York: Harper, 2009).
3. Donna Freitas, *Sex and the Soul.*
4. Mark Regnerus and Jeremy Uecker, *Premarital Sex in America: How Young Americans Meet, Mate, and Think about Marrying* (New York: Oxford University Press, 2010).

5. Kathleen A. Bogle, *Hooking Up: Sex, Dating, and Relationships on Campus* (New York: New York University Press, 2008).

6. Laura Sessions Stepp, *Unhooked: How Young Women Pursue Sex, Delay Love and Lose at Both* (New York: Riverhead Books, 2007).

7. Kimmel, *Guyland*.

8. Freitas, *Sex and the Soul*; Donna Freitas, *The End of Sex: How Hookup Culture Is Leaving a Generation Unhappy, Sexually Unfulfilled, and Confused about Intimacy* (New York: Basic Books, 2013).

9. Regnerus and Uecker, *Premarital Sex in America*, 51–100.

10. National Center for Education Statistics, http://nces.ed.gov/fastfacts/display. asp?id=372 and http://nces.ed.gov/fastfacts/display.asp?id=98.

11. Regnerus and Uecker, *Premarital Sex in America*, 124.

12. Stepp, *Unhooked*.

13. Bogle, *Hooking Up*.

14. Kimmel, *Guyland*, 16–18; Freitas, *The End of Sex*, 4–8.

CHAPTER 4

1. The percentages were rounded to the nearest percentile—all down, it so happens—which is why the four groups equal 99 rather than 100 percent.

2. Melissa A. Lewis, Christine M. Lee, Megan E. Patrick, and Nicole Fossos, "Gender-specific Normative Misperceptions of Risky Sexual Behavior and Alcohol-related Risky Sexual Behavior," *Sex Roles* 57, nos. 1–2 (2007): 81–90; Megan Barriger and Carlos J. Vélez-Blasini, "Descriptive and Injunctive Social Norm Overestimation in Hooking Up and Their Role as Predictors of Hookup Activity in a College Student Sample," *Journal of Sex Research* 50, no. 1 (2013): 84–94; Kyle R. Stephenson and Keiran Sullivan, "The Misperception of Social Norms and Sexual Satisfaction," *Canadian Journal of Human Sexuality* 18, no. 3 (2009): 89–105; Tracy A. Lambert, Arnold S. Kahn, and Kevin J. Apple, "Pluralistic Ignorance and Hooking up," *Journal of Sex Research* 40, no. 2 (2003): 132; Regnerus and Uecker, *Premarital Sex in America*, 118–19, 247; Kimmel, *Guyland*, 209–10.

3. Bogle, *Hooking Up*; Stepp, *Unhooked*; E. L. Paul and K. A. Hayes, "The Casualties of 'Casual' Sex: A Qualitative Exploration of the Phenomenology of College Students' Hookups," *Journal of Social and Personal Relationships* 19, no. 5 (2002): 639–61; Catherine M. Grello, Deborah P. Welsh, and Melinda S. Harper, "No Strings Attached: The Nature of Casual Sex in College Students," *Journal of Sex Research* 43, no. 3 (2006): 255–67; John Marshall Townsend and Timothy H. Wasserman, "Sexual Hookups Among College Students: Sex Differences in Emotional Reactions," *Archives of Sexual Behavior* 40, no. 6 (2011): 1173–81; Elizabeth Victor, "Mental Health and Hooking Up: A Self-discrepancy Perspective," *The New School Psychology Bulletin* 9, no. 2 (2012): 24–34; W. F. Flack et al., "Risk Factors

and Consequences of Unwanted Sex Among University Students: Hooking Up, Alcohol, and Stress Response," *Journal of Interpersonal Violence* 22, no. 2 (2007): 139–57; Maria Gavranidou and Rita Rosner, "The Weaker Sex? Gender and Post-traumatic Stress Disorder," *Depression & Anxiety* 17, no. 3 (May 2003): 130–39; Justin R. Garcia et al., "Casual Sex: Integrating Social, Behavioral, and Sexual Health Research," in *Handbook of the Sociology of Sexualities*, ed. John D. DeLamater and Rebecca F. Plante (New York: Springer Cham, 2015), 203–21.

4. Jesse Owen, Frank D. Fincham, and Jon Moore, "Short-Term Prospective Study of Hooking Up Among College Students," *Archives of Sexual Behavior* 40, no. 2 (2011); Shannon Snapp, Ehri Ryu, and Jade Kerr, "The Upside to Hooking Up: College Students' Positive Hookup Experiences," *International Journal of Sexual Health* 27, no. 1 (2015): 43–56.

5. Zhana Vrangalova, "Does Casual Sex Harm College Students' Well-Being? A Longitudinal Investigation of the Role of Motivation," *Archives of Sexual Behavior* 44, no. 4 (2014): 954; Melina M. Bersamin et al., "Risky Business: Is There an Association between Casual Sex and Mental Health Among Emerging Adults?" *Journal of Sex Research* 51, no. 1 (2013): 49.

6. Marina Epstein et al., "Anything from Making Out to Having Sex: Men's Negotiations of Hooking Up and Friends with Benefits Scripts," *Journal of Sex Research* 46, no. 5 (2009): 414–24; Justin R. Garcia and Chris Reiber, "Hookup Behavior: A Biopsychosocial Perspective," *Journal of Social, Evolutionary, and Cultural Psychology* 2, no. 4 (2008): 198; Freitas, *Sex and the Soul*, 101–102; Freitas, *The End of Sex*, 97–115; Kimmel, *Guyland*, 280–82; Regnerus and Uecker, *Premarital Sex in America*, 163–66.

7. Garcia et al., "Casual Sex"; Garcia et al., "Sexual Hookup Culture," 161–76; Snapp, Ryu, and Kerr, "The Upside to Hooking Up," 43–56.

8. Jesse J. Owen, Frank D. Fincham, and Jon Moore, "Hooking Up Among College Students: Demographic and Psychosocial Correlates," *Archives of Sexual Behavior* 39, no. 3 (2010): 653–63.

9. Jesse Owen and Frank D. Fincham, "Young Adults' Emotional Reactions After Hooking Up Encounters," *Archives of Sexual Behavior* 40, no. 2 (2011): 327.

10. Owen, Fincham, and Moore, "Short-Term Prospective Study," 339.

11. Owen and Fincham, "Young Adults' Emotional Reactions," 327.

CHAPTER 5

1. Johann Baptist Metz, *Faith in History and Society: Toward a Practical Fundamental Theology* (New York: Seabury Press, 1980), 70–71.

2. Metz, *Poverty of Spirit*, 31.

3. Ibid., 25.

4. Ibid., 27.

5. Ibid., 11–12.

6. Ibid., 25.

7. Ibid., 11.

8. Martin Luther, *The Large Catechism,* in *The Book Of Concord: The Confessions of the Evangelical Lutheran Church,* trans. and ed. Theodore G. Tappert et al. (Philadelphia: Fortress, 1959), 365.

9. Johann Baptist Metz, "Bread of Survival: The Lord's Supper of Christians as Anticipatory Sign of an Anthropological Revolution," in *Love's Strategy: The Political Theology of Johann Baptist Metz,* ed. John K. Downey (Harrisburg: Trinity Press International, 1999), 55.

10. Metz, *Faith in History and Society,* 19. In other words, religious and philosophical ideas (the purpose of life and human fulfillment, moral virtues and the good life, the common good, care for the marginalized) and values (love, friendship, empathy, gratitude, play, etc.) are now relegated to the private realm of persons' individual tastes and opinions.

11. Christian Smith and Melinda Lundquist Denton, *Soul Searching: The Religious and Spiritual Lives of American Teenagers* (Oxford: Oxford University Press, 2005). Kenda Creasy Dean, *Almost Christian: What the Faith of Our Teenagers Is Telling the American Church* (Oxford: Oxford University Press, 2010).

12. Johann Baptist Metz, *The Emergent Church: The Future of Christianity in a Postbourgeois World* (New York: Crossroad, 1981), 4–6.

13. Metz, *Faith in History and Society,* 47.

14. John Downey, "Can We Talk? Globalization, Human Rights, and Political Theology," in *Missing God?: Cultural Amnesia and Political Theology,* ed. John K. Downey, Jürgen Manemann, and Steven T. Ostovich (Berlin: Lit Verlag, 2007), 147.

15. Ibid., 222.

16. Ibid., 209.

17. Metz, *The Emergent Church,* 35.

18. Metz, "Bread of Survival," 54.

CHAPTER 6

1. Metz, *Poverty of Spirit,* 4–5.

2. Ibid., 4.

3. Ibid., 11–12.

4. Ibid., 13.

5. Ibid., 10–11.

6. Ibid., 11.

7. Ibid., 37.

8. Ibid., 5.

9. Richard M. Gula, *The Good Life: Where Morality and Spirituality Converge* (New York, Paulist Press, 1999), 27.

10. R. Beiter et al., "The Prevalence and Correlates of Depression, Anxiety, and Stress in a Sample of College Students," *Journal of Affective Disorders* 173 (2015): 90–96;

Richard Kadison and Theresa Foy DiGeronimo, *College of the Overwhelmed: The Campus Mental Health Crisis and What to Do about It* (San Francisco, CA: Jossey-Bass, 2004); Jean M. Twenge, *Generation Me: Why Today's Young Americans Are More Confident, Assertive, Entitled—And More Miserable than Ever Before* (New York: Atria, 2006).

11. Of course, Christianity is not the only religion that offers wisdom related to self-acceptance, resistance, and suffering. Buddhist thinkers, for instance, corroborate Metz's insight that becoming fully human involves acknowledging limitations and suffering. Pema Chodron's *Wisdom of No Escape*, for example, begins by naming the "common misunderstanding" among human beings that "the best way to live is to try to avoid pain and just try to get comfortable.... A much more interesting, kind, adventurous, and joyful approach to life is to begin to develop our curiosity, not caring whether the object of our inquisitiveness is bitter or sweet." See Pema Chodron, *The Wisdom of No Escape And the Path of Loving Kindness* (Boulder, CO: Shambhala Publications, 2010), 3. More specifically, Buddhist thinkers acknowledge that fleeing human vulnerability and "clinging" to what we like produces suffering because change is the essence of the universe. Within their well-known framework of noble truths, Buddhists express this with remarkable simplicity: Whereas the first noble truth regards suffering as an unavoidable part of human life, the second truth names resistance, "the fundamental operating mechanism of what we call the ego," as its cause (Chodron, *Wisdom of No Escape*, 40). Thus, Buddhist paths to enlightenment are practices geared toward open, honest, mindful awareness and "acceptance" of reality.

12. Johann Baptist Metz and Jean-Pierre Jossua, *Theology of Joy* (New York: Herder and Herder, 1974), 8.

13. Metz and Jossua, *Theology of Joy*, 197.

14. Parker J. Palmer, *Let Your Life Speak: Listening for the Voice of Vocation* (San Francisco, CA: Jossey-Bass, 2000), 10.

15. Thomas Merton, *New Seeds of Contemplation* (New York: New Directions, 1961), 31.

16. Palmer, *Let Your Life Speak*, 16–17.

17. Merton, *New Seeds of Contemplation*, 32.

18. Ibid., 33.

19. Palmer, *Let Your Life Speak*, 6.

20. Ibid., 42.

21. Ibid., 35.

22. Ibid., 71.

23. Richard Rohr, *Breathing under Water: Spirituality and the Twelve Steps* (Cincinnati, OH: St. Anthony Messenger Press, 2011), 33.

24. Ibid., 8–9.

25. Palmer, *Let Your Life Speak*, 29.

26. Thomas Merton, *No Man Is an Island* (New York: Harcourt Brace, 1955), 127.

27. Metz, *Poverty of Spirit*, 39.
28. Palmer, *Let Your Life Speak*, 12.
29. Metz, *Faith in History*, 143.
30. Ibid., 134–35.
31. Ibid., 19.
32. Ibid., 98.
33. Ibid., 90.
34. Ibid., 93.
35. Merton, *New Seeds of Contemplation*, 53–54.

CHAPTER 7

1. Metz, *Poverty of Spirit*, 45.
2. Ibid., 45.
3. Ibid., 45.
4. Metz, *Faith in History and Society*, 93.
5. Ibid., 93.
6. Ibid.,163.
7. Ibid., 113.
8. Downey, "Can We Talk?," 137.
9. Johann Baptist Metz, "Christians and Jews after Auschwitz," in *Love's Strategy: The Political Theology of Johann Baptist Metz*, ed. John K. Downey (Harrisburg: Trinity Press International, 1999), 47.
10. Metz, *The Emergent Church*, 97.
11. Metz, *Poverty of Spirit*, 44.
12. Ibid., 33–34.
13. J. B. Metz and translate by John K. Downey, "Facing the World: A Theological and Biographical Inquiry," *Theological Studies* 75, no. 1 (2014), 33.
14. Metz, *Poverty of Spirit*, 32–33.
15. When analyzing students' descriptions of vulnerability, I found that 218 phrases had a negative association, 123 had a positive association, and 38 had a neutral association. In regard to women's responses, 8% mentioned positive associations, 49% mentioned negative associations, and 43% mentioned positive and negative associations. For men, 7% mentioned positive associations, 67% mentioned negative associations, and 27% mentioned both positive and negative associations.
16. In this brainstorming exercise on vulnerability, students only revealed their gender when submitting papers.

CHAPTER 8

1. Margaret A. Farley, *Just Love: A Framework for Christian Sexual Ethics* (New York: Continuum International, 2006), 209.

2. Ibid., 212.

3. Ibid., 212.

4. Ibid., 214.

5. Ibid., 213.

6. Ibid., 200.

7. Ibid., 207.

8. Ibid., 216.

9. Ibid., 214–31.

10. The percentages of students in this survey do not equal 100 because a minority of students did not directly answer the question.

11. Lisa Wade, "Are Women Bad at Orgasms?," in *Gender, Sex, and Politics*, ed. Shira Tarrant (New York: Routledge, 2016), 227–58; L. Hamilton and E. A. Armstrong, "Gendered Sexuality in Young Adulthood: Double Binds and Flawed Options," *Gender & Society* 23, no. 5 (2009): 599; Paul and Hayes, "The Casualties of 'Casual' Sex," 654–55; Caroline Heldman and Lisa Wade, "Hookup Culture: Setting a New Research Agenda," *Sexuality Research and Social Policy* 7, no. 4 (2010): 325–26.

12. Hamilton, "Gendered Sexuality"; Garcia et al., "Casual Sex."

13. Elizabeth Armstrong, Alison Fogarty, and Paula England, "Orgasm in College Hookups and Relationships," in *Families as They Really Are*, ed. Barbara Risman (New York: W.W. Norton, 2010), 377.

14. Gail Dines, *Pornland: How Porn Has Hijacked Our Sexuality* (Boston: Beacon Press, 2010).

15. Michael E. Levin, Jason Lillis, and Steven Hayes, "When Is Online Pornography Viewing Problematic Among College Males? Examining the Moderating Role of Experiential Avoidance," *Sexual Addiction & Compulsivity: The Journal of Treatment & Prevention* 19, no. 3 (August 22, 2012): 168–80; Jill Manning, "The Impact of Internet Pornography on Marriage and the Family: A Review of the Research," *Sexual Addiction & Compulsivity* 13, nos. 2–3 (2006): 131–65; Julie M. Albright, "Sex in America Online: An Exploration of Sex, Marital Status, and Sexual Identity in Internet Sex Seeking and Its Impacts," *Journal of Sex Research* 45, no. 2 (2008): 175–86; A. Baltazar et al., "Internet Pornography Use in the Context of External and Internal Religiosity," *Journal of Psychology and Theology* 38, no. 1 (2010): 32–40; Nicola M. Döring, "The Internet's Impact on Sexuality: A Critical Review of 15 Years of Research," *Computers in Human Behavior* 25, no. 5 (2009): 1089–1101; Michael P. Twohig, Jesse M. Crosby, and Jared M. Cox, "Viewing Internet Pornography: For Whom Is It Problematic, How, and Why?" *Sexual Addiction & Compulsivity* 16, no. 4 (2009): 253–66; Vincent Cyrus Yoder, Thomas Virden, and Kiran Amin, "Internet Pornography and Loneliness: An Association?" *Sexual Addiction & Compulsivity* 12, no. 1 (2005): 19–44.

16. Michael E. Levin, Jason Lillis, and Steven Hayes, "When Is Online Pornography Viewing Problematic Among College Males? Examining the Moderating Role of Experiential Avoidance," *Sexual Addiction & Compulsivity: The Journal of Treatment & Prevention* 19, no. 3 (August 22, 2012): 168–80; Jill Manning, "The Impact of

Internet Pornography on Marriage and the Family: A Review of the Research," *Sexual Addiction & Compulsivity* 13, nos. 2–3 (2006): 131–65; Julie M. Albright, "Sex in America Online: An Exploration of Sex, Marital Status, and Sexual Identity in Internet Sex Seeking and Its Impacts," *Journal of Sex Research* 45, no. 2 (2008): 175–86; A. Baltazar et al., "Internet Pornography Use in the Context of External and Internal Religiosity," *Journal of Psychology and Theology* 38, no. 1 (2010): 32–40; Nicola M. Döring, "The Internet's Impact on Sexuality: A Critical Review of 15 Years of Research," *Computers in Human Behavior* 25, no. 5 (2009): 1089–1101; Michael P. Twohig, Jesse M. Crosby, and Jared M. Cox, "Viewing Internet Pornography: For Whom Is It Problematic, How, and Why?" *Sexual Addiction & Compulsivity* 16, no. 4 (2009): 253–66; Vincent Cyrus Yoder, Thomas Virden, and Kiran Amin, "Internet Pornography and Loneliness: An Association?" *Sexual Addiction & Compulsivity* 12, no. 1 (2005): 19–44; Christina Rogala and Tanja Tyden, "Does Pornography Influence Young Women's Sexual Behavior?" *Women's Health Issues* 13, no. 1 (2003): 39–43.

17. Tara Emmers-Sommer and Ryan J. Burns, "The Relationship Between Exposure to Internet Pornography and Sexual Attitudes Toward Women," *Journal of Online Behavior* 1, no. 4 (2005): 1–16; Neil M. Malamuth, Tamara Addison, and Mary Koss, "Pornography and Sexual Aggression: Are There Reliable Effects and Can We Understand Them?" *Annual Review of Sex Research* 11 (2000): 26–91; Vanessa Vega and Neil M. Malamuth, "Predicting Sexual Aggression: The Role of Pornography in the Context of General and Specific Risk Factors," *Aggressive Behavior* 33, no. 2 (2007): 104–17.

18. Christopher Kilmartin and Alan Berkowitz, *Sexual Assault in Context: Teaching College Men about Gender* (Holmes Beach, FL: Learning Publications, 2001).

19. K. C. Davis et al., "Rape-Myth Congruent Beliefs in Women Resulting from Exposure to Violent Pornography: Effects of Alcohol and Sexual Arousal," *Journal of Interpersonal Violence* 21, no. 9 (2006): 1208–23; Jeanette Norris et al., "Victim's Response and Alcohol-Related Factors as Determinants of Women's Responses to Violent Pornography," *Psychology of Women Quarterly* 28, no. 1 (2004): 59–69.

20. Dines, *Pornland*, 75–78; Pamela Paul, *Pornified: How Pornography Is Transforming Our Lives, Our Relationships, and Our Families* (New York: Times Books, 2005).

21. Malamuth et al., "Pornography and Sexual Aggression," 26–91; John D. Foubert, Matthew W. Brosi, and R. Sean Bannon, "Pornography Viewing Among Fraternity Men: Effects on Bystander Intervention, Rape Myth Acceptance and Behavioral Intent to Commit Sexual Assault," *Sexual Addiction & Compulsivity* 18, no. 4 (2011): 212–31; Dines, *Pornland*, 84–98; Emmers-Sommer and Burns, "The Relationship Between Exposure," 1–16.

22. Sut Jhally, Andrew Killoy, and Joe Bartone, *Dreamworlds 3: Desire, Sex & Power in Music Video*, Media Education Foundation, 2007.

23. Ibid.

24. Maureen Palmer et al., *Sext Up Kids*, Dream Street Pictures, Canadian Broadcasting Corporation, and Media Education Foundation, 2012.

25. Cristina L. H. Traina, *Erotic Attunement: Parenthood and the Ethics of Sensuality between Unequals* (Chicago: University of Chicago Press, 2011), 72–73.

26. Kelly Brown Douglas, *Sexuality and the Black Church: A Womanist Perspective* (Maryknoll, NY: Orbis Books, 1999); Miguel De La Torre, *A Lily Among the Thorns: Imagining a New Christian Sexuality* (San Francisco, CA: John Wiley, 2007).

27. Chris Weedon, *Feminist Practice and Poststructuralist Theory* (Oxford: Blackwell, 1987), 108.

28. Douglas, *Sexuality and the Black Church*, 21.

29. Ibid., 22–23.

30. The contemporary porn industry, for instance, unabashedly perpetuates these historical dehumanizing stereotypes of black male and female sexuality and bodies and legally profits from the vicious sexual abuse of female black bodies. See Dines, *Pornland*, 121–40.

31. Jhally, *Dreamworlds 3*.

32. Ibid.

33. Ibid.

34. De La Torre, *A Lily Among the Thorns*, 37.

35. Dines, *Pornland*, 121–40.

36. Marvin Mahan Ellison and Kelly Brown Douglas, *Sexuality and the Sacred: Sources for Theological Reflection* (Louisville, KY: Westminster John Knox Press, 2010), 76–93, 245, 248.

37. Marvin Mahan Ellison, *Erotic Justice: A Liberating Ethic of Sexuality* (Louisville, KY: Westminster John Knox Press, 1996), 77.

38. J. R. Garcia et al., "Touch Me in the Morning: Intimately Affiliative Gestures in Uncommitted and Romantic Relationships." Paper presented at the Annual Conference of the Northeastern Evolutionary Psychology Society, New Paltz, New York, 2010.

39. Garcia et al., "Sexual Hookup Culture," 168.

40. Peggy J. Kleinplatz et al., "The Components of Optimal Sexuality: A Portrait of 'Great Sex,'" *Canadian Journal of Human Sexuality* 18, no. 1–2 (2009): 1–13.

41. Jenny A. Higgins et al., "Sexual Satisfaction and Sexual Health Among University Students in the United States," *American Journal of Public Health* 101, no. 9 (2011): 1643–54.

42. Elizabeth A. Armstrong, Paula England, and Alison C. K. Fogarty, "Accounting for Women's Orgasm and Sexual Enjoyment in College Hookups and Relationships," *American Sociological Review* 77, no. 3 (2012): 435–62.

43. Ibid., 455.

CHAPTER 9

1. White House Task Force to Protect Students from Sexual Assault, "Sample Language and Definitions of Prohibited Conduct for a School's Sexual Misconduct Policy," April 4, 2014. https://www.justice.gov/ovw/page/file/910276/download.

2. Research studies have found that LGBTQ students report significantly higher rates of sexual assault than their heterosexual peers. See Katie M. Edwards et al., "Physical Dating Violence, Sexual Violence, and Unwanted Pursuit Victimization: A Comparison of Incidence Rates among Sexual-Minority and Heterosexual College Students," *Journal of Interpersonal Violence* 30, no. 4 (2014): 580–600; David Cantor, Bonnie Fisher, Susan Chibnall, Reanne Townsend, Hyunshik Lee, Carol Bruce, and Gail Thomas, *Report on the AAU Campus Climate Survey on Sexual Assault and Sexual Misconduct* (Rockville, MD: Westat, 2015).

3. Christopher Krebs et al., *The Campus Sexual Assault Study*, Report no. 221153, October 2007 (Washington, DC: National Institute of Justice): 1–111.

4. Ibid.

5. S. B. Sorenson, M. Joshi, and E. Sivitz, "Knowing a Sexual Assault Victim or Perpetrator: A Stratified Random Sample of Undergraduates at One University," *Journal of Interpersonal Violence* 29, no. 3 (2013): 394–416.

6. My students, a graduate student, and I interviewed student volunteers at my university about their perspectives and analyses of hookup culture, sexual violence, and what constitutes a sexually just campus. Students signed consent forms granting me permission to use their interviews for educational and research purposes. I received IRB approval from my Midwestern university to collect and analyze student interviews on hookup culture for research and educational purposes. The IRB determined that the data met the criteria for the Exempt from Review category under Federal Regulation 45CFR46.

7. Heidi Zinzow et al., "Drug- or Alcohol-Facilitated, Incapacitated, and Forcible Rape in Relationship to Mental Health Among a National Sample of Women," *Journal of Interpersonal Violence* 25, no. 12 (2010): 2217–236.

8. David Lisak and Paul M. Miller, "Repeat Rape and Multiple Offending Among Undetected Rapists," *Violence and Victims* 17, no. 1 (2002): 73–84.

9. Meichun Mohler-Kuo et al., "Correlates of Rape While Intoxicated in a National Sample of College Women," *Journal of Studies on Alcohol* 65, no. 1 (2004): 37–45.

10. Antonia Abbey et al., "Alcohol and Sexual Assault," *Alcohol Research and Health* 25, no. 1 (2001): 43–51.

11. Charlene Muehlenhard and Melaney Linton, "Date Rape and Sexual Aggression in Dating Situations: Incidence and Risk Factors," *Journal of Counseling Psychology* 34, no. 2 (1987): 187.

12. Elizabeth Tomsich et al., "Violent Victimization and Hooking Up Among Strangers and Acquaintances on an Urban Campus: An Exploratory Study," *Criminal Justice Studies* 26, no. 4 (2013): 433–54. Heldman and Wade, "Hookup Culture," 323–33; K. M. Klipfel, S. E Claxton, and M. H. M. van Dulmen, "Interpersonal Aggression Victimization Within Casual Sexual Relationships and Experiences," *Journal of Interpersonal Violence* 29, no. 3 (2014): 557–69.

13. Flack et al., "Risk Factors and Consequences of Unwanted Sex," 139–57.

14. Charles Whitfield et al., "Adverse Childhood Experiences and Hallucinations," *Child Abuse & Neglect* 29, no. 7 (2005): 797–810.

15. Patricia Tjaden and Nancy Thoennes, *Extent, Nature, and Consequences of Rape Victimization: Findings from the National Violence Against Women Survey*, NIJ Research Report, U.S. Department of Justice, Office of Justice Programs, National Institute of Justice (Washington, DC: National Institute of Justice, 2006).

16. World Health Organization, "Violence against Women," posted September 2016, www.who.int/mediacentre/factsheets/fs239/en/.

17. M. Black et al., "National Intimate Partner and Sexual Violence Survey: 2010 Summary Report," November 2011, National Center for Injury Prevention and Control Centers for Disease Control and Prevention, Atlanta, Georgia.

18. Antonia Abbey and Pam McAuslan, "A Longitudinal Examination of Male College Students' Perpetration of Sexual Assault," *Journal of Consulting and Clinical Psychology* 72, no. 5 (2004): 747–56; Heidi Zinzow and Martie Thompson, "Factors Associated with Use of Verbally Coercive, Incapacitated, and Forcible Sexual Assault Tactics in a Longitudinal Study of College Men," *Aggressive Behavior* 41, no. 1 (January 2015): 34–43; Martie Thompson, Kevin Swartout, and Mary Koss, "Trajectories and Predictors of Sexually Aggressive Behaviors during Emerging Adulthood," *Psychology of Violence* 3, no. 3 (2013): 247–59; Mary Koss, Christine Gidycz, and Nadine Wisniewski, "The Scope of Rape: Incidence and Prevalence of Sexual Aggression and Victimization in a National Sample of Higher Education Students," *Journal of Consulting and Clinical Psychology* 55, no. 2 (1987): 162–70; J. Warkentin and C. Gidycz, "The Use and Acceptance of Sexually Aggressive Tactics in College Men," *Journal of Interpersonal Violence* 22, no. 7 (2007): 829–50.

19. Heidi Zinzow and Martie Thompson, "A Longitudinal Study of Risk Factors for Repeated Sexual Coercion and Assault in U.S. College Men," *Archives of Sexual Behavior* 44, no. 1 (2014): 213–22.

20. Lisak and Miller, "Repeat Rape and Multiple Offending"; Steven Collings, "Sexual Aggression: A Discriminant Analysis of Predictors in a Non-Forensic Sample," *South African Journal of Psychology* 24, no. 1 (1994): 35–38.

21. H. Cleveland, M. Koss, and J. Lyons, "Rape Tactics from the Survivors' Perspective: Contextual Dependence and Within-Event Independence," *Journal of Interpersonal Violence* 14, no. 5 (1999): 532–47.

22. Zinzow and Thompson, "Factors Associated with Use of Verbally Coercive, Incapacitated, and Forcible Sexual Assault Tactics," 34–43.

23. Ibid., 40.

24. David Lisak, "Understanding the Predatory Nature of Sexual Violence," *Sexual Assault Report* 14, no. 4 (March/April 2011): 49–57; David Lisak and National Judicial Education Program to Promote Equality for Women and Men in the Courts, *The "Undetected" Rapist* (New York: National Judicial Education Program, 2000).

25. Zinzow and Thompson, "Factors Associated with Use of Verbally Coercive, Incapacitated, and Forcible Sexual Assault Tactics," 40; Krebs, C. P. et al., "College Women's Experiences with Physically Forced, Alcohol- or Other Drug-Enabled, and Drug-Facilitated Sexual Assault Before and Since Entering College." *Journal Of American College Health* 57, no. 6 (May 2009): 639–47; Jennifer B. Warkentin, and Christine A. Gidycz, "The Use and Acceptance of Sexually Aggressive Tactics in College Men," *Journal of Interpersonal Violence* 22, no. 7 (2007): 829–50.

26. Sarah Mcmahon, "Rape Myth Beliefs and Bystander Attitudes Among Incoming College Students," *Journal of American College Health* 59, no. 1 (2010): 3–11; Kathryn M. Ryan, "Further Evidence for a Cognitive Component of Rape," *Aggression and Violent Behavior* 9, no. 6 (2004): 579–604; M. Christina Santana et al., "Masculine Gender Roles Associated with Increased Sexual Risk and Intimate Partner Violence Perpetration among Young Adult Men," *Journal of Urban Health* 83, no. 4 (2006): 575–85.

27. Ryan, "Further Evidence for a Cognitive Component of Rape," 586. Alan Berkowitz, "College Men as Perpetrators of Acquaintance Rape and Sexual Assault: A Review of Recent Research," *Journal of American College Health* 40, no. 4 (1992): 175–81; Ruth E. Mann and Clive R. Hollin, "Sexual Offenders' Explanations for Their Offending," *Journal of Sexual Aggression* 13, no. 1 (2007): 3–9; P. Ouimette, and D. Riggs, "Testing a Mediational Model of Sexually Aggressive Behavior in Nonincarcerated Perpetrators," *Violence and Victims* 13, no. 2 (Summer 1998): 117–30; Thompson et al., "Trajectories and Predictors," 247–59.

28. Joetta Carr and Karen Vandeusen, "Risk Factors for Male Sexual Aggression on College Campuses," *Journal of Family Violence* 19, no. 5 (2004): 279–89.

29. Jennifer Wheeler, William George, and Barbara Dahl, "Sexually Aggressive College Males: Empathy as a Moderator in the "Confluence Model" of Sexual Aggression," *Personality and Individual Differences* 33, no. 5 (2002): 759–75.

30. Walter Dekeseredy and Patrik Olsson, "Adult Pornography, Male Peer Support, and Violence Against Women," in *Technology for Facilitating Humanity and Combating Social Deviations: Interdisciplinary Perspectives*, ed. Miguel A. Garcia-Ruiz, Miguel Vargas Martin, and Arthur Edwards (Hershey, PA: Information Science Reference, 2011), 34–50; Kimmel, *Guyland*.

31. Lisak and Miller, "Repeat Rape and Multiple Offending," 73–84.

32. John Foubert, Johnatan T Newberry and Jerry Tatum, "Behavior Differences Seven Months Later: Effects of a Rape Prevention Program," *Journal of Student Affairs Research and Practice* 44, no. 4 (2007): 1125–46; Catherine Loh et al., "A Prospective Analysis of Sexual Assault Perpetration: Risk Factors Related to Perpetrator Characteristics," *Journal of Interpersonal Violence* 20, no. 10 (2005): 1325–48.

33. Ryan, "Further Evidence for a Cognitive Component of Rape," 592.

34. Carr and Vandeusen, "Risk Factors for Male Sexual Aggression," 279–89.

35. After Matt disclosed the sexual assault, I spoke with campus security concerning legal obligations I might have to report the assault and disclose the name of the assault perpetrator. I was told that campus security could "do nothing" in this case, as the university did not officially count or pursue incidents of sexual assault unless reported by the sexual assault survivor herself. Such a policy undoubtedly kept University A's sexual assault statistics artificially low.

36. I explain this program in chapter 11.

37. R. Campbell, E. Dworkin, and G. Cabral, "An Ecological Model of the Impact of Sexual Assault on Women's Mental Health," *Trauma, Violence, & Abuse* 10, no. 3 (2009): 225–46; Heather Littleton, Amie Grills-Taquechel, and Danny Axsom, "Impaired and Incapacitated Rape Victims: Assault Characteristics and Post-Assault Experiences," *Violence and Victims Violence* 24, no. 4 (2009): 439–57; Erin Eadie, Marsha Runtz, and Julie Spencer-Rodgers, "Posttraumatic Stress Symptoms as a Mediator between Sexual Assault and Adverse Health Outcomes in Undergraduate Women," *Journal of Traumatic Stress* 21, no. 6 (2008): 540–47.

38. Bonnie Fisher, Francis Cullen, and Michael Turner, *The Sexual Victimization of College Women*, Report no. NCJ 182369, U.S. Department of Justice, Office of Justice Programs, National Institute of Justice (Washington, DC: Bureau of Justice Statistics, 2000), 1–39.

39. American Association of University Professors, "Campus Sexual Assault: Suggested Policies and Procedures," *Academe* 99, no. 4 (Jul/Aug 2013): 93.

40. Carlo Faravelli et al., "Psychopathology After Rape," *American Journal of Psychiatry* 161, no. 8 (2004): 1483–85.

41. Kari's comments are taken from my 2010–2012 interview project on hookup culture. Kristin wrote about her rape experiences in her class reflection. Both survivors gave me permission to disclose their experiences for research and educational purposes.

42. Campbell et al., "An Ecological Model," 225–46; Gretchen Clum, Karen Calhoun, and Rachel Kimerling, "Associations Among Symptoms of Depression and Posttraumatic Stress Disorder and Self-Reported Health in Sexually Assaulted Women," *Journal of Nervous and Mental Disease* 188, no. 10 (2000): 671–78.

43. American Psychiatric Association, *Diagnostic and Statistical Manual of Mental Disorders*, 5th ed. (Arlington, VA: American Psychiatric Association, 2013).

44. Campbell et al., "An Ecological Model," 225–46; Sarah Ullman, "Ten-Year Update on 'Review and Critique of Empirical Studies on Rape Avoidance,'" *Criminal Justice and Behavior* 34, no. 3 (2007): 411–29; Sarah Ullman and Leanne Brecklin, "Sexual Assault History, PTSD, and Mental Health Service Seeking in a National Sample of Women," *Journal of Community Psychology* 30, no. 3 (2002): 261–79.

45. Judith Herman, *Trauma and Recovery* (New York: Basic Books, 1992), 28–42.

46. Audrey Miller et al., "Stigma-Threat Motivated Nondisclosure of Sexual Assault and Sexual Revictimization: A Prospective Analysis," *Psychology of Women Quarterly* 35, no. 1 (2011): 119–28.

47. Ibid., 120.

48. H. Risser, M. Hetzel-Riggin, C. Thomsen, and T. McCanne, "PTSD As a Mediator of Sexual Revictimization: The Role of Reexperiencing, Avoidance, and Arousal Symptoms," *Journal of Traumatic Stress* 19, no. 5 (2006): 687–98.

49. Dean Kilpatrick et al., "Violence and Risk of PTSD, Major Depression, Substance Abuse/Dependence, and Comorbidity: Results from the National Survey of Adolescents," *Journal of Consulting and Clinical Psychology* 71, no. 4 (2003): 692–700; Judith Becker et al., "Depressive Symptoms Associated with Sexual Assault," *Journal of Sex & Marital Therapy* 10, no. 3 (1984): 185–92; M. Audrey Burnam et al., "Sexual Assault and Mental Disorders in a Community Population," *Journal of Consulting and Clinical Psychology* 56, no. 6 (1988): 843–50; Gretchen Clum, Pallavi Nishith, and Patricia Resick, "Trauma-Related Sleep Disturbance and Self-Reported Physical Health Symptoms in Treatment-Seeking Female Rape Victims," *Journal of Nervous and Mental Disease* 189, no. 9 (2001): 618–22; Diana Elliott, Doris Mok, and John Briere, "Adult Sexual Assault: Prevalence, Symptomatology, and Sex Differences in the General Population," *Journal of Traumatic Stress* 17, no. 3 (2004): 203–11; H. L. Littleton et al., "Rape Acknowledgment and Post-assault Experiences: How Acknowledgment Status Relates to Disclosure, Coping, Worldview, and Reactions Received from Others," *Violence and Victims* 21 (2006): 761–78.

50. Edward C. Chang and Jameson K. Hirsch, "Social Problem Solving Under Assault: Understanding the Impact of Sexual Assault on the Relation between Social Problem Solving and Suicidal Risk in Female College Students," *Cognitive Therapy and Research* 39, no. 3 (2015): 403–13.

51. Laura Boeschen et al., "Experiential Avoidance and Post-Traumatic Stress Disorder," *Journal of Aggression, Maltreatment & Trauma* 4, no. 2 (2001): 211–45; H. Filipas, "Child Sexual Abuse, Coping Responses, Self-Blame, Posttraumatic Stress Disorder, and Adult Sexual Revictimization," *Journal of Interpersonal Violence* 21, no. 5 (2006): 652–72.

52. Lily disclosed her experience of rape during my 2010–2012 interview project on hookup culture. Megan wrote about her rape experience in her class reflection. Both survivors gave me permission to disclose their experiences for research and educational purposes.

53. Jennifer Beste, *God and the Victim: Traumatic Intrusions on Grace and Freedom* (Oxford: Oxford University Press, 2007), 46.

54. C. Mengo, and B. Black, "Violence Victimization on a College Campus: Impact on GPA and School Dropout," *Journal of College Student Retention: Research, Theory & Practice* 18, no. 2 (2015): 234–48; Connie J. Kirkland, *Academic Impact of Sexual Assault* (Fairfax, VA: George Mason University, 1994).

55. C. Jordan, J. Combs, and G. Smith, "An Exploration of Sexual Victimization and Academic Performance Among College Women," *Trauma, Violence, & Abuse* 15, no. 3 (2014): 191–200; Majel Baker et al., "Sexual Victimization History Predicts

Academic Performance in College Women," *Journal of Counseling Psychology* 63, no. 6 (2016): 1–8.

56. Melissa Griffin, Jeffrey Wardell, and Jennifer Read, "Recent Sexual Victimization and Drinking Behavior in Newly Matriculated College Students: A Latent Growth Analysis," *Psychology of Addictive Behaviors* 27, no. 4 (2013): 966–73; R. Duncan, "Childhood Maltreatment and College Drop-Out Rates: Implications for Child Abuse Researchers," *Journal of Interpersonal Violence* 15, no. 9 (2000): 987–95.

57. Baker et al., "Sexual Victimization History."

58. Derek Summerfield, "Addressing Human Response to Trauma in War and Atrocity," in *Beyond Trauma: Cultural and Societal Dynamics*, ed. R. Kleber, C. Figley, and B. Gersons (New York: Plenum Press, 1995), 19. See also Richard Tedeschi, and Lawrence Calhoun, "The Posttraumatic Growth Inventory: Measuring the Positive Legacy of Trauma," *Journal of Traumatic Stress* 9, no. 3 (1996): 455–71.

59. Bessel A. Van Der Kolk and Alexander C. McFarlane, "Trauma and Its Challenge to Society," in *Traumatic Stress: The Effects of Overwhelming Experience on Mind, Body, and Society*, ed. Bessel A. Van Der Kolk, Alexander C. McFarlane, and Lars Weisæth (New York: Guilford Press, 2007), 28–29.

60. Herman, *Trauma and Recovery*, 7–8.

CHAPTER 10

1. Krebs et al. *The Campus Sexual Assault Study.*

2. Megan A. Alderden and Sarah E. Ullman, "Creating a More Complete and Current Picture: Examining Police and Prosecutor Decision-Making When Processing Sexual Assault Cases," *Violence against Women* 18, no 5 (2012): 540; RAINN, "Campus Sexual Violence: Statistics," 2016, Rape, Abuse and Incest National Network, www.rainn.org/statistics/criminal-justice-system.

3. Heather Littleton, Danny Axsom, and Amie Grills-Taquechel, "Sexual Assault Victims' Acknowledgment Status and Revictimization Risk," *Psychology of Women Quarterly* 33, no. 1 (2009): 34–42.; H. Littleton, C. Radecki Breitkopf, and A. Berenson, "Beyond the Campus: Unacknowledged Rape Among Low-Income Women," *Violence Against Women* 14, no. 3 (2008): 269–86.

4. C. Cleere, and S. Lynn, "Acknowledged Versus Unacknowledged Sexual Assault Among College Women," *Journal of Interpersonal Violence* 28, no. 12 (2013): 2593–611.

5. Heidi Zinzow et al., "The Role of Rape Tactics in Risk for Posttraumatic Stress Disorder and Major Depression: Results from a National Sample of College Women," *Depression and Anxiety* 27 (2010): 714.

6. Littleton et al., "Sexual Assault Victims' Acknowledgment," 35.

7. Marjorie Sable et al., "Barriers to Reporting Sexual Assault for Women and Men: Perspectives of College Students," *Journal of American College Health* 55, no. 3 (2006): 157–62.

8. Michelle Davies, Paul Pollard, and John Archer, "Effects of Perpetrator Gender and Victim Sexuality on Blame Toward Male Victims of Sexual Assault," *Journal of Social Psychology* 146, no. 3 (2006): 275–91; Kathy Doherty and Irina Anderson, "Making Sense of Male Rape: Constructions of Gender, Sexuality and Experience of Rape Victims," *Journal of Community & Applied Social Psychology* 14, no. 2 (2004): 85–103.

9. Sable et al., "Barriers to Reporting Sexual Assault," 160.

10. S. E. Ullman, and C. J. Najdowski, "Prospective Changes in Attributions of Self-Blame and Social Reactions to Women's Disclosures of Adult Sexual Assault," *Journal of Interpersonal Violence* 26, no. 10 (2010): 1934–62.

11. L. Orchowski, A. Untied, and C. Gidycz, "Social Reactions to Disclosure of Sexual Victimization and Adjustment Among Survivors of Sexual Assault," *Journal of Interpersonal Violence* 28, no. 10 (2013): 2005–23.

12. All of the survivors I knew who filed a report at University A were women.

13. For more information on Kristin's comments, see note 41, chapter 9.

14. Courtney Ahrens, "Being Silenced: The Impact of Negative Social Reactions on the Disclosure of Rape," *American Journal of Community Psychology* 38, nos. 3–4 (2006): 263–74; M. Relyea, and S. Ullman, "Unsupported or Turned Against: Understanding How Two Types of Negative Social Reactions to Sexual Assault Relate to Postassault Outcomes," *Psychology of Women Quarterly* 39, no. 1 (2013): 37–52; Jacqueline Golding, Sharon Wilsnack, and M. Lynne Cooper, "Sexual Assault History and Social Support: Six General Population Studies," *Journal of Traumatic Stress* 15, no. 3 (2002): 187–97.

15. Jon Krakauer. *Missoula: Rape and the Justice System in a College Town* (New York: Anchor Books, 2015).

16. Kirby Dick, and Amy Ziering, *The Hunting Ground: The Inside Story of Sexual Assault on American College Campuses*, distributed by Weinstein Company, Anchor Bay Entertainment, 2015; Krakauer, *Missoula*.

17. Lauren P. Schroeder, "Cracks in the Ivory Tower: How the Campus Sexual Violence Elimination Act Can Protect Students from Sexual Assault," *Loyola University Chicago Law Journal* 45 (May 2015): 1195–243.

18. Krakauer, *Missoula*.

19. Beth Pearsall, "Sexual Assault: An Unspoken Barrier to Higher Ed," *AAUW Outlook* 108, no. 3 (2014): 20.

20. Fisher et al., *Sexual Victimization of College Women*, 1–39, 10.

21. Dick and Ziering, *The Hunting Ground*; Krakauer, *Missoula*.

22. J. D. Scott Lewis, Saundra K. Schuster, Brett A. Sokolow, and Daniel C. Swinton, *Equity Is Such A Lonely Word*. Rep. NCHERM Group, LLC and ATICA, 2014, https://www.ncherm.org/wordpress/wp-content/uploads/2012/01/2014-Whitepaper-FINAL.pdf.

23. Russlyn Ali, "Dear Colleague Letter," Department of Education Office for Civil Rights, April 4, 2011, http://www2.ed.gov/about/offices/list/ocr/letters/colleague-201104.html.

24. Kristin Lombardi, "A Lack of Consequences for Sexual Assault," Center for Public Integrity, February 24, 2010, www.publicintegrity.org/2010/02/24/4360/lack-consequences-sexual-assault.

25. Todd Lighty, Stacy St. Clair, and Jodi S. Cohen, "Few Arrests, Convictions in Campus Sex Assault Cases," *Chicago Tribune*, June 22, 2011, http://www.chicagotribune.com/news/ct-met-campus-sexual-assaults-0617-20110616-story.html.

26. Tyler Kingkade, "Fewer Than One-Third of Campus Sexual Assault Cases Result in Expulsion," *Huffington Post*, September 29, 2014, www.huffingtonpost.com/2014/09/29/campus-sexual-assault_n_5888742.html.

27. Carly Parnitzke Smith and Jennifer J. Freyd, "Institutional Betrayal," *American Psychologist* 69, no. 6 (2014): 575; Carly Parnitzke Smith and Jenniver J. Freyd, "Dangerous Safe Havens: Institutional Betrayal Exacerbates Sexual Trauma," *Journal of Traumatic Stress* 26, no. 1 (February 2013): 119–24; R. Campbell, "Rape Survivors' Experiences with the Legal and Medical Systems: Do Rape Victim Advocates Make a Difference?" *Violence Against Women* 12, no. 1 (2006): 30–45.

28. Smith and Freyd, "Dangerous Safe Havens," 119–24.

29. Edward Chang et al., "Hope Under Assault: Understanding the Impact of Sexual Assault on the Relation Between Hope and Suicidal Risk in College Students," *Journal of Social and Clinical Psychology* 34, no. 3 (2015): 221–38.

30. For more information on Kari's comments, see note 41, chapter 9.

31. Melinda Henneberger et al., "Reported Sexual Assault at Notre Dame Campus Leaves More Questions than Answers," *National Catholic Reporter*, March 26, 2012, www.ncronline.org/news/accountability/reported-sexual-assault-notre-dame-campus-leaves-more-questions-answers.

32. Ibid.

33. Ibid.

34. Jack Flynn, "Trey Malone, Late Amherst Student's Sexual Assault Case Never Reported to District Attorney's Office, Officials Say," November 13, 2012. http://www.masslive.com/news/index.ssf/2012/11/the_northwest_district_attorne.html.

35. The Good Men Project, "Lead a Good Life, Everyone: Trey Malone's Suicide Note," November 5, 2012, https://goodmenproject.com/ethics-values/lead-a-good-life-everyone-trey-malones-suicide-note.

36. Lisa Barrios et al., "Suicide Ideation Among U.S. College Students: Associations with Other Injury Risk Behaviors," *Journal of American College Health* 48, no. 5 (2000): 229; David J. Drum, Chris Brownson, Adryon Burton Denmark, and Shann E. Smith, "New Data on the Nature of Suicidal Crises in College Students: Shifting the Paradigm," *Professional Psychology: Research and Practice* 40, no. 3 (2009): 214, 215; "Crisis on Campus: The Untold Story of Student Suicides," College Degree Search, April 6, 2015, http://www.collegedegreesearch.net/student-suicides/.

37. White House Task Force to Protect Students from Sexual Assault, "Not Alone: The First Report of the White House Task Force to Protect Students from Sexual

Assault," https://obamawhitehouse.archives.gov/the-press-office/2014/04/29/
fact-sheet-not-alone-protecting-students-sexual-assault; Russlyn Ali, "Dear
Colleague Letter," Department of Education Office for Civil Rights, April 4, 2011,
http://www2.ed.gov/about/offices/list/ocr/letters/colleague-201104.html.

CHAPTER 11

1. California State Legislature, S. Bill 967, Chapter 748, Sess. of 2011 (Cal. 2014), https://
   leginfo.legislature.ca.gov/faces/billNavClient.xhtml?bill_id=201320140SB967.
2. Jaclyn Friedman, "Consent Is Not a Lightswitch," posted November 9, 2010, http://
   amplifyyourvoice.org/u/yes_means_yes/2010/11/09/consent-is-not-a-lightswitch.
3. Jessica Bennett, "Campus Sex . . . with a Syllabus," *New York Times*, January 10, 2016,
   www.nytimes.com/2016/01/10/fashion/sexual-consent-assault-college-campuses.
   html?smid=fb-nytimes&smtyp=cur&_r=1.
4. Affirmative Consent Project, "Affirmative Consent Laws (Yes Means Yes) State
   by State | Affirmative Consent/Stopping Campus Sexual Assault," posted 2016,
   http://affirmativeconsent.com/affirmative-consent-laws-state-by-state/.
5. Jacob Bucher and Michelle Manasse, "When Screams Are Not Released: A Study
   of Communication and Consent in Acquaintance Rape Situations," *WWCJ
   Women & Criminal Justice* 21, no. 2 (2011): 123–40.
6. Melanie Boyd, "The Case for Affirmative Consent," *Huffington Post*, December
   17, 2014, http://www.huffingtonpost.com/melanie-boyd/the-case-for-affirma-
   tive-consent_b_6312476.html.
7. Michelle J. Anderson, "Campus Sexual Assault Adjudication and Resistance to
   Reform," *The Yale Law Journal* 125 (2016): 1979.
8. Rachael O'Byrne, Susan Hansen, and Mark Rapley, "If a Girl Doesn't Say 'No' . . .:
   Young Men, Rape and Claims of 'Insufficient Knowledge,'" *Journal of
   Community & Applied Social Psychology* 18, no. 3 (2008): 168–93; Susan Hansen,
   Rachael O'Byrne, and Mark Rapley, "Young Heterosexual Men's Use of the
   Miscommunication Model in Explaining Acquaintance Rape," *Sexuality Research
   and Social Policy* 7, no. 1 (2010): 45–49; Rachel O'Byrne, Mark Rapley, and Susan
   Hansen, "'You Couldn't Say "No," Could You?' Young Men's Understandings
   of Sexual Refusal," *Feminism & Psychology* 16, no. 2 (2006): 133–54; Melanie
   Beres, "Sexual Miscommunication? Untangling Assumptions about Sexual
   Communication between Casual Sex Partners," *Culture, Health & Sexuality* 12,
   no. 1 (2010): 1–14.
9. Western Michigan University, "FIRE Sexual Assault Peer Educators," posted
   2016, https://wmich.edu/healthcenter/healthpromotion/fireplace/peer-fire.
   David Burt, "Peer Educators to Tackle Sexual Consent," *Yale Daily News*,
   September 4, 2011, http://yaledailynews.com/blog/2011/09/14/peer-educa-
   tors-to-tackle-sexual-consent/; University of the Pacific, "Student 2 Student

Healthy Relationships Peer Educators," posted 2016, www.pacific.edu/ Campus-Life.html.

10. To see video examples, see "Videos + Campaigns," Culture of Respect, 2016, http://cultureofrespect.org/the-resources/videos-photos.

11. Men Can Stop Rape, "A Comprehensive Approach: The Strength Campaign," Men Can End Rape, www.mencanstoprape.org/A-Comprehensive-Approach-The-Strength-Campaign/.

12. Alia Wong, "The Renaissance of Student Activism," *The Atlantic*, May 21, 2015, www.theatlantic.com/education/archive/2015/05/the-renaissance-of-student-activism/393749/.

13. In 2011, the Department of Education's Office of Civil Rights issued the "Dear Colleague Letter," which offered a revised set of Title IX guidelines about how colleges and universities must respond to sexual assault allegations. Universities not in compliance would risk losing federal funding. This letter informed universities that using the "clear and convincing" standard when adjudicating sexual assault cases is inconsistent with the standard of proof established for violations of civil rights lawsuits, and is thus not equitable under Title IX. Instead, the Department of Education reinterated that schools must adjudicate these cases using a "preponderance of the evidence" standard. This standard, which means that an incident more likely than not occurred, is normally used in civil court cases, including sexual harassment lawsuits. See Ali, "Dear Colleague Letter."

14. As I complete final edits for *College Hookup Culture and Christian Ethics*, Donald Trump is in the early months of his presidency. Pertinent to this discussion, we know that concerns about his views toward women and treatment of women were repeatedly raised during the presidential campaign, and some of his top priorities have been to roll back Obama era federal regulations. Thus, it is currently unclear whether the Title IX initiatives begun under President Obama will be maintained. Trump's selection of Betsy DeVos as Department of Education secretary raises further concerns. At her confirmation hearing, DeVos did not commit to upholding the revised Title IX regulations. Her prior $25,000 donation to FIRE (the Foundation for Individual Rights in Education) also raises concerns that she will overturn revised Title IX regulations. This organization has sued the Obama administration to raise the standard of proof for victims of sexual assault in university judicial board hearings. FIRE advocates for the highest standard of proof—"beyond a reasonable doubt standard"—which is only used when life and liberty are at stake in criminal cases. FIRE has also opposed affirmative consent legislation. See Anna Orso, "Trump's Education Pick Donated to Philly Group with Controversial Campus Rape Stance," PolitiFact, January 19, 2017, http://www.politifact.com/pennsylvania/statements/2017/jan/19/bob-casey/trumps-education-pick-donated-philly-group-controv/.

15. White House, "Fact Sheet: The 'It's On Us' Campaign Launches New PSA, Marks One-Year Since Launch of 'It's On Us' Campaign to End Campus Sexual Assault,"

press release, September 1, 2015, www.whitehouse.gov/the-press-office/2015/
09/01/fact-sheet-its-us-campaign-launches-new-psa-marks-one-year-launch.

16. Jody Clay-Warner, "Avoiding Rape: The Effects of Protective Actions and Situational Factors on Rape Outcome," *Violence and Victims* 17, no. 6 (2002): 691–705.

17. U.S. Department of Justice, "Bystander-Focused Prevention of Sexual Violence." NotAlone.gov, October 12, 2016, www.notalone.gov/assets/bystander-summary.pdf.

18. White House Task Force to Protect Students from Sexual Assault, "Not Alone: The First Report of the White House Task Force," September 19, 2014. For an update on best practices, the 2016 Biennial Report to Congress analyzes 109 universities that received grants to address campus sexual assault and summarizes their preliminary findings on investigating and adjudicating sexual assault. Their recommendations to improve a campus' response to sexual assault included a need to improve offender accountability. They recognize there is still a need to "increase awareness of sexual assault, dating violence and stalking among all student groups" and "to expand mandatory education to all students." Furthermore, the report found that many victims were not sufficiently aware of or willing to use the services and options available to them. See United States Department of Justice Office on Violence Against Women, *The 2016 Biennial Report to Congress on the Effectiveness of Grant Programs Under the Violence Against Women Act*, https://www.justice.gov/ovw/page/file/933886/download.

The White House Task Force also published its preliminary findings in 2017. See White House Task Force to Protect Students from Sexual Assault, "The Second Report of the White House Task Force to Protect Students from Sexual Assault," January 5, 2017. https://www.whitehouse.gov/sites/whitehouse.gov/files/images/Documents/1.4.17.VAW%20Event.TF%20Report.PDF.

19. According to the 2017 report, "Addressing Gender-Based Violence on College Campuses," schools must develop uniform and consistent sanctions for sexual assault in order to ensure the safety of the entire campus community and foster a sense of trust among students that their school will respond to allegations of sexual assault fairly and treat survivors with respect and dignity. The report states: "The impacts of overlooking, poorly responding to, or inadequately investigating incidents of GBV [gender-based violence] are immense. The violence can escalate, placing the victim, other students, and faculty at risk, and officer safety can be compromised as well. The victim may begin to miss class, grades may begin to decline, and the victim may drop out of school and experience other detrimental effects. . . . Most troubling, is that when these crimes are overlooked or the victim disengages with the criminal process and doesn't file a report, the perpetrator is empowered and continues to engage in criminal behaviors with no consequences leaving the campus community at risk for future victimizations (49)." See "Addressing Gender-Based Violence on College Campuses: Guide to a Comprehensive Model," Office on Violence Against Women, Department of Justice Grant no. 2015-TA-AX-K063, (2017): 1–93.

20. Lombardi, "A Lack of Consequences."

21. Yale University, "Yale Sexual Misconduct Policies and Related Definitions," posted May 10, 2016, http://smr.yale.edu/sexual-misconduct-policies-and-definitions; Duke University, "Student Sexual Misconduct Policy and Procedures: Duke's Commitment to Title IX," posted 2016, https://studentaffairs.duke.edu/conduct/z-policies/student-sexual-misconduct-policy-dukes-commitment-title-ix; Vassar College, "Sexual Assault & Violence Prevention," posted March 11, 2015, http://savp.vassar.edu/policies/sexual-misconduct.html; Dartmouth University, "Unified Disciplinary Procedures for Sexual Assault by Students and Student Organizations," posted March 1, 2016, www.dartmouth.edu/sexualrespect/policies/unified-sexual-assault-policy.html; Princeton University, "University-wide Regulations," posted August 2, 2016, www.princeton.edu/pub/rrr/part1/index.xml#comp13); University of Iowa, "Sanctioning Guidelines for Sexual Assault," posted 2016, https://dos.uiowa.edu/policies/sanctioning-guidelines-for-sexual-assault/; University of North Carolina, "Policy on Prohibited Discrimination, Harassment and Related Misconduct—Equal Opportunity and Compliance Office," posted 2016, http://eoc.unc.edu/our-policies/ppdhrm/; Northwestern University, Equal Opportunity and Compliance Office, "Policy on Sexual Misconduct," posted September 2016, www.northwestern.edu/sexual-misconduct/docs/sexual_misconduct_policy.pdf.

22. "Addressing Gender-Based Violence on College Campuses," 1–93.

23. See Farley's analysis of how our understandings of sexuality remain "immersed in the economy of defilement" in Farley, *Just Love*, 177.

24. John Stoltenberg, *Refusing to Be a Man: Essays on Social Justice* (London: UCL Press, 2000), 22.

APPENDIX

1. I received IRB approval from this midwestern university to collect and analyze my students' written work provided that I delete names and all identifying information of students. The IRB determined that the data met the criteria for the Exempt from Review category under Federal Regulation 45CFR46.

2. Carl Auerbach and Louise Silverstein, *Qualitative Data: An Introduction to Coding and Analysis* (New York: New York University Press, 2003).

3. Since I did not want to invade my students' privacy, I did not ask students to disclose their sexual orientation or economic class. On consent forms granting or denying me permission to use their written work for educational or research purposes, students only disclosed their gender and racial identity. Thus, my study cannot analyze the effects of class on students' involvement in party culture.

Bibliography

Abbey, Antonia, and Pam McAuslan. "A Longitudinal Examination of Male College Students' Perpetration of Sexual Assault." *Journal of Consulting and Clinical Psychology* 72, no. 5 (2004): 747–56.

Abbey, Antonia, Tina Zawacki, Philip O. Buck, A. Moique Clinton, and Pam McAuslan. "Alcohol and Sexual Assault." *Alcohol Research and Health* 25, no. 1 (2001): 43–51.

"A Comprehensive Approach: The Strength Campaign." Men Can End Rape. At http://www.mencanstoprape.org/A-Comprehensive-Approach-The-Strength-Campaign/.

"Addressing Gender-Based Violence on College Campuses: Guide to a Comprehensive Model. Office on Violence Against Women." Department of Justice, Grant No. 2015-TA-AX-K06 (2017): 1–93.

Affirmative Consent Project. "Affirmative Consent Laws (Yes Means Yes) State by State." Posted 2016. At http://affirmativeconsent.com/affirmative-consent-laws-state-by-state/.

Ahrens, Courtney E. "Being Silenced: The Impact of Negative Social Reactions on the Disclosure of Rape." *American Journal of Community Psychology* 38, nos. 3–4 (2006): 263–74.

Albright, Julie M. "Sex in America Online: An Exploration of Sex, Marital Status, and Sexual Identity in Internet Sex Seeking and Its Impacts." *Journal of Sex Research* 45, no. 2 (2008): 175–86.

Alderden, Megan A., and Sarah E. Ullman. "Creating a More Complete and Current Picture: Examining Police and Prosecutor Decision-Making When Processing Sexual Assault Cases." *Violence Against Women* 18, no. 5 (2012): 540.

American Association of University Professors. "Campus Sexual Assault: Suggested Policies and Procedures." *Academe* 99, no. 4 (July/August 2013): 92–100.

American Psychiatric Association. *Diagnostic and Statistical Manual of Mental Disorders*, 5th ed. Arlington, VA: American Psychiatric Association, 2013.

Anderson, Michelle J. "Campus Sexual Assault Adjudication and Resistance to Reform." *Yale Law Journal* 125 (2016): 1940–2005.

Armstrong, Elizabeth, Paula England, and Alison Fogarty. "Accounting for Women's Orgasm and Sexual Enjoyment in College Hookups and Relationships." *American Sociological Review* 77, no. 3 (2012): 435–62.

Armstrong, Elizabeth, Alison Fogarty, and Paula England. "Orgasm in College Hookups and Relationships." In *Families as They Really Are*, edited by Barbara Risman, 362–77. New York: W.W. Norton, 2010.

Auerbach, Carl, and Louise Silverstein. *Qualitative Data: An Introduction to Coding and Analysis.* New York: New York University Press, 2003.

Baker, Majel R., Patricia A. Frazier, Christiaan Greer, Jacob A. Paulsen, Kelli Howard, Liza N. Meredith, Samantha L. Anders, and Sandra L. Shallcross. "Sexual Victimization History Predicts Academic Performance in College Women." *Journal of Counseling Psychology* 63, no. 3 (2016): 685–92.

Baltazar, Alina, Herbert W. Helm, Duane McBride, Gary Hopkins, and John V. Stevens Jr. "Internet Pornography Use in the Context of External and Internal Religiosity." *Journal of Psychology and Theology* 38, no. 1 (2010): 32–40.

Barriger, Megan, and Carlos J. Vélez-Blasini. "Descriptive and Injunctive Social Norm Overestimation in Hooking Up and Their Role as Predictors of Hookup Activity in a College Student Sample." *Journal of Sex Research* 50, no. 1 (2013): 84–94.

Barrios, Lisa, Sherry A. Evertt, Thomas Simon, and Nancy D. Brener. "Suicide Ideation Among U.S. College Students: Associations with Other Injury Risk Behaviors." *Journal of American College Health* 48, no. 5 (2000): 220–33.

Becker, Judith V., Linda J. Skinner, Gene G. Abel, Roz Axelrod, and Eileen C. Treacy. "Depressive Symptoms Associated with Sexual Assault." *Journal of Sex & Marital Therapy* 10, no. 3 (1984): 185–92.

Beiter, R., R. Nash, M. Mccrady, D. Rhoades, M. Linscomb, M. Clarahan, and S. Sammut. "The Prevalence and Correlates of Depression, Anxiety, and Stress in a Sample of College Students." *Journal of Affective Disorders* 173 (2015): 90–96.

Bennett, Jessica. "Campus Sex. . . . with a Syllabus." *New York Times*, January 10, 2016. At www.google.com/?gws_rd=ssl#q=Bennett,+Jessica.+2016.+%E2%80 %9CCampus+Sex+%E2%80%A6+With+A+Syllabus%E2%80%9D.+Nytimes. Com&tbm=shop.

Beres, Melanie. "Sexual Miscommunication? Untangling Assumptions About Sexual Communication Between Casual Sex Partners." *Culture, Health & Sexuality* 12, no. 1 (2010): 1–14.

Berkowitz, Alan. "College Men as Perpetrators of Acquaintance Rape and Sexual Assault: A Review of Recent Research." *Journal of American College Health* 40, no. 4 (1992): 175–81.

Bersamin, Melina M., Byron L. Zamboanga, Seth J. Schwartz, M. Brent Donnellan, Robert S. Weisskirch, Su Yeong Kim, V. Bede Agocha, Susan Krauss Whitbourne, and S. Jean Caraway. "Risky Business: Is There an Association between Casual

Sex and Mental Health among Emerging Adults?" *Journal of Sex Research* 51, no. 1 (2013): 43–51.

Beste, Jennifer. *God and the Victim: Traumatic Intrusions on Grace and Freedom.* American Academy of Religion Academy Series. Oxford: Oxford University Press, 2007.

Black, M. C., K. C. Basile, M. J. Breiding, S. G. Smith, M. L. Walters, M. T. Merrick, J. Chen, and M. R. Stevens. "National Intimate Partner and Sexual Violence Survey: 2010 Summary Report." November 2011. National Center for Injury Prevention and Control, Centers for Disease Control and Prevention, Atlanta, Georgia.

Boeschen, Laura E., Mary P. Koss, Aurelio Jose Figueredo, and James A. Coan. "Experiential Avoidance and Post-Traumatic Stress Disorder." *Journal of Aggression, Maltreatment & Trauma* 4, no. 2 (2001): 211–45.

Bogle, Kathleen A. *Hooking Up: Sex, Dating, and Relationships on Campus.* New York: New York University Press, 2008.

Boyd, Melanie. "The Case for Affirmative Consent." *Huffington Post*, December 17, 2014. At http://www.huffingtonpost.com/melanie-boyd/the-case-for-affirmative-consent_b_6312476.html.

Bucher, Jacob, and Michelle Manasse. "When Screams Are Not Released: A Study of Communication and Consent in Acquaintance Rape Situations." *WWCJ Women & Criminal Justice* 21, no. 2 (2011): 123–40.

Burnam, M. Audrey, Judith A. Stein, Jacqueline M. Golding, Judith M. Siegel, Susan B. Sorenson, Alan B. Forsythe, and Cynthia A. Telles. "Sexual Assault and Mental Disorders in a Community Population." *Journal of Consulting and Clinical Psychology* 56, no. 6 (1988): 843–50.

Burt, David. "Peer Educators to Tackle Sexual Consent." *Yale Daily News*, September 4, 2011. At http://yaledailynews.com/blog/2011/09/14/peer-educators-to-tackle-sexual-consent/.

California State Legislature. S. Bill No. 967, Legislative Counsel's Digest (2014) (enacted). Approved by the governor and filed with the Secretary of State, September, 28, 2014. At https://leginfo.legislature.ca.gov/faces/billNavClient.xhtml?bill_id=201320140SB967.

Campbell, R. "Rape Survivors' Experiences with the Legal and Medical Systems: Do Rape Victim Advocates Make a Difference?" *Violence Against Women* 12, no. 1 (2006): 30–45.

Campbell, R., E. Dworkin, and G. Cabral. "An Ecological Model of the Impact of Sexual Assault on Women's Mental Health." *Trauma, Violence, & Abuse* 10, no. 3 (2009): 225–46.

Cantor, David, Bonnie Fisher, Susan Chibnall, Reanne Townsend, Hyunshik Lee, Carol Bruce, and Gail Thomas. *Report on the AAU Campus Climate Survey on Sexual Assault and Sexual Misconduct.* Rockville, MD: Westat, 2015.

Carr, Joetta L., and Karen M. Vandeusen. "Risk Factors for Male Sexual Aggression on College Campuses." *Journal of Family Violence* 19, no. 5 (2004): 279–89.

Chang, Edward C., and Jameson K. Hirsch. "Social Problem Solving Under Assault: Understanding the Impact of Sexual Assault on the Relation between Social Problem Solving and Suicidal Risk in Female College Students." *Cognitive Therapy and Research* 39, no. 3 (2015): 403–13.

Chang, Edward C., Tina Yu, Zunaira Jilani, Erin E. Fowler, Elizabeth A. Yu, Jiachen Lin, and Jameson K. Hirsch. "Hope Under Assault: Understanding the Impact of Sexual Assault on the Relation Between Hope and Suicidal Risk in College Students." *Journal of Social and Clinical Psychology* 34, no. 3 (2015): 221–38.

Chodron, Pema. *The Wisdom of No Escape And the Path of Loving Kindness.* Boulder, CO: Shambhala Publications, 2010.

Clay-Warner, Jody. "Avoiding Rape: The Effects of Protective Actions and Situational Factors on Rape Outcome." *Violence and Victims* 17, no. 6 (2002): 691–705.

Cleere, C., and S. J. Lynn. "Acknowledged versus Unacknowledged Sexual Assault Among College Women." *Journal of Interpersonal Violence* 28, no. 12 (2013): 2593–611.

Cleveland, H. H., M. P. Koss, and J. Lyons. "Rape Tactics From the Survivors' Perspective: Contextual Dependence and Within-Event Independence." *Journal of Interpersonal Violence* 14, no. 5 (1999): 532–47.

Clum, Gretchen A., Karen S. Calhoun, and Rachel Kimerling. "Associations Among Symptoms of Depression and Posttraumatic Stress Disorder and Self-Reported Health in Sexually Assaulted Women." *Journal of Nervous and Mental Disease* 188, no. 10 (2000): 671–78.

Clum, Gretchen A., Pallavi Nishith, and Patricia A. Resick. "Trauma-Related Sleep Disturbance and Self-Reported Physical Health Symptoms in Treatment-Seeking Female Rape Victims." *Journal of Nervous and Mental Disease* 189, no. 9 (2001): 618–22.

Collings, Steven J. "Sexual Aggression: A Discriminant Analysis of Predictors in a Non-Forensic Sample." *South African Journal of Psychology* 24, no. 1 (1994): 35–38.

Davies, Michelle, Paul Pollard, and John Archer. "Effects of Perpetrator Gender and Victim Sexuality on Blame Toward Male Victims of Sexual Assault." *Journal of Social Psychology* 146, no. 3 (2006): 275–91.

Davis, K. C., Jeanette Norris, William H. George, Joel Martell, and Julia R. Heiman. "Rape-Myth Congruent Beliefs in Women Resulting from Exposure to Violent Pornography: Effects of Alcohol and Sexual Arousal." *Journal of Interpersonal Violence* 21, no. 9 (2006): 1208–223.

Dartmouth University. "Unified Disciplinary Procedures for Sexual Assault by Students and Student Organizations." Posted March 1, 2016. At www.dartmouth.edu/sexualrespect/policies/unified-sexual-assault-policy.html.

Dean, Kenda Creasy. *Almost Christian: What the Faith of Our Teenagers Is Telling the American Church.* Oxford: Oxford University Press, 2010.

Dekeseredy, Walter S., and Patrik Olsson. "Adult Pornography, Male Peer Support, and Violence Against Women." In *Technology for Facilitating Humanity and Combating*

Social Deviations Interdisciplinary Perspectives, edited by Miguel A. Garcia-Ruiz, Miguel Vargas Martin, and Arthur Edwards, 34–50. Hershey, PA: Information Science Reference, 2011.

De La Torre, Miguel. *A Lily among the Thorns: Imagining a New Christian Sexuality*. San Francisco, CA: John Wiley, 2007.

Dick, Kerby, and Amy Ziering. *The Hunting Ground: The Inside Story of Sexual Assault on American College Campuses*. Weinstein Company, Anchor Bay Entertainment, 2015.

Dines, Gail. *Pornland: How Porn Has Hijacked Our Sexuality*. Boston: Beacon Press, 2010.

Doherty, Kathy, and Irina Anderson. "Making Sense of Male Rape: Constructions of Gender, Sexuality and Experience of Rape Victims." *Journal of Community & Applied Social Psychology* 14, no. 2 (2004): 85–103.

Döring, Nicola M. "The Internet's Impact on Sexuality: A Critical Review of 15 Years of Research." *Computers in Human Behavior* 25, no. 5 (2009): 1089–101.

Douglas, Kelly Brown. *Sexuality and the Black Church: A Womanist Perspective*. Maryknoll, NY: Orbis Books, 1999.

Downey, John. "Can We Talk? Globalization, Human Rights, and Political Theology." In *Missing God?: Cultural Amnesia and Political Theology*, edited by John K. Downey, Jürgen Manemann, Steven T. Ostovich, 125–38. Berlin: Lit Vertag, 2007.

Drum, David J., Chris Brownson, Adryon Burton Denmark, and Shanna E. Smith. "New Data on the Nature of Suicidal Crises in College Students: Shifting the Paradigm." *Professional Psychology: Research and Practice* 40, no. 3 (2009): 213–222.

Duke University. "Student Sexual Misconduct Policy and Procedures: Duke's Commitment to Title IX." Posted 2016. At https://studentaffairs.duke.edu/conduct/z-policies/student-sexual-misconduct-policy-dukes-commitment-title-ix.

Duncan, R. D. "Childhood Maltreatment and College Drop-Out Rates: Implications for Child Abuse Researchers." *Journal of Interpersonal Violence* 15, no. 9 (2000): 987–95.

Eadie, Erin M., Marsha G. Runtz, and Julie Spencer-Rodgers. "Posttraumatic Stress Symptoms as a Mediator between Sexual Assault and Adverse Health Outcomes in Undergraduate Women." *Journal of Traumatic Stress* 21, no. 6 (2008): 540–47.

Edwards, K. M., K. M. Sylaska, J. E. Barry, M. M. Moynihan, V. L. Banyard, E. S. Cohn, W. A. Walsh, and S. K. Ward. "Physical Dating Violence, Sexual Violence, and Unwanted Pursuit Victimization: A Comparison of Incidence Rates Among Sexual-Minority and Heterosexual College Students." *Journal of Interpersonal Violence* 30, no. 4 (2014): 580–600.

Elliott, Diana, Doris Mok, and John Briere. "Adult Sexual Assault: Prevalence, Symptomatology, and Sex Differences in the General Population." *Journal of Traumatic Stress* 17, no. 3 (2004): 203–11.

Ellison, Marvin Mahan. *Erotic Justice: A Liberating Ethic of Sexuality*. Louisville, KY: Westminster John Knox Press, 1996.

Ellison, Marvin Mahan, and Kelly Brown Douglas. *Sexuality and the Sacred: Sources for Theological Reflection.* Louisville, KY: Westminster John Knox Press, 2010.

Emmers-Sommer, Tara, and Ryan J. Burns. "The Relationship Between Exposure to Internet Pornography and Sexual Attitudes Toward Women." *Journal of Online Behavior* 1, no. 4 (2005): 1–16.

Epstein, Marina, Jerel P. Calzo, Andrew P. Smiler, and L. Monique Ward. "Anything From Making Out to Having Sex: Men's Negotiations of Hooking Up and Friends With Benefits Scripts." *Journal of Sex Research* 46, no. 5 (2009): 414–24.

Faravelli, Carlo, Alice Giugni, Stefano Salvatori, and Valdo Ricca. "Psychopathology After Rape." *American Journal of Psychiatry* 161, no. 9 (2004): 1483–85.

Farley, Margaret A. *Just Love: A Framework for Christian Sexual Ethics.* New York: Continuum International, 2006.

Filipas, H. H. "Child Sexual Abuse, Coping Responses, Self-Blame, Posttraumatic Stress Disorder, and Adult Sexual Revictimization." *Journal of Interpersonal Violence* 21, no. 5 (2006): 652–72.

Fisher, Bonnie S., Francis T. Cullen, and Michael G. Turner. *The Sexual Victimization of College Women.* Report no. NCJ 182369, U.S. Department of Justice, Office of Justice Programs, National Institute of Justice. Washington, DC: Bureau of Justice Statistics, 2000.

Flack, W. F., K. A. Daubman, M. L. Caron, J. A. Asadorian, N. R. D'Aureli, S. N. Gigliotti, A. T. Hall, S. Kiser, and E. R. Stine. "Risk Factors and Consequences of Unwanted Sex Among University Students: Hooking Up, Alcohol, and Stress Response." *Journal of Interpersonal Violence* 22, no. 2 (2007): 139–57.

Flynn, Jack. "Trey Malone, Late Amherst Student's Sexual Assault Case Never Reported to District Attorney's Office, Officials Say." November 13, 2012. At http://www.masslive.com/news/index.ssf/2012/11/the_northwest_district_attorne.html.

Foubert, John D., Matthew W. Brosi, and R. Sean Bannon. "Pornography Viewing Among Fraternity Men: Effects on Bystander Intervention, Rape Myth Acceptance and Behavioral Intent to Commit Sexual Assault." *Sexual Addiction & Compulsivity* 18, no. 4 (2011): 212–31.

Foubert, John D, Johnatan T. Newberry, and Jerry Tatum. "Behavior Differences Seven Months Later: Effects of a Rape Prevention Program." *Journal of Student Affairs Research and Practice* 44, no. 4 (2007): 1125–46.

Freitas, Donna. *The End of Sex: How Hookup Culture Is Leaving a Generation Unhappy, Sexually Unfulfilled, and Confused about Intimacy.* New York: Basic Books, 2013.

Freitas, Donna. *Sex and the Soul: Juggling Sexuality, Spirituality, Romance, and Religion on America's College Campuses.* Oxford: Oxford University Press, 2008.

Friedman, Jaclyn. "Consent Is Not a Lightswitch." Posted November 9, 2010. At http://amplifyyourvoice.org/u/yes_means_yes/2010/11/09/consent-is-not-a-lightswitch.

Garcia, Gina A., Marc P. Johnston, Juan C. Garibay, Felisha A. Herrera, and Luis G. Giraldo. "When Parties Become Racialized: Deconstructing Racially Themed Parties." *Journal of Student Affairs Research and Practice* 48, no. 1 (2011): 11–16.

Garcia, Justin R., and Chris Reiber. "Hookup Behavior: A Biopsychosocial Perspective." *Journal of Social, Evolutionary, and Cultural Psychology* 2, no. 4 (2008).

Garcia, Justin R., Chris Reiber, Sean G. Massey, and Ann. M. Merriwether. "Sexual Hookup Culture: A Review." *Review of General Psychology* 16, no. 2 (2012): 161–76.

Garcia, Justin R., Chris Reiber, A. M. Merriwether, L. L. Heywood, and H. E. Fisher. "Touch Me in the Morning: Intimately Affiliative Gestures in Uncommitted and Romantic Relationships." Paper presented at the Annual Conference of the NorthEastern Evolutionary Psychology Society, New Paltz, New York, 2010.

Garcia, Justin R., Susan M. Seibold-Simpson, Sean G. Massey, and Ann M. Merriwether. "Casual Sex: Integrating Social, Behavioral, and Sexual Health Research." In *Handbook of the Sociology of Sexualities*, edited by John Delamater and Rebecca Plante, 203–22. New York: Springer Cham, 2015.

Gavranidou, Maria, and Rita Rosner. "The Weaker Sex? Gender and Post-traumatic Stress Disorder." *Depression & Anxiety* 17, no. 3 (May 2003): 130–39.

Golding, Jacqueline M., Sharon C. Wilsnack, and M. Lynne Cooper. "Sexual Assault History and Social Support: Six General Population Studies." *Journal of Traumatic Stress* 15, no. 3 (2002): 187–97.

Good Men Project. "Lead a Good Life, Everyone: Trey Malone's Suicide Note." At https://goodmenproject.com/ethics-values/lead-a-good-life-everyone-trey-malones-suicide-note.

Grello, Catherine M., Deborah P. Welsh, and Melinda S. Harper. "No Strings Attached: The Nature of Casual Sex in College Students." *Journal of Sex Research* 43, no. 3 (2006): 255–67.

Griffin, Melissa J., Jeffrey D. Wardell, and Jennifer P. Read. "Recent Sexual Victimization and Drinking Behavior in Newly Matriculated College Students: A Latent Growth Analysis." *Psychology of Addictive Behaviors* 27, no. 4 (2013): 966–73.

Hamilton, Laura, and Elizabeth A. Armstrong. "Gendered Sexuality in Young Adulthood Double Binds and Flawed Options." *Gender & Society* 23, no. 5 (2009): 589–616.

Hansen, Susan, Rachael O'Byrne, and Mark Rapley. "Young Heterosexual Men's Use of the Miscommunication Model in Explaining Acquaintance Rape." *Sexuality Research and Social Policy* 7, no. 1 (2010): 45–49.

Heldman, Caroline, and Lisa Wade. "Hookup Culture: Setting a New Research Agenda." *Sexuality Research and Social Policy* 7, no. 4 (2010): 323–33.

Henneberger, Melinda, Lisa C. Barrios, Sherry A. Everett, Thomas R. Simon, and Nancy D. Brener. "Reported Sexual Assault at Notre Dame Campus Leaves More Questions than Answers." *National Catholic Reporter*, March 26, 2012. At https://www.ncronline.org/news/accountability/reported-sexual-assault-notre-dame-campus-leaves-more-questions-answers.

Herman, Judith Lewis. *Trauma and Recovery*. New York: Basic Books, 1992.

Higgins, Jenny A., Margo Mullinax, James Trussell, J. Kenneth Davidson, and Nelwyn B. Moore. "Sexual Satisfaction and Sexual Health Among University Students in the United States." *American Journal of Public Health* 101, no. 9 (2011): 1643–54.

Its On Us. Cultural movement. At www.itsonus.org/#spread_the_word.

Jhally, Sut, Andrew Killoy, and Joe Bartone. *Dreamworlds 3: Desire, Sex & Power in Music Video*. Media Education Foundation, 2007. At http://www.mediaed.org/transcripts/Dreamworlds-3-Transcript.pdf.

Jordan, C. E., J. L. Combs, and G. T. Smith. "An Exploration of Sexual Victimization and Academic Performance Among College Women." *Trauma, Violence, & Abuse* 15, no. 3 (2014): 191–200.

Kadison, Richard, and Theresa Foy DiGeronimo. *College of the Overwhelmed: The Campus Mental Health Crisis and What to Do About It*. San Francisco, CA: Jossey-Bass, 2004.

Kilmartin, Christopher, and Alan Berkowitz. *Sexual Assault in Context: Teaching College Men about Gender*. Holmes Beach, FL: Learning Publications, 2001.

Kilpatrick, Dean G., Kenneth J. Ruggiero, Ron Acierno, Benjamin E. Saunders, Heidi S. Resnick, and Connie L. Best. "Violence and Risk of PTSD, Major Depression, Substance Abuse/dependence, and Comorbidity: Results from the National Survey of Adolescents." *Journal of Consulting and Clinical Psychology* 71, no. 4 (2003): 692–700.

Kimmel, Michael S. *Guyland: The Perilous World Where Boys Become Men*. New York: Harper, 2009.

Kingkade, Tyler. "Fewer Than One-Third of Campus Sexual Assault Cases Result in Expulsion." *Huffington Post*, September 29, 2014. At www.huffingtonpost.com/2014/09/29/campus-sexual-assault_n_5888742.html.

Kirkland, Connie J. *Academic Impact of Sexual Assault*. Fairfax, VA: George Mason University, 1994.

Kleinplatz, Peggy J., A. Dana Menard, Marie-Pierre Paquet, Nicolas Paradis, Meghan Campbell, Dino Zuccarino, and Lisa Mehak. "The Components of Optimal Sexuality: A Portrait of 'Great Sex.'" *Canadian Journal of Human Sexuality* 18, nos. 1–2 (2009): 1–13.

Klipfel, K. M., S. E. Claxton, and M. H. M. Van Dulmen. "Interpersonal Aggression Victimization Within Casual Sexual Relationships and Experiences." *Journal of Interpersonal Violence* 29, no. 3 (February 2014): 557–69.

Koss, Mary P., Christine A. Gidycz, and Nadine Wisniewski. "The Scope of Rape: Incidence and Prevalence of Sexual Aggression and Victimization in a National Sample of Higher Education Students." *Journal of Consulting and Clinical Psychology* 55, no. 2 (1987): 162–70.

Krakauer, Jon. *Missoula: Rape and the Justice System in a College Town*. New York: Anchor Books, 2015.

Krebs, Christopher P., Christine H. Lindquist, Tara D. Warner, Bonnie S. Fisher, and Sandra L. Martin. *The Campus Sexual Assault (CSA) Study*. Report no. 221153,

October 2007. Washington, DC: National Institute of Justice. At www.ncjrs.gov/ pdffiles1/nij/grants/221153.pdf.

Krebs, Christopher P., Christine H. Lindquist, Tara D. Warner, Bonnie S. Fisher, and Sandra L. Martin. "College Women's Experiences with Physically Forced, Alcohol- or Other Drug-Enabled, and Drug-Facilitated Sexual Assault Before and Since Entering College." *Journal of American College Health* 57, no. 6 (2009): 639–47.

Lambert, Tracy A., Arnold S. Kahn, and Kevin J. Apple. "Pluralistic Ignorance and Hooking Up." *Journal of Sex Research* 40, no. 2 (2003): 129–33.

Levin, Michael E., Jason Lillis, and Steven C. Hayes. "When Is Online Pornography Viewing Problematic Among College Males? Examining the Moderating Role of Experiential Avoidance." *Sexual Addiction & Compulsivity: The Journal of Treatment & Prevention* 19, no. 3 (August 22, 2012): 168–80.

Lewis, Melissa A., Christine M. Lee, Megan E. Patrick, and Nicole Fossos. "Gender-specific Normative Misperceptions of Risky Sexual Behavior and Alcohol-related Risky Sexual Behavior," *Sex Roles* 57, nos. 1-2 (2007): 81–90.

Lewis, Scott J. D., Saundra K. Schuster, Brett A. Sokolow, and Daniel C. Swinton, *Equity Is Such A Lonely Word*. Rep. NCHERM Group, LLC and ATICA, 2014. At https:// www.ncherm.org/wordpress/wp-content/uploads/2012/01/2014-Whitepaper-FINAL.pdf.

Lighty, Todd, Stacy St. Clair, and Jodi S. Cohen, "Few Arrests, Convictions in Campus Sex Assault Cases." *Chicago Tribune*, June 22, 2011. At http://www.chicagotri-bune.com/news/ct-met-campus-sexual-assaults-0617-20110616-story.html.

Lisak, David. "Understanding the Predatory Nature of Sexual Violence." *Sexual Assault Report* 14, no. 4 (March/April 2011): 49–57.

Lisak, David, and Paul M. Miller. "Repeat Rape and Multiple Offending Among Undetected Rapists." *Violence and Victims* 39, no. 6 (2002): 73–84.

Lisak, David., and National Judicial Education Program to Promote Equality for Women and Men in the Courts. *The "Undetected" Rapist*. New York: National Judicial Education Program, 2000.

Littleton, Heather, Danny Axsom, C. Breitkopf, and A. Berenson. "Rape Acknowledgment and Post-assault Experiences: How Acknowledgment Status Relates to Disclosure, Coping, Worldview, and Reactions Received from Others." *Violence and Victims* 21 (2006): 761–78.

Littleton, Heather, Danny Axsom, and Amie Grills-Taquechel. "Sexual Assault Victims' Acknowledgment Status And Revictimization Risk." *Psychology of Women Quarterly* 33, no. 1 (2009): 34–42.

Littleton, Heather, Amie Grills-Taquechel, and Danny Axsom. "Impaired and Incapacitated Rape Victims: Assault Characteristics and Post-Assault Experiences." *Violence and Victims* 24, no. 4 (2009): 439–57.

Littleton, Heather, C. Radecki Breitkopf, and A. Berenson. "Beyond the Campus: Unacknowledged Rape Among Low-Income Women." *Violence Against Women* 14, no. 3 (2008): 269–86.

Loh, Catherine, Christine A. Gidycz, Tracy R. Lobo, and Rohini Luthra. "A Prospective Analysis of Sexual Assault Perpetration: Risk Factors Related to Perpetrator Characteristics." *Journal of Interpersonal Violence* 20, no. 10 (2005): 1325–48.

Lombardi, Kristen. "A Lack of Consequences for Sexual Assault." Center for Public Integrity. Posted February 24, 2010. At www.publicintegrity.org/2010/02/24/ 4360/lack-consequences-sexual-assault.

Luther, Martin. "The Large Catechism." In *The Book of Concord: The Confessions of the Evangelical Lutheran Church*, translated and edited by Theodore G. Tappert et al., 357–461. Philadelphia, PA: Fortress, 1959.

Malamuth, Neil M., Tamara Addison, and Mary Koss. "Pornography and Sexual Aggression: Are There Reliable Effects and Can We Understand Them?" *Annual Review of Sex Research* 11 (2000): 26–91.

Mann, Ruth E., and Clive R. Hollin. "Sexual Offenders' Explanations for Their Offending." *Journal of Sexual Aggression* 13, no. 1 (2007): 3–9.

Manning, Jill C. "The Impact of Internet Pornography on Marriage and the Family: A Review of the Research." *Sexual Addiction & Compulsivity* 13, nos. 2–3 (2006): 131–65.

Mcmahon, Sarah. "Rape Myth Beliefs and Bystander Attitudes Among Incoming College Students." *Journal of American College Health* 59, no. 1 (2010): 3–11.

Mengo, C., and B. M. Black. "Violence Victimization on a College Campus: Impact on GPA and School Dropout." *Journal of College Student Retention: Research, Theory & Practice* 18, no. 2 (2015): 234–48.

Merton, Thomas. *New Seeds of Contemplation.* New York: New Directions, 1961.

Merton, Thomas. *No Man Is an Island.* New York: Harcourt, Brace, 1955.

Metz, Johann Baptist. "Bread of Survival: The Lord's Supper of Christians as Anticipatory Sign of an Anthropological Revolution." In *Love's Strategy: The Political Theology of Johann Baptist Metz*, edited by John K. Downey, 53–63. London, England: Bloomsbury T&T Clark, 1999.

Metz, Johann Baptist. "Christians and Jews after Auschwitz." In *Love's Strategy: The Political Theology of Johann Baptist Metz*, edited by John K. Downey, 39–52. London, England: Bloomsbury T&T Clark, 1999.

Metz, Johann Baptist. *The Emergent Church: The Future of Christianity in a Postbourgeois World.* New York: Crossroad, 1981.

Metz, Johann Baptist. *Faith in History and Society: Toward a Practical Fundamental Theology.* New York: Seabury Press, 1980.

Metz, Johann Baptist. *Poverty of Spirit.* New York: Paulist Press, 1998.

Metz, Johann Baptist, and translated by John K. Downey. "Facing the World: A Theological and Biographical Inquiry." *Theological Studies* 75, no. 1 (2014): 23–33.

Metz, Johann Baptist, and Jean-Pierre Jossua. *Theology of Joy.* New York: Herder and Herder, 1974.

Miller, Audrey, Erika Canales, Amanda Amacker, Tamika Backstrom, and Christine Gidycz. "Stigma-Threat Motivated Nondisclosure of Sexual Assault and Sexual

Revictimization: A Prospective Analysis." *Psychology of Women Quarterly* 35, no. 1 (2011): 120.

Mohler-Kuo, Meichun, George W. Dowdall, Mary P. Koss, and Henry Wechsler. "Correlates of Rape While Intoxicated in a National Sample of College Women." *Journal of Studies on Alcohol* 65, no. 1 (2004): 37–45.

Muehlenhard, Charlene L., and Melaney A. Linton. "Date Rape and Sexual Aggression in Dating Situations: Incidence and Risk Factors." *Journal of Counseling Psychology* 34, no. 2 (1987): 186–96.

Norris, Jeanette, Kelly Cue Davis, William H. George, Joel Martell, and Julia R. Heiman. "Victim's Response and Alcohol-Related Factors as Determinants of Women's Responses to Violent Pornography." *Psychology of Women Quarterly* 28, no. 1 (2004): 59–69.

Northwestern University. "Policy on Prohibited Discrimination, Harassment and Related Misconduct." Equal Opportunity and Compliance Office, January 13, 2014. At www.northwestern.edu/sexual-misconduct/docs/sexual_misconduct_policy.pdf.

Northwestern University. "Policy on Sexual Misconduct." Posted September 2016. At www.northwesern.edu/sexual-misconduct/docs/sexual_misconduct_policy.pdf.

O'Byrne, Rachael, Susan Hansen, and Mark Rapley. "If a Girl Doesn't Say 'No'...: Young Men, Rape and Claims of 'Insufficient Knowledge.'" *Journal of Community & Applied Social Psychology* 18, no. 3 (2008): 168–93.

O'Byrne, Rachael, Mark Rapley, and Susan Hansen. "'You Couldn't Say "No," Could You?' Young Men's Understandings of Sexual Refusal." *Feminism & Psychology* 16, no. 2 (2006): 133–54.

Orchowski, L., A. Untied, and C. Gidycz. "Social Reactions to Disclosure of Sexual Victimization and Adjustment Among Survivors of Sexual Assault." *Journal of Interpersonal Violence* 28, no. 10 (2013): 2005–23.

Orso, Anna. "Trump's Education Pick Donated to Philly Group with Controversial Campus Rape Stance." PolitiFact, January 19, 2017. At http://www.politifact.com/pennsylvania/statements/2017/jan/19/bob-casey/trumps-education-pick-donated-philly-group-controv/.

Ouimette, P. C., and D. Riggs. "Testing a Mediational Model of Sexually Aggressive Behavior in Nonincarcerated Perpetrators." *Violence and Victims* 13, no. 2 (Summer 1998): 117–30.

Owen, Jesse, and Frank D. Fincham. "Young Adults' Emotional Reactions After Hooking Up Encounters." *Archives of Sexual Behavior* 40, no. 2 (2011): 321–30.

Owen, Jesse J., Frank D. Fincham, and Jon Moore. "Hooking Up Among College Students: Demographic and Psychosocial Correlates." *Archives of Sexual Behavior* 39, no. 3 (2010): 653–63.

Owen, Jesse, Frank D. Fincham, and Jon Moore. "Short-Term Prospective Study of Hooking Up Among College Students." *Archives of Sexual Behavior* 40, no. 2 (2011): 331–41.

Palmer, Maureen., Rick. LeGuerrier, Timothy M. Hogan, Ann-Marie MacDonald, John Collins, Marcel. Gallant, Jac Gautreau. *Sext Up Kids.* Dream Street Pictures, Canadian Broadcasting Corporation, and Media Education Foundation, 2012.

Palmer, Parker J. *Let Your Life Speak: Listening for the Voice of Vocation.* San Francisco, CA: Jossey-Bass, 2000.

Paul, E. L., and K. A. Hayes. "The Casualties of 'Casual' Sex: A Qualitative Exploration of the Phenomenology of College Students' Hookups." *Journal of Social and Personal Relationships* 19, no. 5 (2002): 639–61.

Paul, Pamela. *Pornified: How Pornography Is Transforming Our Lives, Our Relationships, and Our Families.* New York: Times Books, 2005.

Pearsall, Beth. "Sexual Assault: An Unspoken Barrier to Higher Ed." *AAUW Outlook* 108, no. 3 (2014): 20. At http://online.qmags.com/OL1014#pg22&mode2.

Poteat, V. Dave, and Lisa B. Spanierman. "Modern Racism Attitudes Among White Students: The Role of Dominance and Authoritarianism and the Mediating Effects of Racial Color-Blindness." *Journal of Social Psychology* 152, no. 6 (2012): 758–74.

Princeton University. "University-wide Regulations." Posted August 2, 2016. At www.princeton.edu/pub/rrr/part1/index.xml#comp13.

Rape, Abuse, & Incest Nationl Network (RAINN). "Campus Sexual Violence: Statistics, 2016." At www.rainn.org/statistics/campus-sexual-violence.

Regnerus, Mark, and Jeremy Uecker. *Premarital Sex in America How Young Americans Meet, Mate, and Think about Marrying.* New York: Oxford University Press, 2010.

Relyea, M., and S. E. Ullman. "Unsupported or Turned Against: Understanding How Two Types of Negative Social Reactions to Sexual Assault Relate to Postassault Outcomes." *Psychology of Women Quarterly* 39, no. 1 (2013): 37–52.

Risser, H., M. Hetzel-Riggin, C. Thomsen, and T. McCanne. "PTSD As a Mediator of Sexual Revictimization: The Role of Reexperiencing, Avoidance, and Arousal Symptoms." *Journal of Traumatic Stress* 19, no. 5 (2006): 687–98.

Rogala, C, and T. Tyden. "Does Pornography Influence Young Women's Sexual Behavior?" *Women's Health Issues* 13, no. 1 (2003): 39–43.

Rohr, Richard. *Breathing Under Water: Spirituality and the Twelve Steps.* Cincinnati, OH: St. Anthony Messenger Press, 2011.

Ryan, Kathryn M. "Further Evidence for a Cognitive Component of Rape." *Aggression and Violent Behavior* 9, no. 6 (2004): 579–604.

Sable, Marjorie R., Fran Danis, Denise L. Mauzy, and Sarah K. Gallagher. "Barriers to Reporting Sexual Assault for Women and Men: Perspectives of College Students." *Journal of American College Health* 55, no. 3 (2006): 157–62.

Santana, M. Christina, Anita Raj, Michele R. Decker, Ana La Marche, and Jay G. Silverman. "Masculine Gender Roles Associated with Increased Sexual Risk and Intimate Partner Violence Perpetration among Young Adult Men." *Journal of Urban Health* 83, no. 4 (2006): 575–85.

Scharen, Christian Batalden, and Aana Marie Vigen. *Ethnography as Christian Theology and Ethics.* London: Continuum, 2011.

Schroeder, Lauren P. "Cracks in the Ivory Tower: How the Campus Sexual Violence Elimination Act Can Protect Students from Sexual Assault." *Loyola University Chicago Law Journal* 45 (May 2015): 1195–243.

Smith, Carly Parnitzke, and Jennifer J. Freyd. "Dangerous Safe Havens: Institutional Betrayal Exacerbates Sexual Trauma." *Journal of Traumatic Stress* 26, no. 1 (February 2013): 119–24.

Smith, Carly Parnitzke, and Jennifer J. Freyd. "Institutional Betrayal." *American Psychologist* 69, no. 6 (2014): 575–87.

Smith, Christian, and Melinda Lundquist Denton. *Soul Searching: The Religious and Spiritual Lives of American Teenagers.* Oxford: Oxford University Press, 2005.

Snapp, Shannon, Ehri Ryu, and Jade Kerr. "The Upside to Hooking Up: College Students' Positive Hookup Experiences." *International Journal of Sexual Health* 27, no. 1 (2015): 43–56.

Sorenson, S. B., M. Joshi, and E. Sivitz. "Knowing a Sexual Assault Victim or Perpetrator: A Stratified Random Sample of Undergraduates at One University." *Journal of Interpersonal Violence* 29, no. 3 (2013): 394–416.

Stephenson, Kyle R., and Keiran Sullivan. "The Misperception of Social Norms and Sexual Satisfaction." *Canadian Journal of Human Sexuality* 18, no. 3 (2009): 89–105.

Stepp, Laura Sessions. *Unhooked: How Young Women Pursue Sex, Delay Love and Lose at Both.* New York: Riverhead Books, 2007.

Stoltenberg, John. *Refusing to Be a Man: Essays on Social Justice.* London: UCL Press, 2000.

Summerfield, Derek. "Addressing Human Response in War and Atrocity." In *Beyond Trauma: Cultural and Societal Dynamics,* edited by R. Kleber, C. Figley, and B. Gersons, 17–29. New York: Plenum Press, 1995.

Tatum, Beverly Daniel. "Why Are All the Black Kids Sitting Together in the Cafeteria?" And Other Conversations about Race. New York: Basic Books, 1997.

Taylor, Charles. "Modern Social Imaginaries." *Public Culture* 14, no. 1 (2002): 91–124.

Tedeschi, Richard G., and Lawrence G. Calhoun. "The Posttraumatic Growth Inventory: Measuring the Positive Legacy of Trauma." *Journal of Traumatic Stress* 9, no. 3 (1996): 455–71.

Thompson, Martie P., Kevin M. Swartout, and Mary P. Koss. "Trajectories and Predictors of Sexually Aggressive Behaviors during Emerging Adulthood." *Psychology of Violence* 3, no. 3 (2013): 247–59.

Tjaden, Patricia, and Nancy Thoennes, *Extent, Nature, and Consequences of Rape Victimization: Findings From the National Violence Against Women Survey.* NIJ Research Report, U.S. Department of Justice, Office of Justice Programs, National Institute of Justice. Washington, DC: National Institute of Justice, 2006.

Tomsich E. A., L. M. Schaible, C. Marie Rennison, and A. R. Gover. "Violent Victimization and Hooking Up among Strangers and Acquaintances on an Urban Campus: An Exploratory Study." *Criminal Justice Studies* 26, no. 4 (2013): 433–54.

Townsend, John Marshall, and Timothy H. Wasserman. "Sexual Hookups Among College Students: Sex Differences in Emotional Reactions." *Archives of Sexual Behavior* 40, no. 6 (2011): 1173–81.

Traina, Cristina L. H. *Erotic Attunement: Parenthood and the Ethics of Sensuality Between Unequals.* Chicago: University of Chicago Press, 2011.

Twenge, Jean M. *Generation Me: Why Today's Young Americans are more Confident, Assertive, Entitled—And More Miserable than Ever Before.* New York: Atria. 2006.

Twohig, Michael P., Jesse M. Crosby, and Jared M. Cox. "Viewing Internet Pornography: For Whom Is It Problematic, How, and Why?" *Sexual Addiction & Compulsivity* 16, no. 4 (2009): 253–66.

Ullman, Sarah E. "Ten-Year Update on 'Review and Critique of Empirical Studies on Rape Avoidance.'" *Criminal Justice and Behavior* 34, no. 3 (2007): 411–29.

Ullman, Sarah E., and Leanne R. Brecklin. "Sexual Assault History, PTSD, and Mental Health Service Seeking in a National Sample of Women." *Journal of Community Psychology* 30, no. 3 (2002): 261–79.

Ullman, S. E., and C. J. Najdowski. "Prospective Changes in Attributions of Self-Blame and Social Reactions to Women's Disclosures of Adult Sexual Assault." *Journal of Interpersonal Violence* 26, no. 10 (2010): 1934–62.

University of Iowa. "Sanctioning Guidelines for Sexual Assault." Posted 2016. At https://dos.uiowa.edu/policies/sanctioinng-guidelines-for-sexual-assault/.

University of North Carolina. "Policy on Prohibited Discrimination, Harassment, and Related Misconduct—Equal Opportunity and Compliance Office." Posted 2016. At http://eoc.unc.edu/our-policies/ppdhrm/.

University of the Pacific. "Student 2 Student Healthy Relationships Peer Educators." At www.pacific.edu/Campus-Life/Diversity-and-Inclusion/Womens-Resource-Center/Student-2-Student-Peer-Educators.html.

U.S. Department of Justice. "Bystander-Focused Prevention of Sexual Violence." October 12, 2016. At www.notalone.gov/assets/bystander-summary.pdf.

U.S. Department of Justice Office on Violence Against Women. *The 2016 Biennial report to Congress on the Effectiveness of Grant Programs Under the Violence Against Women Act.* 2016. At https://www.justice.gov/ovw/page/file/933886/download.

Vassar College. "Sexual Assault & Violence Prevention." Posted March 11, 2015. At http://savp.vassar.edu/policies/sexual-misconduct.html.

Vega, Vanessa, and Neil M. Malamuth. "Predicting Sexual Aggression: The Role of Pornography in the Context of General and Specific Risk Factors." *Aggressive Behavior* 33, no. 2 (2007): 104–17.

Victor, Elizabeth. "Mental Health and Hooking Up: A Self-Discrepancy Perspective." *The New School Psychology Bulletin* 9, no. 2 (2012): 24–34.

"Videos + Campaigns." Culture of Respect. 2016. At http://cultureofrespect.org/the-resources/videos-photos/.

Vrangalova, Zhana. "Does Casual Sex Harm College Students' Well-Being? A Longitudinal Investigation of the Role of Motivation." *Archives of Sexual Behavior* 44, no. 4 (2014): 945–59.

Wade, Lisa. "Are Women Bad at Orgasms?" In *Gender, Sex, and Politics*, edited by Shira Tarrant, 227–37. New York: Routledge, 2016.

Wade, Lisa. "Sex on Campus isn't What You Think: What 101 Student Journals Taught Me." *The Guardian*, August 23, 2016. At https://www.theguardian.com/us-news/2016/aug/23/sex-on-campus-hookup-culture-student-journals.

Warkentin, J. B., and C. A. Gidycz. "The Use and Acceptance of Sexually Aggressive Tactics in College Men." *Journal of Interpersonal Violence* 22, no. 7 (2007): 829–50.

Weedon, Chris. *Feminist Practice and Poststructuralist Theory.* Oxford: B. Blackwell, 1987.

Wermund, Benjamin. "DeVos' Donations Spark Questions About her Stance on Campus Sexual Assault." Politico, January 9, 2017. At http://www.politico.com/story/2017/01/betsy-devos-education-sexual-assault-233376.

Western Michigan University. "FIRE Sexual Assault Peer Educators:Fighting Ignorance and Rape Through Education. At https://wmich.edu/healthcenter/healthpromotion/fireplace/peer-fire.

Wheeler, Jennifer G., William H. George, and Barbara J. Dahl. "Sexually Aggressive College Males: Empathy as a Moderator in the 'Confluence Model' of Sexual Aggression." *Personality and Individual Differences* 33, no. 5 (2002): 759–75.

White House. "The 'It's On Us' Campaign Launches New PSA, Marks One-Year Since Launch of 'It's On Us' Campaign to End Campus Sexual Assault." Fact sheet, September 1, 2015. At www.whitehouse.gov/the-press-office/2015/09/01/fact-sheet-its-us-campaign-launches-new-psa-marks-one-year-launch.

White HouseTask Force to Protect Students From Sexual Assault. "Not Alone: The First Report of the White House Task Force to Protect Students from Sexual Assault." https://obamawhitehouse.archives.gov/the-press-office/2014/04/29/fact-sheet-not-alone-protecting-students-sexual-assault.

White House Task Force to Protect Students from Sexual Assault. "The Second Report of the White House Task Force to Protect Students from Sexual Assault." January 5, 2017. At https://www.whitehouse.gov/sites/whitehouse.gov/files/images/Documents/1.4.17.VAW%20Event.TF%20Report.PDF.

Wong, Alia. "The Renaissance of Student Activism." *The Atlantic*, May 21, 2015. At www.theatlantic.com/education/archive/2015/05/the-renaissance-of-student-activism/393749/.

World Health Organization. "Violence Against Women." Fact sheet, September 2016. At www.who.int/mediacentre/factsheets/fs239/en/.

Yale University. "Yale Sexual Misconduct Policies and Related Definitions." At http://smr.yale.edu/sexual-misconduct-policies-and-definitions.

Yoder, Vincent Cyrus, Thomas B. Virden, and Kiran Amin. "Internet Pornography and Loneliness: An Association?" *Sexual Addiction & Compulsivity* 12, no. 1 (2005): 19–44.

Zinzow, H. M., H. S. Resnick, A. B. Amstadter, J. L. Mccauley, K. J. Ruggiero, and D. G. Kilpatrick. "Drug- or Alcohol-Facilitated, Incapacitated, and Forcible Rape in Relationship to Mental Health Among a National Sample of Women." *Journal of Interpersonal Violence* 25, no. 12 (2010): 2217–36.

Zinzow, Heidi M., Heidi S. Resnick, Jenna L. Mccauley, Ananda B. Amstadter, Kenneth J. Ruggiero, and Dean G. Kilpatrick. "The Role of Rape Tactics in Risk for Posttraumatic Stress Disorder and Major Depression: Results from a National Sample of College Women." *Depression and Anxiety* 27 (2010): 708–15.

Zinzow, Heidi M., and Martie Thompson. "A Longitudinal Study of Risk Factors for Repeated Sexual Coercion and Assault in U.S. College Men." *Archives of Sexual Behavior* 44, no. 1 (2014): 213–22.

Zinzow, Heidi M., and Martie Thompson. "Factors Associated with Use of Verbally Coercive, Incapacitated, and Forcible Sexual Assault Tactics in a Longitudinal Study of College Men." *Aggressive Behavior* 41, no. 1 (January 2015): 34–43.

Index

affirmative sexual consent, 217–19,
    222–28, 254–55, 291–95
aggression, 165, 209, 285
  and its association with
    pornography, 260–61
  masculinity and, 30, 55, 71, 80, 255
  predatory behavior of college men,
    39, 43, 47, 50–51, 89, 287
  in unequal sex, 66, 234–35, 247, 293
alcohol. *See also* hooking up
  binge drinking, 19–21, 34, 38–39,
    62–67, 116–17, 121–22, 161, 268
    drinking games, 21, 24, 27, 29,
    49, 103–4
  as an escape, 63–65, 160–64,
    168–69, 210
  happiness and, 102–7, 113–24
  and incapacitation, 48–49, 67, 255,
    287, 295, 311n5, 315n3
    tactics, 44–47, 65–66, 256–67
  and lack of accountability for
    behavior, 65–66, 161–62,
    258–60, 275–88
  and lack of women's sexual
    agency, 47, 57–60, 226, 258,
    263, 266–70
  as liquid courage, 35–39, 64

motivations for consuming, 48–51,
    62–66, 161–64, 178–81, 200
party expectations and, 17–68,
    113–17, 178–81
predatory behavior and, 44–47,
    65–67, 109, 259–64, 276–77
pregaming and, 3, 19–21, 57, 118
regret and, 44, 67, 106–10
sexual assault and, 59, 256–64,
    276–77, 315n3
sexual consent and, 217, 293,
    295, 312n5
unhappiness and, 67, 105–10, 123
anxiety, 169–70, 268
  hookups and, 106, 122
  relieved by alcohol, 63, 169–71
  sexual assault and, 275, 280–85
  success and, 136, 209
athletes, 10, 133
  hookup culture and, 17, 34
  as a powerful social group on
    campus, 74, 81–83, 95–96
  and sexual assault, 264, 280–81, 284,
    289, 296
authenticity, 155–56, 172–88,
    197–205, 303
autonomy, 145, 216–17, 294

CPSIA information can be obtained
at www.ICGtesting.com
Printed in the USA
BVHW030715140619
550974BV00002B/3/P

9 780190 268503